# DAVID,

# KING OF ISRAEL

*HIS LIFE AND ITS LESSONS.*

BY THE

REV. WILLIAM M. TAYLOR, D.D.,
MINISTER OF THE BROADWAY TABERNACLE, NEW YORK CITY.

**Fredonia Books**
**Amsterdam, The Netherlands**

David, King of Israel:
His Life and its Lessons

by
Rev. William M. Taylor, D. D.

ISBN: 1-58963-493-4

Copyright © 2001 by Fredonia Books

Reprinted from the 1874 edition

Fredonia Books
Amsterdam, The Netherlands
http://www.fredoniabooks.com

All rights reserved, including the right to reproduce this book, or portions thereof, in any form.

In order to make original editions of historical works available to scholars at an economical price, this facsimile of the original edition of 1874 is reproduced from the best available copy and has been digitally enhanced to improve legibility, but the text remains unaltered to retain historical authenticity.

# PREFACE.

THE Psalms of David are the throbbing heart of Holy Scripture. But they can not be fully understood unless we read them in the light of the experiences out of which they sprung. Hence the life of the son of Jesse must be ever interesting to the devout student of the Word of God; and many have undertaken to set it forth in distinctness before the modern reader.

In adding another to the works already existing on this portion of sacred history, I have no other apology to offer than that which arises out of the interest, amounting almost to a fascination, which it has long had for myself. I have endeavored to give vividness and reality to the far-off past, and to draw from it lessons of "doctrine, of warning, of reproof, of correction, of instruction in righteousness" for the present. In attempting to do this I have availed myself of all the light which I could obtain from every quarter. I have not consciously evaded any difficulty, or strained any statement; and while I have carefully noted my obligations to others, I can not forbear expressing in this place my indebtedness to Dean Stanley's "Lectures on the Jewish Church," and the Bible dictionaries of Kitto, Smith, and Fairbairn.

Such as it is, I desire to lay my work at the feet of Him "whose I am and whom I serve;" and if it shall in any measure increase my reader's interest in the Old Testament Scriptures, or add to his enjoyment of the sacred Psalter, or minister to his spiritual profit, I shall be abundantly rewarded.

BROADWAY TABERNACLE, *September* 30, 1874.

# CONTENTS.

| | | PAGE |
|---|---|---|
| I. | The Anointing at Bethlehem | 9 |
| II. | Medicinal Music | 24 |
| III. | The Conflict with Goliath | 41 |
| IV. | David and Jonathan | 58 |
| V. | The Escape from Gibeah to Ramah | 75 |
| VI. | The Valley of Deceit | 93 |
| VII. | Songs in the Night | 112 |
| VIII. | Cave Songs | 133 |
| IX. | Nabal | 153 |
| X. | Ziklag, Endor, and Gilboa | 170 |
| XI. | Hebron and Jerusalem | 191 |
| XII. | The Bringing up of the Ark | 210 |
| XIII. | Nathan's Message | 230 |
| XIV. | David's Administration | 245 |
| XV. | The Great Transgression | 264 |
| XVI. | The Bereavement | 283 |
| XVII. | The Revolt of Absalom | 299 |
| XVIII. | Absalom's Defeat and Death | 320 |
| XIX. | The Restoration of David to his Throne | 338 |
| XX. | Famine and Pestilence | 360 |
| XXI. | Even-song | 379 |
| XXII. | The Coronation of Solomon | 399 |
| XXIII. | Last Words | 415 |
| *INDEX* | | 435 |

# DAVID, KING OF ISRAEL.

## I.

*THE ANOINTING AT BETHLEHEM.*

1 SAMUEL xvi., 1-13.

IN entering upon the consideration of the life-story of David, King of Israel, it is needful that we have a clear conception of the state of affairs in the land at the time when he first appears upon the scene.

Samuel, to whose history the interest of every reader is drawn with a peculiar fascination, was now an old man; and had, in a great measure, retired from public life to his home at Ramah, where, however, he still presided over one of those educational institutions which in the Old Testament are called "schools of the prophets." He had judged Israel for twenty years with prudence, impartiality, and success, and was in every way as worthy as ever of the veneration and confidence of the community. But moved, partly by the fact that his sons did not walk in his footsteps, and partly also by that ostentatious rivalry of their neighbors, which is the bane of states as well as of families, the tribes desired a king. This request at first greatly distressed the aged prophet, but after consulting God upon the subject he was led to acquiesce in the proposal, and at a solemn gathering of the people he addressed them in a strain of mingled tenderness and reproof, took them to witness that he had managed their affairs with moderation and integrity, and then summoned them to appoint their king, not however by popular election, but by lot, thereby reminding them that he who should be set over them would be, after all, only the vicar and representative of their true King, Jehovah. The whole narrative impresses us with a sense of the dignity and self-control of Samuel; and we see that he was a truly patriotic and self-sacrificing man, willing to be any thing, or to do any thing, for the sake of his people and his God.

The man on whom the lot at this time fell was Saul, the son of Kish, of the tribe of Benjamin. He had an imposing appearance, great martial prowess, and considerable intellectual ability, and if he had been willing to sink his personal ambition in the service of the Lord, he might have become truly great, but ever and anon he rebelled against and overpassed what may be called the constitutional restraints of the theocratic monarchy; and so he lost the great opportunity of his life, and left behind him a name around which the saddest associations hover, and to which no real nobility belongs.

At first his appointment to the regal office was the occasion of discontent, and almost mutiny, among the people; but the promptitude and valor which he evinced in the rescue of the citizens of Jabesh-gilead secured to him the willing homage of his subjects. His reverence for God, however, was not equal to his daring on the field of battle, and he fretted and chafed under what he regarded as the interference of Jehovah with his management of public affairs.

On at least two memorable and testing occasions he showed his determination to take his own way, in defiance of the commands of the Almighty.

The first of these was in connection with an effort to rid the people of the vexatious bondage under which they were held by the Philistines, who still maintained several garrisons in the midst of the Promised Land, from which they came forth ever and anon to plunder and murder the inhab-

## The Anointing at Bethlehem.

itants. Jonathan, Saul's noble son, had taken the stronghold of Geba; and the king, desirous of following up this success by a general assault upon the enemy, summoned the people to Gilgal. It would appear, however, that Samuel had, in the name of Jehovah, forbidden him to do any thing until he had arrived and offered sacrifice, and that he had appointed the seventh day for that purpose. In the mean time, the Philistines, hearing of the movements of the Israelites, had assembled in great force, and came up to offer battle. Their appearance occasioned a panic among the Israelites, and Saul's soldiers were deserting on every hand, so that, in his view, it became necessary to act at once. Hence, on the seventh day, though Samuel had not yet come, Saul, thinking to stay the panic that had set in, and perhaps also imagining that he would raise himself in the estimation of the army, assumed the office of priest, and offered sacrifice with his own hands.

He had scarcely finished when Samuel arrived; and having heard what the king had done, the prophet sorrowfully, yet sternly, said, "Thou hast done foolishly: thou hast not kept the commandment of the Lord thy God, which he commanded thee: for now would the Lord have established thy kingdom upon Israel forever. But now thy kingdom shall not continue: the Lord hath sought him a man after his own heart, and the Lord hath commanded him to be captain over his people, because thou hast not kept that which the Lord commanded thee."*

The second similar occasion was in connection with a commission which Saul received to destroy the Amalekites, who were ancient foes of Israel, and whose extermination was needful to the establishment of the great theocracy. The order was very severe. No one was to be spared, and

---

* 1 Sam. xiii., 13, 14.

all the cattle were to be destroyed. But Saul faltered in carrying it out. From a spirit of self-glory he spared Agag, the chief, that he might grace his triumphant return to Gibeah. In the same arrogant disposition, he set up a memorial of his victory near Carmel; and preferring his own way to God's, he spared the flocks and herds under pretense of making a great offering to Jehovah. Again, however, he was confronted by Samuel, who upbraided him with his self-will, and gave utterance to that great principle which had in it the forecast of the Gospel, "To obey is better than sacrifice, and to hearken than the fat of rams." Thereafter the prophet repeated his solemn announcement, "Because thou hast rejected the word of the Lord, he hath also rejected thee from being king." This declaration deeply affected Saul, and he sought by every means to draw from Samuel some revocation. In the earnestness of his appeal he even laid hold upon the prophet's mantle, but, from the rending of the garment in the royal hand, Samuel only took occasion to repeat the prediction in another form, saying, "The Lord hath rent the kingdom of Israel from thee this day, and hath given it to a neighbor of thine, that is better than thou."* Still, commiserating the humiliated monarch, the prophet yielded to his entreaty so far as to continue to honor him that day before the people, but after he had with his own hands put to death the chief of the Amalekites, Samuel withdrew to his retirement in Ramah; and so far as the record bears he saw Saul again no more, save for a brief space at Naioth, until that night of terror and dismay at Endor, when he came forth from his grave to say to him, "To-morrow shalt thou and thy sons be with me."

Alas! for Saul. With many elements of greatness about him, and having withal such a disposition that those who

---

* 1 Sam. xv., 22, 23, 28.

were most intimately connected with him could not help liking him, he was yet the creature of impulse, swaying evermore between his better and his worse nature. Now he was among the sons of the prophets entering enthusiastically into their occupations, and catching the spirit of their service; and anon he was carried away by some caprice of self-conceit, or some freak of personal inclination, to do what was utterly inconsistent with the position which he occupied, as the servant of the Lord upon the throne of Israel. Had he yielded to the promptings of his nobler self, and the drawings of God's Spirit, he might have been one of the grandest characters in sacred history; but he allowed his lower nature to predominate, and though to the last we have occasional outflashings of his old generosity and religiousness, these were but like the glimmerings of an expiring lamp, which went out in a darkness so profound as to sadden the heart of every beholder. As Dean Stanley has truly remarked, "His religion was never blended with his moral nature—his religious zeal was always breaking out in wrong channels on irregular occasions in his own way;" and again "it broke out in wild, ungovernable acts of zeal and superstition, and then left him a prey more than ever to his own savage disposition."* With splendid opportunities and great abilities, he yet failed to profit by either, because he knew not "the day of his visitation," and because he repudiated the conditions within which alone he could have risen to greatness. Yet there was a strange charm about him too. Even as in our own day we may know some reckless youth, with frank, impetuous disposition, and occasional impulses to right things, who is making shipwreck of himself, and whom, in spite of his folly, we can not help liking, so we are drawn toward Saul notwithstanding his wickedness, and we can well understand how Samuel

---

* "The Jewish Church," vol. ii., pp. 21, 24.

felt when he "mourned" over him. He had hoped so much from him; he had seen so much that was lovable about him; and yet he had been so sadly disappointed in him, that we do not wonder at his sorrow. Haply, too, he was cherishing the expectation that he might yet come to himself, and redeem the promise of his earlier time. But it was not so to be, for now the command comes to the prophet, "How long wilt thou mourn for Saul, seeing I have rejected him from reigning over Israel? fill thine horn with oil, and go, I will send thee to Jesse the Beth-lehemite: for I have provided me a king among his sons."

The town to which Samuel was now sent was but a little one among the thousands of Judah, and up to this time had not come into any great prominence in the history of the tribe. It is about five miles south of Jerusalem, a little to the east of the road that leads to Hebron. It stands upon the summit and slopes of a narrow ridge, which projects eastward from the central chain of the Judean mountains. The sides of the hill below the village are carefully terraced, and even in modern times they are occupied with fertile vineyards; while in the valleys beneath, and on a little plain that lies to the eastward, there are some corn-fields whose produce, perhaps, gave the name Bethlehem, or house of bread, to the town with which they were connected. Beyond these fields is the wilderness of Judea, the chief features of which are white limestone hills, thrown confusedly together, with deep ravines winding in and out among them.

The place never was of any great political importance in the land, but around it cluster associations which, throughout eternity, will make its name illustrious. In the immediate neighborhood, memorial of the tenderest sorrow of Jacob's life, was the tomb of Rachel. In yonder corn-fields Ruth gleaned after the reapers of Boaz, on those never-to-be-forgotten harvest-days which so materially changed the circumstances of the alien woman, and made her the ancestress of a royal line, whose representative sits now at God's right hand. On the slopes of these hills David was watching his father's flocks on the occasion before us; and here, too, were announced to shepherds, as they tended their charge by night, the glad tidings of the birth of Him who "has brought life and immortality to light."

It was an appropriate training-place for the future king and bard of Israel, and no occupation could have been more conducive to the development in him of those qualities of prudence, promptitude, and prowess which his after-life required, than that of a shepherd. Its solitude would cast him upon the companionship of God; and when the night unveiled the glory of the stars, he would become familiar with the grandeur of the heavens, thus storing his mind with lofty thoughts and holy musings, which, either then or at a later day, came forth glorified and made immortal by the music of his verse. Nor was this all: his unceasing labors and occasional conflicts with wild animals from the neighboring wilderness would give him physical strength; while, again, his proximity to the tribe of Benjamin would call forth in him a desire to outrival, in their friendly matches, the skill of those eminent marksmen "who could sling at a hair-breadth and not miss," and so, all unconsciously to himself, prepare him for the work which lay before him.

But we must not anticipate. When Samuel received his commission he was filled with dismay, and said, "How can I go? if Saul hear it, he will kill me." This fear on the part of one who was usually so brave may indicate, either that the mental malady with which Saul was latterly afflicted had already begun to show itself in fierce outbreaks of passionate cruelty, or that he had somehow manifested that unscrupulous disregard of human life which he evinced at a later date on more than one occasion, and more particularly when he caused the seventy priests of Nob to be put to death. But the Lord's will must be done. So he is commanded to allay suspicion by summoning the inhabitants of Bethlehem to a sacrifice. Here, however, was no subterfuge. There would have been disingenuousness if he had professed to offer sacrifice, while he really meant to do nothing of the kind; but he did carry out his design in that matter, though for prudential considerations he made no public allusion to the other commission with which he was intrusted. If any surprise be felt at the offering of sacrifice, in a place other than that appointed in the Mosaic law, the explanation is to be found in the fact that the ark of the covenant of the Lord was not at this time in the Tabernacle, but in the city of Kirjath-jearim, and so the Tabernacle had ceased for the present to be the only place of the nation's worship.*

The appearance of the prophet approaching the city, and driving a heifer before him, created quite a sensation among the people. They feared that in some way they had offended God, and that he had sent his servant to denounce them and to bring some punishment upon their heads. Thus natural is it for men whose consciences tell of guilt, to fear when any thing reminds them of Jehovah. Hundreds of years after this, when the heavenly light was seen in the same place by the shepherds, they too were "sore afraid;" but there was as little ground for fear in the one case as in the other; for in both there was a provided sacrifice, and in both the mission was one of peace; yea, as Samuel came to anoint David to be a king, so the angel-heralded Jesus appeared "to make us kings and priests unto our Lord and his Father."

Having exhorted them to make suitable preparations for the sacred service, and having gone through the necessary ritual observances, the prophet invited Jesse and his sons to

---

* See Keil on 1 Samuel, p. 168.

## The Anointing at Bethlehem.

take their places at the feast with which the sacrifice concluded; but just as they were about to sit down, he looked intently at the young men to see which of them was the Lord's anointed. The eldest attracted his attention by his countenance and his stature, and he said within himself, "This must be he;" but God, reminding him, perhaps, of the same features about Saul, declared that he had refused him, because he read in his heart unfitness for the royal office. Similarly the rest were passed, until, in great perplexity, Samuel said to Jesse, "Are here all thy children?" The answer revealed to him that the youngest was in the field following the sheep, whereupon he affirmed that they could not proceed until he appeared, and directed that he should be sent for immediately.

While, therefore, they await the return of the messenger, we may briefly give you all that we can gather from the page of Scripture of the genealogy and position of Jesse and his family. From the table at the end of the book of Ruth, taken in connection with that prefixed to the gospel of Matthew, we learn that Jesse was the ninth, in direct descent, from Judah, the son of Jacob; and as in the first chapter of the book of Numbers we have the name of Nahshon, the fifth in that lineage, with the title "prince of the house of Judah" attached to it, we may fairly presume that the family was of great importance in the tribe. We know, too, that Boaz, the grandfather of Jesse, was a wealthy magnate in Bethlehem; and so we may conclude that Jesse was, if not the chief man in the place, at least one of its most influential inhabitants. In the tables to which I have referred the names of two Gentile women occur—Rahab of Jericho, and Ruth of Moab —and it is by no means improbable that the connection of his ancestors with Gentile nations may have had, when he came to know it, a considerable influence on the mind of David, while, perhaps, it contributed in after-days to his choice of Moab as an asylum for his parents when it was no longer safe for them to remain in Bethlehem.

The family of Jesse consisted of eight sons and two daughters. David was the youngest child; and so great a difference was there between his age and those of some of the elder ones, that the sons of his sister Zeruiah seem to have been brought up as boys along with him, and were through life associated with him—not always to his advantage. Of his mother we know almost nothing; her name has nowhere been preserved for us in sacred history. Some have supposed that she was Jesse's second wife, and others have not scrupled to place her in a less honorable relationship; with no good ground, however, so far as I can see. David in his Psalms styles himself, on more than one occasion, "the son of God's handmaid;" and this leads us to believe that she had a holy influence upon him, and that it was most likely from her lips that he first heard the wondrous story of God's former dealings with his people, as well as the simple, pathetic pastoral of Ruth. His father is not referred to by him in any such way as to evince that he owed, either intellectually or spiritually, very much to him. Indeed, as one has said, Jesse "seems to have been a sort of dull country squire, with not many thoughts beyond his sheep, and not many aspirations beyond the advancement of himself and family. He manifestly thought very little of his youngest son; perhaps because he was a quiet, thoughtful, pious lad, who liked better to make hymns and sing them, than to pursue those arts by which his older brothers were seeking to push their way in the world."[*] But he had a firm hold on his mother's heart; and we can imagine how, when he came home at night fatigued by the day's toils, she

---

[*] Dr. W. L. Alexander, of Edinburgh: "Christian Thought and Work," pp. 256, 257.

would soothe and solace him, and minister to his wants, bringing with her some well-saved dainty which she knew he would prize ; how, when he spoke to her some of his musings over the realities of the world unseen, she would enter into his views and feelings, and deepen every salutary impression ; and how, when he sung to her some simple song which he had made that day while following the flock, she would shield him from the ridicule of his brothers, and give him, in her loving appreciation of his verse, a new inspiration, firing his heart with the ambition of some day producing such poetry that "the world would not willingly let it die."

But yonder he comes! with his shepherd's crook in his hand, his face flushed with the exertions he has been making to obey his father's call, his auburn hair* flowing in the breeze, and a light flashing from his fair, bright eyes. We can easily picture him to ourselves as, with bashful surprise, he felt the holy oil suffuse his head, and saw it flow even to the skirts of his garments.

We are not informed whether Samuel explained to him, or to his father, the meaning of this sacred rite. The likelihood is that he did not, because his words would have been sure in some way or other to have reached the ears of Saul, and then all his prudential measures would have been taken in vain. But David would receive all needful knowledge from another quarter, for "the Spirit of the Lord came upon him from that day forward." Not with stormful gust, like that which swept over the soul of Saul when he met the children of the prophets, and which speedily passed away; but with the gentle silence of the opening dawn which brightens into perfect day, the Spirit came into David's heart, and soon, by his secret, supernatural suggestions, he would dis-

---

* 1 Sam. xvii., 42.

cover for what purpose the prophet had emptied his horn of oil upon his head.

It was a crisis in his history. He entered from that moment upon a higher stage of life than that on which heretofore he had stood. The light-hearted boy became a thoughtful youth, forecasting the duties and responsibilities of his future career; but, far from considering the tending of his sheep a work too menial for one on whom the consecrating oil had been shed, he went back to it, seeing in it a new significance as a preparative for the nobler labors that lay before him. He sought to fit himself for the loftier sphere by continuing faithfully to discharge the duties of the humbler; and while he was far from putting away from him the exaltation which was in store for him, he was content to wait until it was God's time for him to rise to it. The revelation of the future neither soured his heart at the present, nor turned him away from the work he was required to do. The day that was passing over him only acquired new importance in his eyes because of the revelation of the future which had been given him; and he was not the less watchful as a shepherd, but rather the more, because he knew that there was a throne before him.

How much is there in all this to instruct us who believe in Jesus Christ! By the holy anointing of the Spirit we too have been designated for a throne, but let us not be high-minded because of that. Let us rather continue here at the daily work which he has set us, grappling manfully with the spiritual enemies by whom we are beset, even as David slew the lion and the bear that came to his flock, and soothing our spirits the while with the music of a psalm, even as David sang while following his sheep. Then, when it is God's time for us to rise, we shall hear his voice saying to us, "Come up hither," and shall discover that, by the daily discipline of duty done in the name of the Lord Jesus, we have been making ourselves ready for the throne on which we shall be placed.

The narrative over which we have thus come, introductory though it be, is rich in practical suggestiveness; but we can stay now to give point to only two or three reflections.

We may see in the history of Saul, which we have briefly summarized, how important it is that we should make the most of the opportunities which God puts before us. There came to the son of Kish a tidal time of favor, which, if he had only recognized and improved it, might have carried him, not only to greatness, but to goodness. But he proved faithless to the trust which was committed to him, and became in the end a worse man than he would have been, if no such privileges had been conferred upon him. We can not read his history without observing how, as his life wore on, the good features in his character disappeared, and he who once promised to bear much goodly fruit had in the end "nothing but leaves," and was blighted by the curse of barrenness. His career is a melancholy illustration of the truth of the Saviour's words, "From him that hath not, shall be taken away even that he hath." Let the young take note of the lesson and the warning. Whether you know it or not, God has given you special opportunities, and according as you deal with these he will deal with you. There have been times, mayhap, when you too were "among the prophets," and felt within you the stirrings and strivings of the Holy Spirit; but what has been the result? Were you changed thereby merely into "other" men; or did you become "new creatures" in Christ Jesus? Depend upon it, after all such experiences you can not continue quite as you were before. If you have not been the better for them, you must be the worse, and if they come again, beware how you deal with them! Once, long after, Saul came again under influences and impressions similar to those which he felt at the beginning of his career; but he let that day of grace also pass, and in the end he felt that God had departed from him. Let it not be so with you. "Quench not the Spirit" by your follies and your sins, but yield yourselves up to God through Jesus Christ, and live always and only for him; so shall the opportunities which he has given you become the steps on that great life-ladder up which you climb to heaven. See that you know the "day of your visitation;" and that you may make no mistake, where mistake is so fatal, let every day be to you a day of grace. Determine by the help of God's Spirit to make the best of it for the development within you of a holy character, and for the promotion around you of the good of souls. God has anointed you to rule over your own spirits, and to bring them "into captivity to the obedience of Christ;" but if you despise this glorious royalty, and give yourselves over to iniquity, he will despise you, and give you over to destruction.

We may see, again, in Jehovah's expostulation with Samuel concerning Eliab, the solemn truth that in the eye of the All-seeing the heart is the man. "God looketh on the heart." It makes little matter, therefore, what the outward appearance is, while, if the heart be wrong, nothing can be right. There is much, no doubt, in the bodily development to attract the eye, and I would not undervalue attention to the symmetrical discipline of the physical frame. Yet muscularity is not Christianity, and bodily beauty is not holiness. The character, therefore, ought to be the principal object of your attention. Not how you look, but what you are, ought to be the first care of your lives; for if you have a selfish disposition, a sordid soul, or a sinful life, your outward beauty will be like "a jewel in a swine's snout," and your bodily vigor will only be like the strength of a safe in which nothing worth preserving is locked up. Let your aim be to be holy; and if you will only turn in faith to Jesus, and follow in the footsteps of his example, your soul will become beautiful in Jehovah's eyes, and your life will become, even in the view of your fellow-men, bright with a glory which is not of earth.

We may see once more, from the anointing of David, that we need a special preparation for the service of God. In the old economy, the prophet, the priest, and the king were set apart to their offices by the pouring of oil upon their heads; and this was, as the history before us makes apparent, the symbol of the conferring upon them of the Holy Ghost. Under the New Testament dispensation there are no such offices, or, rather, every believer is himself, in a subordinate sense, a king, priest, and prophet, all in one. Now, for the services which we are as such to render to God and to our fellow-men we need a special unction of the Holy Ghost. Be it ours, therefore, to make earnest application for this supreme anointing. We have each his own work to do, but we shall fail to do it rightly, unless the Spirit of glory and of God do rest upon us. To-night, like another Samuel, I am sent to tell you that God is willing to consecrate you as his "kings and priests;" that you may serve him in the Gospel of his Son, alike in your daily labor and your sacred exercises. Despise not, I pray you, this baptism of the Holy Ghost. Uncover your heads for this heavenly oil; open your hearts for the admission of this celestial influence; and hear these words from the mouth of Him who solemnly ordains you to this ministry of life: "Know ye not that your body is the temple of the Holy Ghost which is in you, which ye have of God, and ye are not your own? For ye are bought with a price: therefore glorify God in your body, and in your spirit, which are God's."

## II.

### *MEDICINAL MUSIC.*

1 SAMUEL xvi., 14-23.

AFTER Samuel's rebuke at Gilgal, Saul appears to have become more abandoned than ever. He brooded over his rejection as if it had been a wrong done to him; and though in his inmost heart he felt that he had sinned, he would neither make acknowledgment of his transgression, nor return to a proper mind. He became moody, irritable, vindictive, and gloomy, a source of misery to himself, and a cause of anxiety and terror to all who were around him. The moral balance of his nature, weak and unsteady as it had always been, seems now to have been almost destroyed, and even his intellect became beclouded, for he exhibited symptoms closely akin to those of mental aberration.

The cause and nature of the malady with which he was afflicted are described in the narrative by these two phrases: "The Spirit of the Lord departed from Saul," and "An evil spirit from the Lord troubled him." There is thus both a privative and a positive proposition, and it is extremely difficult to determine what precisely is indicated by their combination. In regard to the negative or privative declaration to the effect that "the Spirit of the Lord had departed from Saul," we may take it to mean that God withdrew from him all those special aids which, in connection with his anointing to the royal office, had been conferred upon him. Perhaps, also, we may include in it the taking away from him of those gracious influences of the Holy Spirit without which a man becomes, in the saddest and solemnest of all senses, "aban doned." This is what Paul has described as a "being given over to a reprobate mind, to do those things which are not convenient;" and what, in the simple Saxon of our common speech, we call "a being left to one's self." The Saviour has said, "From him that hath not shall be taken away even that he hath." Now, in Saul, as we have already hinted, we have a deeply suggestive instance of the execution of this sentence. He had received not one talent only, but many; yet he failed to improve them, and so they were taken from him, and he was left, in a large degree, the mental and moral wreck of his former self. He was deprived of all the special gifts which had been conferred upon him, and set free from all those restraining influences which had been exerted upon him, and which had kept him from those aggravated iniquities into which he afterward fell.

This was sad enough, for, as Delany says, "No man needs a heavier chastisement from Almighty God than the letting loose of his own passions upon him."* Still the positive expression, "An evil spirit from the Lord troubled him," would appear to indicate that there was something more, and more dreadful even than this, though what that something was, it is not easy now to determine. On such a subject it would be the height of folly for any man to dogmatize; but just as in the case of Job, the Lord permitted Satan to visit him with calamity and evil, with the view of bringing out thereby more vividly before men's eyes the saintliness of the patriarch's character; and as in that of Paul, a messenger of Satan, in the shape of a thorn in the flesh, was permitted to buffet him lest he should be exalted above measure; so here, it seems to me, that God made use of an evil spirit in order to inflict judicial punishment upon Saul; and, for my own part, I do

---

* "Historical Account of the Life and Reign of David, King of Israel," vol. i., p. 26.

not see any thing more mysterious in such an employment of evil spirits in the present state, than there is in the idea that these spirits shall in some terrible way intensify the misery of the lost in the world to come. We have here, then, as we think, something like a case of demoniacal possession, having its root and origin in the moral perversion of the soul itself. It would be wrong, indeed, to assert that in all cases of that sort described in Scripture, the malady was the consequence of special sin in the individual afflicted by it; nevertheless, as Trench has remarked, "It should not be lost sight of, that lavish sin, superinducing, as it often would, a weakness of the nervous system, wherein is the special bond between the body and the soul, may have laid open those unhappy ones to the fearful incursions of the powers of darkness."* And, from the peculiar language here employed, there is hardly room for doubt that, by the mysterious judicial permission of God, and as a punishment for his stubborn rebellion, such a spirit now laid hold on Saul, widening and deepening the gulf of separation which already existed between him and Jehovah. He that will do evil of his own choice is ultimately given over to evil as his master. This is the dreadful law, and in the present instance that mastery was maintained by the personal agency of one of those spiritual beings which are subordinate to the prince of darkness. Farther than this on such a subject we dare not venture, only we may take to ourselves the lesson of warning with which it is fraught, and learn to be on our guard, lest, refusing the guiding influence of God's Holy Spirit, we too should be given over to the dominion of Satan; for though demoniacal possession in its ancient form has disappeared from among us, it is yet too sadly possible for the prince of darkness to hold us captives at his will, and to rule in those

---

* "Notes on the Miracles," p. 161.

high places within us, in which God alone should be enthroned.

The servants of Saul, devoted to him by that personal attachment of which we have already seen a remarkable instance in Samuel himself, were deeply concerned on his account, and did every thing that they could think of, to alleviate his misery and cheer his spirit. But it was of no avail. At length, becoming convinced that the thing was of God, they bethought themselves of some special remedy; and one would have imagined that, as they saw so clearly the divine hand in the malady, they would have counseled their lord to return in submission to Jehovah, and to call in the aid of Samuel. But, whether they feared that such advice would have been unwelcome, and might therefore rather have tended to aggravate the evil, or whether they were themselves so defiant of God as deliberately to pass him over in their thoughts, we can not tell. All we know is, that they had recourse not to a spiritual, but to a material remedy. They suggested music; and if the disease had been merely a physical thing, they had prescribed well, for there is a virtue in "the concord of sweet sounds" to soothe the fretting brain and calm the troubled nerves; and men in every age, from the invention of musical instruments till now, have in such cases availed themselves of its aid with much effect. Interesting instances in illustration of this are given in abundance, by those who have made this subject a special study. We may mention a few. Seneca tells us that Pythagoras quieted the troubles of his mind with a harp; and in Pindar Æsculapius figures as healing acute disorders with soothing songs. "A story, too, is told of Farinelli, the famous singer, being sent for express to Madrid, to try the effect of his magical voice on the King of Spain (Philip the Fifth), who was then buried in the profoundest melancholy, proof against every appeal to exertion, living without signs of life in a darkened chamber, the unresisting prey of dejection beyond relief. The vocalist was desired by the physicians to sing in an outer room, which for a day or two he did, without any effect upon the royal patient. But at length it was noticed that the king seemed partially roused from his stupor, and became an evident listener; next day tears were seen starting from his eyes; the day after he ordered the door of his chamber to be left open; and at last "the perturbed spirit entirely left him, and the medicinal voice of Farinelli effected what no other medicine could." Similarly, we find that in literature and the drama kindred effects are ascribed to music. Readers of Scott will remember how a frenzied Highlander is soothed into self-restraint by the minstrelsy of Annot Lyle. Goethe makes the first bar of an air by Gretchen suffice to lull the sorrows of young Werther, who protests that "instantly the gloom and madness which hung over him were dispersed, and he breathed freely again." And Robert Browning has these beautiful lines, as the utterance of one who is listening to sweet sounds:

> "My heart! they loose my heart, those simple words;
> Its darkness passes, which naught else could touch,
> Like some dank snake that force may not expel,
> Which glideth out to music sweet and low."*

But it is more pertinent to our present purpose to remind you that, when Elisha's spirit had been fretted and chafed by the presence of the wicked Jehoram, he called for a minstrel, and under the soothing strains of his music he so regained his wonted composure that the Spirit of the Lord came upon him. Now this last instance may fitly illustrate all that music could do for Saul. It could not effect a permanent cure. It simply created a temporary alleviation.

---

* For these and many similar allusions, see "Scripture Texts Illustrated," by Francis Jacox. First series, pp. 55–60.

The words of Delany here seem to me most judicious. "We have reason," says he, "to believe, nor will the best philosophy forbid us, that quieting the perturbations of the mind is absolutely necessary toward receiving the sacred influences of the Spirit of God; and if so, then we may fairly conclude that the same state of mind which fits us for the influence of good spirits as naturally unfits us for the influence of such as are evil; and therefore the same power of music which quieted Elisha's rage (and indignation against the idolatrous Jehoram), and fitted him for the agency of the Holy Spirit of God, might for the same reason, by quieting Saul's unruly passions, unfit him for the agency of the evil spirit which troubled him, and of consequence work his cure for that time."* Hence, though it did not go to the root of the evil, the suggestion of Saul's servants was valuable so far as pointing to a temporary mitigation of the calamity. Their advice seems to have been given in one of the monarch's lucid intervals; and it so met his approval that he at once gave the command, "Provide me now a man that can play well, and bring him to me." On making inquiry, it was found that one of the servants of his house had met David, and had either heard him play, or had heard of his great musical ability, and on his report a messenger was at once dispatched to Jesse desiring the immediate attendance of his youngest son at Gibeah. Notice the description that is here given of the youthful shepherd: "Cunning in playing, and a mighty, valiant man, and prudent in matters (or, as the margin has it, in speech), and a comely person, and the Lord is with him." We are not surprised to find here mention made of his skill in music and his comeliness in person, but it is not so easy to account for the fact that he is styled "a

---

* "Historical Account of the Life of David, King of Israel," vol i., p. 28.

mighty valiant man, and a man of war;" and from the difficulty which these words present, it has been supposed that by some accident there has been a transposition of two sections of the narrative at this particular portion of the book of Samuel. To put the case clearly before you, we must anticipate one or two of the incidents in the succeeding chapter. Observe, then, that it is said that after David's performances on the harp, Saul made him his armor-bearer; and again, that after the conflict between him and Goliath, Saul asked, "Whose son is this youth?" as if he had been, up till that moment, ignorant of every thing about him. It is hence inferred by some that the narrative on which we are now engaged has fallen out of its proper place, and that it should be taken in after the next chapter, or rather between the ninth and tenth verses of the eighteenth chapter. But this seems to me to be a violent cutting of the knot, while, in reality, it does not free us from the difficulty; for if the description of David by Saul's servant in the section before us were given after the duel with the giant, it is inconceivable that no mention should have been made of that great victory; while again, after the events of that memorable day, it is improbable that Saul should not have known and recognized who David was from his servant's description of him; and as after that deed of prowess David was the special object of Saul's jealousy, his presence would have tended rather to aggravate, than to mitigate, the malady from which he suffered. On the whole, therefore, though the narrative is by no means free from difficulties, I prefer to take it in the order here given, the rather as there is nothing in any of the Hebrew manuscripts, or in any of the ancient versions, to indicate that a transposition has occurred.

But what, then, is the meaning of the words "a mighty man of valor," and "a man of war," as applied to a youth like David? I answer that the reference may be to his successful encounters with wild beasts in the keeping of his flocks, or to his valiant resistance of the wandering Arabs, who then, like the modern Bedouins, roamed through the land, making prey of every thing on which they could lay their hands. Stories of David's youthful prowess, as well as of his skill in music and his pre-eminent piety, must have been common in the neighborhood, so that already he had a reputation for bravery before he faced Goliath; and probably it is to his local renown for such encounters that Eliab refers when, on David's appearance in the Valley of Elah, he taunts him with having left his sheep, and upbraids him with having come for no other purpose than to see the battle. The phrase "prudent in matters," means also, "skillful in words;" and so it may refer either to his signal sagacity, or to his ability in the composition of extempore verses, with which, like the Italian improvisator, and the minstrels of the Scottish border of a later day, he accompanied the music of his harp.

In any case, the description so pleased Saul that he sent a messenger to Jesse forthwith, saying, "Send me David thy son, which is with the sheep." We can not tell with what feelings Jesse received this command. What could Saul want with his son? Could there be any evil hanging over his house? or was it, that the visit of Samuel to him was now about to bear visible fruits? Between these two anticipations of fear and hope his mind would vibrate; and as he laded the ass with the simple present that David was to bear to Saul, we can imagine with what unwonted fervor he would commend his youngest-born to the keeping of his God. But who may describe the feelings that swelled up in the heart of the young shepherd himself? When, as he followed his sheep, he thrilled the strings of his much-loved lyre, he had little idea that it was by his harp he was first to be brought into prominence in the land; and now as he sets out for Gibeah, and thinks of the anointing that he had received from Samuel's hands, and of the future that lay all untrodden before him, I can almost imagine him anticipating some of his later strains, and saying, "Hold up my goings in thy paths, that my footsteps slip not. Lead me in thy truth, and teach me: for thou art the God of my salvation; on thee do I wait all the day."* "Truly," as Kitto says, "it is a pleasant picture to conceive the future king of Israel stepping lightly along behind the ass, with his shepherd staff and scrip, and entertained as he went by the gambols of the kid. His light harp was no doubt slung to his back; and it is likely that he now and then rested under a tree and solaced his soul with its music. His fearless temper would not allow him to look forward to the result of his journey with misgivings; or if a doubt crossed his mind, he found sufficient rest in confidence in God."†

The distance from Bethlehem to Gibeah was a little short of twelve miles, and the road lay down the valley of Rephaim, near to the stronghold of Zion, which was still held by the Jebusites. As he passed Moriah's rocky ridge, did there come into his young heart any premonition of the day when his own palace should crown the hill of Zion, and the threshing-floor of Araunah should be consecrated for Jehovah's temple? We can not tell; but often, I doubt not, in after times, as he looked abroad from the heights of Jerusalem, or from the roof of his palace, there would rise up before him the remembrance of this early journey, when, with his lowly present and his humble harp he went to begin the world at the court of Saul; and, as then, he thought of God's favor to him through all the intervening years, I can almost hear him saying, "O how great is thy goodness, which thou hast laid up for them that fear thee; which thou hast wrought for

---

* Psa. xvii., 5; xxv., 5.   † "Daily Bible Illustrations," vol. iii., p. 229.

them that trust in thee before the sons of men! Thou shalt hide them in the secret of thy presence from the pride of man: thou shalt keep them secretly in a pavilion from the strife of tongues. Blessed be the Lord: for he hath showed me his marvelous kindness in a strong city."*

Arrived at Gibeah, David was at once presented to Saul, upon whom he made such a favorable impression that he was taken forthwith into his regard, and appointed as one of his armor-bearers; nay more, the king desired his constant presence at the court, and sent to Jesse, saying, "Let David, I pray thee, stand before me; for he hath found favor in my sight." And ever as some new attack of his malady seized him, David was there with his harp and holy hymns to soothe his soul, and "Saul was refreshed, and was well, and the evil spirit departed from him." To borrow the lines of James Montgomery,† in his "World before the Flood," and substituting in them the name of David for that of Jubal, we may thus describe the scene:

> "David with eager hope beheld the chase
> Of strange emotions hurrying o'er his face,
> And waked his noblest numbers to control
> The tide and tempest of the maniac's soul.
> Through many a maze of melody he flew;
> They rose like incense, they distilled like dew,
> Passed through the sufferer's breast delicious balm,
> And soothed remembrance till remorse grew calm."

But it was only a temporary relief after all. A more wondrous triumph was yet destined to be wrought by that same harp when, tuned to words by God's own inspiration given, it should not only soothe the soul of the singer himself, but also give forth notes that would reach through all time, and

---

* Psa. xxxi., 19–21.

† For this application of Montgomery's lines, I am indebted to Blaikie's "David, King of Israel," p. 37.

lift the devout spirit above all evil influences. How often have these holy lyrics done for men a grander work than that wrought by this music on the mind of Saul! Luther felt their influence when, inspirited by their strains, he went forth to his great reforming work; and the souls of many anxious ones have been quieted by their trustful utterances when their hearts, like Eli's, "trembled for the ark of God." The lone widow has dried her tears as she has listened to the music of the words, "God lives! blessed be my rock, and let the God of my salvation be exalted." The helpless orphan has been directed to a friend above, as this soft strain has fallen on his ear, "When my father and my mother forsake me, then the Lord will take me up." The desponding saint has seen the heavens grow bright above him while he heard these trustful notes: "Why art thou cast down, O my soul? and why art thou disquieted within me? hope thou in God: for I shall yet praise him, who is the health of my countenance, and my God." The dying one has felt as if the glory-gate was already opening to him while the melody of these words has distilled like the dew over his spirit: "As for me, I will behold thy face in righteousness: I shall be satisfied, when I awake, with thy likeness." Yea, mightiest achievement of all, it was a strain from David's harp which upheld the Redeemer's soul when from the depths of his infinite agony he cried, "My God, my God, why hast thou forsaken me?" Truly, as well as eloquently, has one said, "The temporary calm which the soft notes of David's harp spread over the stormy soul of Saul was but a superficial emotion compared with the holy rest on the bosom of their God to which the Psalms have guided many an anxious and weary sinner. The one was like the passing emotion of an oratorio, the other is the deep peace of the Gospel."[*]

---

[*] Blaikie's "David, King of Israel," p. 38.

Pausing here for the present, let us bring together a few inferences from our subject which may be profitable for doctrine and practice. We can not help observing, then, in the first place, how God works out his purposes through the agency of men who are acting according to their own free choice. Evermore, as we read history, or look back upon our own experience, we see distinctly marked these two things, the plan of God, and the liberty of man. We can not get rid of either, nor can we see how they can be perfectly harmonized; yet there they are, constantly running parallel to each other, and forming, so to say, the two lines of rail on which the chariot of human progress rolls along. It was the design of the Lord that David should sit upon the throne of his people, and it was needful thereto that the young shepherd should, in some way or other, be introduced to the court of Saul, while, at the same time, it was essential that the circumstances of his introduction should excite no suspicion as to his future career. Now, see how all this was brought about. David, in his devotion to his harp, had no thought of thereby rising to the royal favor; the servant who mentioned his name to Saul had no idea of the fact that he was already anointed to be Saul's successor; yet each, in his own way, and by working out the choice of his own free-will, was helping on the fulfillment of the purpose of God. So it is still, the only difference being that, in ordinary history, we are not always thus permitted to see the different agencies at work. Usually we are like men looking on the watch-dial and reading off results, according as the fingers indicate. Here, however, we are privileged to look within, and to see how the various instrumentalities work together to bring about the outward and visible effect. But we must not forget that in every thing, as really as in this history, God's providence is working itself out through the free agency of men, though at the moment they may not be thinking of him at all. Oh, matchless mystery, whereby these two apparent opposites are held in harmony! Oh, most consoling truth, whereby in all circumstances we are reminded that "all things work together for good to them that love God, to them who are the called according to his purpose!"

But passing from this mysterious theme, let me hold up before the young people of my audience the example of David here, that they may be stimulated to improve their leisure time in acquiring some useful information, or in learning some useful art. While David followed the sheep, he had ample time at his disposal, but instead of letting it go by in idleness, or frittering it away in spasmodic study, now of this thing and now of that, he specially concentrated his attention on the art of music, until he acquired rare skill and excellence in playing upon the harp; and it was through this self-taught attainment that he was first called forth into public life. Now it is of immense consequence, that the young people of these days should clearly see the necessity under which they are laid, of acting in a similar manner. I speak, observe, of leisure time, and any thing which I may say is not to be misconstrued into an admonition to neglect business for other pursuits. By no means. David did not neglect his sheep for his harp. He was as ready to encounter the lion and the bear as he was to play upon his lyre; but with his work he combined the cultivation of music in his spare moments. And I earnestly exhort you, my youthful hearers, to have some one study or pursuit on hand to which you devote your leisure hours.

I advocate this on the ground of economy. As things are with most of you, your spare moments go you can not tell how. To-day they are given to one thing, to-morrow to another; so that with this continual social and mental dissipation, it would be difficult for most to tell, either what they have done or what they have learned, out of business hours last week. And yet they have been occupied all the while. "As they were busy here and there," at one thing or another, the week "was gone," and they have nothing to show for it; whereas, if they had systematically devoted their hours of leisure to the prosecution of some plan in some department of self-culture, they would have acquired something which would remain with them, and be of signal service to them in after-life. Bind together your spare hours, therefore, by the cord of some definite purpose, and you know not how much you may accomplish. Gather up the fragments of your time, that nothing may be lost.

I advocate this on the ground of recreation. Some, indeed, may be apt to say that they have no strength for the prosecution, after the labors of the day, of such a work as that to which I would incite them. But not to say that there is nothing more wearisome than idleness, unless it be the dissipation of pleasure, I would remind you that the truest relaxation is a change of employment.

> "A want of occupation is not rest,
> A mind quite vacant is a mind distressed."

No doubt there must be some physical recreation, but for rest to the mind we need something else than exercise for the body; we need occupation for the mind itself in some other sphere of thought, and this can be best obtained by the systematic prosecution of some favorite pursuit. Try it, young men, and you will acquire from it buoyant elasticity of mind, while at the same time you will obtain substantial information, or proficiency in some elegant art.

I advocate this on the ground of self-protection. Idleness is the mother of vice, and it is a sadly suggestive fact that a man is commonly either made or marred for life by the use which he makes of his leisure time. It is not at business, or at work, that temptation first assails a youth; it is when he is at leisure; and commonly when he falls into iniquity in business it is in order that he may procure the means of indulging in the vicious habits which he has learned during his leisure. If, therefore, you would keep temptation at a distance from you, and deprive the haunts of iniquity of the power to attract you, seek to give yourself to some favorite study in your spare hours, with all the ardor and energy of your nature; and when one comes to entice you into sin, you will be able to say, "I am doing something better, and I can not go with you."

I advocate this use of your spare time, lastly, as a preparative for future eminence. It is interesting to observe how many have passed through this very gate to usefulness and honor. Hugh Miller raised himself from the position of a working mason by his devotion, first to geology, and afterward to literature, in his leisure moments; and Michael Faraday, while a book-binder's apprentice, was reading chemical books, and making electrical machines in his evening hours—thereby laying the foundations of that great work which as a man of science he was afterward to accomplish. You can not all become Millers or Faradays indeed, but, by following their example, you will attain to something nobler than you otherwise could reach, and make the best of yourselves for God and for the world.

It may seem to many as if in speaking thus I were drawing a merely secular lesson from a sacred theme; but to the Christian there is nothing secular. He wants to make the most of himself and of his opportunities for Christ, and he must learn this lesson, else when occasions come he will not be able to avail himself of them. The men who have been unsuccessful on the earth have failed, not for want of opportunities of succeeding, but because they were never ready to avail themselves of the opportunities which did come to them; and this unreadiness may be traced to the frittering away by them of their leisure hours in strenuous idleness, or in frivolous amusement, or in vicious indulgence.

Again, as we see David setting out from Bethlehem, we are reminded of the feelings, the difficulties, and the dangers which are usually attendant upon the first leaving of the father's house. I have not attempted to describe to you what David's emotions were as he parted from father and mother, and looked forward to the delicate position which he was to occupy; but I can not help employing this incident to remind the young people who may have come to this great commercial centre from a distant home, that there are parents looking after them with longing solicitude, and earnestly beseeching God to bless them. It may be, indeed, that in some instances the parents from whom they have parted are now in glory; yet I am sure that they all look back to their early abode with the tenderest feelings, and regard it as surrounded with the holiest associations. Are you living now, my young friends, as those parents would have you? Would you care to have your mother perfectly acquainted with all you did last week? How does your present life look when you think of your father now in heaven?

It may be, too, that there are some here preparing to leave their father's house, and go like Abraham, hardly knowing whither, save only that duty calls them. Let me entreat them to go in Abraham's faith, and above all to secure that, as in the case of David here, the Spirit of the Lord shall rest upon them, making them prudent in matters. With this possession, no matter where we go, all will be well. Without it, no matter what worldly prosperity may attend us, we shall be poor indeed. They are never far from home who take God with them, for he is himself their dwelling-place.

Finally, we may learn, from Saul's experience, how transient is the relief which mere earthly influences can give in the case of a moral and spiritual disease. David's music went so far, but it did not touch the root of the evil. Only when Saul returned to God would God return to him. He needed a new heart; and no earthly music, even from David's harp, could give him that. So let us be admonished by his folly. Vain are all merely worldly prescriptions for the sin-burdened and depraved soul. Well-meaning friends may say to the anxious sinner, "Go to the opera, come to the theatre, visit this and the other place of amusement;" but it is all to no purpose. These may give temporary relief, but in the silence of the solitary chamber the agony of heart comes back more violently than before. There is but one who can hush its troubled perturbations into peace, and that is He "who stilled the rolling lake of Galilee." To Him, therefore, O anxious one, betake thyself, and He will give thee a new heart, which will be itself like a well-tuned harp, whose strings will vibrate evermore with holy harmony in thy secret ear! He will make thee independent of all outward influences, by giving thee quietude and holiness within. To Him, then, make thy way; for has He not said. "Come unto me, all ye that labor and are heavy laden, and I will give you rest?"

## III.

### *THE CONFLICT WITH GOLIATH.*

1 SAMUEL xvii.

AFTER David's music had produced such a beneficial effect upon Saul, the young shepherd seems to have returned to his former charge upon the slopes of Bethlehem. This may appear strange, especially after the statement that "the king loved him greatly," and made him his armor-bearer. But if we take a correct view of the character of Saul, and consider how at a later date he vibrated between the two extremes of inordinate admiration and spiteful persecution of David, our surprise will cease, and we shall have in David's departure from Gibeah at this time only another illustration of that fickleness and instability for which Saul was so remarkable. With his restoration to health, his love for David cooled; or, perhaps, he did not care to be constantly reminded of his malady by the continuous presence of the young minstrel, and so he sent him to his home again.

How long David remained at Bethlehem before the occurrence of the events narrated in this seventeenth chapter, we are not informed, and it is vain to make any attempt at conjecture. All we know is that he was brought again into prominence in connection with the renewal of hostilities between Saul and the Philistines: and as this is the first occasion on which we come into contact with that ancient and warlike people, we may pause a few moments to gather into one brief paragraph the main features of their history and character.

Coming, as the ablest critics have generally agreed, from Egypt,* they occupied the strip of country lying along the south-east coast of Palestine, and comprising a confederacy of five united yet independent towns — Gaza, Ashdod, Ashkelon, Gath, and Ekron. When the children of Israel took possession of the land, this territory was given, by lot, to the tribe of Judah; but it was not until the days of David that they could be said actually to possess it; and, indeed, all through the history of the Jews, there was danger of collision between them and this fierce nation. They had early attained to great skill in the arts alike of war and peace; they probably possessed a navy, for they had harbors at Gath and Ashkelon; they were eminent as smiths and armorers; and their images of golden mice and emerods, referred to in one of the early chapters of the first book of Samuel, imply an acquaintance with the work of the founder and the goldsmith. We are told, in the first chapter of the book of Judges, that Judah took Gaza, Ashkelon, and Ekron, with their coasts; but the resources of the Philistines were such that they speedily regained their territory and asserted their supremacy. In the days of Shamgar, Jephthah, and Samson, they held the Jews in hard and cruel bondage; and it was only under Samuel that the chosen people had been able in any serious degree to break their power. Even after that, however, they re-asserted their dominion, and were able successfully to dispute with Saul the ownership of the soil, and so to cripple the tribes, that there was no proper implement of war to be found among them, save only in the hands of Saul and Jonathan. The mode of warfare pursued by them was of the guerilla description  They made a series of sudden raids on unprotected places for purposes of plun-

---

* See the article PHILISTINES, in Smith's "Dictionary of the Bible;" and also that on the same subject in Fairbairn's "Imperial Bible Dictionary."

## The Conflict with Goliath.

der. They seized some commanding position, which they strongly fortified, and from that they sent out bands of marauders to spoil the surrounding district. This system of incursions kept the Israelites in constant anxiety; and when the alarm of the approach of their oppressors was given, the people betook themselves to hiding-places, or fled across the Jordan. It was in the storming of such a fortress as I have described that Jonathan won his first laurels as a warrior, and though, as a result of his success at that time, the nation had enjoyed a brief season of repose, the chapter before us represents the land as ringing once again with the alarm of war.

The Philistines, hearing perhaps of Samuel's separation from Saul, and encouraged by that circumstance, and by their possession of a famous champion, had taken the field again. They encamped at Shochoh, which belonged to Judah, between Shochoh and Azekah, in Ephes-dammim; and the children of Israel, in response to the summons of Saul, made their rallying-point in the Valley of Elah—literally, the valley of the terebinth-tree, the name having been probably given to it because of the plentifulness of such trees in the vicinity. "The valley," says Dr. Porter, "is now called Wady-es-sumpt, because it abounds in acacias. It is a remarkable fact, and tends to throw light on the origin of the ancient name, that one of the largest terebinths in Palestine may be seen in a branch of the valley, only a few miles distant from the scene of the battle." The valley itself, according to the same authority, "runs in a north-westerly direction, from the mountains of Judah, through the low hills at their base, into the plain of Philistia, which it enters a little north of the site of Gaza. The ruins of Shochoh, now called Shuweikeh, cover a natural terrace on the left bank of the valley; and Azekah appears to have stood on a conical hill some two miles distant on the same bank. Between them, on the slope of the ridge, the Philistines encamped; and opposite them, on the right bank, were the Israelites. The distance between the armies was about a mile; and the vale beneath is flat and rich. Through the centre winds a torrent-bed, the banks fringed with shrubbery of acacia, and the bottom covered with 'smooth stones.' The ridges on each side rise to the height of about five hundred feet, and have a uniform slope, so that the armies ranged along them could see the combat in the valley."\* The place was about twelve miles south-west of Jerusalem, and therefore probably not more than seven or eight miles from Bethlehem.

In the army with Saul were the three eldest sons of Jesse: Eliab, Aminadab, and Shammah. It was the law of Israel, that in times of war each able-bodied man between certain ages was to carry arms; and so, whenever a summons was given, suspense would reign in every home. On the present occasion, however, as the war was defensive, and as the lives and property of the people depended on the character of the resistance that was offered to their enemies, there would probably be no great difficulty in securing a large army; yet the parents of such as went to the front would naturally feel much solicitude concerning their safety. We do not wonder, therefore, that Jesse was anxious to know how things went with his sons. Indeed, considering his comparative proximity to the two encampments, it was the most natural thing in the world that he and his wife should desire to send some home comforts to their sons. Accordingly he took David from his sheep, and dispatched him to Elah, with an ephah of parched corn, and ten loaves for his brothers, and ten cheeses for the officer of their company. He instructed him also "to take their pledge," that is, as I suppose, to bring with him in his hand some token or pledge of their safety in

---

\* Kitto's "Cyclopædia," by Alexander, article ELAH.

## THE CONFLICT WITH GOLIATH.

the camp. So, leaving his sheep with a keeper, David hastened to Elah, and arrived just as the battle-cry was being raised in both armies, and the ranks of each stood in formal array against the other. Seeing this state of matters, the eager youth left his baggage at the wagon-line by which the camp was surrounded, and ran to look for his brothers. Scarcely had he found them, and asked them of their welfare, when there stalked forth from the front of the Philistian line the tall champion of Gath named Goliath. This man, probably a descendant of the Anakim, is described as six cubits and a span in height. The cubit was originally the length from the elbow to the point of the middle finger, and is commonly taken as about eighteen or nineteen inches. Accepting the smaller of these as correct, the stature of Goliath would be about nine feet nine inches. Josephus and the Septuagint, however, read four cubits and a span, and this would reduce his height to six feet nine inches.* This enormous height apparently did not interfere with the development of his strength, for the weight of his armor was such as could have been borne only by one of Herculean might. Taking the shekel at half an ounce avoirdupois, his coat of mail must have been one hundred and fifty-six pounds in weight, and the head of his spear must have been eighteen pounds twelve ounces.

It is not surprising, therefore, that when he came forth into the space between the armies and defied Israel, consternation and dismay took hold upon the soldiers of Saul. Nor was this the first occasion, on which he had made his appearance thus. For forty days he had come repeating his boastful and

---

\* Keil on 1 Samuel, p. 173, says: "His height was six cubits and a span, *i. e.*, according to a calculation made by Thenius, about nine feet two inches Parisian measure—a great height, no doubt, though not altogether unparalleled, and hardly greater than that of the great-uncle of Iren, who came to Berlin in the year 1857."

insulting words : "Why are ye come out to set your battle in array? Am not I a Philistine, and ye servants to Saul? choose you a man for you, and let him come down to me. If he be able to fight with me, and to kill me, then will we be your servants : but if I prevail against him, and kill him, then shall ye be our servants, and serve us. I defy the armies of Israel this day ; give me a man, that we may fight together." To this challenge there was not spirit enough among the Israelites to make response. Saul was probably restrained from personally accepting it by motives of dignity ; but we can not read the record without contrasting his silence, and the utter hopelessness of his army, on this occasion, with the enthusiasm which he displayed, and the bravery which they manifested that day at Jabesh-gilead, when they drove their enemies before them like chaff before the wind. We read, indeed, of the royal promise to enrich the man who should slay his enemy, and to give him his daughter in marriage, and to make his father's house free in Israel ; but there is no word of any calling upon God, or any application to the high-priest, that with his Urim and Thummim he might give direction from on high. Suggestive silence this! Saul was still self-reliant and defiant ; and so this was to be the occasion of bringing his successor forth before the people's eyes.

David, young as he was, was astonished at what he saw and heard. Apparently he had no fear of the giant, but he did wonder at the craven-heartedness of his fellow-countrymen. He asked again and again into the particulars, and was so specially minute in his inquiries about what Saul had promised to the victor, that his eldest brother began to surmise that he was himself purposing to accept the challenge, and said to him, in a sneering, cynical, elder-brotherly fashion, "Why camest thou down hither? and with whom hast thou left those few sheep in the wilderness? I know thy pride, and the naughtiness of thine heart ; for thou art come

## THE CONFLICT WITH GOLIATH.

down that thou mightest see the battle." But David did not allow himself to be provoked; he ruled his spirit for the time—a harder task and a yet nobler achievement even than the conquest of the giant, and he simply said, "What have I now done? Is there not a cause?" At length, however, as he talked with one and another, the report spread out that there was one who would fight the giant, and finally it was told to Saul, who sent for him, and sought to dissuade him from his purpose, saying, "Thou art not able to go against this Philistine to fight with him; for thou art but a youth, and he a man of war from his youth." But the young shepherd was not to be daunted thus. Rehearsing his deeds of valor in the defense of his flock, and tracing his successes on these occasions to the help of God, he said, "The Lord that delivered me out of the paw of the lion, and out of the paw of the bear, he will deliver me out of the hand of this Philistine." This was precisely the spirit that was needed for the stern encounter; and Saul, recognizing in it that in which he was himself so deficient, at once made answer, "Go, and the Lord be with thee!" At first the king proposed that he should array himself in the royal armor; but David was not at home in that, and, with a true stroke of military genius, he determined to go forth with the weapons with which he was most familiar. He took his shepherd's staff in his left hand, and his sling in his right, and having his sachel suspended from his neck, he went out in front of the lines. As he crossed the dry bed of the brook, he selected some smooth stones, one of which he fixed in his sling, and the others he dropped into his bag. It has been commonly supposed that, in laying aside Saul's armor and preferring his own sling, David was giving up every advantage, and that the chances of his success were materially lessened by the fact that he was thus, comparatively speaking, defenseless. But that is a mistake. The genius of David was made manifest in the choice of his weapons, and so soon as he had determined to use the sling the issue was not doubtful. The giant was open to attack only on the forehead; but then he was cased in such heavy armor that he could not move with swiftness, and so he could prove a formidable foe only when he was fighting at close quarters. David, on the other hand, was free, and could run with swiftness and agility; while using the sling he could begin the attack from a distance, and out of the range of his adversary's weapons. So far, therefore, as weapons were concerned, the advantage was clearly on David's side, provided only he could preserve his precision of aim and steadiness of hand. He was like one armed with a rifle, while his enemy had only a spear and a sword; and if only he could take sure aim, the result was absolutely certain. Goliath, however, despised his simple weapons, and in spiteful indignation cursed him by his gods, saying also, "Come to me, and I will give thy flesh unto the fowls of the air, and to the beasts of the field." Nothing daunted, David made reply: "Thou comest to me with a sword, and with a spear, and with a shield: but I come to thee in the name of the Lord of hosts, the God of the armies of Israel, whom thou hast defied. This day will the Lord deliver thee into mine hand; and I will smite thee, and take thine head from thee; and I will give the carcasses of the host of the Philistines this day unto the fowls of the air, and to the wild beasts of the earth; that all the earth may know that there is a God in Israel. And all this assembly shall know that the Lord saveth not with sword and spear: for the battle is the Lord's, and he will give you into our hands." As modern warfare is conducted, such a colloquy as this between two combatants seems to be ridiculous; but every one who is familiar with Homer's "Iliad," either in the original, or in one of its spirited translations, will see a wonderful similarity between the speeches of Goliath and David, and those which the father

## THE CONFLICT WITH GOLIATH.

of poetry puts into the mouths of his heroes in similar circumstances.*

But now the time for parley is at an end, Goliath is advancing to meet his antagonist, and David, seeing that his only opportunity is to strike him while yet he is at a distance, makes haste and runs. As he runs, he re-adjusts the stone in his sling; and taking unerring aim, he sends it whizzing to its mark in the forehead of the giant, who forthwith fell with his face to the ground. Then rushing forward, he took the sword of his adversary and cut off his head, which he carried with him as a trophy of victory. When the Philistines saw that their champion was dead, they turned and fled; but the Israelites pursued them hotly even to the gates of Ekron, and the victory was complete.

Two things mentioned as consequent upon this encounter are apt to perplex the general reader. The first is, that David took the Philistine's head to Jerusalem, and put his armor in his tent. Now it is said by some that Jerusalem was not yet in the hands of the Israelites, but only came into their possession years afterward, when David conquered the Jebusites. But, as obviating this difficulty, we may remind you that it was not Jerusalem that David took from the Jebusites, but rather the stronghold of Zion, which was only a part of Jerusalem; and it is quite likely that before it was taken by David the other portions of the city were occupied by the Jews. Or perhaps the reference may simply be to Nob, the site of the Tabernacle, which, though in the territory of the tribe of Benjamin, was yet so near to Jerusalem as to be within sight of it. Then, as to the putting of the armor in his tent by David, we are not to suppose that this was meant by him as its ultimate destination, but

---

* See, in particular, the speeches of Glaucus and Diomede, in the sixth book of the "Iliad:" "Come hither," says Glaucus, "that you may quickly reach the goal of death."

we may well enough understand that it was put there for safety until he should have an opportunity of laying it up before the Lord in the Tabernacle; while, if any should be surprised that he should have a tent in the camp, considering that he had only come casually from Bethlehem, we may remove their astonishment by suggesting that, after so signal a victory as that which he had been honored to achieve, every thing would be done to show him gratitude, and we may be sure that a tent would be put at his disposal. The second and more formidable difficulty is in connection with Saul's inquiry after David. We read that he said to Abner, "Whose son is this youth? And Abner said, As thy soul liveth, O king, I can not tell. And the king said, Inquire thou whose son the stripling is. And as David returned from the slaughter of the Philistine, Abner took him, and brought him before Saul with the head of the Philistine in his hand. And Saul said to him, Whose son art thou, thou young man? And David answered, I am the son of thy servant Jesse the Bethlehemite." Now how shall we account for Saul's non-recognition of David after having had him formerly at his court, and numbered among his armor-bearers? Some would get rid of the difficulty by alleging that there has been a transposition of the narrative here, and that the account of David's minstrel visit to Gibeah should come in after the record of the incidents which have been before us now; but for the reasons which I formerly advanced, I can not accept this theory. Others think that in the state of mind in which Saul was when David played before him on the harp, he would not be able to take any particular notice of him, and therefore when he saw him again might not recognize him. While others still suppose that the purpose of Saul's question was not to know who David was, but to inquire into the character and condition of his family, that he might make good the promise which he had made to the man that should slay the Philistine, to the effect that he would give him his daughter in marriage, and make his father's house free in Israel. This is the solution proposed by Keil, who says: "It was not the name of David's father alone that he wanted to discover, but what kind of a man he really was; and the question was put not merely in order that he might grant him exemption from taxes, but also that he might attach such a man to his court, since he inferred, from the courage and bravery of the son, the existence of similar qualities in the father. It is true that David merely replied, 'The son of thy servant Jesse the Bethlehemite;' but it is evident from the expression in chapter xviii., 1: 'When he had made an end of speaking unto Saul,' that Saul conversed with him still further about his family affairs, since the very words imply a lengthened conversation."* Dr. Kitto, however, is perhaps nearer the truth when he suggests that, in the interval between David's appearance at court and his fighting with the giant, he had passed from early youth into manhood, and so grown, as it were, out of Saul's recognition. Here are his words: "You would scarcely know him for the same person that you saw some three years ago; he was then a growing youth, but he has now attained to greater fullness of stature, and to more firmly knit limbs; above all, his beard has grown, and to those who, like us, remove the beard as soon as it appears, the great difference produced by the presence of this appendage on the face of one who a year or two ago was a beardless youth, is scarcely conceivable."† That was written by the good doctor thirty-one years ago. I imagine that in the interval we have had a good deal of experience in the mat-

---

\* Kiel on 1 Samuel, p. 178, note.

† Kitto's "Daily Bible Illustrations," vol. iii., p. 240. See, also, this whole subject very fairly argued, though there is a leaning to the transposition theory, in "The Land and the Book," p. 568. English edition.

ter to which he refers, and may therefore be the better prepared to accept his explanation as the correct one.

In the Greek version of the Old Testament made by the Seventy, there is an apocryphal Psalm, numbered the 151st, which purports to have been written by David on the occasion of this victory; but it has nothing in it either of the beauty or the grandeur of David's odes, and is probably a mythical production made by some ordinary person on reading the history, and attempted by him to be palmed off as the work of the young hero.* Yet, though there was no special ode composed by David on this occasion, we can see in many of his lyrics traces of the influence which this, his first great victory, produced upon him. Thus I can not doubt that he remembered the whole incidents of this eventful day, when he sang these words: "I will not trust in my bow, neither shall my sword save me. In God we boast all the day long, and praise thy name forever."† And again, "There is no king saved by the multitude of a host: a mighty man is not delivered by much strength. Our soul waiteth for the Lord: he is our help and our shield."‡ Nor can I help remarking that in this recognition of God, and confidence in him, with which David entered upon public life, we have the root of the difference between him and Saul. You never hear Saul expressing his trust in God, as David did when he went forth to meet Goliath; whereas, as we proceed in the history, we shall find that with David it was habitual. The tendency of Saul's life was toward himself: any thing inconsistent with that in him, or about him, was but fitful and spasmodic. But it was just the reverse with David. The leaning of his soul was toward God, and though at times self and sin sadly and terribly asserted their power, yet these times

---

* See, for a translation of this Psalm, Stanley's "Jewish Church," vol. ii., p. 56.
† Psalm xliv., 6, 8.  ‡ Psalm xxxiii., 16, 20.

were only occasional, and out of keeping with the usual course and current of his character. His sins, like Saul's impulses toward good things, were but occasional eruptions of that which it was the habit of his soul to repress; his piety, like Saul's impiety, was the principle of his life. And herein we account for the acceptance of the one, and the rejection of the other, as the occupant of the throne of Israel.

But it is time now that we should seek for some practical guidance from this subject for our daily lives, and for the better understanding of the Gospel of Christ. Every reader of the narrative will see many points in which it both touches and illustrates New Testament themes. Thus, without going the length of adopting the view that David was in all this a type of Christ, we can not see him confronting the giant with his sling and stone, and consummating his destruction with his own sword, without being reminded of a greater than he who foiled the prince of darkness with a triple thrust of the sword of the Spirit which is the Word of God, and who "through death destroyed him that had the power of death, and delivered them who through fear of death were all their lifetime subject to bondage."

Again: when we think of the tribal inheritance of Judah, still in a large degree retained by the Philistines, who ever and anon arose to reclaim it all, and sometimes nearly succeeded, we have a striking analogy to the heart of the believer, wherein, though he has given himself to Jesus, and has been renewed by the Holy Spirit, divers sins and lusts do still contend for the mastery; and sometimes one of them, attaining Goliath-like proportions, threatens to enslave him altogether. Who has not felt himself thus menaced by some fierce passion? Each of us has his own giant to fight, and here, too, it must be single combat, with no one to help us but Him who went forth with the stripling David. With some of us it is temper; with some avarice; with some ap petite; with some ambition; but whatever it be, let us learn to resist it courageously, relying on the might of the Lord Jesus Christ, and the victory will be ours.

Or, yet again, in contending with external evils, we may sometimes feel that they have assumed such magnitude as to appall us. Thus, which of us is not brought almost to a stand-still, when he surveys the ignorance, infidelity, intemperance, and licentiousness by which we are surrounded? It seems to us sometimes, in moments of depression, as if these evils, and perhaps the last of them the worst, were stalking forth defiantly before the armies of the living God, and laughing them, Goliath-like, to scorn; and our courage is apt to cool as we contemplate this show of force. But we must not allow these feelings to prevail. The God of David liveth, and he will still give us success. The great danger that besets the Christian at such times is that of attempting to fight with the world's weapons. The worldling will always overcome him when he does so, because the Christian in such armor is not at home. He can not use it unscrupulously as the worldling does; and the moment he undertakes to employ it, he seals his own defeat. Let him go forth with the cross of Christ in his hand, and by that he will conquer; but if he seek a lower weapon, and try to fight with force of law, or with earthly philosophy, or with mere social expedients, he will inevitably fail. What David's sling and stone were in the Valley of Elah, that is the cross of Christ in the theological controversies, and social wranglings, and moral antagonisms of our age; and so long as we preach Christ crucified, it matters not though men ridicule it as foolishness, it shall prove to be "the power of God and the wisdom of God." "The weapons of our warfare are not carnal, but" (though they are not carnal—nay, just because they are not carnal) "mighty, through God, to the pulling lown of strongholds." Arrayed in the armor of the world, the Christian will be weaker than the weakest of his adversaries; but let him be but panoplied from the spiritual armory of God, and he will be mightier than the mightiest of his foes.

But leaving these general applications of this many-sided story, we may learn from the bearing of David all through, two or three valuable lessons, with the enumeration of which I shall for the present conclude. There is, first, an example of meekness. When the haughty and scornful Eliab assailed him with taunting words, the young shepherd kept his temper, and we feel how difficult that must have been for him, when, as we read the story, our own hearts rise in burning indignation at the spirit which the elder brother evinced. Probably this was not the first time that Eliab attempted to lord it over him, for unhappily it is only too common for the seniors in a family to tyrannize over and torment the juniors; but David kept himself calm, and like Another, in a yet more trying hour, "when he was reviled, he reviled not again." "He that ruleth his spirit is greater than he that taketh a city;" and to my thinking this calmness of soul under Eliab's taunt was a greater thing in David than his boldness before the giant. I do not, of course, in thus emphasizing David's meekness, extenuate the rudeness of Eliab. On the contrary, it was worthy of all reprobation, but David felt that he was called not to fight with Eliab in this matter, but with himself, and so he held his peace. Let us try to imitate his example, and when we are assailed in our home, or beyond it, with scorn and derision, let us remember that our real conflict in such a case is not with the scorner, but with ourselves. Let our effort be put forth not to silence him, but to control ourselves, and then we shall succeed in obtaining a victory over both.

But we have here again an example of faith. David believed God, and his name might fitly have been included by Paul in that illustrious catalogue which he has given us in the eleventh chapter of the Hebrews. He was not afraid of Goliath, because he saw God beside himself. And one great reason why his faith was now so strong was that he remembered God's former kindness to him. He thought of the day when he prevailed over the lion and the bear, and he reasoned that the God who had heard his prayer and helped him then, would assist him now. Similarly, in all difficult enterprises, let us Christians realize that God is with us ; and to this end let us recall those former occasions when he has strengthened and delivered us. We have all had former deliverances of some kind, and particularly we have all been redeemed by the great price of the blood of Christ. Let us think of that when we have dangerous work to do, and we shall be nerved to do it bravely. "He that spared not his own Son, but delivered him up for us all, how shall he not with him also freely give us all things?" "This is the victory that overcometh the world, even our faith."

Finally, we have here an example of humility. David's purpose, in all he did (and this shows how thoroughly Eliab had misunderstood him), was not to display himself, but to honor God. Mark these words: "That all the earth may know that there is a God in Israel. And all this assembly shall know that the Lord saveth not with sword and spear: for the battle is the Lord's." Here was the secret of David's victory. He went to do God's will. He sought not to glorify himself, but to serve Jehovah ; and by this trait in his character he takes his place in the noblest brotherhood of heroes of whom sacred history makes mention. As we read these words we think of Elijah, on the brow of Carmel, confronting the hosts of Baal, and saying, in his fervent prayer, "Let it be known this day that thou art God in Israel—hear me, that this people may know that thou art the Lord God." We think of John the Baptist turning away from the temptation that was set before him to proclaim himself Messiah, saying, "He must increase, but I must decrease." We think of Peter calling to the wondering crowd that thronged around the lame man who had been cured, "Why marvel ye at this, or why look ye so earnestly at us, as though by our own power or holiness we had made this man to walk?" We think of Paul writing from Rome, with his chained hand, to the Philippians, and saying, "According to my earnest expectation, and my hope that in nothing I shall be ashamed, but that with all boldness as always so now also Christ shall be magnified in my body, whether it be by life or by death." David, Elijah, John, Peter, Paul—where are the men who have done more valiantly in the world than they? and yet they did it by putting God uppermost, and seeking his glory first. That was the secret of their success, and that we are not like them in that is the explanation of our failure. We succeed in little, because we are aiming after our own honor, and not after the honor of the Lord. This keeps us from entering at all on many fields of usefulness, and prevents us from working with a right loyal, hearty, and self-sacrificing spirit, even in the best directions. And yet how little we secure honor to ourselves after all ! The men who are always grasping after greatness and distinction never get them—they only degrade and belittle themselves by their efforts; while they who put the Lord Jesus first, and seek his glory, become at length sharers in his divine renown. "Them that honor me, I will honor." This is the great law. Let us, therefore, merge self in him; let us, whether in pulpit, or pew, or home, or counting-house, or senate-chamber, or hall of judgment, hide ourselves behind the Lord Jesus; and then, working from love to him, we too shall do valiantly: and though our weapons be no more than a sling and a stone, the spiritual adversaries with whom we may contend, gigantic though they be, shall fall before us, for "we shall be more than conquerors through Him that loved us."

## IV.

### *DAVID AND JONATHAN.*

#### 1 Samuel xviii., 1-30.

DAVID'S interview with Saul after the slaughter of the giant must have lasted a considerable time, and must have embraced other subjects than his parentage; for its result was that Jonathan, the king's son, was so favorably impressed by him, that he took him to his special regard, and formed with him a league of friendship, which for sincerity, constancy, and romantic pathos is unrivaled in the annals of history, whether sacred or profane. As we have already seen, there were in David both physical and moral qualities, which tended to win for him the affection of those with whom he came into contact. His ruddy complexion, beautiful countenance, and well-knit frame would immediately evoke a warrior's admiration, while, in his encounter with the giant, he had exhibited such a mingling of courage, prudence, and humility as must have captivated the chivalrous heart of Jonathan. Perhaps, also, in the conversation, some flashes of his poetic genius might gleam forth, or some evidence of his piety might appear, to increase the attraction; but in any case, "the soul of Jonathan was knit with the soul of David, and Jonathan loved him as his own soul." As a substantial token of this affection, he gave to David "his robe and his garments, even to his sword, and his bow and his girdle." It is not said that David gave him any thing in return, but it is likely that there was some exchange made between them, and that the present of David to Jonathan was of so little value, comparatively speaking, that no mention is here made of it. At all events, such interchanges of gifts were not uncommon between friends in ancient times, and Homer gives us some instances that may illustrate what is here recorded. In particular he tells that Glaucus exchanged armor with Diomede, "golden for brazen, the value of a hundred oxen for the value of nine."* Perhaps, therefore, there was some similar reciprocity here, as the seal of the new-born affection between Jonathan and David.

According to the common chronology, Jonathan was considerably older than David; but there was such community of sentiment between them on the highest and most important of all matters, and such similarity of tastes generally, as fitted them for each other's fellowship. They were one in their faith in God, and in their devotion to his will; for on the memorable occasion when Jonathan went forth, with his armor-bearer as his sole companion, to attack the Philistine stronghold, he said, in a spirit of sublimest trust, "It is all one to the Lord to save by many or by few;" and in afterdays, when he parted from David for the last time, in the wilderness of Ziph, we are told that "he strengthened David's hand in God." Then they had both a genius for military leadership, and this would help in some measure to cement their friendship.

But though all this must be admitted, and though we do not wish in the least degree to disparage David in this matter, yet there are special considerations which must be taken into account, and which are peculiarly to the credit of Jonathan. I can not allude to them all without, in some degree, anticipating the narrative; but it is so important to have a clear and distinct idea of the whole intimacy between these two remarkable men, that I may be excused for referring at

---

* "Iliad," book vi., lines 232-236.

this early stage to incidents which will come up for review at a later portion of the history.

In the outset, then, we can not fail to be impressed with the disinterested nature of this friendship, as far as Jonathan was concerned. The king's son had, humanly speaking, at this date nothing to gain from the shepherd of Bethlehem. Jonathan might be of great service to David, but it was scarcely likely that David could do very much for him. His taking of David to his heart, therefore, was a purely unselfish thing. It was the outgoing of his affections toward an object to which they were attracted, and all his joy was in yielding to the charm by which he was influenced. Too frequently the favorites of kings, and perhaps more frequently of king's sons, have been those who have risen to their position by pandering to the prejudices, or toadying to the weaknesses, or, worse than either, by ministering to the vices, of those by whom they were valued. But Jonathan had no such reasons for binding David to him. He saw in the young hero a congenial soul and a true man. He was attracted by his piety, his patriotism, and his prowess, and he yielded up his heart to him in the unselfish impulse of disinterested affection.

Again: this friendship was not tainted on Jonathan's side by the slightest trace of envy or jealousy. There are, I fear, few such friendships between those who are nearly equals in eminence in the same profession. The proverb says that "two of a trade can never agree," and it takes high-toned principle to rejoice in the rise, to an equal position with ourselves, of one who is in the same calling with us. Provided there be a sufficient distance between us, either in excellence, or in success, the difficulty is not greatly felt on either side. The young statesman, just entering on public life, has neither jealousy nor envy of the veteran leader, who has by genius and perseverance made his way to the front rank of politicians, and the leader, in his turn, feels it easy to be cordial and encouraging to the youthful aspirant. But let the one see the other as nearly as possible on a level with himself, even in his own chosen department of excellence, and feel that probably he must soon consent to be second to him, and the case is altered. Then, almost in spite of themselves, jealousies and envyings will spring up between them; they will look askance at each other, and though they may not break out into open foes, there will be, what I may call, a sort of armed watchfulness between them, and a very little matter will set them in direct antagonism. The nearer individuals come into competition with each other, the greater is their tendency to be spiteful toward each other. It is easy to be a patron, and, stooping down from a lofty height, to take by the hand some struggling beginner; it is easy, too, to be an admiring pupil of one who is acknowledged to be a great way above us; but it is a much harder, and therefore a much nobler, thing to be the warm appreciative friend of one who is in the same calling with ourselves, and who is bidding fair to outshine and surpass us. But it was just this hard and noble thing that Jonathan did, when he took to his heart the youthful David. He did not seem to care that the duel with the giant would, in the after-history of the nation, be seen to rival his own brilliant achievement at Geba. He did not think of himself at all; but having found a man whom he could love and trust, he "grappled him to his soul with hooks of steel." Nay, even when he came to discover that David was the predestined occupant of his father's throne, the heart of Jonathan was never alienated from him. He accepted the lot which was before him, and rejoiced in it for David's sake, saying only "Thou shalt be king in Israel, and I shall be next unto thee."* I have

---

* 1 Sam. xxiii. 17.

a high idea of David's magnanimity, but I doubt whether it could have equaled this of Jonathan ; and so, in the matter of this friendship, I am disposed to give the palm to the son of Saul. And I greatly mistake if, as you read the record, you shall not grow into the belief which I have long entertained, that there are few characters in Old Testament history which, for genuineness, chivalry, self-sacrifice, and constancy at once to his father and his friend, can be put into comparison with Jonathan.

This leads me to say, further, that we are deeply impressed with the fidelity with which, on Jonathan's part, this friendship was maintained even in the face of personal dangers. When Saul's heart was stirred against David, and was filled with murderous intent regarding him, Jonathan was placed in a very difficult and perplexing position. He was called to decide between his father and David, yet he was true to his friend, without being unfilial to Saul. In David's absence he stood forth in his defense before the king, and once so provoked the royal indignation, that his own life was endangered. Still he adhered to David after all this ; and there are few more touching incidents recorded in history than that of their parting by the stone Ezel, when "they kissed one another, and wept one with another until David exceeded ;"* or that of their last interview, in the forest of Ziph, when, though the son of Jesse was fleeing from his father, " Jonathan strengthened his hand in God."† That is the stoutest cable which can stand the strain of the fiercest storm, and truly heroic must that friendship have been which lasted through such dangers and heart perplexities as did this of Jonathan for David. Nor, to be just to David, ought I to forget to add that it was on his part intensely appreciated. It was his solace as a fugitive and exile ; it

---

\* 1 Sam. xx., 41. † 1 Sam. xxiii., 16.

kept him repeatedly from laying violent hands on Saul; it disposed him long afterward to show kindness to the children and children's children of his early friend; and on that dark day when, in filial devotion to his father, the warrior fell on Mount Gilboa, "slain on his own high places," it inspired him to sing his lament, in that plaintive ode, which, by its passionate outburst of grief, has given even to this present age its grandest funeral music.

Having dwelt so long on this beautiful union between two congenial spirits, you will forgive me if, before proceeding to less agreeable themes, I say a few words on the principles which ought to regulate our choice of friends. It is for the most part in early life that lasting companionships are formed, and their influence on the course and complexion of the after career can scarcely be overestimated. "He that walketh with wise men shall be wise; but the companion of fools shall be destroyed." There are few ways of pitching one's tent "toward Sodom" so common, or so insidious as the selection of improper friends. Let me earnestly counsel you all, therefore, and especially the young, to secure first, and before all others, the friendship of the Lord Jesus. Give your hearts in confidence and love to him. Trust him as your Saviour. Follow him as your example. Imbibe his principles. Obey his precepts. Seek to possess his spirit, and to secure his regard. Remember the words which he spake to his first followers : "Ye are my friends if ye do whatsoever I command you. Henceforth I call you not servants, for the servant knoweth not what his lord doeth, but I have called you friends; for all things that I have heard of my Father, I have made known unto you." Aim first at securing this confidential intercourse with the Lord Jesus Christ, through the study of his Word, and earnest prayer to the Father in his name. Then make this, your fellowship with Jesus, the test by which you determine whether or not you will accept the earthly friendships which are offered to you. You can not withdraw from all dealings of every sort with the ungodly, for then must you go out of the world altogether; but into the inner circle of your friends let none be admitted who do not love supremely the Lord who has redeemed you, and who can not "strengthen your hand in God." Make this the indispensable prerequisite to your intimate companionship. If he who seeks to become your friend would endeavor to undermine your religious principles, or to loosen the bonds that unite you to the members of your Father's house, or to lead you into places and practices in which you would lose the fellowship of Christ, then turn away from him, and say, "My soul, come not thou into their secret; into their assembly mine honor be not thou united."

But even among Christians, seek for your friends those who have the greatest affinity with you, and in whom you can find your own weaknesses of character most materially strengthened. There must be some points of contact and resemblance between you and your friend, otherwise there can be no real companionship; but there must also be certain elements of diversity, otherwise the one can be no help to the other. If the one be merely the echo of the other, the friendship will be tame and profitless to both; but if in the individuality of each there be qualities which the other lacks, and if these are allowed by both to have free play in their mutual fellowship, great good to both will be the result. This was the nature of that companionship, the record and memorial of which has been given to the world by Tennyson, in his "In Memoriam;" and the ideal of friendship is sketched by him in these lines:

> "He was rich where I was poor;
> And he supplied my want the more,
> As his unlikeness fitted mine."

It may seem, however, that in giving the advice which I am

now enforcing I were making friendship impossible, inasmuch as, if we are to look for those who are thus richer than ourselves, the benefit must be entirely one-sided. But it is not so; for we may be as greatly superior to our friend in some things as he is to us in others, and he may receive as much from us in some departments as we may obtain in others from him. Thus the relationship will become mutually helpful. How many instances of such reciprocity have occurred in history! John and Peter, Barnabas and Paul, Luther and Melancthon, have proved at once the possibility and the advantage of such a friendship as I have suggested; and as we see each pair shining like binary stars in the firmament of history—two, and yet in a great sense one—we have before us at once a model and a motive. On this subject I know few things in our literature finer, or more instructive, than the lines which Cowper has devoted to its elucidation. I commend them all to your careful study, and select only the following stanzas, by way of whetting your appetite for the rest:

"No friendship will abide the test
That stands on sordid interest,
  And mean self-love erected;
Nor such as may a while subsist
'Twixt sensualist and sensualist,
  For vicious ends connected.

"Who hopes a friend, should have a heart
Himself, well furnished for the part,
  And ready on occasion
To show the virtue that he seeks;
For 'tis a union that bespeaks
  A just reciprocation.

"Pursue the theme, and you shall find
A disciplined and furnished mind
  To be at least expedient;
And after summing all the rest,
Religion ruling in the breast,
  A principal ingredient."

But we must turn now, with whatever reluctance, to contemplate Saul's treatment of David. Immediately after the conquest of Goliath, the king seemed to be friendly enough to the young victor. He was in no haste, indeed, to perform the promises which he had made previous to the encounter, but he took him with him to Gibeah, and would let him return no more to his father's house. He made him also one of his chief captains; and such was the amiability of David, that his exaltation, far from exciting the enmity of the monarch's former servants, was approved of and rejoiced in by them. This very popularity, however, was destined, in a short time, to turn the heart of Saul against him, and a very simple occasion was sufficient to rouse his anger and revenge. After their successful campaign against the Philistines, the Israelitish troops returned in formal triumph through many of the cities. They were met generally at the gates by companies of women, who, playing on the tabret and dancing to their own music, chanted also in responsive chorus rhythmic lines appropriate to the occasion. At the end of every strophe there came this refrain, sung by answering companies: "Saul hath slain his thousands, and David his ten thousands." Very likely there was nothing more meant by this than an expression of joy at the nation's deliverance, with such exaggeration as strong emotion is always prone to indulge in; but the sensitive soul of Saul, now all the more inclined to be suspicious, since Samuel had foretold the taking of the kingdom from him, took offense at the implied preference of David to himself, and seeing, perhaps for the first time, in the youthful Bethlehemite that "neighbor better than himself" to whom his kingdom was to be given, he murmured thus moodily to himself: "They have ascribed unto David ten thousand, and to me they have ascribed but thousands; and what can he have more but the kingdom?" The thought was gall and wormwood to his heart, and from that moment the determination to checkmate David, and get rid of him by any means, no matter how unscrupulous, became the ruling passion of his life. Let it be observed, too, that there was in this not only hatred of David, but also a defiant determination to circumvent and defeat the published purpose of the Almighty. I am particular to draw your attention to this point, because it is this, that especially marks the depth to which Saul had sunk. Samuel had foretold that the kingdom was to be given to another, and now that there is a sort of prophetic premonition in his own heart that David was his appointed successor, he is only thereby roused to more active antagonism, and seeks to make the fulfillment of the prophecy impossible. As Herod, long afterward, deliberately inquired what the meaning of a prophecy was, in order that he might set himself to falsify it, so Saul here defiantly sets himself to defeat Jehovah. It was a strange perversity. If the prediction had not come from God, why should he have cared at all about it? but if it had come from God, could all his efforts prevent its fulfillment? Ah me! how vain the endeavor to beat back the Almighty! and how terrible that confession of defeat which came from Saul on that weird night when, beside the cottage of Endor, he cried, "Bring me up Samuel!" But it was then too late, and Samuel came only to pronounce his doom.

The first effect of Saul's jealousy was a relapse of his malady, under the influence of which he was in a kind of rapture, like that of the prophets when the Spirit came upon them; but in his case it was a spirit of evil, and not the Spirit of the Lord. David, seeing that he was troubled as before, took his harp and tuned it to sweetest music; but instead of being soothed thereby, the maniac monarch became only the more enraged, and twice aimed a javelin at the head of the musician, who escaped only by dexterously evading its point.

This violence of his frenzy soon spent itself, but it settled down into a deliberate purpose to compass David's destruction, not at first directly, but by roundabout contrivances. First, he put him into a position in which he expected that by his inexperience he would provoke such opposition as might end in his death. But David behaved himself wisely, and nothing came out of that plan. Then, after promising to give him Merab, his elder daughter, to wife, he insulted him by bestowing her upon Adriel, the Meholathite, expecting, probably, that David would thereby be roused to do or say something that might be construed into treason, and so furnish a legal pretext for his being put to death. But neither did he succeed in this. Thereafter he discovered that Michal, his second daughter, had fallen in love with David, and, in a most diabolical spirit, he resolved to sacrifice her most tender feelings to his own vindictive malice, by attempting to make her a snare to him. He caused some of his servants privately to sound David, who in the most prudent fashion intimated that he was by no means eager to be the king's son-in-law, since he was a poor man, and could not give any thing like a dowry suitable for a king's daughter. In the East it was usual, and, I believe, is so still, for the bridegroom to give a large present to his father-in-law, in acknowledgment of the blessing which he expects to receive in his wife; and it is to this, probably, that David alludes when he says, "Seemeth it to you a light thing to be a king's son-in-law, seeing that I am a poor man and lightly esteemed?" On hearing a report of this conversation, Saul saw in the very poverty of David a means of revenging himself; and he cunningly and cruelly intimates to him that he would accept, as a dowry for Michal, the proof, "furnished after the barbarous fashion of the times," that he had slain a hundred of the enemies of Israel. His intention in all this was to secure, as far as human calculations could secure, David's death, while yet not Saul, but the Philistines, would be the ostensible authors of the mischief. But he was again disappointed, for He who went forth with Othniel when he won the daughter of Caleb went forth again with David; so that before the appointed time he returned with evidence that two hundred of the Philistines had fallen before his company. After this there could be no possible pretext for delaying the marriage: so Michal became the wife of David; and though the connection was not such as permanently contributed either to David's happiness or holiness, we can not deny to her the praise of standing faithful to him for a time, even at the expense of her father's indignation. She would not allow herself to become the instrument of Saul's revenge, and in the perplexing position in which she was placed, she took for the time, without any hesitation, the part of her husband. This only exasperated her father more; and as in all the matters to which he put his hand David's wisdom and bravery were conspicuous, and his name became renowned, Saul's hatred increased yet more and more, until at length an open rupture became unavoidable.

Here, however, it will be convenient to pause, that we may gather up some lessons for our modern life from this ancient chapter of sacred history.

In the first place we may see the evil of centring our thoughts and plans entirely on ourselves. This was the root of Saul's misery. He was one of the most ardent *selfists* that ever lived. He had made self his god. He looked only and always at his own interests. "How will this affect me?" was his constant question as each new event transpired; and whensoever he imagined that he was to be injured by any other man's elevation or advancement, he was stirred up to seek his ruin. Thus he was ever moody and unhappy. He hugged himself to his heart, and as a punishment God left him to himself, and no companionship could have been more miserable. But this was not the worst. His self-devotion generated envy, hatred, malice, and even murder in his heart. Because, in a woman's song, David had apparently been set above him, he is filled with rage, and schemes for the destruction of one who had in former days been a blessing to him; who had rid him of one of the fiercest of his foes; and who in his inmost heart was loyal to him as the Lord's anointed. Behold how foul a progeny may spring from one parent evil passion! Men are apt to regard self-worship as a little thing, and in its lower form of self-conceit they think that it is worthy only to be laughed at; but when it is permitted to get the mastery, it may work incalculable mischief. Who can tell how many alienations, heart-burnings, jealousies, plottings against others' welfare, and even murders, grow out of this root? The man who is determined to be first can brook no competitor, and is led to wish all rivals out of his way. Let us be on our guard in this respect, and cultivate rather the noble magnanimity of Jonathan, than the narrow and miserable selfishness of Saul. How different (I can not but indulge the fancy) Saul's afterlife might have been had he only fostered David, and taken him lovingly to his heart! Instead of the ceaseless hunting of his son-in-law, which from this point darkens his name, we might then have read of their happy fellowship and mutual help. He might not have been able to retain the crown in his family, but he might have enjoyed peace in his own days, and in the common devotion of Jonathan and David to his interests he might have been relieved from the cares and anxieties of his office. Thus in quiet enjoyment the years might have rolled over him at Gibeah, and then at last, instead of setting in blood behind the mountains of Gilboa, his sun might have gone down in peace, and Jonathan and David might have lived to fill in the beautiful outline of mutual service to each other, and common devotion to their country and their God, which the one had sketched when he said unto the other, "Thou shalt be king in Israel, and I shall be next unto thee." But the reality was just the reverse of all this. The absorbing selfishness of Saul embroiled the land in civil discord, leaving it open as a prey to its ever-watchful enemies. It imbittered his own heart; it made his home a scene of strife and debate; it chased away from him one of his most faithful servants and most daring captains; and, in the end, it sent him forth in isolation, God-deserted, to meet his doom on the field of battle by his own hand. Behold the retribution! The man who schemed and planned so constantly for the pre-eminence and profit of himself perishes at last by his own sword. But is it not always so, in a very real and solemn sense? The selfish man is ever a moral suicide. He poisons his own happiness; he kills his own joy; he destroys his own soul. "Whosoever will save his life shall lose it; and whosoever will lose his life for my sake shall find it." Behold here the far-reaching character of the Saviour's words. He that is determined at all hazards to seek only and always his own interests, shall lose that to which he is so devoted; but he that, for the Saviour's sake, is willing to lose every thing, or to be any thing, shall have the highest degree of honor, and his salvation too. He who is always thinking of his own happiness and planning for it, is thereby doing his best to drive all happiness from him. But he who, out of regard to God in Christ, holds himself subordinate to the Master, and rejoices in the prosperity of all around him, thinking nothing of himself, shall have the highest happiness and the purest joy.

When, in the midnight hour, you lie awake and wish for sleep, the more you try expedients to bring it to your pillow, the more it seems to flee from your pursuit. But when you turn your mind away from it altogether, and think on something quite apart from yourself, then with muffled footstep the angel of the night steals into your chamber, and "steeps your senses in forgetfulness." And so, like sleep, happiness and pre-eminence, the more you seek them, and the more anxious you are to obtain them, fly the farther away from you; but when, caring nothing for them, you seek the good of others and the glory of God, they will come in unobserved and wreathe you with their laurels. How deeply philosophical, therefore, as a recipe for happiness, not to put it in a stronger form, is the apostolic injunction, "Look not every man upon his own things, but every man also upon the things of others."

But the Christian has a higher reason for obeying that command than any to which I have yet adverted. In Christ he has himself an interest, and property in every other Christian. Hence he may reasonably rejoice in the eminence of every other believer, inasmuch as the greatness of one is the greatness of all. "All things are his, whether Paul, or Apollos, or Cephas"—and so he can rejoice in the distinctive excellences of each. The man whose heart holds only himself is not a Christian, and must be made miserable and wicked by his devotion to himself; but he who has the Christian public spirit to see and own that Christ and his cause are infinitely greater than himself, will rejoice in the appearance of every young David who comes forward to grapple with the gigantic evils of his time, and will gladly bid him welcome to his heart and home.

We may see here, in the second place, that the servant of God may expect to encounter adversity in an early stage of his career. David was not to be cradled for his future work in the lap of luxury. He was "to learn in suffering what he taught in song." He was not to be like "a bird on a bough, singing forth free and off-hand, never knowing the troubles of other men;" but, led through trials of his own, he was stimulated and inspired to sing of them in strains which, because they came "from the heart of man, speak to all men's

## DAVID AND JONATHAN.

hearts." Early, therefore, was he brought into trial; and there are not a few of his Psalms which seem to take their tone from these first experiences of difficulty. Take, for example, the following: "In the time of trouble he shall hide me in his pavilion: in the secret of his tabernacle shall he hide me; he shall set me up upon a rock." "Pull me out of the net that they have laid privily for me: for thou art my strength." "For I have heard the slander of many: fear was on every side: while they took counsel together against me, they devised to take away my life. But I trusted in thee, O Lord: I said, Thou art my God. My times are in thine hand: deliver me from the hand of mine enemies, and from them that persecute me."* From all this let us learn to prepare for trial. It may come in unexpected forms, and from unexpected quarters, but let us be always ready to meet it; for he who is the friend of God must lay his account with being treated as an enemy by the ungodly.

Lastly, we may learn here that the wisest course in time of danger is to do faithfully our daily duty, and leave our case with God. David went about his work, behaved himself wisely, and let God take care of him. On other occasions, as we shall see, he had sometimes recourse to questionable expedients, and sinful practices, for self-protection; but in the present instance he walked steadily on in the right path, and we may rely that he verified the truth of the words which he afterward wrote: "Trust in the Lord, and do good; so shalt thou dwell in the land, and verily thou shalt be fed. Delight thyself also in the Lord; and he shall give thee the desires of thine heart. Commit thy way unto the Lord; trust also in him; and he shall bring it to pass. And he shall bring forth thy righteousness as the light, and thy judgment as the noonday."† Let us follow this example when we are in trou-

---

\* Psa. xxvii., 5; xxxi., 4, 13-15.   † Psa. xxxvii., 3-5.

ble, and either God will protect us from our enemies, or he will enable us so to meet their enmity as to glorify him. On no account let us compromise ourselves and dishonor him by deserting our post, or employing questionable or sinful means for preserving ourselves. Faith is not real within us unless it develop courage; and he who sins to save himself from harm is lacking in boldness, because he is deficient in faith. No matter what may come upon you, therefore, do what you clearly see to be your duty, and take with you this song of Norman M'Leod's to cheer you as you do it:

> "Courage, brother! do not stumble,
> Though thy path is dark as night
> There's a star to guide the humble—
> Trust in God, and do the right!
>
> "Let the road be long and dreary,
> And its ending out of sight,
> Foot it bravely, never weary—
> Trust in God, and do the right!
>
> "Perish policy and cunning;
> Perish all that fears the light,
> Whether losing, whether winning,
> Trust in God, and do the right!
>
> "Some will hate thee, some will love thee,
> Some will flatter, some will slight;
> Cease from man and look above thee—
> Trust in God, and do the right!
>
> "Simple rule and safest guiding,
> Inward peace and inward light:
> Star upon our path abiding—
> Trust in God, and do the right!"*

---

\* "A Life-Story, with Characters and Comments;" a Lecture given by the late Dr. Norman M'Leod, in Exeter Hall, London.

## V.

## *THE ESCAPE FROM GIBEAH TO RAMAH.*

1 SAMUEL xix.

BAFFLED in his schemes for bringing about indirectly the death of David, Saul at length gave positive orders to Jonathan, and to all his servants, that they should kill him. But, in issuing these commands to Jonathan, he was unwittingly taking the course which was most likely to defeat the end he had in view; for, in a way alike honorable to his head and heart, that noble man set himself at once to secure David's safety. He did not, indeed, stand forth at the moment in open defense of his friend. He knew his father too well to think of adopting such a course as that, while David was unwarned; for, in one of those sudden outbursts of temper to which he was so liable, Saul might, on the instant of Jonathan's interference, have sent to order David's execution. Accordingly, without speaking to any one upon the subject, Jonathan went privately to David, and put him on his guard. He requested him, moreover, to hide in a certain secret place in the field well known to both of them, and promised that he would lead his father out into the same neighborhood in the morning, and would there engage him in such a conversation as would reveal the state of his heart regarding David. This arrangement was made, as it would appear, not that David might overhear for himself the words of Saul, but that he might be close at hand, so that, if the worst should happen, no time should be lost in finding him and sending him away to a place of safety.

True to his word, Jonathan brought Saul to the appointed

spot, and warmly expostulated with him on David's behalf. He dwelt on his utter innocence of any disaffection toward the king, alluded to the fact that, at the risk of his life, he had rid the country of one of its most formidable enemies, and referred in the most delicate manner to the joy which had thrilled Saul's own heart on the memorable day in the Valley of Elah. Nor was this all; the piety of the chivalrous prince comes out in his ascription to God of the glory of David's exploit, and in his plain and thorough condemnation of the sin which his father would commit, if he were to shed the innocent blood of the young hero, to whom he and the people owed so much.

This appeal so moved the heart of Saul that he swore, apparently too with all sincerity, that David should not be slain; and so, for the time, David, to whom Jonathan at once reported the substance of his conversation with the king, was re-assured, and returned to his place at court. I do not know many instances in which we have such a manifestation of prudence and principle combined, as we have in the case of this expostulation of Jonathan with his father. Prudence did not go so far as to make him silent about the sin which Saul was purposing to commit; principle was not so asserted as to arouse his father's indignation. Neither was weakened by the other; but both were so admirably interblended as to produce the result on which his heart was set.

Saul's good-will to David, however, was not of long continuance. His envy was soon renewed, and that in a way which recalls the occasion of his first estrangement from the shepherd hero. The Philistines had resumed hostilities against the Israelites; and in the battles which ensued, David again so distinguished himself as to awaken the enthusiastic admiration of the people. This, coming to the ears of Saul, stirred up the old jealousy of his disposition, and that, in its turn, brought on a new attack of his mysterious malady. Again "the evil spirit from the Lord troubled him." Sitting in his palace with his spear in his hand, he was a source of terror to all around him; but David, unhindered by any recollection of former danger, and desirous only of soothing the monarch's heart, went in as aforetime and played the harp before him. This time, however, music was of no avail. Nay, it seemed only to rouse him to more vehement ferocity, for he attempted to smite David with his javelin; but, dexterously evading the blow, he slipped out of the royal presence, leaving the spear quivering in the wall, to tell of the danger from which he had escaped.

This incident opened David's eyes to the imminent peril in which he stood, and he fled to his own house. But not even there was he safe from the fury of his infatuated persecutor, for Saul sent men to surround his dwelling and bring him to him for destruction. This design, however, was defeated by Michal, who learning, probably from some inmate of her father's house, what was in progress, or, perhaps, knowing her father so well as to be sure of what he would do next, insisted on sending David off at once. She let him down from the window before Saul's messengers had arrived, and then, that she might gain time for him before they started after him, she took an image and placed it in bed, covering its head with a goats'-hair veil, and lyingly told her father's emissaries that David was sick. They returned with this report to the king, who insisted that David should be brought to him even on his bed. This, of course, led to the discovery of the trick that Michal had played off upon them all; and Saul, turning upon her with the disappointed fury of a wild beast which has been cheated of its prey, said to her, "Why hast thou deceived me so, and sent away mine enemy, that he is escaped?" But her only reply was the utterance of a lie, which came new-minted from her fertile brain: "He said unto me, Let me go; why should I kill thee?"

Now out of this narrative a curious question arises, not only affecting the character of Michal, but also opening up a subject which is closely connected with the domestic religion of the Jews. What was this image that Michal employed to personate David? and how are we to account for the presence of such a thing in David's house? The word rendered image is in the margin given in its Hebrew form, "teraphim;" and perhaps the best way to bring the whole subject before you will be to put together the most important of those passages in which it occurs.

The first mention of it is in connection with the record of Jacob's flight from the house of Laban, on which occasion we are told that Rachel had stolen her father's images (or teraphim), and concealed them in her tent;* and it is probable that Jacob referred to these and similar objects of superstitious veneration, when he ordered all in his encampment to put away the strange gods that were among them.

The next time the word occurs is in the very singular history contained in the seventeenth and eighteenth chapters of the book of Judges, which tells how Michah, an Ephraimite, set up in his house a kind of domestic chapel, in which were an ephod and teraphim; how he got a Levite to be his priest; and how the Danites came and took away both his priest and his images to Dan, where they set them up for themselves, and where, in after-ages, this small seed of superstitious error developed into the worship of the golden calf set up by Jeroboam, the son of Nebat.

The next passage in which the word occurs, and which clearly shows that the use of such an image was sinful, is in 1 Sam. xv., 23, where Samuel, in his denunciation of Saul,

---

* Gen. xxi., 25-35.

says: "Rebellion is as the sin of witchcraft, and stubbornness is as iniquity and idolatry" (or, as the term is, teraphim). The next, after the narrative that has been before us, is in 2 Kings xxiii., 24, where we are told that "the workers with familiar spirits, and the wizards, and the images (or teraphim), and the idols, and all the abominations that were spied in the land of Judah and in Jerusalem, did Josiah put away." The next is in the prophecies of Hosea iii., 4, where it is said, "The children of Israel shall abide many days without a king, and without a prince, and without a sacrifice, and without an image, and without an ephod, and without teraphim." Some have supposed that here we have a kind of tacit approval of teraphim; but when we read the following verse, we discover that this is not the case, for it is there said, "Afterward shall the children of Israel return," intimating that all the things enumerated belonged to a superstitious and unspiritual worship. The last reference to teraphim which I shall specify is in the tenth chapter of Zechariah, second verse, "For the idols [teraphim] have spoken vanity, and the diviners have seen a lie, and have told false dreams," etc. From all these passages, then, it appears that the teraphim were images having some sort of resemblance to the human form; that they are found as far back as the time of Jacob; that they were consulted oracularly; that their use continued down to the days of Zechariah at least; and that, though the more lax of the priests and rulers might tolerate their existence, and even themselves employ them, the prophets from Samuel downward denounced the employment of them as inconsistent with a right idea of the spirituality of God. Observe, however, wherein the special sin of the use of these teraphim consisted. It was not polytheism, the worship of gods many and lords many; neither was it the worship of a god other than the true God; but it was the worship of the trus God, under and through the visible representation of an image. In other words, it was not a violation of the first commandment, which says, "Thou shalt have no other gods before me;" but it was a violation of the second, which forbids the use of any image, even in the worship of the true God. The distinction may seem a subtle one, but all the more on that account it needs to be accurately made, especially as it is one of the main points of difference between the Protestant and the Romanist. Both of these alike profess to worship the one God—Father, Son, and Holy Ghost; but the Protestant will have no visible teraphim, while the Romanist employs them without scruple. Now, as the use of such things was forbidden, even under the extremely ritualistic system of Moses, it must be still more inconsistent with the simplicity and spirituality of Gospel worship. The employment of such images not only tends to idolatry, but, indeed, partakes of it, and is altogether contrary to the dictum of our Divine Master: "God is a spirit, and they that worship him must worship him in spirit and in truth."

But if this be so, if even in the Old Testament times the employment of such factitious aids to devotion was forbidden, how comes it that we have here teraphim in David's house? Perhaps the history of Rachel and Jacob may furnish the explanation. Jacob was entirely ignorant that his wife had carried away Laban's teraphim; and David here may have been equally innocent of all complicity in this kind of worship. In our domestic arrangements it would not be possible, perhaps, for a wife to indulge in such a mode of religious service without the cognizance of her husband, but it might be quite easily managed in an Eastern dwelling. Now, if this explanation be accepted, it will help to account for the weakness which Michal here and at other times in her history displayed. She was not like David in the highest and most momentous things. She loved him, indeed, and, as we see, was eager to save his life; but her love for him was earthly and selfish. She was captivated by the brave and beautiful young warrior, but she had no right appreciation of the best parts of David's character. She had no oneness with him in his truest and noblest self. Hence the deceitfulness which she manifested in the plan she took to aid his escape and to expedite his flight; hence also, at a later day, her easy acquiescence in her father's arrangement, which, in violation of the sanctity of marriage, took her from David and gave her to another. No doubt she loved David; indeed, as one has said, her affection for him had "started forth with what we might almost deem an unmaidenly promptness." But her affection could not stand the strain of trial. It was not like that of Jonathan, because it had not, like Jonathan's, its root in devotion to the Lord. She could not and did not follow her husband through persecution and exile and danger, because she was not one with him in God. She could tell lies for David, but she had not the courage and the faith to go with him into suffering, or to tell the truth for him. So long as fortune favored him, she was found beside him, helping him, too, in her own way; but when he went forth a fugitive, to be hunted like a partridge upon the mountains, she did not say to him, "Whither thou goest I will go, and where thou lodgest I will lodge," for she could not say, "Thy God shall be my God." Want of sympathy in spiritual matters between husband and wife is always a painful thing, and frequently a perilous. The noblest marriage is not that which secures a great alliance, or a fashionable equipage, or an ample fortune, but that which is made "in the Lord."

But we must resume the narrative. To this episode in David's life the 59th Psalm, as we learn from its title, refers; and it is interesting to note, not only the strength of faith which it evinces, but also the plea by which, in it, he enforces his petition for deliverance. Again and again he calls God his "defense" and "shield," and asks that the machinations of his enemies may be confounded, so that "men may know that God ruleth in Jacob, unto the ends of the earth." Very graphically, also, does he describe the movements of Saul's messengers, comparing them as, under the cloud of darkness, they went round and round his dwelling, to the dogs, which, every Oriental traveler tells us, are still the nuisance and the danger of all Eastern cities after night-fall. And then, at the close of the ode, already anticipating his escape, he gives expression to joyful assurance in these beautiful words: "I will sing of thy power; yea, I will sing aloud of thy mercy in the morning: for thou hast been my defense and refuge in the day of my trouble. Unto thee, O my strength, will I sing; for God is my defense, and the God of my mercy."

Leaving Gibeah, David made his way to Ramah, that he might refresh his soul by converse with Samuel; but the prophet, thinking, perhaps, that his house would be no safe retreat for one who was fleeing from Saul, took him with him to Naioth in the immediate neighborhood, where there was a school of the prophets, and where Saul would probably be restrained from laying hands upon the fugitive. This school had, in all likelihood, been instituted by Samuel himself, for the purpose of training young men for becoming the instructors of the nation, and perhaps, also, under the idea that out of the bands thus educated there might, from time to time, arise some whom God might commission as his specially-inspired messengers to his people. Similar establishments we find at a later date in sacred history, at Bethel and Gilgal; and it is supposed that in connection with the existence of such seminaries there was maintained, from the days of Samuel till the close of the Old Testament canon, a continuous succession of prophets in the land. Not, indeed, that God confined himself to those who were trained in these schools. When he had a word to say to the people, or a work to do among them, he was never circumscribed in the area from which he took his instruments. But that he usually employed as his special messengers those who were educated in these schools may, I think, be inferred from the words of Amos, who speaks of it as a thing unusual and strange, that he was no prophet, nor the son of a prophet, but a plain herdman of Tekoah, taken from following the flock. These ancient colleges were under the superintendence of a recognized prophet, such as Samuel or Elisha, who was called the father, while the students were styled his children. They were places of study and devotion, yet they were not monasteries, as we now understand that word, seeing that the youths were allowed to marry. They seem to me to have resembled rather the seminary of the ancient Culdee Church, the ruins of which still awaken the interest of the traveler in the island of Iona, and which was not only a place of retreat and study, but also a great missionary centre, from which laborers went forth in every direction to do the work of God. The chief subject which engaged the attention of the students was the law of Moses and its interpretation, but along with that, though subsidiary to it, they practiced music and sacred poetry. In such a place, therefore, David would find himself in congenial society, and the influence of his sojourn there must have been both soothing and salutary to his spirit. We do not know that he had ever met Samuel since the day when he was anointed at Bethlehem, and we may be sure that the venerable prophet, while comforting him under his present trials, would give him many valuable instructions as to the principles which should regulate his conduct when he should come into the kingdom. As he had communed with Saul on the house-top at the period of his anointing, so now again he would enter with David into an ample explanation of the terms on which the sceptre was given to him—an explanation made all the more sadly clear by allusion to the mistakes which Saul had committed, and the terrible consequences to which these had led. In connection with this matter, too, we may well suppose that Samuel would speak of his own wide experience as a magistrate, giving him maxims and advice which would never be forgotten; while, continually, the good old man would commend him to the keeping of that God who, through his own long and active life, had sustained and protected him.

Besides this intercourse with Samuel, the pursuits of the sons of the prophets, alike in their practice of music and poetry, and in the study of the Word of God, were just such as David would most thoroughly enjoy, and as would most materially tend to soothe his spirit after the trials through which he had just passed, and brace it for the difficulties which lay before him. I do not presume to fix either the date or the authorship of all the productions, which have been brought together into the one book of the Psalms, but if the 119th Psalm came from the pen of David, as multitudes believe, then I do not wonder that many have connected its composition, with his residence in the school of the prophets at Naioth. The calm in which he then found himself, and the studies which he then prosecuted, might well have led his musings in the direction of that alphabetic ode, while there are in it not a few expressions which, to say the least, may have particular reference to the dangers out of which he had so recently escaped, and by which he was still threatened. Such, for example, are the following: "Princes also did sit and speak against me: but thy servant did meditate in thy statutes." "The proud have had me in derision: yet have I not declined from thy law." "Trouble and anguish have taken hold on me: yet thy commandments are my delights." Then, in regard to his present enjoyment, we may quote these lines: "O how love I thy law! it is my meditation all the day." "The law of thy mouth is better unto me than thousands of gold or silver;" and in reference to God's dealings with him, he says, "I know, O Lord, that thy judgments are right, and that thou in faithfulness hast afflicted me." "It is good for me that I have been afflicted; that I might learn thy statutes." But why need I enlarge here? I might well quote the entire Psalm, pervaded as it is with love of the Word of God, and confidence in God himself. Let me commend it to your prayerful study, as a perfect store-house of suggestive thoughts and devout aspirations. In allusion to its peculiarity of structure, in accordance with which it is divided into as many parts as there are letters in the Hebrew alphabet, and each verse of every part begins, in the Hebrew, with the letter which marks the part to which it belongs, Bishop Cowper has called it "a holy alphabet, so plain that children may understand it, and so rich and instructive that the wisest and most experienced may learn something from it."* This witness is true, and if only each day of our lives we were to fix in our memories one verse of this admirable production, and make it the subject of our meditation in our intervals of rest, we should grow in every thing that adorns the Christian character, and become both more devout in the closet, and more holy in the transaction of our daily business.

But not even the sanctity that surrounded the residence of the sons of the prophets could shield David from the vengeance of Saul, for so soon as he discovered where his son-in-law had found an asylum, the king sent messengers to apprehend him. By the mysterious power of God's Holy Spirit, however, when these men came to Naioth, and saw the sons of the prophets at their daily service, they came under

---

* Quoted by Plumer, in "Studies in the Book of Psalms," p. 1018.

a peculiar influence, which impelled them to do as the students did. This was told to the king, who sent others in their stead, and to them it happened in like manner. The same thing occurred with a third company of messengers; and at length, instead of learning from all this that God had David under his special protection, and giving up his mad intent, Saul became so exasperated that he set out himself for Naioth, determined to be the executioner of his own commands. But lo! as he drew near the village, even before he came into the company of the prophets, he was himself laid hold of by the Spirit of God, and as in the early days of his reign he prophesied—yea, he was filled with the Spirit so that he stripped off his outer garments, and lay on the ground, as in a trance, until the following morning. Thus, again, the proverb which had obtained currency at the beginning of his reign was revived, and men said once more, "Is Saul also among the prophets?" Thus, also, by the restraining might of God's Spirit, he was again kept from laying violent hands upon David.

In reviewing the narrative over which we have come, we are impressed with the proof, which is here furnished, of the diversified resources, which Jehovah has at command for the protection of his people. Again and again Saul attempts to take David's life, but always without success; and each time the means by which David was delivered are different. At first he is defended by God's blessing on his own valor against the Philistines; then he is indebted for his safety to the mediation of Jonathan; then to the agency of Michal; and finally to the miraculous work of God's own Holy Spirit. In the subsequent portion of the history, we shall find that the same principle holds, and that in each new peril he is preserved by some new instrumentality. When God purposes to protect a man, he is at no loss for the means of carrying out his design. He may find them in what seems to us mortals the most unexpected places, and they may work in what appears to us to be a very strange—it may be, also, a very sinful manner; yet the purpose is accomplished, while yet the liberty of the different agents is not infringed. David was at this time, in a very peculiar sense, the ward of God's providence, and he was kept in safety. By the experiences through which he had passed, he was able afterward to sing, "The angel of the Lord encampeth round about them that fear him, and delivereth them;" and from the occurrences which we have been considering, we may learn that God will keep us alive, so long as we are needed in his service. "A man is immortal till his work be done." If in the purpose of God there is still something to be accomplished by any one, he bears a charmed life until that be fulfilled. This, of course, must not be understood as implying that we should use no means to insure our own safety, far less that we should recklessly and wantonly rush into danger; but it does imply, that when we have taken all proper precautions, we are to trust in God, and wait the issue. Either they will be fruitless, and then there will be the consciousness that the end is come, and that our reward is near; or they will be successful, and anew the glorious truth shall be demonstrated to every beholder, that man's extremity is God's opportunity. The good man should never despair, for either God will glorify himself in his protection, or he will glorify God in suffering for his name's sake; and in either case the issue shall be well. "God's providence is his inheritance."

But our review leads us to remark further, on the foolish and unbelieving deceit which Michal practiced for David's deliverance. It was unbelieving, for it was equivalent to an assertion on her part that God could not save her husband except by her sin; it was foolish, for, after all, it did not accomplish very much for David, and only exasperated Saul.

Having told one lie, she needed to give that probability, by a clumsy piece of acting; and then she had to sustain the whole by another falsehood, which contained in it such a reflection on her husband's character, as no true-hearted wife would have allowed herself to make, even in jest. I can not but think that Michal's deception here, taken in connection with her possession of the image, as I suppose, in a clandestine way, is an indication of a low moral tone; and while she is certainly to be commended for the promptitude with which she urged David to flee, we must condemn her for the falsehood which she told, and the deceit which she practiced in connection with his flight. Some, indeed, may say that she did no more than Rahab did for the spies at Jericho; and that since Rahab's faith is praised, we are surely too severe in condemning Michal. But then we must bear in mind that Rahab was a heathen, and that her mode of life was such as was fitted only to harden her in heathenism and sin; while Michal was brought up under all the privileges of the Mosaic law. What Rahab did in sending forth the spies in peace, betokened that she had faith; what she did in telling a lie for their sakes, showed how weak her faith was, after all; but that she had any faith whatever was a marvelous thing, considering her position. With Michal, on the other hand, it was different, and she must be judged by a different standard. To borrow an illustration from the history, on a part of which we are engaged—when the Philistines handled the sacred ark of the covenant, no death came to them, for they knew no better; but when the men of Bethshemish looked into it, they were smitten down by the outflashing of the sword of Jehovah—even as Uzzah was at a later date; for they ought to have known its sanctity.*
And so there might be, comparatively speaking little mor-

---

* 1 Sam. vi., 10-21.

al guilt in the doing by a heathen of a thing which, when done by a Jewess, was worthy of severe condemnation. I know, indeed, that we must not judge Michal by the Gospel standard. Still, even in the light of the law of Moses, she was to blame for her deceit, and to us who have the cross of Christ before us, and the Sermon on the Mount sounding in our ears, nothing can be more evident than that it is never necessary to commit sin. It is always wrong to do wrong. No circumstances or motives, no extenuations or palliations, can ever change wrong into right. There is no Darwinianism in morals. There is here no transmutation possible. Wrong is wrong, and right is right, for evermore. And if, in criticising a character in real history it is warrantable to refer to the creations of the novelist, I would place side by side with Michal here, the Jeanie Deans of Walter Scott, that you may see the contrast between cunning unscrupulousness and inflexible integrity. I reckon that delineation, founded as it is in its main outlines on fact, as one of the noblest that ever came from the mind of its author; and in the honor which we are constrained to pay to her, who would not tell a falsehood to save her sister's life, though she walked hundreds of miles afterward to deliver her from the gallows, you may see, also, how much we blame Michal for her unbelieving deceit.* Be it ours, my brethren, to stand unflinchingly by the right, for the sake of Him who is himself the right. Every deceit is a dishonor to him, as well as to ourselves, and death is preferable to such dishonor.

---

* The parallel here is scarcely perfect, since the heroine of the tale was put upon her oath in a court of justice, while Michal was questioned only in the ordinary manner. The casuistry of this and similar cases is canvassed in a note to Froude's "History of England," vol. ii., p. 65. That author admits that he does not see his way to a conclusion as to the degree of guilt attaching to such a kind of unveracity as this; but he fails to show, if falsehood be ever venial, within what limits it is to be restrained.

Again: in reviewing this chapter, we are impressed with the gracious long-suffering of God with sinners. When Saul was laid hold of by God's Spirit, the desire of the Lord was not merely to restrain him from injuring David, but also to visit him again with that particular blessing which he had received at the beginning of his reign. It was a gracious, as well as a miraculous, visitation to him. Anew the Holy Ghost was striving within him. Once again he had the opportunity of turning to God. His heart was moved. He was almost persuaded; the tide was at the flood again with him, and if he had taken it, he might have finished his life in another manner; but no: he allowed it to ebb, and it never flowed again! Yet see the goodness of God to him in giving him this new opportunity, while, at the same time, you observe the danger in which those are placed who let such opportunities go unimproved.

There may be some within the sound of my voice to-night whose experience is akin to Saul's. They, too, can look back upon a former time—some era of great revival, perhaps—when they were drawn to the truth, and took a prominent place in the Church and its services; but a sad declension came, and for many years they had no care for any thing spiritual or eternal. They were devoted to ease and self-indulgence, making enjoyment their constant idol. But now, again, in their riper years, with mayhap the hoary locks of age beginning to appear upon them, their old feelings are coming back upon them. They are attracted as of yore to God's house; they enjoy his ordinances; they are moved many times to tears by the preaching of his Word; they are disposed to serious devoutness in God's worship, and to earnest holiness, in the family, and in the world. But as yet they have gone no farther. Oh, let me beseech them to follow all this up by taking the one decisive step of giving themselves unreservedly and at once to the Lord, lest, when the fervor of their present enthusiasm shall have gone, they may be left farther from God than they ever were before. Not always will God forbear with the vacillations of a changeful heart; not always will his Spirit strive with men. Oh! drive him not away by your carelessness and self-will, but open your soul to his influences, and yield yourself up to his loving service. Ere this spring-tide of opportunity falls, it may be never to rise again, let it carry you on its bosom into the harbor of salvation.

Finally, mark here, how men who are themselves godless observe and criticise the characters of those who join themselves with the people of God. "Is Saul also among the prophets?" said the wits of Israel, when they heard of what occurred at Naioth. Now this might have been as honorable to Saul, as it came to be dishonorable to him, if only he had in his after history proved himself sincerely resolved to do the will of God. Thus, when we say of another Saul, "Is Paul also among the apostles?" we mean no reproach to the man of Tarsus, but only desire thereby to magnify the riches of divine grace, which transformed him from a persecutor of the Church into a preacher of the Gospel; and had this occasion been the turning-point in the history of the King of Israel, as the prostration at Damascus was the crisis in the life of the Christian apostle, the proverb before us would have been one of honor, and not of disgrace. Unhappily, however, by his after conduct Saul gave occasion to men to speak of his insincerity and wickedness, and so, "Saul among the prophets" is, even yet, jeeringly said by us, when we mean to indicate that a godless, Christless man has found his way into the membership or ministry of the Church. Now this proverb, thus understood, is two-edged. It speaks to those who are as yet outside of the Church, and says to them, "If you are not really and truly Christ's; if you do not love the Lord and desire to serve him, then do not seek to enter the Church." But it speaks also to those who are within, and says to them, "If in your hearts you are conscious that you are none of Christ's, and if in your conduct you are dishonoring his name, then go out from the Church. It is not for such as you; and your continuance in it will only make men say, 'Is Saul also among the prophets?' They who have named the name of Christ should depart from iniquity." The reputation of Christ, in the world of to-day, is very much in the hands of those who profess to be his followers. Let us see to it, that, so far from allowing it to suffer from our conduct, we add new adornment to his Gospel by the saintliness of our lives, and compel men to take knowledge of us that we have been with Jesus.

## VI.

### *THE VALLEY OF DECEIT.*

1 Samuel xx.–xxii.

TAKING advantage of the miraculous restraint which was put upon Saul at Naioth, David left the school of the prophets, and hasted back to Gibeah.

Here, on the return of the monarch, it would seem that, under the influence of his recent experiences, his heart was somewhat softened toward his son-in-law; for Jonathan, in the interesting interview which is described so fully in the twentieth chapter of 1 Samuel, speaks at first with the greatest confidence of David's safety; and David himself, even in his distress, takes it for granted that his presence would be expected at the customary banquet on new-moon. But he had seen so many vacillations in Saul, that he was not disposed to build much upon his present gracious mood. Nay, rather, from brooding morbidly over Saul's treatment of him, to the entire exclusion from his mind of God's constant care over him, he fell into despair, and ran into a course of reckless deceit which brought the most fearful consequences in its train.

It may appear strange, that all this should have happened immediately after his pleasant and profitable sojourn with Samuel, at the school of the prophets. But perhaps the very contrast between his happiness at Naioth, and his continual suspense at Gibeah, where he felt himself to be like one standing on the very edge of an active volcano, may help to account for his depression. In any case, it is by no means an uncommon experience, that times of great spiritual elevation are followed by periods of deep dejection. Every height has its hollow; and as Peter went from the first Lord's Supper to his denial of the Master, David went from Naioth to Nob, and from Nob to Gath. It is a suggestive incident, bidding us be always on our guard against temptation, and then, most of all, when we have been enjoying the most exalted privileges.

In his distress David sought for Jonathan, and poured his complaint into the ear of his friend, telling him that Saul was seeking his life, with such sleepless assiduity, "that there was but a step between him and death." The king's son was taken by surprise, and expressed his belief that David was allowing his fear to overmaster, not his faith only, but his judgment also. Still, seeing how seriously his companion was taking matters, he offered to do any thing which he could suggest, in the way either of discovering Saul's intentions toward him, or of delivering him from any danger which might be hanging over him. So an agreement was made to the following effect: The next day was new-moon, on which it was the regular custom for Saul to entertain the captains of his host. On such an occasion it was David's duty to be present; but this time he would take the opportunity of going to Bethlehem, to the yearly feast of his father's household; and Jonathan would see, by Saul's remarks upon his absence, how he felt toward him. Then, on the third day, David would return to a hiding-place, known to both of them, by the stone Ezel in the field, where Jonathan, under color of practicing his favorite sport of archery, would let him know how matters were. If he said to the boy who went with him to fetch his arrows, "See they are beyond thee," David would know that mischief was determined against him by the king; if he said, "They are on this side of thee," he would understand that all was well, and that he was perfectly safe.

## THE VALLEY OF DECEIT.

In the formation of this agreement, the hearts of the two friends were greatly moved; and the faith which Jonathan manifested in David's future, contrasts very strongly with the despondency which was shown by David himself. How deeply touching, for example, are these words of Jonathan: "Thou shalt not only while yet I live show me the kindness of the Lord, that I die not: but also thou shalt not cut off thy kindness from my house forever: no, not when the Lord hath cut off the enemies of David every one from the face of the earth. And Jonathan caused David to swear again, because he loved him: for he loved him as he loved his own soul."

On the feast day, as David had anticipated, Saul observed his absence; but, imagining that it was caused by one or other of those ceremonial defilements, which might make him unclean until the evening, he made no remark. On the morrow, however, the absence being repeated, the king asked, in a tone of displeasure, "Wherefore cometh not the son of Jesse to meat, neither yesterday nor to-day?" In reply, Jonathan stated that, with his permission, David had gone to Bethlehem, to the annual home-feast of his family; whereupon Saul went into a paroxysm of passion, saying, in the most insulting and blood-thirsty manner, to Jonathan, "Thou son of the perverse rebellious woman, do not I know that thou hast chosen the son of Jesse to thine own confusion, and unto the confusion of thy mother's nakedness? for as long as the son of Jesse liveth upon the ground, thou shalt not be established, nor thy kingdom. Wherefore now send and fetch him unto me, for he shall surely die." But though Jonathan knew, as well as Saul, that David was destined to sit upon the throne, he was not thereby either estranged from him, or desirous of his death. So he stood up bravely in his friend's defense, asserting his innocence, and asking why he should be slain. This, however, only added fuel to the flame of Saul's evil passion, for he made answer by hurling a javelin at the head of his son. That was enough. Loving and dutiful as Jonathan was, he could stand it no longer, but rose in great indignation from the table, and at the appointed time went, in bitter humiliation, to the trysting-stone, where David lay concealed, to tell him what had occurred. By the preconcerted signal, he let him know that all hope of reconciliation with his father was at an end. But he could not leave his friend without a parting embrace. So, giving his bow and quiver to his attendant, with instructions to carry them into the city, he remained behind, and David came forth from his hiding-place, "and fell on his face to the ground, and bowed himself three times: and they kissed one another, and wept one with another, until David exceeded. And Jonathan said to David, Go in peace, forasmuch as we have sworn both of us in the name of the Lord, saying, The Lord be between me and thee, and between my seed and thy seed forever. And he arose and departed: and Jonathan went into the city." We attempt no remark on this touching scene, but content ourselves with setting it in vivid distinctness before your view as one of the most thrilling illustrations of devoted friendship that the world has ever witnessed.

The parting which we have just described occurred, most probably, on the afternoon of the sixth day of the week, and David, eager to enter at once into a secure asylum, employed the brief season before the sunset should usher in the Sabbath, in hastening forward to Nob, where the Tabernacle at that time was pitched. This place has not been certainly identified by modern travelers. It is supposed by some to have been on one of the shoulders of the Mount of Olives, and, from other references to it in the Old Testament, it seems at least certain that it was in the immediate neighborhood of Jerusalem, and within sight of Mount Zion.* This

---

* See, for example, Isaiah x., 32.

## THE VALLEY OF DECEIT.

being the case, it could not well have been more than five or six miles from Gibeah; David, therefore, could reach it with ease before the commencement of the Sabbath, and, once there, he would be quite secure, as "no one could travel thither after him on the Sabbath, neither could any one who might be at Nob when he came go to Gibeah (on that day), to give intelligence of his arrival." The place was inhabited by a colony of priests numbering more than fourscore, at the head of whom was Ahimelech the high-priest, the son of Ahitub. When David presented himself at the Tabernacle, having first left his companions in some place of retreat,† the prelate was astonished that he, the king's son-in-law, and a distinguished warrior, should be traveling unattended, and he said to him, "Why art thou alone, and no man with thee?" In reply, David told a cunning falsehood, representing that Saul had sent him on a secret mission, and begged to be furnished with such provisions as might be at hand. The priest, ignorant, to all appearance, of the new feud between Saul and David, and seeing no improbability in the story which was told him, made answer that he had nothing but the shew-bread which had that day been removed to make way for a new supply, and which it was lawful for the priests alone to eat. Nevertheless, in a case of extremity like that of David, he declared his readiness to give him that, provided that he and his men had not been defiled. Having been satisfied on that point, he gave David the hallowed bread, and then, in response to another request, he put into his hand Goliath's sword. This act of Ahimelech, in giving the sacred bread to David, has been referred to with com-

---

Kitto's "Daily Bible Illustrations," vol. iii., p. 281.

† It has been supposed by some, that the reference made by David to his attendants was a falsehood as great as that which he told about the object of his journey; but the words of the Lord Jesus, when he alludes to this incident, relieve him from that accusation.

mendation by the Lord Jesus,* and was used by him as a vindication of his working miracles on the Sabbath. His allusion to the whole circumstances implies that, where two obligations come apparently into collision, the lower must give place to the higher, and that there is nothing in the sight of God more sacred than the saving of life, or the helping of suffering humanity, or the salvation of a soul.

But his words, while sustaining the action of the high-priest, do not in the least degree extenuate the sin of David. Some indeed, like Delany, do not hesitate to vindicate him even for the deception which he practiced here; but David himself, at a later period, deeply bewailed his falsehood, and, even at the time at which he told it, a circumstance occurred which made his heart beat loud with the upbraidings of conscience, and darkened his soul with the forebodings of disaster. For in the Tabernacle with him, detained from traveling by the recurrence of the Sabbath, was Doeg, an Edomite, the chief shepherd of King Saul; and David had a too sure presentiment that the monarch would by him be speedily informed of the whole affair, and would take ruthless revenge on all concerned. But there was another there whom David had forgotten, else he had never told the lie which wrought such havoc in the holy settlement. God was there! Had the hunted fugitive but realized *that*, it would have kept him from deceit, and the face of the Edomite would not have troubled him. He who feareth God needs be afraid of no one else, but when one is committing iniquity he starts at his own shadow. "The thief doth fear each bush an officer." At another time David would have met Doeg unabashed, but now his heart misgives him at his presence, and he wishes to escape his observation.

---

* Matthew xii., 3; Mark ii., 25; Luke vi., 3, 4.

## The Valley of Deceit.

> "Thus oft it haps that when within
> They shrink at sense of secret sin,
> A feather daunts the brave;
> A fool's wild speech confounds the wise,
> And proudest princes veil their eyes
> Before their meanest slave."*

David remained at Nob no longer than was absolutely necessary, and on the morning of the first day of the week he took the path down through the valley, afterward called by the name of Jehoshaphat, past the Jebusite stronghold of Zion, and away most probably through the very battle-field where he had slain Goliath, on to the city of Gath, where he wished to put himself under the protection of Achish, who was at that time the head of the Philistian confederacy.

This was a strange, an almost insane, procedure on the part of David; yet, if we will but remember that at this juncture he had lost his faith in the protection of Jehovah, we shall easily see how he came to act as he did. The other tribes by whom the Israelites were surrounded were at peace with Saul, hence none of them would have been likely to risk a quarrel with him by taking David under their protection. But the Philistines were the traditional enemies of the Jews; hence, if he could ingratiate himself with them, he might find a secure retreat at the court of their leader. This idea, promising at first view, seems to have been adopted by David without due reflection on the consequences which might follow from his acting upon it, or on the conditions on which alone it was possible for him to receive assistance from the enemies of his nation. Had he considered for a moment, he might have seen that, even if the Philistines should receive him hospitably, his very acceptance of their kindness would seriously compromise him

---

* Scott's "Marmion."

in after-years. Besides, he might have known that he could expect the Philistines to defend him, only on the understanding that he should make common cause with them, and take up arms against his own countrymen.

Hence, even as a policy, this flight to Gath was a blunder, and David was only saved from its dangers and entanglements by the opposition to him of the lords of the Philistines, whose national instinct told them that he could not but be their constant enemy. They had heard of his popularity among his own people, after the slaying of their gigantic chieftain; they had been informed of Saul's jealousy of him; they knew, too, in some way or other, that he had been already designated as Saul's successor, and therefore they regarded him with undisguised hostility, and loudly expressed their dissatisfaction with Achish for permitting him to remain in their land. These feelings were very probably intensified when they saw the sword of Goliath in David's hand, and very soon the indications which met him on every hand, that he was most unwelcome, filled his heart with dismay. His great object then became to get away in safety. He feared that they might forcibly detain him, and consign him to imprisonment in some one of their fortresses. Indeed, from the heading of the 56th Psalm, as well as from the words of Achish in the narrative, it would seem that they did apprehend him; so he had recourse to a questionable expedient to make himself appear contemptible, and altogether unworthy of the consideration of his enemies. He feigned madness, going about scribbling on the doors of the gate, and letting his spittle fall upon his beard; and so well did he counterfeit, that Achish held him up to the scorn of his courtiers, who were all at length glad to be rid of his presence. Thus was David taught that "it is an evil thing and a bitter to forsake the Lord of Hosts." He had lost his faith in Jehovah, and put his confidence in Achish, and nothing more salutary could have happened to him than such a reception as that which was given to him at Gath. When a youth is going on a wrong course, the best thing that can befall him is failure and disgrace, and the worst thing that can come to him is what the world calls success. If he succeed, the probability is that he will go farther astray than ever; but if he fail, there is hope that he will return to the right path, and seek alliance with Jehovah. This last was the case with David in the instance before us, if at least we may judge of the effect which his experience produced upon him, from the songs which he wrote with special reference to the incidents at which we have been looking. The titles of the 34th and 56th Psalms connect these odes with David's residence in Gath; and though there are few acknowledgments of sin in them, yet they indicate that, as the result and outcome of his trials, he was led to look away from all earthly helpers to the Lord alone. "This poor man cried, and the Lord heard him and saved him out of all his troubles." Perhaps, too, there may be an implied condemnation of the course which he had been pursuing, and a virtual resolution to abstain from it in the future, when he says, "What man is he that desireth life, and loveth many days, that he may see good? Keep thy tongue from evil, and thy lips from speaking guile. Depart from evil, and do good; seek peace, and pursue it." And it is scarcely possible to doubt that, from his own penitence for the sins of which he had just been guilty, and his own experience of God's favor when he returned to him, he was led to sing, "The Lord is nigh unto them that are of a broken heart; and saveth such as be of a contrite spirit. Many are the afflictions of the righteous: but the Lord delivereth him out of them all." How interesting, too, it is to picture him to ourselves as, journeying from Gath, and, taking the way that led to the cave in which he was to find for a time a home, he sings, "Thou tellest my wanderings: put thou my tears into thy bottle: are they not in thy book? When I cry unto thee, then shall mine enemies turn back: this I know; for God is for me. In God will I praise his word: in the Lord will I praise his word. In God have I put my trust: I will not be afraid what man can do unto me. Thy vows are upon me, O God: I will render praises unto thee. For thou hast delivered my soul from death: wilt not thou deliver my feet from falling, that I may walk before God in the light of the living?" Said I not truly that David's repulse from Gath was the best thing that could have happened him? It sent him back into the arms of God, and in these notes of trust there is again the spirit of him who laid Goliath low.

Leaving Achish, David went back to his native land, and found an asylum in the cave of Adullam. This is now generally identified with a cave in the side of a deep ravine, some five or six miles south-west of Bethlehem, and called the Wady Khureitun. Dr. Thomson, in "The Land and the Book,"\* speaks thus of it: "Leaving our horses in the charge of wild Arabs, and, taking one for a guide, we started for the cave, having a fearful gorge below, gigantic cliffs above, and the path winding along a shelf of rock narrow enough to make the nervous among us shudder. At length, from a great rock hanging on the edge of this shelf, we sprang, by a long leap, into a low window which opened into the perpendicular face of the cliff. We were then within the hold of David, and creeping, half doubled, through a narrow crevice for a few rods, we stood beneath the dark vault of the first chamber of this mysterious and oppressive cavern. Our whole collection of lights did little more than make the darkness visible. After groping about as long as we had time to spare, we returned to the light of day, fully convinced that

---

\* English Edition, pp. 606, 607.

with David and his lion-hearted followers inside, all the strength of Israel under Saul could not have forced an entrance—would not even have attempted it." If this, then, were the cave, it is quite probable that, from its proximity to Bethlehem, David was already familiar with it. But be that as it may, in this or in some other similar cavern, he took up his abode, establishing himself in a kind of independent chieftainship, and, while religiously refraining from all attacks on Saul, ready to defend himself from every assault. Nor was he left alone. His brethren and kinsmen joined his standard, and others, to the number of about four hundred, became his followers. They were a motley multitude, each individual having his own special reason for the course he took. Some came because their circumstances were so bad, that any change, even though it were into a cave, was an improvement; others came because they were so deeply drowned in debt that they could escape slavery only by becoming military adventurers; while others were impelled to join the company because they were imbittered either by their own personal sorrows, or by oppression at the hands of Saul. But all alike were attracted to David because he was a brave, dashing leader, destined, in the end, to be king over Israel.

But there were two who came to the cave very specially on David's account. The first was Gad, the seer, of whom now, for the first time, mention is made in the sacred narrative. Perhaps he had made David's acquaintance during his recent sojourn at Naioth, in the school of the prophets; and now, prompted by his own generous heart, or mayhap obedient to the suggestion of the venerable Samuel, he came, in the time of the young hero's necessity, to cheer and counsel him during his outlawry.

The other was Abiathar, the son of Ahimelech, the high-priest who came from Nob, telling of a terrible tragedy which

Saul had enacted there, and claiming the protection of the son of Jesse.

The story which he told, supplemented by such details as the record itself furnishes, was briefly this: Hearing of David's escape to Gath, and of his re-appearance in Judah, Saul made complaint of the lukewarmness of his servants in carrying out his commands against his rival, and affirmed that they were all in league with Jonathan in the interests of David. Upon this, Doeg the Edomite came forward and told how, on a certain Sabbath when he was at Nob, Ahimelech, the high-priest, had given David food, and had presented him with Goliath's sword. He also alleged that he had, by means of the Urim and Thummim, "inquired of the Lord" for him. Of this last there is no record in the narrative, and it was probably added with malignant intent by Doeg, for consultation of the sacred oracle was reserved for great occasions, and was generally regarded as the exclusive privilege of the head of the nation. Hence "the inquiring of the Lord" for David would be construed by Saul, especially in the temper in which he then was, as a transference of his allegiance by the high-priest from Saul to David. The moment the king heard of it, therefore, he sent for the priests, and asked if the assertion of Doeg was correct. Ahimelech replied in a strain of astonishment, like one who knew nothing of the deceit which had been practiced upon him, and indignantly denied that he had consulted the oracle for David. What he had done he had done as a mere act of humanity, and under the impression that he was assisting one who was traveling with haste, on the urgent business of the king himself. But his defense was made in vain, for Saul gave instant orders that the whole colony of the priests at Nob should be put to death. No Israelite, however, would execute a command which doomed the anointed of the Lord to destruction, and so to Doeg, the foreigner, who had played the mean part of informer, the horrible commission was given. It was a work all too well suited to his disposition, and he executed it with such sanguinary ferocity that only one out of the whole number escaped. This was Abiathar, who managed also to carry with him the ephod, with the Urim and Thummim, with which he came to David in the cave. When David heard the tale of blood which he had to tell, he was filled with the deepest sorrow, and cried out, in the bitterness of his remorse, "I knew it that day when Doeg the Edomite was there, that he would surely tell Saul. I have occasioned the death of all the persons of thy father's house. Abide thou with me; fear not: for he that seeketh my life, seeketh thy life: but with me thou shalt be in safeguard." Thus was Saul filling up the cup of his iniquities; thus, too, unconsciously on the part of all concerned, God was fulfilling that terrible doom which he pronounced in the ear of the young Samuel, when first he was called to the prophetic office, and which declared that all the house of Eli should be cut off.

The cave of Adullam, though a place of perfect security, was yet very far from being an abode of comfort; and though David could not but be cheered by the presence and fellowship of his parents with him there, yet he loved them too well to think of allowing them, in their old age, to share his perils and privations. Hence, with beautiful and delicate consideration for their comfort and security, he sought from the King of Moab an asylum for them with him, until his own calamities were overpast. In making this selection for them, he was probably influenced by his remembrance of the fact that Naomi and her family had found in that land a place of sojourn, and that Ruth, his ancestress, around whose name such tender associations clustered, was herself a Moabitess. But whatever his motives were in the choice of the place to which he sent them, we can not but admire his filial thoughtfulness and devotion; and we rejoice to see that, under the shield of the warrior, there still beat the loving heart of a son.

Here, however, we must break off the interesting story, and pause a little to gather up the lessons which we may learn from this, the first chapter in David's life that is darkened by the shadow of his own evil-doing.

Behold, then, in the first place, how far one will go on in sin who has lost his faith in God. This, as it seems to me, is the root from which all the iniquity which we have been to-night describing sprung. Even when David was with Jonathan, immediately after his return from Naioth, he had said, "There is but a step between me and death;" and after parting with his friend, he appears to have given up all hope of ever sitting upon the throne of Israel, and to have acted as if he regarded it as impossible even for God to fulfill to him all that he had promised. His unbelief made him reckless; and having lost his hold on God, his feet slipped, and he fell into grievous sin. Both in the Tabernacle at Nob, and in the city of Gath, at the court of Achish, he was in this desponding and sinful spirit; and this accounts for the deceit, both in words and conduct, of which he was guilty. There is nothing will keep a man from sin more surely than confidence in God; but despair is the most dangerous condition into which one can fall. While faith and hope last, there will be energy, and watchfulness, and purity; but with despair come recklessness and folly. WE ARE SAVED BY HOPE; but when we despair of God's help, we run into extremes of wickedness. When a merchant is in difficulties, there is no great danger so long as he believes that he can retrieve himself, and hopes that he will come out all right. But when he falls into despair, he becomes regardless alike of God or man, and runs headlong into practices of which in other circumstances he would never have thought, thereby destroying alike his character and future. But it is quite similar in spiritual matters. When a man falls into despair, he is ready for any sin, and runs blindly and rashly forward upon destruction. Hence, if we would abide in holiness, we must continue in faith. So long as Peter looked to Jesus and trusted in him, he could walk on the waters in safety; but when he turned his eyes from the Master's face, and let them rest upon the waves beneath him, he began to despair, and despair made him sink. We can walk anywhere in safety, at the command of Christ, so long as we have confidence in him; but when we lose our faith, we lose our security. "Believe in the Lord Jesus Christ, and thou shalt be saved," is true not only of the punishment which our sins have merited, but also, and with equal, if not indeed with greater emphasis, of the dangers by which through life we are beset. The greatest sin you can commit against God is to despair of his grace; but it is also the greatest sin you can commit against yourself, for it carries in it the germ of manifold iniquity. If, therefore, you would keep yourself unspotted from the world, be careful to preserve your faith in the promises, the power, and the salvation of the Lord Jesus.

Behold, in the second place, in this history, how impossible it is to arrest the consequences of our evil actions. David lied to Ahimelech, probably thinking not only to secure his own safety thereby, but also to keep the priest from being involved with him in the displeasure of Saul. But mark what ensued. Eighty-five priests, together with all the inhabitants of Nob, "both men and women, children and sucklings," were put to death for this sin of which he, and not they, had been guilty. I have no doubt that when David heard of all this, he would willingly have given all that he had, ay, even his hopes of one day sitting on the throne of Israel, if he could have recalled the evil which he had spoken, and undone its dismal consequences. But it was impossible. The lie had gone forth from him; and having done so, it was no longer under his control, but would go on producing its diabolical fruits. And so it is yet. We can not arrest the consequences of the evil which we do. Whether we will or not, it will continue to work on. We may, indeed, repent of our sin ; we may even, through the grace of God for Christ's sake, have the assurance that we are forgiven for it ; but the sin itself will go on working its deadly results. You may as soon think of staying an avalanche midway in its descent from the Alpine ridge, and so saving the village in the valley from destruction, or of stopping the bullet midway in its flight, from the musket to the heart of him who will be destroyed by it, as think of arresting the consequences of the evil which you once have done. A man, let us suppose, has written an infidel book, or a book whose sole design was to destroy the purity and corrupt the modesty of youth. In course of time, however, he becomes himself a convert to the Christian faith, and has the assurance that all his sins, the writing of the book among the rest, are forgiven. But he can not recall the past. He can not take back that book. It has circulated, it may be, by thousands. Its poison has gone into many hearts. It has made many skeptics, who are living and propagating its abominable errors. Or it has tainted many souls, who are doing their very utmost to carry out its principles, and destroy the sanctity of our home life, and the solemnity of the marriage-vow. Yet its author can not put a stop to all this. The thing has gone from him, and is now no more under his control. Or, again, one gathers around him a knot of companions who are largely moulded by his influence. He teaches them intemperance. He introduces them into haunts of sensuality and impurity. He shakes their faith in the Word of God, and leads them on to glory in their shame. But after a while he is taken, in God's providence, to some other city, where Jesus lays hold of him by his grace, and brings him to his feet. He is converted, he is forgiven, he is himself renewed and sanctified; but he can not undo the mischief of his former evil influence. That is working still! ay, and it will continue to work through one and another, long after his body is beneath the sod, and his soul is with his Saviour. Ah! what a thought have we here! and how earnest it ought to make the unconverted to give themselves to Christ at once, lest, by their continuance in their present course, they should be storing up for themselves sorrows in the days that are to come. The calf that Jeroboam set up gave an idolatrous cast to all the after-history of Israel, and wrought the nation's undoing at the last; and could he, perchance, have foreseen the misery of the captives long years after, when, in consequence of his sin, they were led away to privation and exile, we may well believe that he would sooner have suffered martyrdom himself than have caused such distress to others. Those who heard the lectures of the greatest living English historian, during his recent visit to these shores, will not soon forget how solemnly he said, "that often, in the providence of God, the full consequences of an evil course fall not upon the head of him who was guilty of it, but on those who in after-days are his representatives," and added, amidst a stillness which showed how fully his audience understood his reference, "If Sir John Hawkins, in the day when he went negro-hunting on the coast of Africa, could have foreseen Gettysburg, he would sooner that his ship and all on board had gone to the bottom, than that he should have done any thing to produce such a terrible result." But this holds spiritually as well. The one sin of a Christian, in a moment of unbelief and temptation, may be the ruin of many souls. And when it is once committed, its consequences can not be arrested. In view of this awful consideration, and reflecting on the issues that may already have come from some action of our own, or that may hang on some individual transgression in the future, which of us is not constrained to offer these petitions: "Deliver me from blood-guiltiness, O God, thou God of my salvation." "Hold up my goings in thy paths, that my footsteps slip not."

Finally, behold in David's tender provision for his parents an example of the care which we ought to have for father and mother. There are few things more delightful than to see a son or a daughter lovingly supporting an aged parent; and, on the other hand, there is nothing more worthy of our scorn and reprobation than the conduct of those who leave their parents to the cold charity of an unfeeling world. "He that provideth not for his own, and especially for those of his own house, hath denied the faith, and is worse than an infidel." If you have a father or mother in circumstances that require your assistance, count it a high honor and glorious privilege to render it. Never think that they are a burden, or allow yourself to grudge what you are doing for them. Consider how much you have owed in earlier days to them, and do not be ashamed of them. They may not be quite so polished in their manners as those are among whom now you move; they may not be so correct in their speech as those are with whom you are meeting every day; but if you are a son worthy of the name, you will give them the post of honor when they come to your home, and you will count it the happiest thing in your lot that you are able to lighten for them the load of years. It is a poor, paltry, pitiful puppyism that is ashamed of a parent—a feeling unworthy of a man, not to say of a Christian.

Nor is it only in the matter of support that we should show our regard to our parents. We should reverence them when we are beside them, and when we go to a distance from them we should be regular and full in our correspondence with them, letting them know all about us, and making them feel that we appreciate their interest in us. Is there a son here, to-night, who has allowed many months to roll past without sending a single line to his father or his mother, to tell how he fares? Let the blush of shame suffuse his face as he thinks of his thoughtlessness. You may not have much occasion to remember your home. In the bustle of the workshop, or of the store, or of the counting-room, many things force themselves upon your attention, and you do not miss your home. But your mother, having no such multiplicity of things to divert her mind, is thinking upon you all the day long; and as the postman goes his round each morning, she looks out expecting a note from you. But, alas! each day she turns away disappointed, saying, with a heavy heart, "Can he have forgotten his mother?" Don't let this occur again. Go at once and send her a cheery, hearty letter, if possible with a check or a post-office order in it, as a tangible evidence of your affection. Her loneliness will be irradiated by the sunshine of your kindness; her heart will be warmed by the assurance of your continued love; and your own soul will be benefited by the doing of a filial deed. "Honor thy father and thy mother, that thy days may be long upon the land which the Lord thy God giveth thee."

## VII.

### *SONGS IN THE NIGHT.*

I SAMUEL xxii., 5—xxiii., 1-28.

DURING the days of his outlawry at the hands of Saul, David was specially guarded and guided by Jehovah. Indeed, in so far as the direction of his movements was concerned, he enjoyed at this time very peculiar privileges. As we have already seen, Gad the seer was among his adherents; and when Abiathar, the high-priest, joined his standard, he brought with him the Urim and Thummim, those mystic treasures of the ephod which were the means by which the answers of the sacred oracle were given. David had thus two distinct channels of direct communication with Jehovah; and whenever the mind of God was made known to him, either through the one or the other, he set himself to obey it. Sometimes, indeed, as we shall see with regret, he allowed himself to be carried away by his own evil inclinations, but these were exceptions to the general tenor of his life—like the backward eddies of the Niagara whirlpool in a river whose course, as a whole, is still toward the sea—for his habit was to follow where Jehovah led.

It is to be noted here as an interesting fact, that in the hold of Adullam and in the wilderness of Judah, we have, side by side, representatives of the oracular and the prophetical methods of the communication of the will of God to men; and that, in the life of David, as a whole, we have the era of the transition from the one to the other. Up till this time the priest had been the most important personage in the nation, and the only recognized channel through which

God indicated his will to the people. True, there had been great outstanding prophets, like Moses and Samuel; but the former was an exception to all rules as being the leader of the Exodus; and the latter, from his training under Eli, was as much a priest as he was a prophet. True, again, in the time of the Judges there was Deborah, the prophetess; but she was raised up, in connection with a particular crisis in the history of her people. The general system, however, was, that when the head of the nation, whether judge or king, wished, at any special emergency, to ask counsel of the Lord, the inquiry was made through the priest, and the answer was given by the Urim and Thummim. But now the prophet, as a standing official personage, comes into prominence, and the mind of God begins to be made known through his human individuality, and not through any such visible media as those which were connected with the priestly breastplate.

In the hold and in the wilderness, David received divine directions through both channels, but gradually, even in his life, the breastplate oracle disappears or falls into desuetude; and from the reign of Solomon downward we have no mention made of its employment in the Jewish annals. In the same gradual manner the prophet waxes into pre-eminence, Gad and Nathan preparing the way for Elijah and Elisha, and these, in their turn, giving place to Isaiah and Jeremiah, who were succeeded, in the days of the exile, by Ezekiel and Daniel; and in the era of the Restoration by Haggai, Zechariah, and Malachi.

Now, if we think out this subject a little more fully, we shall see that in the life of David a distinct forward step was taken in the education of the people of God, from the first rudiments of external symbolism, on toward that system of spiritual simplicity under which we now live in the Gospel dispensation. In that course of education, the Urim and

Thummim were themselves an advance on what had gone before. It is not easy, indeed, to say definitely what the Urim and Thummim were. The words denote "Light and Perfection," and they were the names given to some things connected with the dress of the Jewish high-priest. Over the white tunic which he wore when he came nigh to the shekinah, he had the blue robe of the ephod; then, over that he wore the ephod itself, made of white twined linen, inwrought with blue, and purple, and scarlet, and gold; then, over the ephod he placed the breastplate, on which were twelve precious stones, corresponding to the tribes of Israel; then, in the breastplate, apparently as something different from it, were put the Urim and Thummim. But what these were — whether other precious stones, or, as some suppose, symbolic figures of truth and righteousness, like those which were worn by the Egyptian judges—we are nowhere informed. Still, whatever they were, through them, in some visible manner, God gave his answer to the head of the nation, when he was specially applied to in any time of perplexity. In almost all the recorded cases of the use of the Urim and Thummim, the questions which were put were military or strategical; one question only was answered at a time, and the response, in every instance, was very brief, amounting frequently to little more than "Yes" or "No."

There was in all this, of course, much of the visible and material. Yet there was in it, also, a distinct advance, in so far as the demand for faith was concerned, over that which was made by the pillar and the cloud in the Arabian desert. These latter symbols were always before the eyes of all the people. While following them, therefore, they were walking not so much by faith as by sight; but when these were withdrawn, and the glory of the shekinah hid from view, the media of communication were concealed beneath the high-priest's breastplate, and there was more occasion for faith.

This call for faith was increased when the Urim and Thummim ceased, and the prophets came speaking in God's name, giving gradually fewer and fewer specific directions as to particular matters, and more and more proclaiming great spiritual principles. And now there is, more than ever, a demand for faith, when, under the New Testament economy, the way into the holiest is made manifest to every believer, and the answers to the soul's inquiries are given not by any objective oracle, but by the Christian's study of God's Word, as that is interpreted by the providences that are without him, and the Spirit of God that is dwelling within him. Hence, when we read the history of David's sojourn in the cave, or of his wanderings in the wilderness, and see the priest Abiathar on his right hand, and the prophet Gad on his left, we feel that we are standing on one of the great landing-places of that stairway of education, up which God led his people from the childhood of walking by sight, to the glorious liberty, and graceful movement, of that spiritual manhood which walks continually by faith.

These considerations, interesting as they are in a mere historical point of view, are valuable also as tending to keep us from regretting that now we have no such oracle as that which, as we shall see to-night, David consulted again and again with signal advantage to himself. Some may think that it would have been better had the Urim and Thummim held their place till now! And, I suppose, we can all look back on critical times in our history, when we would have given all we had in the world for some such infallible indication of God's will as to our duty, as that which David received. But we had the throne of grace to go to in prayer; and as we gathered what God's mind was, from the consideration of his Word, the leadings of his Spirit, and the indications of his providence, we were guided as truly as David was: and, now that we have passed the crisis, and can look at it from the other side, we feel that we were benefited by the experience, and that we are to-day stronger in all the elements of Christian manhood, than we should have been if, without any mental or spiritual activity of our own, God had told us, in so many words, what we were to do. When Jesus said to his followers, "It is expedient for you that I go away," he meant that they would become in every respect nobler men, if they went forward believing in the unseen Christ whose Spirit was in their hearts, than they would have been if he had remained beside them saying to each one, "Do this." In the one case they would have been merely his servants, doing his commands in so many individual directions. In the other case he would be, if I may so say, repeating or incarnating himself anew in every one of them; and they would become, each one in his own measure, another representative of Christ, working as he would have wrought, speaking as he would have spoken, and acting as he would have acted. Now similarly here, we have lost the external Urim and Thummim; but we have in its stead the internal and indwelling Holy Ghost, by whose agency within us, supplemented and interpreted by God's Word, and providence without us, our prayers are answered as really as David's were by the mystic oracle.

I have dwelt thus long on this subject, both because of its connection with the history that is before us, and because of its importance from its bearing on the gradual preparation which, all through the Jewish history, God was making for the introduction of the Gospel of Christ—but I hasten now to the incidents recorded in the chapter of David's life to which we have this evening come.

When he was in the hold of Adullam, as we learn from the fifth verse of the twenty-second chapter, David was recommended by Gad to betake himself to the territory of Judah, and he went immediately to the forest of Hareth; but

## Songs in the Night.

as every trace of this forest has disappeared, we have now no means of identifying its locality. More interesting to us by far than any mere question of topography, however, is the fact that in connection with his wanderings at this time David composed that exquisitely beautiful Psalm, which has been a song to the people of God in the house of their pilgrimage ever since, and which is numbered as the 63d in the sacred Psalter. Read it in the light of the circumstances out of which it sprung, and you will see in it new loveliness, and feel a new power coming from it. Mark the intense longing for a closer fellowship with God with which it begins: "O God, thou art my God; early will I seek thee: my soul thirsteth for thee, my flesh longeth for thee in a dry and thirsty land, where no water is; to see thy power and thy glory, so as I have seen thee in the sanctuary." Behold how even in his desolation—perhaps just because of his desolation—he feels the value of spiritual blessings, and praises God for them: "Because thy loving-kindness is better than life, my lips shall praise thee. Thus will I bless thee while I live: I will lift up my hands in thy name." Then, in the sleeplessness of the night, as the wind sighs through the forest trees, and the dreariness of his position is apt to sink him into despondency, observe the antidote which he employs to counteract those influences: "My soul shall be satisfied as with marrow and fatness; and my mouth shall praise thee with joyful lips: when I remember thee upon my bed, and meditate on thee in the nightwatches." And in the final strain, see how, reasoning from the past, already rich to him, young though he still was, in memories of deliverance, he looks forward with confidence to the future, when he should be set free from all his enemies, and, as the king upon the throne, should rejoice in God, "Because thou hast been my help, therefore in the shadow of thy wings will I rejoice. My soul followeth hard after thee  thy right hand upholdeth me. But those that seek my soul to destroy it, shall go into the lower parts of the earth. They shall fall by the sword; they shall be a portion for foxes. But the king shall rejoice in God; every one that sweareth by him shall glory: but the mouth of them that speak lies shall be stopped." Happy they, who in their trials find such consolations as David then experienced; for, even in the midst of their troubles, they are more to be envied than the men of the world when their "corn and their wine do most abound."

While the outlawed leader and his band were at Hareth, some messengers came to tell that the Philistines had resumed their marauding practices at Keilah, where they were carrying away the grain, night after night, from the threshing-floors. This gives us a glimpse into the state of the country at the time, and shows us also the nature of the position which David and his men occupied in the estimation of their fellow-countrymen. The Philistines, as we have repeatedly seen, were by no means subdued by the Israelites. They were still able to harass and annoy them; and watching their opportunity, they came down in the harvest-time upon the threshing-floors, killing the sentinels, and carrying off the spoil. Now that the people applied to David in such an emergency was a token of their confidence in him. It has been affirmed by many, indeed, that he was at this time a freebooter, living by his sword, and helping himself without scruple to the property of his neighbors; that, in fact, he was a Jewish Robin Hood, or an Israelitish Rob Roy; and that, as Wordsworth sings concerning the Scottish Macgregor,

> "The good old rule
> Sufficed him; the simple plan,
> That they should take who have the power,
> And they should keep who can."

But there is no evidence in support of this, so far, at least, as his position at this time in Judah is concerned. Rather, the fact that, in a crisis like that which came upon the men of Keilah, information of their calamity was at once conveyed to him, seems to indicate that he was recognized as a kind of protector of the people, against the enemies by whom they were so frequently invaded. It is probable, therefore, that he made it a great part of his business, at this time, to defend the lives and property of his fellow-countrymen from the assaults of those unscrupulous robbers, who, like the modern Bedouin, had no regard either for the rights or the existence of others. For this service he naturally expected, and cheerfully received, a recompense from those to whom it was rendered. This recompense came, generally, in the shape of supplies for himself and his men; but the acceptance of such bounty, so rendered, was a very different thing from compelling them to give him a certain tribute, or black-mail, on condition that he should not steal from them himself, and that he should restore what others pilfered.

The view which I have given of David's position at this time is strengthened by the circumstances, which are narrated in connection with Nabal, and which will be considered more fully hereafter. I may only at present quote, in corroboration of my theory, the words of Nabal's servants to Abigail, when describing David and his men. They say, "The men were very good unto us, and we were not hurt; neither missed we any thing as long as we were conversant with them, when we were in the fields. They were a wall unto us both by night and day, all the while we were with them keeping the sheep."

Now, if this be a correct account of the matter, we can easily understand why David was told of the outrage which had been committed upon Keilah, and why the impulse of his heart was to go at once to its assistance. But he would not move without consulting the oracle, both because he wished to be himself quite certain that he was taking the path of duty, and because he was desirous of securing the confidence of his men. The reply of the Urim and Thummim was favorable to his undertaking the expedition, but still the hearts of his followers failed, for they said, " Behold, we be afraid here in Judah : how much more then if we come to Keilah against the armies of the Philistines." Judah here means the mountain district of that tribal territory, since Keilah was a city in the plain. The confidence of David's men was in the hills, but he himself looked higher, even to Him " who made the heavens and the earth." So, to re-assure them, he inquired again at the oracle, and having received the same answer, only with added emphasis in regard to success, he went down to save the city, and recover the property of its inhabitants.

The expedition was crowned with decisive success, and, relying on the gratitude of those whom he had served, he went with his men into the city. It was a fortified place with walls and gates, and when Saul heard that he had taken up his abode in it, he immediately conceived the plan of laying siege to it, and catching David in it as in a trap. He said, " God hath delivered him into mine hand " (so piously sometimes can people speak, even when they are plotting blackest crimes), " for he is shut in, by entering into a town that hath gates and bars." But not thus was David to be destroyed ; for by some means he had received information as to Saul's intentions, and he had recourse at once to the oracle on the breastplate of Abiathar. He put two questions, from the answers to which he learned that Saul would besiege the city, and that the men of Keilah would deliver him up into the hands of his persecutor. Therefore, leaving Keilah, he and his company went forth "whithersoever they could go." One is disposed to be very bitter and indignant at the ingratitude of those whom David had so signally befriended ; yet we must not forget that Saul was still the king, that he had many resources at his command, and that, with the massacre of Nob before their minds, the people of Keilah had nothing but destruction to expect, if they showed any kindness whatever to the son of Jesse. Even with all these risks, however, a chivalrous and grateful people would have suffered any thing rather than give their deliverer up. But the men of Keilah were neither chivalrous nor grateful. They regarded their own interests as supreme. Like many in our own day, they might profess to aim after the greatest happiness of the greatest number, but when you came to analyze their views, you would find that with them, to use the words of Joseph Hume, "the greatest number was number one!" It was not for their advantage to serve David, and they did not serve him; and I am free to say, that all my observation and experience convince me that a large proportion of the present generation would have done as they were willing to do. Of course that does not excuse them, but it should make us cautious as to what we say in their condemnation, lest, haply, we may some day be judged out of our own mouths. Gratitude, chivalry, enthusiasm for the cause of the wronged—what are words in the mouths of many to-day but words? they sound well, and they are very fine so long as they cost nothing; but let adherence to them put property or life in peril, and too many would cling to the property and the life, and let the others go. Ye who condemn the inhabitants of Keilah because they were willing to betray David, how long would you show gratitude at the risk of the loss of all things? It was a disgrace to them that they would not stand by him who had delivered them; but is it any thing less to us, when we allow our worldly interests to blind us to the obligations under which we lie to those who befriended us in our time of need? Is it any thing less to us when, for the sake of fashion, or fortune, or fame, we turn our backs upon the Christ, who has borne the agony of Gethsemane and Calvary on our behalf? Idolatry of self is as hideous now as it was in David's time. Let those who are guilty of it, therefore, look here, and, in the pitiful poltroonery of the men of Keilah, they will see how mean and contemptible they are.

But the ingratitude of men only threw David back upon the faithfulness of God. It is generally supposed that the 31st Psalm was composed by him, in connection with the events which we have just rehearsed, and, though there is nothing in the title of that ode to give certainty to such an opinion, yet the internal evidence in the song itself is very strong in its behalf. Thus, when you remember that Keilah was a walled city, and that Saul's purpose was to shut him up in it, you may see a reference to these things in the following words: "Thou hast known my soul in adversities; and hast not shut me up into the hand of the enemy: thou hast set my feet in a large room." So, again, without any straining of the meaning, there may be an allusion to Keilah in this verse, "Blessed be the Lord: for he hath showed me his marvelous kindness in a strong city." Now, if on these and similar grounds, we connect this Psalm with the events of the narrative before us, there is much in it to reveal David's spiritual exercise at this time. With what absolute trust he puts himself into Jehovah's hands, saying, "Into thine hand I commit my spirit: thou hast redeemed me, O Lord God of truth;" and again, "I trusted in thee, O Lord: I said, Thou art my God. My times are in thy hand." How earnestly he pleads for deliverance, pouring out his soul in sorrowful rehearsal of all his troubles! And then, in the last section of the Psalm, added, if we may indulge the conjecture, after his escape, how joyfully he praises God for his goodness and chides himself for his despondency! "For I said in my haste, I am cut off from before thine eyes: nevertheless thou heardest the voice of my supplication when I cried unto thee. O love the Lord, all ye his saints: for the Lord preserveth the faithful, and plentifully rewardeth the proud doer. Be of good courage, and he shall strengthen your heart, all ye that hope in the Lord." Trial thus is rich in results, not alone to him who bears it, but to others who come after him. He leaves words of cheer behind him, which, falling on the ears of others, sustain and soothe them in like circumstances. The stream that followed the Israelites in their wanderings through the wilderness, had its source in the smitten rock; and if you trace up every rich experimental psalm which has refreshed God's people in their weary heritage, to its source, you will find it in some trial-smitten heart. David was sent on through the valley of sorrow, in advance of others, that he might furnish those who followed with songs in their night of trouble; and if it is ever permitted to the spirits of the blessed in Heaven to know what is going on here below, then, when David from his celestial seat heard the Redeemer on the cross relieve his agony and dismiss his soul from its fleshly tabernacle, in the words of this Keilah Psalm, "Into thine hands I commit my spirit," he would feel that it was worth undergoing all the miseries of his persecution ten thousand times over, to have been thus instrumental, even in the smallest degree, in sustaining the heart of Jesus in that climax of his anguish.

But we must hasten forward. When Saul learned that David had gone from Keilah, he forbore to begin the siege, and David betook himself to the wilderness, daily pursued by Saul, and at length finding a refuge for the time in the neighborhood of Ziph. This was a town in the highland district of Judah. In the book of Joshua it is named between Carmel and Juttah, and from the narrative before us we learn that there was in its neighborhood a wood and a wilderness. The wood has vanished, but the wilderness remains, and the name Ziph is found, to this day, belonging to a rounded hill of about one hundred feet high, which is situated about three miles south of Hebron. About half a mile to the east of this hill are some ruins, which Dr. Robinson pronounced to be those of Ziph, but it is more probable that the hill itself was the site of the city.

In the adjoining wood David had a covert from observation, so that he eluded the vigilance of Saul. But what the enmity of Saul could not do, the love of Jonathan accomplished, for by some means he got to know where David was, and in this wood, sweet because stolen, and memorable because the last that was ever held between the two friends on earth, a most affecting interview was held. As we read these words: "Jonathan strengthened David's hands in God, and he said unto him, Fear not: for the hand of Saul my father shall not find thee; and thou shalt be king over Israel, and I shall be next unto thee," our hearts thrill with admiration of the son of Saul. What magnanimity! what piety! what affection! what humility! have we in these words; and who is not disposed to say, amidst the trials and sufferings of earth, Oh for such a friend! Yet there is a better friend even than he; and if we will but make a covenant with Jesus, he will strengthen our hand in God, and be to us a richer comforter than Jonathan was to David.

But while Saul's son was proving his steadfastness to David, the men of Ziph were plotting his destruction. They sent and told Saul of his hiding-place, and he, in a strain of grossest adulation, thanked them for their information, and asked them to give him particular directions as to his movements, that he might come and take him. Very soon they found out, and told Saul that he was in the wilderness of Maon—a name which, almost unchanged, is given now to a conical hill about seven miles south of Hebron, so that probably that is the very place here called the Hill of Maon. When Saul heard this, he followed David, and, from the description given, we gather that the position of things was something like the following: David was on one side of the hill; Saul and his men were on the other; but, with the view of making sure of his adversaries' destruction, Saul caused his army to surround the entire base of the mountain, and determined to remain there until, by sheer necessity, David would be compelled to surrender himself into his hands.

But David had a protector of whom Saul took no thought, and to him he made appeal, for, as we learn from its title, it was while he was thus surrounded by Saul's forces that he wrote and sang the 54th Psalm. I can not refrain from quoting it entire. "Save me, O God, by thy name, and judge me by thy strength. Hear my prayer, O God; give ear to the words of my mouth. For strangers are risen up against me, and oppressors seek after my soul: they have not set God before them. Behold, God is mine helper: the Lord is with them that uphold my soul. He shall reward evil unto mine enemies: cut them off in thy truth. I will freely sacrifice unto thee: I will praise thy name, O Lord; for it is good. For he hath delivered me out of all trouble: and mine eye hath seen his desire upon mine enemies." That is the prayer; now read the history, and you have the answer to it: "But there came a messenger unto Saul, saying, Haste thee, and come; for the Philistines have invaded the land. Wherefore Saul returned from pursuing after David, and went against the Philistines: therefore they called that place Sela-hammahlekoth"—the *Rock of Divisions*, as it is given in the margin, or, as some prefer to render it, the *Rock of Escape*.

Thus as, at a later date, Rabshakeh was drawn off from his attack on Hezekiah by hearing a rumor of an assault on his own land, and the prayer of the good Jewish king for deliverance was answered; so here, David was set free, because Saul and his men were needed elsewhere, to repel an invasion of the Philistines. Many would call this a mere coincidence;

but the unprejudiced reader can not fail to see in it an answer to David's supplication, and it was doubtless in the spirit of heartfelt gratitude to God that he called the mountain by this significant name.

Now, in reviewing the history over which we have come, we have clearly brought before us the good man's resort in perplexity. Even the most careless must be struck with the frequent recurrence in this chapter of the phrase, "David inquired of the Lord;" and although we have now no Urim and Thummim, yet we have the Throne of Grace, to which we can ever repair, with the assured confidence that God will hear our cry, and send us an answer which shall meet our need.

Many objections, indeed, have been brought, in these days, against the possibility of God's answering prayer except by miracle; and learned treatises have been written on both sides of this important question. To me, however, it seems as if there were no room for much argument upon the subject, for if a man does not believe that there is a personal God, standing in the relation of a father to his people on the earth, there is no use to reason with him about prayer. You have to begin with him farther back, and convince him first of the folly of his atheism. If, again, a man does really and truly believe that God is, and is the father of his people, you will not need to argue with him; for as the son goes to his father, he will repair to God, and expect that God's fatherhood is a reality, and not a mere name. He will say, and no philosophy in the world will prevent him, if God is my father, then, since my earthly father hears my cry and gives me an answer, much more will my heavenly. The whole debate about prayer, therefore, is but a skirmish on one of the far outposts of the field whereon the war between belief and unbelief is waging. The real question is about God's existence and fatherhood. Until men can say, believingly, "Our Father," they will never pray; when they can say that sincerely, they will pray in spite of all scientific difficulties.

But it is well occasionally to remind scientific objectors of one of the first principles of their own inductive philosophy. After Newton had elaborated one of his theories, a friend discovered something that seemed to be inconsistent with it, and was almost afraid to mention it to him; but when the philosopher heard it, he only said, "It may be so. We must see whether what you say is a fact. There is no arguing against a fact." Now here is a prayer offered by David, and an answer given in the turning of Saul's force into another direction, and there was no miracle. But you say that was three thousand years ago; we want something that has occurred among ourselves. Be it so. Then take these two instances—the most recent that have come within my own information. Being in Springfield, Massachusetts, ten days ago, I saw a letter written from a Western city to a convict in the State-prison of Massachusetts, by one who had been himself for some time an inmate of that jail. The person to whom he wrote had committed burglary, but was hopefully converted in the prison, and had tried to benefit some of his fellow-prisoners. His correspondent had been impressed with his words, and was wishing, after his release, to live another life. With this object he went West, but found it hard to get on. His money was gone; there seemed to him only two alternatives—either starvation, or crime; but—and here I must tell the story in his own words, rude though they may seem to ears polite: "I thought of what you once said about a fellow's calling on the Lord when he was in hard luck, and I thought I would try it once, anyhow; but when I tried it, I got stuck on the start, and all I could get off was, 'Lord, give a poor fellow a chance to square it for three months, for Christ's sake. Amen;' and I kept a-thinking of it over and over as I went along. About an hour after that I was in Fourth Street; and this is what happened: As I was walking along I heard a big noise, and saw a horse running away with a carriage, with two children in it. I grabbed up a piece of box-cover from the sidewalk, and ran in the middle of the street, and, when the horse came up, I smashed him over the head as hard as I could drive. The board split to pieces, and the horse checked up a little, and I grabbed the reins, and pulled his head down until he stopped." He then tells how the gentleman to whom the children belonged rewarded him very handsomely, and, after hearing his story, befriended him, and helped him into a respectable situation where he could earn an honest living; so that he is now not only a good citizen, but an humble Christian.*

From Springfield I went on to Boston, and there a well-known member of the American Board showed me the autobiography of the Japanese youth Joseph, who has been in this country for some years, and was lately the secretary of Mr. Tenako, the member of the Japanese Embassy who was especially charged with the subject of education. In his own country, Joseph's father was secretary to one of the native princes, and he himself was an officer of two swords, and had a good education, being acquainted with two or three languages. A friend lent him an American Common School Geography in the Chinese language and a Chinese Bible, and these two books opened up a new world to him. He described what he felt on reading the first verse of Genesis, which unfolded to him an entirely new view of things, and then he went on to tell how the desire to know Western civilization and Christianity took possession of his soul. His first prayer

---

* Since the above was written, the whole letter here referred to has been printed in the *Illustrated Christian Weekly* newspaper for one of the weeks in August, 1873.

was, "O God, if thou have eyes, look for me. O God, if thou have ears, hear me. I want to know Bible. I want to be civilized with Bible." He left his home, and went to Hakodadi, with the view of getting somehow to America, to learn this knowledge. He went thence to China, and in the port to which he went, he was led by God's providence to a ship which was bound for Boston, and which was owned by a good man whose heart was interested in the cause of Christ. That gentleman, on the arrival of his ship, hearing the captain's account of Joseph, was interested in him; and his wife undertook to have him educated at her own expense. He went first to Andover, and then to Amherst; became a member of the Christian Church, and an excellent scholar; and when the Japanese Embassy came to this country, he who, like Joseph, had been sent on before them, was prepared to be their interpreter; and who shall say what he is yet destined to do for his benighted nation?* Thus, winding round the roots of that great revolution in Japan which has so astonished and gladdened the hearts of us all, we find the prayers of this earnest youth who was thirsting for the knowledge of God. I might say much on many subjects which this little history suggests, but I bring it up now as a fact, indicating how really, and without a miracle, through God's ordinary providence, prayer is answered. Truly, "more things are wrought by prayer than this world dreams of." Let no man, therefore, ridicule and reason you out of prayer. Here is the charter: "If any of you lack wisdom, let him ask of God, that giveth to all men liberally, and upbraideth not; and it shall be given him. But let him ask in faith, nothing wavering: for he that wavereth is like a wave of the sea driven with the wind and tossed. For let not that man

---

* This youth, now the Rev. Joseph Nee Sima, has been now (1883) for some years a missionary in his native land, under the direction of the American Board.

think that he shall receive any thing of the Lord." "Ask, and it shall be given you; seek, and ye shall find; knock, and it shall be opened unto you."

But we have, in this chapter of David's history, also a beautiful illustration of the fruitfulness of trial when it is rightly borne. It prunes the vine of the spiritual life, so that the clusters that grow on it attain to larger development. This is true of all the graces. But to-night I wish especially to show you how David's times of trial were emphatically and peculiarly times of song. We have found in the narrative over which we have come, covering only a short space of his life, the origin of no fewer than three of his psalms. That which is most valuable in the writings of any poet is the fruit of some troublous discipline. It is questionable if the world would have ever seen "Paradise Lost," but for the blindness of its author; and it is at least certain, that one of its most touching passages could not have been written but for that terrible privation. Luther's version of the 46th Psalm, which one has called "The Marseillaise of the Reformation," was born out of the stormy life of the great Reformer; and Archbishop Trench, writing of the Thirty Years' War in Germany, has said: "There is one fact most noteworthy, as a sign of the temper in which this great tribulation was met by those who had to drink of its cup of pain deeper, perhaps, than any other, that very many of the most glorious compositions in the hymn-book of Protestant Germany date from the period of the Thirty Years' War; and, most noticeable of all, these contributions are rich, not so much, as one might have expected, in threnes and lamentations, Misereres and cries De Profundis, as in Te Deums and Magnificats, hymns of high hope and holy joy."*

---

\* "Thirty Years' War in Germany," by Archbishop Trench, quoted in Saunders's "Evenings with the Sacred Poets," pp. 140, 141.

Who knows not, also, that Paul Gerhardt's hymn, "Give to the winds thy fears," was the cry of his soul in an hour of greatest extremity; or that the ode of Cowper, beginning, "God moves in a mysterious way," was the last sane utterance of his mind, as the cloud which darkened his reason was settling over his spirit? "The dear cross," said Rist, "has pressed many songs out of me." A friend, speaking to Mr. Whittier about a well-known hymn, and expressing to him his appreciation of it as beyond all his other poems, received this answer from the poet: "I do not wonder at your preference; that hymn was born out of the uttermost anguish of my heart."* Thus the Church has been enriched, and the souls of all its members refreshed, by the recorded experiences of those who have clung to God through trial. Thus, too, we are taught to hold fast by him who supported these sweet singers of the sanctuary, and set

---

\* The poem here referred to is that on page 450 of the first volume of his collected works. Some of its verses have been inserted as a hymn in "The Sabbath Hymn-book." We quote these four stanzas:

> "I ask not now for gold to gild,
>   With mocking shine, a weary frame;
> The yearning of the mind is stilled—
>   I ask not now for fame.
>
> "But, bowed in lowliness of mind,
>   I make my humble wishes known:
> I only ask a will resigned,
>   O Father! to thine own.
>
> "In vain I task my aching brain;
>   In vain the sage's thought I scan;
> I only feel how weak and vain,
>   How poor and blind is man!
>
> "And now my spirit sighs for home,
>   And longs for light whereby to see,
> And like a weary child would come,
>   O Father, unto thee!"

them forth before us, that they might be our helpers. Nay, more: thus are we reminded that the very clasping of Jehovah's hand by the weary and the wayworn believer is itself, in the estimation of God, a holy hymn, a song rising up to him out of the night, and making a deeper impression in his heart, because of the silence and the darkness out of which it emerges. The poetry is not in the verbal expression of the song so much as in the experience it sings; and if sometimes there is a powerful prayer in the falling of a tear, be sure there is as often a sacred song in the light that flashes from the grateful eye, or the smile that radiates the happy countenance of him who is looking unto Jesus. Let us bear trials as David did, trusting in the Lord. Let us go through the world, clinging to Jesus in all our varying experiences; and though we may not be able to write psalms, our lives shall be each a book of hymns, rising gradually up to that new "song of pure concent, aye sung before the sapphire throne with saintly shout and solemn jubilee," "Worthy is the Lamb that was slain to receive power, and riches, and wisdom, and strength, and honor, and glory, and blessing."

## VIII.

### *CAVE SONGS.*

#### 1 Samuel xxiv. ; xxvi.

AFTER their escape from Saul in the wilderness of Maon, David and his men betook themselves to "the strongholds of En-gedi." This place, now identified with "Ain-Jidy," was situated on the western shore of the Dead Sea, about midway between its northern and southern extremities. The name literally signifies "the fountain of the goat," and doubtless had its origin in the fact that the neighborhood abounded in goats, attracted by the verdure which here lines the banks of a stream that issues from the limestone rock about four hundred feet above the level of the lake, at a temperature of 81°, and "rushes down the steep descent, fretted by many a rugged crag, and raining its spray over verdant borders of acacia, mimosa, and lotus."\* The cliffs in the neighborhood are full of natural caverns, in one or more of which the company of David found a lurking-place. These caves, says Dr. Thomson,† "are dark as midnight, and the keenest eye can not see five paces inward; but one who has been long within, and is looking outward toward the entrance, can observe with perfect distinctness all that takes place in that direction."

We can thus easily imagine the gloomy interior. Along the sides of the cavern, enjoying themselves in one or other of the many ways which soldiers have of amusing themselves,

---

\* Smith's "Dictionary," sub voce.
† "The Land and the Book," p. 603, English edition.

the motley multitude of David's men are scattered; while far away in the innermost recesses of the cave, David is to be found alone, or with Gad and Abiathar as his companions, soothing his heart with the strains of his harp, and accompanying the music with the words of the 142d Psalm, which was first sung either here or in Adullam. Let us read it, and see how, as in the pictures of Rembrandt, the very darkness gives to it a character that is all its own. "I cried unto the Lord with my voice ; with my voice unto the Lord did I make my supplication. I poured out my complaint before him ; I showed before him my trouble. When my spirit was overwhelmed within me, then thou knewest my path. In the way wherein I walked have they privily laid a snare for me. I looked on my right hand, and beheld, but there was no man that would know me: refuge failed me ; no man cared for my soul. I cried unto thee, O Lord : 1 said, Thou art my refuge and my portion in the land of the living. Attend unto my cry ; for I am brought very low: deliver me from my persecutors ; for they are stronger than I. Bring my soul out of prison, that I may praise thy name : the righteous shall compass me about ; for thou shalt deal bountifully with me."

There is in all this much of that "rapid stroke as of alternate wings," that "heaving and sinking as of the troubled heart," which Ewald* has so aptly described as the essence of the parallelism of Hebrew poetry ; while in the closing strophe the faith which underlies the whole prayer comes forth, like a daisy emerging from the grass, and opening its petals to the morning sun. The night had made it bend its head, and covered it with dew-drops ; and now, as it lifts itself up to greet the dawn, the tears of the darkness have become the diamonds that encircle its crimson-pointed coronet.

To the same chapter of David's life belongs the 57th

---

* Quoted by Stanley, "Jewish Church," vol. ii., p. 148.

Psalm, which we shall also read. "Be merciful unto me, O God, be merciful unto me: for my soul trusteth in thee: yea, in the shadow of thy wings will I make my refuge, until these calamities be overpast. I will cry unto God most high; unto God that performeth all things for me. He shall send from heaven, and save me from the reproach of him that would swallow me up. God shall send forth his mercy and his truth. My soul is among lions: and I lie even among them that are set on fire, even the sons of men, whose teeth are spears and arrows, and their tongue a sharp sword. Be thou exalted, O God, above the heavens; let thy glory be above all the earth. They have prepared a net for my steps; my soul is bowed down: they have digged a pit before me, into the midst whereof they are fallen themselves. My heart is fixed, O God; my heart is fixed: I will sing and give praise. Awake up, my glory; awake, psaltery and harp: I myself will awake early. I will praise thee, O Lord, among the people: I will sing unto thee among the nations. For thy mercy is great unto the heavens, and thy truth unto the clouds. Be thou exalted, O God, above the heavens: let thy glory be above all the earth."

When the hawk is in the air, the young bird seeks the shelter of the mother's outspread wings. When danger is impending, the child clings to the hand of his father. So, when reproach and persecution come upon David, he takes refuge in his God. How simple is his trust as here expressed! How entire his absorption of his own welfare in God's glory! and then, rising out of this self-abnegation, how lofty the strain of praise with which he concludes! The lark, whose nest is on the ground, rises, singing, as he soars, to the greatest heavenly height, until all but unseen he rains a shower of melody upon the listening earth. So, up from this lowest depth of suffering and distress, David rises to his loftiest ecstasy of praise, shaming the cold-heartedness of many in these days on whose lips "hosannas languish," and in whose hearts devotion all but dies. Nor for himself alone was David led through such experiences. God had set him forth, that in him, a needy and forlorn one in the very extremest degree, he might show his loving-kindness, "for a pattern to them which should hereafter believe on him." Accordingly, these cave Psalms have awakened responsive echoes in the hearts of multitudes in every age. When those of whom the world was not worthy "wandered in deserts and in mountains, and in dens and caves of the earth," no words could so bear up the burden of their hearts to God as those which I have just read. They were chanted, it may be, by Paul and Silas in the prison of Philippi, and by the early Christians in the Roman catacombs. They were sung, in their own rugged yet expressive version, by the Scottish Covenanters, on the bleak hill-side, or in the wild moor-land, or in the dark and lonely cave. When Sir Patrick Hume lay hid in the family sepulchral vault, or in the hole dug for him by his own daughter beneath his house, he tells us that when he had no light, he beguiled the hours by repeating to himself Buchanan's version of the Psalms, which in former days of prosperity he had committed to memory; and Christian sufferers everywhere, in times of revolution or danger, when fleeing before their enemies, have turned instinctively to these odes, and to others of similar character in the sacred Psalter. "There is not a day," says Edwards, in his "Personal Narrative of the Indian Mutiny,"* "in which we do not find something in the Psalms that appears written specially for our unhappy circumstances, to meet the wants and feelings of the day." Thus, as face answereth to face in a glass, so doth the heart of believer to believer in religious experience; and these cave Psalms which David has left, are but like speaking-tubes

---

* "Jewish Church," quoted by Stanley, vol. ii., pp. 145, 165.

in the chamber of affliction, through which we, as well as others, may send up our cry to him who is our Helper.

When Saul had returned from his campaign against the Philistines, and was informed that David had gone to Engedi, he immediately set out with three thousand men, determined to effect his destruction. But, so far from accomplishing his purpose, he was in a singular way put entirely into David's power. Seeking relief from the midday heat, and desiring to refresh himself with slumber, he went, all unwittingly, into the very cavern in which David and his men were concealed. Going from the light and looking inward, it was impossible that he should see them, but accustomed as they had become to the darkness, and looking, as they were from the back part of the cave out toward the dim light at its mouth, they could see him perfectly. David's companions regarded it as a special opportunity of ridding themselves of their adversary, and sought to persuade their leader to kill him. "Behold," said they, "the day of which the Lord said unto thee: Behold I will deliver thine enemy into thine hand, that thou mayest do to him as it shall seem good unto thee." But David could not bring himself so to regard it. There was still to him a "divinity hedging" the king, as the anointed of the Lord, and he would not suffer himself to violate the sanctity of Saul's person. His attitude was entirely defensive, and to slay Saul in cold blood, however much there might have been in Oriental usages to sanction it, would have been in his view not merely murder but sacrilege. No doubt it might be said that God had rejected Saul, and had caused David to be anointed in his room; but that had not given to David the right to deal summarily with Saul: it had only indicated that when, in the course of providence, Saul should be removed, David would be set upon his throne. For this, therefore, David would wait. He would not take providence into his own hands. He would bide God's time, and it should not be said of him that he had come into the kingdom by the assassination of his predecessor. So he stood firm against the entreaties of his men, and would not slay the king. He contented himself with cutting off a portion of Saul's robe, a thing which in the circumstances he could easily do without disturbing his repose. But even this caused him some misgivings of heart, the rather, as perhaps, after he had done it, his men, emboldened by his example, might have felt themselves at liberty to go farther, and lay hands on the king himself. If any such disposition was manifested by them, it was immediately repressed by their leader, and so, altogether unconscious of the danger to which he had been exposed, Saul slept on, until, thoroughly refreshed, he rose and passed out of the cave to join his troops. He was followed by David, with the skirt of his robe in his hand, who cried after him, "My lord, the king!" and bowed before him with his face to the earth.

It was a bold thing to do; and one hardly knows which to admire the more, the magnanimity that spared Saul in the cave, or the valor that braved him and his troops outside of it. But often the bolder course is the wiser, and the courage of a man in placing himself in the very midst of his enemies, so surprises them that they never think of doing him harm. Thus it seems to have been in the present instance; for, as David stands before Saul, and proceeds to plead his cause with him, no one of the royal troops interferes, and the king himself is deeply moved—but it is with sorrow rather than revenge. And it was no marvel that such an effect was produced upon him, for seldom has a more tender, earnest, manly, and candid appeal been made by one man to another, than that which David here addressed to Saul. He complained that the king had listened to unscrupulous men, who had laid to his charge things which his soul abhorred. He denied that he had ever in any way sought the king's hurt, and as a proof he pointed to the skirt which he held in his hand, and which he had taken from the royal robe, when he might just as easily have cut off his head. Then, rising into solemn expostulation, he placed the issue between them on its real merits, by appealing to Jehovah, saying, " The Lord judge between me and thee, and the Lord avenge me of thee: but mine hand shall not be upon thee." He affirmed that he was altogether unworthy even of Saul's enmity, and that the king might find something more dignified to do, than to come out after such an insignificant person as he was. Then, coming round again to their common responsibility to God, he concluded by placing his cause implicitly in the hands of the Lord. As he finished, Saul burst into tears, and cried, " Is this thy voice, my son David? Thou art more righteous than I: for thou hast rewarded me good, whereas I have rewarded thee evil. And thou hast showed this day how that thou hast dealt well with me : forasmuch as when the Lord had delivered me into thine hand, thou killedst me not. For if a man find his enemy, will he let him go well away? wherefore the Lord reward thee good for that thou hast done unto me this day. And now, behold, I know well that thou shalt surely be king, and that the kingdom of Israel shall be established in thine hand. Swear now therefore unto me by the Lord, that thou wilt not cut off my seed after me, and that thou wilt not destroy my name out of my father's house." This oath David willingly took, and Saul, drawing off his men with him, went home. Yet David, reluctant to trust himself to the keeping of one so mercurial and spasmodic as he knew Saul to be, would not forsake his stronghold, but returned into the cave.

And it was well that he did so, for Saul did not long continue in this gracious mood; and a very short while after, we have a scene between him and David not unlike that which we have just witnessed. It is described in the twenty-sixth chapter of 1 Samuel; but it may be convenient to take it now, leaving the intervening narrative to be considered afterward.

In the course of his wanderings David came once again to Hachilah, in the neighborhood of Ziph; and the inhabitants of that city, disappointed, perhaps, at the failure of their former attempt, sent again to Saul to tell him where he was. The result was that Saul came forth with his troops, expecting to take him, as he doubtless would have done on the first occasion, if he had not been called away to attack the Philistines. But, wiser from his former experience, David, this time, did not go to the hill, but abode in the wilderness, keeping ever a vigilant eye upon the movements of his adversary.

At length, one night, accompanied by his nephew, Abishai, David went into the very midst of Saul's encampment while he and his troops were asleep. Abishai counseled that Saul should be slain, and offered to do the treacherous deed himself; but David, true to his reverence for the Lord's anointed, and earnest in his desire not to stain his hands with the blood of his father-in-law, would not consent. He was content to leave the whole controversy between himself and Saul to God, and he would not rashly precipitate its settlement by any crime of his own. "As the Lord liveth," said he, "the Lord shall smite him; or his day shall come to die; or he shall descend into battle, and perish. The Lord forbid that I should stretch forth mine hand against the Lord's anointed." So he restrained Abishai; and counseling him to take only the spear which marked the pillow of the chief, and the cruse of water that was by his side, they stole away from the camp, and returned to their own stronghold. In the morning, David climbed to the ledge of the cliff which overhung the cave in which his men were concealed, and overlooked the valley in which Saul was encamped, and shouting to Abner, the captain of the king's host, he bantered him on the careful watch which he had kept over his master, showing at the same time the spear and the pitcher, as proof that he had himself been at the very side of Saul. When the king heard his voice he was moved as deeply as he had been at En-gedi, and said, "I have sinned: return, my son David; for I will no more do thee harm, because my soul was precious in thine eyes this day: behold, I have played the fool, and have erred exceedingly."

David's response was a renewal of his appeal to God; and Saul parts from him with a benediction: "Blessed be thou, my son David: thou shalt both do great things, and also shalt still prevail." Truly, "When a man's way please the Lord, he maketh even his enemies to be at peace with him." We hear a great deal of David's malignity and revengeful spirit, and I can not, in the light of the New Testament, defend all that he did or said; yet we must not fail to note how here he acted from the noblest magnanimity, and how, long before the words of Paul were written, he verified the truth which they express: "Dearly beloved, avenge not yourselves, but rather give place unto wrath: for it is written, Vengeance is mine; I will repay, saith the Lord. Therefore, if thine enemy hunger, feed him; if he thirst, give him drink: for in so doing thou shalt heap coals of fire on his head. Be not overcome of evil, but overcome evil with good." So far as we know, this was the last meeting between Saul and David; and it is pleasing to think that after all that had occurred, Saul's latest utterance to him was one of benediction; at once a vindication of David's conduct in the past, and a forecast of his glory in the future. Verily, the Psalmist was speaking from his own experience when he said, "Commit thy way unto the Lord; trust also in him: and he shall bring it to pass. And he shall bring forth thy righteousness as the light, and thy judgment as the noonday." But before we pass away from Saul's persecution of

David, an interesting inquiry presents itself, which may be answered by the help of one of the Psalms. How came it, one is tempted to ask, that Saul was thus at one time so friendly to David, and at another filled with such bitter enmity against him? Much of this was owing, doubtless, to the impulsive, wayward, and capricious disposition which, as we have seen, grew upon him after his rejection by Samuel.

But that will not explain it all. An impulse will go on in a man until it exhausts itself; but it will then leave him, at least, indifferent, and something else will be required to account for the rapid reversal of his feelings, when we see him change in a short time from grateful appreciation to fierce antagonism. Where, then, shall we find that something in the case of Saul? The answer seems to me to be furnished by the inscription to the 7th Psalm, which, from its similarity to David's utterances to Saul on the occasions which have been to-night before us, has been by most expositors connected with these events. It is entitled "Shiggaion of David, which he sang unto the Lord, concerning the words of Cush the Benjamite." That is "a dithyrambic ode of David concerning the words of Cush." Now if we adopt the conjecture that Cush was one of Saul's confidential adherents, and that he had set himself deliberately and malignantly to poison his master's mind in reference to David, by inventing all manner of false assertions, and indulging in every variety of significant innuendoes concerning him, we have an explanation at once, of many statements in the narrative, of the vacillations in the disposition of Saul, and of the character of the Psalm to which the title belongs. Thus, at En-gedi, David said to Saul, in apparent allusion to some private slanderers, "Wherefore hearest thou men's words, saying, Behold, David seeketh thy hurt?"[*] And again, at Hachilah, he exclaims,

---

[*] 1 Sam. xxiv., 9.

"If the Lord have stirred thee up against me, let him accept an offering: but if they be the children of men, cursed be they before the Lord; for they have driven me out this day from abiding in the inheritance of the Lord, saying, Go, serve other gods."* So also in one of the two Psalms which I have already brought before you as undeniably belonging to this chapter of his history, the poet, in describing his persecutors, says, "I lie even among them that are set on fire, even the sons of men, whose teeth are spears and arrows, and their tongue a sharp sword."† All this points to the fact that there was at the court of Saul some one whose constant design it was to paint David in the blackest colors, and who for this end did not hesitate to invent the falsest calumnies against him. When the king was alone, away from the influence of this black-hearted sycophant, David's noble and frank ingenuousness produced its appropriate impression on his heart; but when David disappeared, and this Cush resumed his insinuating supremacy, then Saul's heart was again estranged, and he vowed vengeance on the son of Jesse. Of course, if Saul had not been weak, this effect would not have been produced upon him; but, in the circumstances, we can see how the larger measure of the guilt belonged to Cush, and can understand why, while David spared the king, his heart was full of abhorrence of the part which was played by the false-hearted Benjamite. Now, with these considerations in our minds, let us read the Psalm itself. "O Lord my God, in thee do I put my trust: save me from all them that persecute me, and deliver me: lest he tear my soul like a lion, rending it in pieces, while there is none to deliver. O Lord my God, if I have done this; if there be iniquity in my hands; if I have rewarded evil unto him that was at peace with me (yea, I have delivered him that without cause is

---

\* 1 Sam. xxvi, 19. † Psa. lvii., 4.

mine enemy)—[a parenthetic allusion to his allowing Saul to escape, even though he had him in his power]; let the enemy persecute my soul, and take it; yea, let him tread down my life upon the earth, and lay mine honor in the dust. Arise, O Lord, in thine anger, lift up thyself because of the rage of mine enemies: and awake for me to the judgment that thou hast commanded. So shall the congregation of the people compass thee about: for their sakes, therefore, return thou on high. The Lord shall judge the people: judge me, O Lord, according to my righteousness, and according to mine integrity that is in me. Oh let the wickedness of the wicked come to an end; but establish the just: for the righteous God trieth the hearts and reins. My defense is of God, which saveth the upright in heart. God judgeth the righteous, and God is angry with the wicked every day. If he turn not, he will whet his sword; he hath bent his bow, and made it ready. He hath also prepared for him the instruments of death; he ordaineth his arrows against the persecutors. Behold, he travaileth with iniquity, and hath conceived mischief, and brought forth falsehood. He made a pit, and digged it, and is fallen into the ditch which he made. His mischief shall return upon his own head, and his violent dealing shall come down upon his own pate. I will praise the Lord according to his righteousness: and will sing praise to the name of the Lord most high."

The similarity of many of the expressions used in this ode to those employed by David in his two appeals to Saul is very great, and fully warrants the belief that the Psalm was composed at the date of the occurrences which have been now before us. In this view it is most interesting, as showing the habitual tendency of David's soul in trial to repair to God. Andrew Fuller has somewhere said that "a man has only as much religion as he can command in the time of trouble;" and by the bearing of David through these calamities we may see how genuine his devotion to Jehovah was.

Traveling once upon a railway car, I had among my fellow-passengers a little laughing child, who romped about and was at home with every body. Had any one come in and looked at her while she was frolicking thus, he would not have been able to tell to whom she belonged, she seemed to be so much the property of every one; but ere long the engine gave a loud, long shriek, as we went rattling into a dark tunnel, and in a moment the child flew, like a bird, to nestle herself in a lady's lap. I knew then who was her mother! So, in the day of prosperity, the good man may go hither and thither, to this side or to that, and there may not be very much about him to tell whose he is; but let him be sent through some dark, damp tunnel of severe affliction, and you will see at once to whom he belongs; for then, David-like, he commits his cause to God and bides the issue. The Spirit of God has written the name of Jesus with invisible ink on the believer's heart, but the fire of tribulation brings out the characters before men's eyes. Still, remember that trial does not make goodness; it only reveals it. We must have it before we can manifest it. Hence, if we would prepare for such an ordeal as that through which David passed, we must in our daily lives cultivate such fellowship with Jehovah, as that which the son of Jesse maintained when he was following his father's sheep.

But going back over the narrative, let us, ere we close, glean for ourselves a few practical lessons from it for our daily guidance. And here an obvious application of the principle on which David acted when Saul was in his power, is that we should never seek success by unwarrantable means. Though David was promised the kingdom, nay, just because he had faith in Him who made the promise, he would not make the body of Saul a step up to the throne. "He that believeth will not make haste." Contrast this conduct of his with that of Rebekah, when, thinking she could manage matters better than God, she stirred up Jacob to seek the birthright by deception, and you will see precisely what I mean when I hold up the procedure of David for approbation and imitation. Rebekah thought she was taking the shortest way to get at that which God had promised, but in reality she sent her son a long way round, entailed upon him much shame and misery, and deprived herself of his presence and fellowship for all her after-life. David, in the view of his followers, might have stepped to the throne of Israel at once by murdering Saul, but he knew better than take such a course as that. The right way may seem the longer, but it is always the safer; and when you get to your destination, you have the satisfaction of an approving conscience, and a favoring God. Now this is a truth which young people, in these days particularly, would do well to remember. There is no temporal object of ambition, indeed, which God has promised to bestow on any one now, as certainly as he covenanted to give to David the throne of Israel. Yet every youth has some kingdom before him which he desires to win; and the restless hurry of our age is such that he becomes infected with the common madness, and is in haste to gain his end. Now, in these circumstances, there are never wanting Abishais who will come and show him a short road to the attainment of his purpose; but it will be over the commission of some sin as real, though perhaps not quite so revolting, as would have been the murder of Saul by David in the cave of Engedi. "See," one says, "here is a glorious opportunity to make your fortune in a day. Never mind, though it does involve the ruin of a rival; you don't owe him any consideration. He would have no regard for you, if your circumstances were reversed;" and so the temptation is to go and do as it is suggested. Or, again, you may have, to use the world's word, the chance to step into a long-coveted office at once, provided only you will covenant to do some mean, ungenerous, or dishonorable thing toward him who at the moment holds it. He has no love for you indeed, and would not hesitate to crush you if you were in his power; but what does that matter? If you yield to such a temptation, you are planting a seed which in after-years will meet you in the shape of manifold retributions, while at the same time you are taking from success that which is ever its truest charm, namely, that it has been honorably and deservedly won. My young friends, will you accept this advice for your guidance through life? Never take a short road to any object when the gate into that road is sin. How much purer would our political and our commercial life become, if men would only consent to act upon that principle! Be not in such hot haste. Keep by the highway of the great King! That will lead you right, though it may sometimes seem to lead you round. Beware of turning to the one hand or to the other, to follow some inviting footpath which seems to shorten the distance. Be sure that will land you in some dismal swamp, wherein you will flounder and struggle for a longer time than it would have taken to go by the proper road, and, when you get to your destination, you will be all over mud! Let no vision of immediate success beguile you to do wrong. Do as God would have you; and leave it to him to bring you to the goal you seek, in his own time. Make haste slowly, and rather resign yourself to the loss of your kingdom, than go to it through shame and sin.

Again: if the view which I have given as to the title of the 7th Psalm, and its connection with the history which we have been considering, be correct, it brings up before us the whole subject of slander.

What a meanly cruel man this Cush must have been! He did not come face to face with David, and allow him the opportunity either of making an explanation or of demanding an investigation; but, like a cowardly assassin, he stabbed him from behind, and whispered his falsehoods into the ear of Saul, with every added embellishment of external mannerism to give them effect. Now, have we nothing like this, even in our own day and in our own circles? Who knows not among his acquaintances some scandal-monger who is forever whispering away some one's reputation with a "They say," or "I'm sure I hope it is not true; but yet, you know, the best of men are but men at the best, and it does look very suspicious, to say the least of it?" Give me rather a hundred open, honorable enemies than one such serpent-tongued and behind-back antagonist as that. Let me see my accusers: let me be brought face to face with any open, above-board statement, at any righteous tribunal; but let me not be set to fight with one who will not come forth from his dark ambush, unless it be to aim another blow when he can do so unseen. It may seem a small matter to the slanderer himself; he may look upon it even as a good joke; but it is a serious business with him whom he assails, for the lie will pass round and round, gathering as it goes, and may, perhaps, entail upon its victim the severest agony.

> "A whisper broke the air—
>    A soft, light tone, and low,
>     Yet barb'd with shame and woe:
>   Now might it perish only there,
>      Nor farther go!
>   Ah me! a quick and eager ear
>     Caught up the little meaning sound!
>   Another voice has breathed it clear,
>     And so it wandered round
>   From ear to lip, from lip to ear,
>   Until it reached a gentle heart,
>     And *that* it broke!"

Think of that when the slanderous story rises to your lips, and be silent!

But though, perhaps, the large part of the blame belonged to Cush, we can not hold Saul guiltless. He ought to have been above receiving private accusations against any man, most of all against one who had done so much for the defense of his country as David had; but, alas! the wish was father to the scandal here. Saul desired some ground on which he might rid himself of David, and so he was ready to believe any evil that might be laid to his charge. If the king had not been willing to hear, Cush would have had no opportunity to speak. In all slander, therefore, the hearer is as bad as the speaker; and if we were only to act as we ought to do when a tale-bearer begins to speak, we should instantly take measures either to silence him or to leave his presence. It is a poor compliment one pays to us when he begins to retail scandal in our ear, because it proves that he believes us to be capable of enjoying it; and certainly no enjoyment could be more diabolical. Hence, if we were to feel rightly in this regard, we would view it as the greatest insult that could be offered to us, when one comes to us with a whispered history that is intended to destroy our confidence in the absent. "Where no wood is, there the fire goeth out;" so, where there is no listener, the scandal-monger's "occupation's gone." But ere I quit this subject, let me direct a moment's attention to the bearing of David under this affliction. He embraces the first opportunity of confronting it, and then he makes his appeal to God, and waits his vindication at the hands of Providence; while, at the same time, he gives expression to the conviction that, sooner or later, the false accuser would be visited for his iniquity, and fall into the pit which he had digged for another. As, in a later history, when Paul was about to be made a victim by an unprincipled governor, who sought only to make the most of his position for his own aggrandizement, he appealed unto Cæsar, thereby removing himself to a higher tribunal in another land, so here, amidst the accusations that were heaped upon him by Cush, David appealed to Heaven, saying, virtually, "There is one that judgeth me, even God." Thus let it be with us in times when we are assailed by slander. We may not expect to get through the world without some of it. Better men than any of us have had much of it to bear; and the better a man is, the greater is the danger of such assaults; for it is only the finest fruit that the birds will peck at, or the wasps destroy! Let us prepare for it, therefore; and when we are called to bear it, let us take it as David took it; nay, higher still, let us take it as it was taken by David's Lord, "who, when he was reviled, reviled not again; when he suffered, he threatened not; but committed himself to him that judgeth righteously."

I add only one other thought: Observe, from the case of Saul, that true repentance is a deeper thing than feeling, and is distinguished by permanence as well as sincerity. Saul says, "I have sinned;" but we must not imagine, because he uses these words, that he has truly repented of his transgressions. Indeed, if you are familiar with the Word of God, you will at once recall a number of instances recorded in it, in which this very expression was employed, but with a different result in almost every case. Thus we hear Pharaoh saying, when the plague of hail had desolated Egypt, "I have sinned;" but the end with him was the hardening of his heart, and his utter destruction. When the lot discovered Achan, and brought out to light the wedge of gold and the Babylonish garment which he had hidden in his tent, he too said, "I have sinned;" but there was nothing in his heart of that spontaneousness which is the essence of all true confession. When Judas came with the pieces of silver, and cast them at the feet of the Pharisees, he too said, "I have sinned;" and very deep and bitter was his consciousness of guilt; but his feeling was remorse, and not repentance, and so he rushed recklessly from the world, vainly seeking a place where he might hide from God. When, after his great sin, David was brought to himself by the expostulation of Nathan, he fell on his knees, and sobbed out the 51st Psalm, part of which is as follows: "Against thee, thee only, have I sinned, and done this evil in thy sight;" and in that jewel of the parables, the story of the Prodigal Son, we hear the starving youth, as he lies in his swineherd's den, soliloquizing thus: "I will arise and go to my father, and will say unto him, Father, I have sinned against heaven, and before thee, and am no more worthy to be called thy son." Now, the mere repetition of these six different ways in which the words "I have sinned" have been employed, will help us to distinguish between genuine and spurious repentance. They differ in the root out of which they spring. The spurious springs from fear, or from a desire to escape punishment; the genuine springs from the contemplation of God—and now of God more especially as he has revealed himself to us in the person and work of Jesus Christ. Which, my hearer, is yours? Have you ever yet said, "I have sinned?" and if you have said it, why have you done so? True repentance is simultaneous with the reception of Christ, and is not to be regarded as a preparation for coming to him. The question has often been asked, indeed, whether faith or repentance comes first, but in reality they may almost be regarded as two ways of describing the same thing. A man truly believes only when he repents; he really repents only when he believes. Faith is the hold which repentance has of Christ; repentance is the view which faith has of sin: Faith is the soul's turning to Christ. But it can not turn to Christ without at the same time also turning from sin, and that is repentance. Faith is the looking eye resting upon Jesus;

Repentance is the tear that gathers and glistens in that eye, as it sees the soul's own sins in the burden which the Redeemer bore. Let us learn to say, "I have sinned" thus at the foot of the cross, and no doubt about the genuineness of our penitence need ever trouble us.

## IX.

### *NABAL.*

#### 1 SAMUEL XXV.

IN the interval between the two meetings of David with Saul, which we considered in our last discourse, the Land of Israel sustained a sore bereavement in the death of the venerable Samuel.

Brought up at the feet of Eli in the Tabernacle at Shiloh, and called while yet a boy to the prophetical office, Samuel had lived almost continuously in the service of the nation, and had gathered to himself the affection and the confidence of the whole community. Seeking not his own glory, but devotedly attached to the people, and eagerly solicitous for the honor of Jehovah, he had been both a civil benefactor and a religious reformer. He rectified the abuses which had sprung up under the wicked sanction of the sons of Eli, and set himself to the administration of even-handed justice among the tribes. He established the practice of holding circuit courts, which has been so largely followed in modern times; and by the decisions which he gave, he redeemed the seat of judgment from the contempt into which it had fallen.

He reorganized the Tabernacle services, and by the influence at once of his teachings and his life, he lifted the priestly office from the depth of infamy to which Hophni and Phineas had sunk it, so that it was no longer true that the most corrupt and degraded looked to it as the last refuge of their destitution, saying, "Put us into the priest's office, that we may eat a piece of bread." He established the schools of the prophets, at which young men were educated for the higher service of the nation; and by his attention to the art of music, he prepared the way for those admirable arrangements for "the service of song in the house of the Lord," which, at a later day, made the name of David illustrious. But perhaps the greatest benefit which he conferred on his fellow-countrymen was in the influence which he exerted over them by his godly example. He lived the truth which he taught, and drew to him increasingly, as the years revolved, the affection of the people. Yea, though in the pride of their heart they had desired a king to rule over them, he had never lost their confidence, but was among them to the last an uncrowned king, to whom, in all seasons of perplexity, they instinctively turned for counsel and assistance. In his later days, indeed, he had retired, in a great measure, into private life, and more especially after the formal rejection of Saul and the anointing of David, he had seldom appeared in public. Still, his very presence among them was a consolation and a defense, and, in the unsettled state of national affairs, the pious members of the community would feel new confidence when they thought of him.

But the time had come when he must die. Humanly speaking, he could ill be spared from a land which was blighted by the sway of a self-willed and unscrupulous monarch, and torn by the distraction of civil strife; but the discord of earth would make the peace of heaven only the more welcome to him, while it intensified the grief of all good men at his loss. To his own children, who walked not in his way, his death would be, perhaps, the breaking of the last restraint that held them from running headlong into uttermost iniquity; to the young men of the school of the prophets, it would be the taking from them of their best and wisest earthly friend; and they would each cry out, like Elisha after the ascending Elijah, "My father! my father! the chariots of Israel and the horsemen thereof." To Saul it might be a relief, as ridding him of one who, alone of all his subjects, feared not to tell him wholesome truth; but to David it would be a sore distress, making him feel as if the one earthly link that bound him to his future kingdom had somehow snapped asunder. He would recall the day when the prophet came to Bethlehem to anoint him, and go back in thought to the happy hours which he had spent with him at Ramah; and as he looked around him at the state of the land, and before him at the difficulties which were barring his way to his predestined throne, we may well conceive him sitting down and singing, out of the depths, the Psalm beginning, "Help, Lord; for the godly man ceaseth; for the faithful fail from among the children of men."* Most appropriate, therefore, was it that all Israel should gather to the good man's burial; and among the crowd of mourners that stood around the tomb at Ramah, we may be sure that there was not one more deeply moved than David.

But his grief for the loss of Samuel, great as it was, could not be allowed to interfere with the taking of those precautions which were needed to insure his own safety. Accordingly, that he might keep out of the way of Saul, he led his men to the wilderness of Paran. This name was given to the entire tract of country south of Judah, extending from the Dead Sea to the peninsula of Sinai and the desert of Egypt; so that in its largest sense it included the deserts of Kadesh and Sin. Nearly all the wanderings of the children of Israel were in the great and terrible wilderness of Paran. But in the present narrative it seems to be restricted to the most northerly portion of this desert, lying to the west of the lower part of the Dead Sea, where the waste changes gradually into an uninhabited pasture-land, in which, at least in

---

* Psalm xii.

spring and autumn, many herds might feed. In this neighborhood was the town of Maon, which was eight miles south-by-east of Hebron; and about one mile to the north of Maon was the village of Carmel, to be carefully distinguished from the promontory and mountain of that name on the shore of the Mediterranean.

In the former of these towns, but with possessions which connected him also with the latter, there dwelt a wealthy man, named, or, perhaps rather nicknamed, Nabal, or the fool, who was distinguished by his niggardly disposition, selfish character, and sottish habits. He might almost have sat for the portrait which our Lord has drawn in the parable of "the rich fool," only in his case the degrading vice of intemperance was added to the grasping passion of avarice. He was a descendant of the noble Caleb, but he had none of Caleb's nature in him. He lived only to increase his goods and to pamper his appetite. Proud of his "three thousand sheep" and his "one thousand goats," he fancied that they gave him a right to snub and despise those who were less fortunate in the world. His wealth had not endowed him with common sense; but, like many in our own day, he imagined that, because he was in affluent circumstances, he might with impunity indulge in rude, ill-mannered sneers at all who were around him. "What did he care for the courtesies or the kindnesses of life? Was not he the great man of the place? Could not he do just as he pleased? And as for what other people thought of him, what did that matter to him? Was not he independent of them all?" Thus, from the murmurs of those around him, he took refuge in the self-complacent soliloquy: "Soul, thou hast much goods laid up for many years; eat, drink, and be merry." The race was not extinct in our Saviour's day. It is not extinct in our own. Let no one suppose, therefore, that when we come upon this Nabal, we are like the geologist when in the crust of the earth he lights upon some huge old megalosaurus, and that we have here the petrified fossil of a kind of animal which was common in the oolite period, but has now entirely disappeared. Not at all! You very likely met him yesterday. You may meet him, perhaps, to-morrow. The man with heavy purse and light head, with full pockets and empty cranium, is everywhere a Nabal; and if, haply, he combines with these the gluttony of the gourmand or the thirst of the drunkard, he will only make the identity more complete.

This purse-proud boor, had contrived (and here, again, the resemblance to the modern specimen of the same species often holds good) to marry a woman "of good understanding, and of a beautiful countenance." I know not how it was brought about. We will be charitable, however, and hope that it was, like other Eastern marriages, a matter of parental arrangement, and that her lofty appreciation of his wealth had nothing at all to do with it. If this were so, then she at least was not so mercenary as some in our enlightened age, who if they can only marry a carriage and pair, do not seem to care whether or not they have a husband of mental ability and moral worth fit to be the companion of their daily lives.

At the time of David's sojourn in this district, Nabal held his annual sheep-shearing. This was equivalent to the harvest of the flock-masters, and was commonly finished with a joyous feast which corresponded to the harvest-home. Generally, therefore, it was a season of liberality and good-will. It was the yearly stock-taking time, and if things had turned out well, if the flocks had increased in number, and the fleeces were up to the average standard of weight and value, the heart of their owner was opened, and he was commonly disposed to show more than usual kindness to all who were in need. In the present instance, David knew that Nabal had peculiar reasons for being satisfied with the returns from his shepherds, for during the sojourn of his troop in the locality, he had constituted himself the guardian of Nabal's property, and, on the testimony of the shepherds, had not only not injured them himself, but had been a wall around them by night and day, so that neither were they injured by any one, nor had they missed any thing all the time that they had been beside them.

Conscious, therefore, of the services which he and his followers had rendered this sheep-farmer, and expecting that in the day of his gladness his heart would be opened to give a substantial reward to his benefactors, David sent ten of his young men to him with a kindly greeting, and a polite request that he would give them some supplies. To their surprise, however, they were met not only with a gruff refusal, but with insulting sneers, which cast the blackest aspersions on the character of their leader. "Who is David?" quoth Nabal, "and who is the son of Jesse? there be many servants nowadays that break away every man from his master. Shall I then take my bread, and my water, and my flesh that I have killed for my shearers, and give it unto men, whom I know not whence they be?"

Stung to the quick by these aggravating words, the young men went to David, and told him how they had been repulsed. Very likely their story lost nothing in the telling. Most probably, indeed, they would infuse something of their own wounded pride into their account; but in any case, when David heard what they said, he became fiercely indignant, and ordering four hundred of his men to arm themselves and follow him, he went forth, vowing the deepest vengeance, and determined not to leave a single survivor of all those who belonged to the ungrateful cynic who had so insulted him.

But this was all wrong; for though David had a clear

moral right to be recompensed for the services which he had rendered to Nabal, he had no legal title to the smallest portion of his property; far less had he any justification for seeking thus to destroy him and his household. We have not a syllable to say in Nabal's vindication; but neither can we utter a word in defense of David for this revengeful purpose. This was not like him who so reined in his spirit when Saul was in his power. It was altogether unworthy of one who had received so many signal tokens of kindness from the Lord. Who was Nabal, that for his rudeness he should let himself be so disturbed? If the man was a fool, then as such his words were beneath contempt, and it would have been much more in harmony with the high-mindedness of the poet-hero if he had taken no notice of his rudeness, and allowed him to rail on. Hence his purpose to destroy Nabal's house was as undignified as it was iniquitous. Human life is a holy thing, and he who takes it away from pride, or passion, or avarice, or lust, commits a foul outrage on the community, and a grievous sin against the Lord. No matter what the character of his victim may be, the man who takes the life of another dishonors God and degrades the law; and it bodes ill for the commonwealth when deeds like these are allowed to be done with impunity.

But by the prompt and prudent management of Abigail, Nabal's wife, David was saved, in this instance, from carrying out his rash intention. It came about in this fashion: One of the shepherds who knew how much they had all been indebted to David and his men, and who feared the consequences of Nabal's rudeness, went at once to Abigail, and stated the case to her. He did not take it upon him to expostulate with his master, "for he knew that he was such a son of Belial that a man could not speak to him." But he had confidence in the sagacity of his mistress, and he besought her to take measures immediately to ward off the evil which would be sure to come upon them all. His appeal was not made in vain, for she made haste, and laded asses with ample stores of provisions; and, sending these on before, she determined to go herself and make an ample explanation and apology to David.

She had not come a moment too soon, for, as she was descending into a covert of the hill on the one side, David and his men were coming down on the other, "nursing their wrath" the while. As soon as she saw them, she lighted from her ass, and, falling at David's feet, in Oriental fashion, she made suit to him in such a manner as to show a rare amount of womanly tact and intellectual ability. Taking all the blame upon herself, she referred to her husband "with that union of playfulness and seriousness which, above all things, turns away wrath."\* "As his name is, so is he; fool (Nabal) is his name, and folly is with him." Then she proceeded, on the supposition that her request had been already granted, to congratulate David that the Lord had withholden him from shedding blood, and she begged his acceptance, for his young men, of the supplies which she had brought. Thereafter, rising from present circumstances, she went on to refer to the future in such a way as to show that she had implicit faith in the prophecies that had gone before concerning David; and in a manner the most delicately adroit she concluded by saying that, when God had given him the kingdom, it should be no grief to him that he had shed blood causeless, or that he had avenged himself. All this was most pertinently put; and when she spake of God's "making David a sure house;" of his soul as "bound in the bundle of life with the Lord his God," and of his enemies as destined to be "slung out, as out of the middle of a sling," we do not wonder that she gained her object. She was a woman; and though we give her

---

\* Stanley's "Jewish Church," vol. ii., p. 79.

full credit for sincerity in all that she said, we can not but admire the dexterous female generalship with which she carried her point in such a way as to leave David with the impression that he was laid by her under a deep obligation. Neither can we overlook the fact, so creditable to her piety, that by the skillful allusion which she made to his revengeful purpose, she deeply touched the conscience of David, and turned his gratitude to her into thanksgiving to God. Only a woman could have managed such a negotiation as this so smoothly and successfully; but only a God-fearing woman would have managed it so as to bring David to a sense of the sinfulness of the act which he had been about to commit.

Nabal, however, was not so much pleased with the result. When Abigail went home, she found him so intoxicated that she said nothing on the subject to him until the morning; but then, when he heard her report, he was so enraged at the loss of his property, or at the thought that his wife had done what he had himself refused to do, that he went into a fit of apoplexy—a disease to which his dissipated habits and the debauch of the previous night had predisposed him, and, after lingering for ten days, he died.

When David heard of his fate, he was anew impelled to express his gratitude to God for having withheld him from the murder which it had been in his heart to commit. This was well; but we are not sure that he was equally to be commended when, with the disposition to connect special calamity with special sin, for which the Jews, as a whole, were distinguished, and against which the Saviour has warned us all, he affected to see in the manner of Nabal's death a righteous retribution for his treatment of himself, and a pleading of the cause of his reproach. For that we do not vindicate him, any more than we do for the means which he employed to console Abigail for her husband's loss, when "he communed with her to take her to him to wife!" Already he was the husband of Michal, and though she had been taken from him by her father Saul, and given to another, that was no excuse for his marrying Abigail now, especially as even before his encounter with Nabal he had taken Ahinoam of Jezreel into a similar relationship. Probably he did this, as Eastern chiefs do to this day, for the purpose of adding to his importance in the estimation of the people; but though polygamy was rather regulated than forbidden by the law of Moses, it is clearly contrary to the primal law of nature, and in David's case, as in the cases of many others, it was followed by disastrous consequences. We shall return to this subject, ere we conclude; meanwhile let us take out of the history which we have to-night reviewed, one or two practical thoughts which may be useful to us in the ordering of our daily lives.

Let us note, then, first, the suggestive contrast which is here presented in the deaths of Samuel and Nabal. On the one hand, we have a good man, taken to his reward after a long life spent in the service of his God, and a whole nation gathers to weep around his tomb. On the other, we have a surly, selfish, sottish man called to his account, and no tear is shed over his grave; but instead, a feeling of relief is experienced by all who were connected with him, for they are all conscious that they will be the happier for his absence. In the one case, the life on earth was but the prelude to a higher, holier, and more useful existence in the heavenly world; in the other, the earthly character was but the germ out of which would spring, in the state beyond, a deeper, darker, and more repulsive wickedness even than that which he had manifested here. I do not think that David wrote the 37th Psalm at this particular date, since, from one expression which it contains, he seems to have penned that ode in his old age; but, whensoever it was written, it is hard for me to believe that he had not before his mind at the time the con trast between Nabal and Samuel which this history so vividly presents. What could be more appropriate to Nabal than these words: "I have seen the wicked in great power, and spreading himself like a green bay tree. Yet he passed away, and lo, he was not: yea, I sought him, but he could not be found." And surely David thought of Samuel when he wrote this verse: "Mark the perfect man, and behold the upright: for the end of that man is peace."

Now, the practical question for us is, To which of these two classes do we belong? Alas! there are many in these days whose lives are inflicting a constant martyrdom on all who have the misfortune to be nearly related to them, and whose deaths, while full of sadness to themselves, would yet be a blessing and a relief to their friends as ridding them of a constant and fearful misery. "A living cross is heavier than a dead one;" and there are few who have to carry a weightier or sharper cross than the wives and families of these Nabals, whose intemperance has brutified them into harsh, unfeeling cruelty. How can you expect the woman who has been beaten and abused by her drunkard husband to feel otherwise than relieved, when death dissolves the union which had brought her such abuse? "I thought you would have been glad when your husband came home," said a little girl to a wife whose husband had just returned from a twelve months' absence at sea; "but instead of that, you look so sad and anxious." Ah! she knew not what a stab her words were giving to her heart, for her husband had returned only to fill her soul with deepest agony. Is there one here to-night who is conscious that he is living such a life as must make all around him miserable — let him see in Nabal how repulsive he looks, and let him turn from his evil ways, and seek to minister to the happiness and holiness of his home. Let him be no more a son of Belial, but indeed a son of God, so that when he passes from the world he may leave behind him those who sincerely mourn his loss, and may himself enter into the enjoyment of heaven's own blessedness.

What a blank is created when the good man dies! Men miss his kindly presence, his wise counsel, his loving words, his liberal deeds, his holy example, and his earnest prayers. It is long before they can become accustomed to his absence; and when some deep grief falls upon them, or some great agony is to be passed through by them, they feel as if they wished him back again to sustain them through the ordeal. But all of him does not depart. He leaves behind him an influence, which, long after he has gone, is active and operative for good.

"Do you see that strip of green yonder?" said one to his companion, as they stood together on a height, surveying the landscape; "I wonder what has caused it?" "I know," was the answer; "there was a brook there once, and its old course is lined with a richer verdure than the surrounding district." Just so, the place where a good man has lived and died is greener from the influence he has exerted over it; and even after his name may have been forgotten by the inhabitants, they may be found in some way moulded by his character. Let it be our aim, brethren, so to walk with Jesus in our daily conduct, that we may have such a hallowed influence on all with whom we come into contact. Let us be earnest in the service of our generation by the will of God. Let us rouse ourselves to zealous activity for the honor of Christ and the benefit of our fellow-men. "It were infamy to die and not be missed." It were foul dishonor to be buried in a grave over which no one cares to shed a tear. But if we would have the death of Samuel, we must live his life; and if we would live his life, we must bear continually in mind the words which Jehovah spoke to Eli by the man of God when Samuel was a child: "Them that honor me

I will honor, and they that despise me shall be lightly esteemed."

Note, in the second place, from this history, that little things are more dangerous to the believer's life than great. David could control himself when in the presence of Saul, and again and again resisted the entreaties of his adherents to put his adversary to death; but when this churlish and altogether contemptible Nabal speaks a few insulting words, he is completely thrown off his guard, and gives way to the most unhallowed anger and blood-thirsty revenge. And it is so with the people of God still. For great things a Christian braces himself up prayerfully, and so he meets them calmly and patiently; but a little thing frets him, and provokes him to testiness and rage, because he deems it too trivial to go to God with, and seeks to encounter it only in his own strength. How common is this experience among us! The loss of a large sum seriously affecting our comfort will be borne with equanimity, for we are driven to meet that upon our knees; but if one should cheat us out of a paltry amount, it will annoy us, and stir us up to envy and revenge, and we will vent our spleen in all manner of attempts to bear down with the full force of law upon our adversary. The death of a child will fill us with sadness, but will be borne by us with believing resignation, because we see God's providence in that; but the accidental upsetting of a tea-urn, or the thoughtless stupidity of a servant, will produce in us an explosion of temper sufficient to shake the whole establishment to its foundation. Is not this too largely the case with us all? and when it is so, how often are we beholden to the Abigail beside us for soothing us down to reason and propriety? Surely we ought to be on our guard against such irritability. And that we may be so efficiently, let us see God's hand in all things; let us turn to God in every thing; and, far from despising small things, let us watch them the more closely the smaller they are, since their very minuteness makes them only the more dangerous. Above all, let us think how unlike this temper is to the meekness of Him by whose name we have called ourselves! Where is the image of Christ in such a disposition? It is only on the surface of the placid lake that you can see, unbroken, the mirrored likeness of the sun; but let it be ruffled by the wind, and forthwith the full rounded image is destroyed, and nowhere can you catch a glimpse of it complete. Not otherwise is it here. The likeness of Christ can be seen only while the Christian preserves his equanimity. In the outburst of temper, the Christ-image is defaced, and the wholesome influence of the character is neutralized.

Besides, how foolish it is to act under the influence of anger! What a dreadful sin David would have committed here, if he had not been providentially restrained! It would be well for us, therefore, to resolve never to act in any matter while the heat of temper is upon us. That is a wise precept which the Chinese have crystallized into a proverb, "Do nothing in a passion; why wouldst thou put to sea in the violence of a storm?" But that is a still wiser of Paul, "Be ye angry, and sin not: let not the sun go down upon your wrath."

Finally, it is impossible to read this chapter without having our minds directed to the whole question of marriage. In the case of Nabal and Abigail we have an illustration of the evils of ill-assorted wedlock; while in the after-relationship which she bore to David, taken in connection with the manifold evils which we shall see resulted from his concubinage, we have a forcible exemplification of the mischiefs and miseries which are always and everywhere the consequences of polygamy. In the Divine intention at the first, the wife was designed to be the helpmeet of the husband, and this was the law. "Therefore shall a man leave his father and his mother, and shall cleave unto his wife: and they shall be one flesh." Whenever and wherever this law has been violated, discord and disaster, in greater or less measure, has been the result. We need only look to the households of Abraham, Jacob, Elkanah, and David to be convinced of this; for if, in the cases of such men, the evils of which we have a record in this book were the consequences of polygamy, where is the man who may hope to be exempted from them, if he persists in following their example? It is nothing that in the law of Moses this sin was sought to be regulated rather than eradicated; for, as the Lord himself has said, Moses suffered this "for the hardness of the hearts" of those over whom he was set; and his laws—in this respect, like those of Solon—were not absolutely the best laws which could have been enacted, but they were the best which the Israelites of his day would have accepted. Now, however, under the Gospel, the sanctity and inviolability of marriage have been re-enacted, and the Lord Jesus has given to it a loftier holiness and a richer significance, by using it as a symbolical illustration of his own relation to "the Church which he hath purchased with his own blood." Rightly viewed, therefore, the marriage of a man and woman is, next after their union to God himself, the most important connection which can be formed on earth, and should not be entered into lightly and unadvisedly, but soberly, discreetly, and in the fear of the Lord. Too often, however, the whole subject is treated in common conversation with the most profane levity, and every allusion which is made to it is met with frivolity as if it were a good joke, instead of being well-nigh the most sacred thing which can engage the attention of the young. If it is not regarded as an affair of convenience or of commerce, it is talked of frequently as a matter of fashion; and the making of a "good match," by which is meant the securing of a fortune, or the entrance upon a high social position, is regarded as of far more importance than the selection of one who shall be a suitable companion, or a daily helper in the Christian life. Even as I speak, I am aware that many may resent my words, as if they were going beyond the province within which multitudes would restrict the proprieties of the pulpit; but having regard to the loose notions which are coming in upon us on this subject, and knowing well how closely it concerns the purity of the Church and the welfare of the nation that the truth concerning it should be preached, I dare not hold my peace. The law of the New Testament is clear, and as one has well said, "the man who wishes to belong to the flock of Christ owns neither Moses nor yet the civil magistrate for his master in this respect." The man and the wife are united until God shall separate them by death. One man to one wife. How important, therefore, that the choice on either side shall be wisely made! It is right to look for mutual adaptation in station, in temper, in education, and in ability. These have all their own importance, but there are two principles which should never be lost sight of. First, let no one enter into this relationship where there is no true love for him or her with whom it is to be formed. That is the law of nature. Second, let no one who is a Christian be united to another who is not also one with Christ. That is the law of grace. "Be ye not unequally yoked together with unbelievers: for what fellowship hath righteousness with unrighteousness? and what communion hath light with darkness? And what concord hath Christ with Belial? or what part hath he that believeth with an infidel?" In a union so close and intimate, it can not but be that an assimilating process will continually go on; and if either party be godless and given to debasing pursuits, then we may say to the other,

"Thou shalt lower to his level day by day,
What is fine within thee growing coarse to sympathize with clay."

And who shall tell how many lives that might otherwise have been beautiful, exalted, and benign, have been marred, and blurred, and mutilated, and degraded, by an improper marriage! This union may be either the brightest blessing or the darkest misery to those who enter into it. What need, then, of care and prayer in the choice of a suitable companion for one's earthly lot! The old Roman punishment which bound to a living man a festering and corrupting corpse, and compelled him to carry it with him wherever he went, was nothing to the self-inflicted misery of those who bind themselves to husbands or to wives who are, like Nabal here, surly, boorish, beastly, and degraded! "Ah, me!" says the venerable Tholuck, "if our youth would but more deeply ponder what it is to choose a partner, to be of one spirit and one flesh with them for the whole of their pilgrimage on earth, their choice would not be made in the false glare of the theatre or the ball-room. *Till death divide you*, would ring perpetually in their souls. In the light of day they would choose, and by the light of God's Word they would try their partner, seek the advice of Christian friends, and not join hands until they were sure of the divine amen."\* God give you grace, my young friends, to ponder well these weighty words!

---

\* "Hours of Christian Devotion; translated from the German of A. Tholuck, D.D., by Robert Menzies, D.D.," p. 471.

## X.

### *ZIKLAG, ENDOR, AND GILBOA.*

1 Samuel xxvii.–xxxi.; 2 Samuel i.

AFTER his interview with Saul at Hachilah, David continued for a time his wandering life in the wilderness of Judah, with his band of followers, which had gradually increased to six hundred men. As originally composed, his company consisted of "those who were in distress, and those who were in debt, and those who were discontented." .Yet even among this motley troop, there were warriors of the utmost bravery, who were destined afterward to be leaders in his army. Such were those three who, on the memorable occasion alluded to in chapter xi. of 1 Chronicles, verses 15–19, while the Philistine garrison was at Bethlehem, when David thirsted for a draught from the well at the gate of that city, from which, in his happy shepherd days, he had often drank, dashed through the host of the enemy, and drew water from the spring, and took it and brought it to their captain. But he would not drink of it, after all; for, with a spirit which combined the purest piety and the loftiest chivalry, he poured it out before the Lord, saying, "My God forbid it me, that I should do this thing: shall I drink the blood of these men, that have put their lives in jeopardy? for with the jeopardy of their lives they brought it." We can not wonder that men loved such a leader, nor is it strange that those who did this daring deed were ever afterward referred to as the three mightiest in his host.

While they were in the hold, others came to him from among the children of Gad; of whom eleven principal lead ers are named as "men of might, and men of war fit for the battle, that could handle shield and buckler, whose faces were like the faces of lions, and were as swift as the roes upon the mountains;" and of whom, "one of the least was over a hundred, and the greatest over a thousand."* This does not imply that they joined David, followed each by a troop varying in number from a hundred to a thousand men, but rather that, after David had come into his kingdom, he promoted them to captaincies in his army. Still, that they came in some considerable force is indicated in the statement, "They went over Jordan in the first month, when it had overflown all his banks; and they put to flight all them of the valleys, both toward the east and toward the west."†

About the same time, also, and probably in the very interval between the episode with Saul at Hachilah and the flight of David to Gath, there came to his standard some of the children of Judah, and some who were connected with Saul's own tribe of Benjamin. When David saw them, he was afraid of treachery, and went forth to meet them, saying, "If ye be come peaceably unto me to help me, mine heart shall be knit unto you: but if ye be come to betray me to mine enemies, seeing there is no wrong in mine hands, the God of our fathers look thereon, and rebuke it." To this their captain, Amasai, made immediate response, "Thine are we, David, and on thy side, thou son of Jesse: peace, peace be unto thee, and peace be to thine helpers; for thy God helpeth thee."‡ And having received this assurance, he received them gladly, and gave them posts of honor in his little army.

But though thus encouraged with the accession of new adherents, David appears shortly after this to have given way

---

\* 1 Chron. xii., 8, 14.   † 1 Chron. xii., 15.   ‡ 1 Chron. xii., 16–18.

to despondency, and almost to despair, for he said, "I shall now perish one day by the hand of Saul; there is nothing better for me than that I should speedily escape into the land of the Philistines; and Saul shall despair of me to seek me any more in the coast of Israel, so shall I escape out of his hand." It is difficult to account for this transition in him from confidence to fear. Something of it might be due to those alternations of emotion which seem to be incidental to our human constitution. We have ebbings and flowings within us like those of the tides; and just as in nature the lowest ebb is after the highest spring tide, so you frequently see, even in the best of men, after some lofty experience of spiritual elevation and noble self-command, an ebbing down to the lowest depth of fear and flight. It was after his happy sojourn in the school of the prophets at Ramah that David went, on the former occasion, to the land of the Philistines; and now it was after he had risen above the cowardly suggestion of his followers to murder Saul in cold blood, and had indeed changed the curse of Saul's enmity into a benediction, that he sinks again into despair.

Something of this change, too, might be owing to the reports brought to him by his recent recruits of the persistent efforts made to poison the mind of Saul against him by the slanderer Cush, to whom we have already referred But, however it may be accounted for, this despair of David's was deeply dishonoring to God, and full of danger to himself. It was dishonoring to God; for had he not then, just as really as he ever had, those promises which had so steadily sustained him in former emergencies, and which had been so signally fulfilled by former deliverances? Had he forgotten the anointing which he received from the hands of Samuel? Was his victory over the giant now entirely ignored by him? Surely he was the very last man who ought to have allowed himself to despair of the love and faithfulness of Jehovah! Yet here he is in the blankest darkness, brooding over his difficulties, and seeking help from the heathen, as if there were no God to call upon, no kingdom to win, no right to be adhered to, and no wrong to be avoided. Still, let us not be too severe on him, lest we thereby condemn ourselves; for, bad as despair was in David, with all his experiences of the goodness of God, it is still worse in us, who have seen the marvelous manifestations of his mercy in the cross of Jesus Christ. If in our times of despondency we can not take hold of this thought, "He that spared not his own Son, but delivered him up for us all, how shall he not with him also freely give us all things?" it ill becomes us to indulge in wholesale denunciation of David here. He that is without sin among us, in this respect, let him cast the first stone at him. For my part, I have been myself so often in the same condemnation, that I am disposed to place myself in the pillory by his side!

But this despair was also dangerous to himself; for, arising as it did from his forgetfulness of God, it kept him from consulting God about his plans. On other important occasions, especially since Abiathar had joined his band, he was careful to inquire at the mystic Urim and Thummim for direction. But here we have no mention made of the sacred oracle, and no record of a single prayer. Hence no good could be expected from an enterprise which was thus inaugurated. That which is begun in prayerlessness must end in misery and humiliation.

Nor was this all. His despair, making him reckless, blinded him to the dangers which he would incur by going to the land of the Philistines. Had he not been panic-stricken, he would surely have remembered his former experiences at the court of Achish, and would have reasoned that if, when he was alone, he was in such peril, he would be much more likely to be seriously endangered when he was accompanied by six hundred men, with their wives and children. But the truth was, there was only one all-absorbing feeling in his soul at this time, namely, the fear of Saul, and he took what seemed to him the readiest way to relieve himself of that danger, without staying for a moment to consider all that his procedure might involve. "He that believeth shall not make haste:" but fear is always in a hurry. Running in wild panic from a dog, one may find himself in the more serious danger of being overturned and trampled upon by the prancing horse as he holds on his course along the street. So he who has lost his confidence in God, and is filled with fear of some calamity, rushes blindly forward seeking present relief, only to fall into a more appalling danger than that from which he flees. Thus it was with David here. As he had calculated, he rid himself of Saul, for we read that he sought no more for David; but by the false step of going over to the Philistines he involved himself in a long course of cruelty and deceit, out of which he came with a tarnished reputation, and a heart grown but too familiar with the crooked policy of expediency and sin.

Achish received him kindly; but while we give him credit for his hospitality, we can not look upon it as altogether disinterested. He knew that David was at enmity with Saul, and seeing so many men accompanying him, he calculated on receiving substantial assistance from him in any military service in which he might engage. Hence, when David requested that he might have a place in some town in the country, that he might dwell there, he gave him Ziklag, a town which had been allotted to the tribe of Judah in the days of Joshua, and which was probably at this time uninhabited, because it had been taken by the Philistines, and its population dispersed.

Here David and his men, with their wives and children, lived for sixteen months, and hither came to him (as we learn from 1 Chronicles xii., 1-7) some of those who were reputed as his mighty men, helpers in the war. "They were armed with bows, and could use both the right hand and the left in hurling stones and shooting arrows out of a bow;" and they were "of Saul's brethren of Benjamin." From Ziklag as a centre, David made incursions on the Geshurites, and the Gezrites, and the Amalekites, living upon the spoils which he took from them, and putting every man, woman, and child among them to death, that no one might remain to tell where he had been; for ever as he returned, he made Achish believe that he had been out against those who were the enemies of the Philistines, and who were either his own countrymen or their friendly allies. Hence Achish made sure of him as a reliable supporter, and calculated that because he had made his own people to abhor him, he would become valuable in his service. Now, there is no possibility of vindicating David for all this. We can not even offer a plausible excuse for him. It is easy to say that, in the circumstances in which he was placed, some allowance must be made for him. But who put him into these circumstances? He was not in Ziklag on God's service. He had not been sent thither by any prophetical command from God. He went of his own accord, and it will not do to make his circumstances when he was there an extenuation of his wickedness. His going thither was in itself a wrong thing; and one sin can never palliate another.

Then as to the falsehood of his life during these months, we must unequivocally and emphatically condemn it. He was seeking all through his own interest, not God's glory. Nay, he was even blind in seeking that, for he might have been sure that, sooner or later, a day of reckoning would come. Mark the prolific progeny that sprang from the one parent sin of unbelief in this dark chapter of David's life. Prayerlessness; desertion of the sphere of duty; theft; murder; falsehood. All these have germinated from the one innocent-looking little seed, loss of confidence in God! Is this thy voice, O David, speaking so falsely in the ear of Achish? Is this the man according to God's own heart? Alas! it is even so. But he is not acting now as God approves. He has forsaken God, and God, for the time being, has left him to himself, to let him see how far without his grace he would run into iniquity, and to let us learn from his example what an evil thing and a bitter it is to forsake the Lord our God.

Very soon a critical time came to David. The Philistines were preparing for that assault on Israel which culminated at Gilboa, and Achish, to show his confidence in David, intimated that he wished him to go with him as his aid-de-camp to battle. Sorely must David have winced under this command; but disguising his dismay, under an evasive answer to this effect, "Thou shalt know what thy servant can do," he made ready his band, and went to Aphek, a place near the plain of Esdraelon, where the Philistines were encamped. But the lords of the Philistines would have none of his presence, and insisted that he and his followers should be sent back to Ziklag. Achish was greatly distressed at this, and made an apology for their rudeness and apparent distrust, to David, who retraced his steps, secretly glad, we may be sure, that he had been so thoroughly delivered from an embarrassing and equivocal position.

As he was leaving Aphek, however, there came to him, as we read again, in the first book of Chronicles (xii., 19–22), from the tribe of Manasseh a goodly number of adherents, of whom no fewer than seven were afterward ranked as captains of thousands in the army of Israel. And indeed it very soon appeared that he had need of all the help which he could obtain. For when they were nearing Ziklag, instead of seeing a happy village, whose streets were full of boys and girls playing in youthful frolic, and whose homes were full of glee, they beheld only a heap of smoking ruins. In the absence of its defenders, the Amalekites had smitten the town and set it on fire, and though they spared the lives of the women and children, they carried them all away captive, in the hope of ransom. Such was the sorrow among David's company, when they looked upon the desolation which the Amalekites had made, that they lifted up their voices and wept; but by-and-by their sadness gave place to anger, as they upbraided their leader for taking them to the Philistine army, and leaving their home unprotected. They even spake of stoning him. This greatly distressed him; but it brought him to his knees and to his faith again. As sometimes the partially intoxicated man will be sobered in a moment by the occurrence of some terrible calamity, so David, who had been living all these months under the narcotic influence of sin, was, by the violence of the Amalekites, and the threatened mutiny of his own men, roused to his nobler self, and "he encouraged himself in the Lord his God." With returning faith came the recognition of the necessity for Jehovah's guidance, and he said to Abiathar, "Bring hither the ephod." From the answer which he received he was encouraged to set out in pursuit of the spoilers, with the assurance that he should without fail recover all. Very suggestive is this contrast. "David said, I shall one day perish by the hand of Saul; there is nothing better for me than that I should speedily escape to the land of the Philistines." "David encouraged himself in the Lord his God, and said unto Abiathar, Bring hither the ephod." On the one hand, despair, leading to prayerlessness and self-will; on the other, faith, leading to prayer and eager willinghood to submit to the guidance of Jehovah. Be it ours to shun the former, and to cultivate the latter.

After a hot pursuit, during which two hundred of his men were obliged to halt and fall out of the ranks, worn out by their long and rapid march, David, directed by a poor Egyptian slave, came up with the Amalekites, and falling upon them when they were feasting and making merry, he so thoroughly destroyed them, that only four hundred young men who rode upon camels escaped out of his hand. Best of all, he recovered all the women and children who had been taken captive, and returned with such loads of spoil that, after satisfying the claims of all his soldiers, he sent presents of it to many of the cities of Judah.

But while he was thus engaged the battle had been raging fiercely between the Philistines and Saul on Mount Gilboa; and though the full consideration of that conflict and its issues belongs rather to the history of Saul than to the life of David, we must ask your indulgence while we seek to set it somewhat vividly before you.

The vale of Esdraelon, whereon so many decisive battles in the world's history have been fought, stretches eastward across central Palestine. It is of a triangular shape, having its apex westward in a narrow pass, through which the river Kishon runs into the Mediterranean Sea. Its northern side is formed by the hills of Galilee; its southern by the hills of Samaria; and from its base on the east, three branch plains, separated from each other by mountain ridges, run still farther eastward on to the Jordan. The northern branch lies between Mount Tabor and Little Hermon; the central branch has Little Hermon on the north and Gilboa on the south; and the southern branch is between Mount Gilboa and Jenim. Now the Philistines, on the present occasion, were in the central one of these three branch plains, and were encamped at the base of Little Hermon, here called Moreh, hard by the well of Harod. Their position was admirably chosen, since, with a gentle slope behind them, they had in front a level place of some two or three miles broad, well fitted for those military chariots on which they so much relied for success.

Saul and his army were on the ridge of Mount Gilboa, clinging to the hills with that instinctive confidence in their strength which the inhabitants of all mountainous districts feel. From his elevated post of observation he could see the whole host of the Philistines; and the sight made him afraid, so that his heart trembled greatly. But to whom could he turn for succor? Samuel was dead; Abiathar and the ephod were with David; and ever, as he thought of God, it was with the feeling that Jehovah had abandoned him. Had there been but one indication of sincere repentance given by him; had he humbled himself in confession of sin before the Lord, or thrown himself on his covenant-keeping faithfulness, there might, even yet, have been deliverance. But though he was profoundly conscious that all his calamities were caused by the fact that he had turned against the Lord, he went and did that which could only widen the distance that was already between them. Instead of calling upon God in penitence and prayer, he sought after forbidden superstitions, and tried to obtain by the help of magic—or perchance even, in his view, of Satan—that assistance which only God could give. Here is the great difference between Saul in his sins, and David in his backslidings. From each of his falls you hear David coming sobbing out a sorrowful confession and appeal like that in the 51st Psalm; in each of Saul's wickednesses you see him assuming the attitude of sterner defiance toward the Almighty; or if there be any sorrow in his heart at all, it is for the loss he has himself sustained, or the suffering he has himself endured, and not for the dishonor which he has done to God. Never, however, has he gone so far as now, when, as Dean Stanley says, "Having swerved from the moral principle which alone could guide it, his religious zeal was turned into a wild and desperate superstition."[*] Having forsaken God, he betook himself to necro-

---

[*] "Jewish Church," ii., 28.

mancy. So he said to his servants, "Seek me a woman that hath a familiar spirit, that I may go to her, and inquire of her;" and they replied, "Behold, there is a woman that hath a familiar spirit at Endor." On receiving this information, he disguised himself, and took his way across the valley past the carefully guarded host of the Philistines, and up over the ridge behind them, until on the other side of that hill he came to the fountain of Dor, in one of the caverns, by the side of which dwelt the woman of whom he was in search. It was a perilous journey, though undertaken under the cover of night; and nothing could have induced Saul to make it, but the agony of the feeling that his last opportunity had come, and that his all was hanging on the venture of the morrow. When he came to the woman, she was reluctant to have any thing to do with him, fearing lest he was laying a trap for her destruction; but on receiving assurances to the contrary, she asked whom she should bring up to him. He replied, "Bring me up Samuel;" and scarcely had his words been uttered, when the apparition of the prophet so startled her that she cried with a loud voice; and, coming to the conviction that it was Saul himself who was beside her, she said, "Why hast thou deceived me? for thou art Saul." Thereafter he bade her fear nothing, and asked what precisely she had seen, for as yet it would appear that nothing had been visible to him. She told him that she saw "gods," or great ones after the manner of gods, ascending out of the earth; and in response to another question, she informed him that Samuel had assumed the appearance of an old man covered with a mantle. As he looked steadfastly at the place indicated by the woman, the apparition shaped itself to his eye; and seeing it was Samuel indeed, he bowed himself to the ground. "Why hast thou disquieted me, to bring me up?" said the mysterious visitant. "I am sore distressed," was the answer; "for the Philistines make war against me, and God is departed from me, and answereth me no more, neither by prophets nor by dreams: therefore I have called thee, that thou mayest make known unto me what I shall do." Oh, the wild wail of this dark misery! There is a deep pathos and a weird awesomeness in this despairing cry; but there is no confession of sin, no beseeching for mercy; nothing but the great, overmastering ambition to preserve himself. The prophet answered him as one who was cognizant of all this: "Wherefore then dost thou ask of me, seeing the Lord is departed from thee, and is become thine enemy? And the Lord hath done to him, as he spake by me: for the Lord hath rent the kingdom out of thine hand, and given it to thy neighbor, even to David: because thou obeyedst not the voice of the Lord, nor executedst his fierce wrath upon Amalek, therefore hath the Lord done this thing unto thee this day. Moreover, the Lord will also deliver Israel with thee into the hand of the Philistines: and to-morrow shalt thou and thy sons be with me: the Lord also shall deliver the host of Israel into the hand of the Philistines." When he heard this dreadful forecast of coming calamity, Saul lost that stern self-possession which he had preserved till then, and fell trembling on the ground; but with many entreaties, his servants and the woman prevailed upon him to arise and partake of a meal which had been hastily extemporized for his necessity, and at length, somewhat refreshed in body, but crushed in spirit, he hastened back to his camp, which he reached before the morning broke.

Concerning this singular chapter in sacred story, two questions have been raised: these, namely—Was there a real appearance of Samuel here? and what precisely was the agency of the woman in the matter? Some have supposed that the whole scene, including the solemn words put into the mouth of Samuel, was the effect of secret management by the woman, aided, perhaps, by ventriloquism, and by one or more confederates. Others, again, have traced the whole thing to the agency of Satan. But to both of these views there are, in my opinion, insuperable objections. There is the fair and obvious purport of the narrative itself, which gives no hint of any unreality in the case. There is, also, the full and particular prediction of the events of the coming day, which we can not conceive that the woman could have given, and which we dare not trace to the agency of Satan. Then, besides these considerations, we must take the weight due to the fact that in the original there is no word corresponding to the English "when" (in verse 12 of chapter xxviii.); and again, that in verse 14, in the clause, "And Saul perceived that it was Samuel," the Hebrew reads, "And Saul perceived that it was Samuel himself." Now this, being an assertion of the narrator, seems to me to settle the matter, and to determine that Samuel was actually there. But if this were so, what had the woman to do with bringing him up? To this I answer: Literally nothing. Observe, as soon as Saul said, "Bring me up Samuel," she saw him, and was dreadfully alarmed by the spectacle. But why should she have been thus terrified, if the whole thing had been only of her own upraising? The truth is, that before she had begun her enchantments, Samuel appeared and startled her out of her cool and cunning self-possession. How, then, do we account for his appearance? I reply, without any hesitation, that he was brought thither by the miraculous agency of God himself. But to this it may be objected that it seems strange that Jehovah should refuse to answer Saul through the recognized channels, and then take this peculiar manner of responding to his appeal. And there is some force in such a statement; but it is to be observed that Saul asked for direction as to what he should do, and that Samuel gives no reply to that entreaty, but only utters words of condemnation. For the rest, the appearance of Samuel, as the result of God's own agency, is a fulfillment, or rather, as one ought, perhaps, to say, an anticipation, of those words spoken long afterward by the prophet Ezekiel (xiv., 7). "For every one of the house of Israel, or of the stranger that sojourneth in Israel, which separateth himself from me, and setteth up his idols in his heart, and putteth the stumbling-block of his iniquity before his face, and cometh to a prophet" (that is, of course, a false prophet) "to inquire of him concerning me; I the Lord will answer him by myself." Just as when Ahaziah sent a messenger to inquire at Baal-zebub, the god of Ekron, Jehovah commissioned his own Elijah to intercept the messenger, and give his own response; so when Saul went to Endor, God anticipated the pretended necromancy of the witch, and sent the real Samuel to pronounce words of doom over the disobedient monarch. Hence the connection of the woman with this vision was merely accidental. She was in no sense its procuring cause. The whole thing is to be traced to God. Even as on the wall of the banqueting-hall wherein Belshazzar was defying Jehovah, by his sacrilegious use of the vessels of the sanctuary, the hand of destiny came forth to write his sentence in mystic characters, which only Daniel could interpret, so now at the cave, to which Saul had come to deal with a familiar spirit, thereby committing, as Trench has said, "the nearest approach to the sin against the Holy Ghost which was possible for one under the old covenant,"* Jehovah confronted him, and, through the mouth of the upraised Samuel, set before him his terrible guilt and its fearful result. Alas for Saul! how changed is he now from that day when Samuel communed with him concerning the kingdom, or when, in the first noble assertion of his royal right, he delivered the men of Jabesh-gilead from their threatened destruction! Did ever promise of so fair a life ripen into such bitter fruit?

---

* "Shipwrecks of Faith," by Archbishop Trench, p. 45.

With the returning day, the battle opened between Israel and the Philistines. Saul was but ill fitted, by the fatigue and excitement of the night, for the fierce affray, and his troops were sorely worsted by their enemies. Their position was badly chosen for the purposes of retreat; and as they ascended the slopes of Gilboa they became conspicuous marks for the dexterous archers among their pursuers. Hence a vast multitude were slain, and among these were the three eldest sons of Saul. The king himself, as the day advanced, was sorely, probably mortally, wounded; and fearing lest, in his weak condition, he should be abused and tortured by the Philistines, he besought his armor-bearer to dispatch him at once. But with natural affection for his master, he refused to obey such a command, and Saul fell upon his own sword; whereupon his servant followed his example, and committed suicide. A wandering Amalekite, who had perhaps been seeking spoil on the battle-field, found the dead body of the monarch, and taking from it the crown and the bracelet by which it was distinguished, hastened with them to Ziklag, and gave them to David. He alleged, besides, that he had himself slain Saul, thinking thereby to win the favor of David for doing him such a service. But he little knew with whom he had to do; for David's reverence for the Lord's anointed could not brook the thought that he should be slain by a wicked Amalekite; so, holding him guilty on his own showing, he put him to death.

Then, as the news of the fate of Saul, and especially of Jonathan, filled his heart, he called his men around him, and, taking his harp, he sang that noble elegy, which, known to his own countrymen as the "Song of the Bow," has been extracted from the book of Jasher by the sacred historian, and embalmed for us in the annals of the chosen people. It is introduced by these words: "Also he bade them teach the children of Judah the use of the bow; behold it is written in

## ZIKLAG, ENDOR, AND GILBOA.

the book of Jasher." The words "the use of" are in italics, as not in the original. So we may read, "He bade them teach the children of Judah the bow;" that is, the song called "The Bow." Now the appropriateness of this title to the song will appear when you mark how prominently the bow is mentioned in one of its strains, and remember that it was specially designed as a memorial of Jonathan, who was famous for his excellence in the use of that weapon. Not only did he belong to the tribe of Benjamin, whose sons were noted archers, but it was with his bow and sling that he won his first victory at Michmash; with his bow he sent the arrows by the stone Ezel, when David parted from him after their mutual covenant; and among the most cherished possessions of the son of Jesse was that bow which, after the slaughter of Goliath, Jonathan had given to him as a token of affection. Hence, from its reference to Jonathan, as well, perhaps, as from the fact that it was designed to be sung by the men of Judah when they were practicing the bow, this lament was called by that name.

The book of Jasher seems to have been a collection of ancient Jewish songs, or ballads, corresponding, in some degree, to the minstrelsy of the Scottish Border, the only other quotation from it in Scripture being the poetical commemoration of the victory of Joshua in the Valley of Ajalon.

It is not needful, surely, that I should enter into a minute analysis of this beautiful ode. It can scarcely be called either a psalm or a hymn. We can hardly even regard it as a specimen of religious poetry. It is rather what Dean Stanley has called "an example of pure poetic inspiration," and as poetry its language is to be interpreted; that is to say, something of poetic license and exaggeration has to be discounted from it when we translate it into prose. It was a testimony of David's life-long attachment to Jonathan, while at the same time his references to Saul indicate that, in the holy presence of death, David had learned to forget and forgive the wrongs which he had received, and desired to dwell only on the good and great qualities of his former antagonist. All after-generations have recognized the lyric grandeur of this noble poem. Over the grave of the Cid, near Burgos, in Spain,* its last stanza is engraved, as the most fitting memento of a mighty man ; and to this day, when a great man is carried to his sepulchre, the most appropriate music for the occasion is found in that exquisite composition which seeks to express in sound this threnody of David, and which is known among us as " The Dead March in Saul."

> " The wild-roe of Israel, slain upon thy high places:
> How are the mighty fallen !
>
> Tell it not in Gath, publish it not in the streets of Askelon;
> Lest the daughters of the Philistines rejoice,
> Lest the daughters of the uncircumcised triumph.
> Ye mountains of Gilboa, nor dew, nor rain be upon you,
> Nor fields of offerings :
> For there the shield of the mighty was vilely cast away,
> The shield of Saul, not anointed with oil.
> From the blood of the slain, from the fat of the mighty,
> The bow of Jonathan turned not back,
> And the sword of Saul returned not empty.
> Saul and Jonathan ! lovely and pleasant !
> In their lives and in their death they were undivided :
> Than eagles they were swifter ! than lions they were stronger !
> Ye daughters of Israel, weep over Saul,
> Who clothed you in scarlet, with other delights ;
> Who put ornaments of gold upon your apparel.
> How are the mighty fallen in the midst of the battle !
>
> O Jonathan, thou wast slain in thine high places.
> I am distressed for thee, my brother Jonathan :
> Very pleasant hast thou been unto me :
> Thy love to me was wonderful, passing that of women.
> How are the mighty fallen, and perished the weapons of war !"

---

* Stanley's "Jewish Church," ii., 37.

ZIKLAG, ENDOR, AND GILBOA.

The Philistines, however, had nothing of the generous magnanimity of David; for when they found the bodies of Saul and his sons, they cut off the head of the king, and stripped off his armor, sending the former to the temple of Dagon, and the latter to the house of Ashtaroth. Then they fixed the headless trunk, along with the bodies of his sons, to the wall of Bethshan, a town at the head of the Valley of Jezreel, looking down into the Valley of the Jordan. And now we have the record of a deed of gratitude which connects the closing act of this sad tragedy with the first brilliant deed of Saul as king in Israel; for the men of Jabesh-gilead, remembering how much they had owed, in their peril, to his promptitude and prowess, arose, and went at night, and took the bodies of Saul and his sons from the wall of Bethshan, and burned them there, and took their bones and buried them under a tree in Jabesh, where they remained, until many years afterward, when David, then an old man, took them, and buried them in the country of Benjamin, in Zelah, in the sepulchre of Kish, his father.

So ends the history of Saul. But we may not pass from it without staying for a moment to point the lesson which it so impressively teaches. It may be given in the words of David himself, at a later date, to Solomon, his son: "Serve God with a perfect heart, and with a willing mind: for the Lord searcheth all hearts, and understandeth all the imaginations of the thoughts: if thou seek him, he will be found of thee: but if thou forsake him, he will cast thee off forever." Some may think, indeed, that, in the record of David's history over which we have passed to-night, we have come upon blacker spots than any which we have found in the biography of Saul. And no doubt, as Archbishop Trench has said, "He was clear of offenses which make some pages of David's history nothing better than one huge blot."* But then

---
* "Shipwrecks of Faith," p. 48.

David knew that he had sinned, and turned from his iniquity in penitent confession unto God. Now we look in vain for any thing like this in Saul. If on any occasion he seems to use the words of regret, they are merely superficial, and come not from the depths of his soul. He cared more for being honored before the people, than for being accepted by the Lord; and even in this last climax of his misery, his concern is not that God may forgive him, but merely that he may vanquish his enemies in battle. In view of all this, we are almost tempted to exclaim, with the eminent prelate from whom I have already quoted, "How much better it would have been to have sinned like David, if only he had repented like David; if a temper resembling at all the temper which dictated the 51st Psalm had found place in him. But all this was far from him. Darkness is closing round him; anguish has taken hold of him; but the broken and the contrite heart, there is no remotest sign of this; no reaching out after the blood of sprinkling. We listen, but no voice is heard like his who exclaimed, 'Purge me with hyssop, and I shall be clean; wash me, and I shall be whiter than snow;' but dark, defiant, and unbelieving, he who had inspired such high hopes goes forward to meet his doom."* Surely, from such a history as that we may well rise with the prayer upon our lips: "Oh for the broken and the contrite heart, which God will not despise!" David's sins sent him weeping to the mercy-seat. Saul's sins sent him defiant and unbending to the cave of Endor: there is the root of the difference between the two.

Again: in the history of Saul we see how, with such a disposition, a man's character will go on deteriorating, until there is little or no good left in it. There was much of nobleness about him when we met him first; but now, alas! as

---

\* "Shipwrecks of Faith," pp. 48, 49.

we see him at Endor, he is the moral wreck of his former self. The enamel of his conscience having once been broken, that noble faculty crumbled gradually away, until at length he committed a sin at thought of which at first he would have shuddered, and which at one time he punished in others with jealous severity. You can see a contrary process to all this in such a man as Jacob, who, though repulsive to every reader in his early history, grows upon us latterly, until we come to rank him among Faith's noblest worthies. Now how shall we explain the difference between the two? We explain it by the difference in the relation of each to God. The one gave back to God all that he had received from him, and, as the result, got it back again himself, exalted and ennobled by the consecration; but the other carried every thing away from God, and endeavored to assert his independence of the Almighty. "They that wait upon the Lord renew their youth;" but they that depart from him become "weary in the greatness of their way," and lose all the elements of noblest manhood. Young men, if you would conserve your purity, your intellectual vigor, and your moral excellence, consecrate them all to God, and keep them all for him. Thus shall you escape the deterioration which else must overtake you, and your path shall be like that of the just, which "shineth more and more, unto the perfect day."

Finally: let us learn from the history of Saul that this life is a probation. God put this man into a kingdom, with splendid opportunities and ample resources; but he did not rise to his responsibility, and these were taken from him. But have we received nothing from the hand of God? To whom do we owe our lives, our Gospel privileges, and our means of serving our generation? Have we improved these? Are we improving them? If not, then let us learn the lesson of this sad life, lest at length the Lord should say over us, as he did over Jerusalem · "If thou hadst known, even thou, at least in this thy day, the things which belong unto thy peace! but now they are hid from thine eyes;" "behold now thine house is left unto thee desolate." Again and again the tide of opportunity may rise, and one may float upon it almost into safety, even as Saul was repeatedly found "among the prophets;" but if such times of visitation are continually slighted by us, we may not count upon their recurrence, for there shall come a day when they shall end forever. Listen, I beseech you, to this word of warning, which comes to us from the mountains of Gilboa, " He that being often reproved hardeneth his neck, shall suddenly be cut off, and that without remedy."

## XI.

### *HEBRON AND JERUSALEM.*

2 SAMUEL ii.–v., 10; 1 CHRONICLES xi.–xii.

THE defeat of the Israelites on Mount Gilboa utterly disconcerted them, and left the Philistines masters of the situation, so that neither the representatives of the house of Saul, nor David and his band, could do very much for the furtherance of the ends which they severally had in view.

What they could do, however, they did promptly. Abner, Saul's cousin, and the captain of his host, fleeing from the field of battle, took with him Ishbosheth, Saul's fourth son, and, crossing the Jordan, settled for the time at Mahanaim, where he proclaimed Ishbosheth king. David, having asked counsel of the Lord, went, by direction of the oracle, to Hebron, where the men of his own tribe rallied to his standard, and anointed him king over themselves. Here we are told that he reigned seven years and six months; but as in the verse immediately following that which gives us this information it is stated that Ishbosheth reigned over Israel two years, there is an appearance of discrepancy between the two declarations; since, if Ishbosheth was anointed at Mahanaim at the time when David set up his court at Hebron, their reigns would be of equal duration. The best solution of the difficulty which I have seen is that given by Mr. Wright,* who says, "Immediately after Saul's death, Abner, we suppose, made Ishbosheth king at Mahanaim over Gilead, that is, over those Israelites east of the Jordan who had not sub-

---

* "David, King of Israel," by Josiah Wright, M.A., pp. 247, 248.

mitted to the Philistines. But it was Abner's aim to drive the invaders utterly out of the land, and to build up again from its ruins the kingdom of Saul. This, however, could not be done at once. The Philistines could only gradually be dislodged, and the enumeration of districts which we have in the ninth verse (2 Sam. ii.) seems to tally with the natural order of the conquests by which Abner's aim was accomplished. First, he drove the Philistines out of the coasts of Asshur; secondly, out of the Valley of Jezreel; then from the mountains of Ephraim; lastly, from the hill fortresses of Benjamin. And having now touched the frontiers of Judah, he caused Ishbosheth to be proclaimed anew over the whole of recovered Israel; for so early do we find all that was not Judah distinguished by this name." Allowing, then, five and a half years for Abner's reconquest of the land, we have two years left for the long war between the house of Saul and the house of David, which ended in the dominion of the latter.

The city in which, by divine direction, David established himself, was not only one of the most ancient in existence, but also one which was encircled with associations which to an Israelite must have been peculiarly sacred. There Abraham, the father of the faithful, sojourned for a considerable portion of his life in Canaan; in the immediate neighborhood was the oak of Mamre, beneath which the patriarch had so often offered sacrifice to Jehovah; and hard by was the cave of Machpelah, in which he buried the remains of Sarah, and in which his own ashes, and those of Isaac and Jacob, were afterward deposited. Hence, of all the cities of Palestine at that date, it must have had the richest attractions to the chosen people; and even yet, in its modern name, El-Khulil—*the Friend*—we can see a reference to him who was styled, by way of eminence, *the Friend of God*. In the days of Joshua the surrounding territory was given to

Caleb, and it was made a city of refuge, and a city of the Levites. It was, besides, one of the places to which David sent a portion of the spoils which he had taken from the Amalekites. Hence, both from its holy associations, its central situation, and the probable favor of its inhabitants toward him, it was a most appropriate place for David's capital.

Here over the little kingdom of Judah he served, so to say, an apprenticeship to monarchy; and from this, in due season, he graduated with honor, as one fitted and entitled to sit upon the throne of Israel in Jerusalem.

It was most probably in connection with his anointing at Hebron that David composed what I may call the Inauguration Psalm, known among us as the 101st. "It is,"* says Dean Stanley, "full of a stern exclusiveness, of a noble intolerance; but not against theological error, not against uncourtly manners, not against political insubordination, but against the proud heart, the high look, the secret slanderer, the deceitful worker, the teller of lies. These are the outlaws from King David's court; these alone are the rebels and heretics that he would not suffer to dwell in his house or tarry in his sight."

The great national celebration which has just been held at Washington† gives this Psalm a peculiar present interest for us; while, alas! the disclosures of the past months make manifest that the resolutions which it expresses are as much required to-day in the case of the chief magistrate of this great republic, as they were in the times at which they were first formed by David. Let us read it with our own legislators, governors, and president in mind; and let us, while we read it, lift up our hearts in prayer for them, that they may all be disposed and strengthened to act according to its principles.

---

\* "Jewish Church," vol. ii., p. 89.

† The inauguration of General Grant to his second term of office, 1873.

"I will sing of mercy and judgment: unto thee, O Lord, will I sing. I will behave myself wisely in a perfect way. O when wilt thou come unto me? I will walk within my house with a perfect heart. I will set no wicked thing before mine eyes: I hate the work of them that turn aside; it shall not cleave to me. A froward heart shall depart from me: I will not know a wicked person. Whoso privily slandereth his neighbor, him will I cut off: him that hath a high look and a proud heart will not I suffer. Mine eyes shall be upon the faithful of the land, that they may dwell with me: he that walketh in a perfect way, he shall serve me. He that worketh deceit shall not dwell within my house: he that telleth lies shall not tarry in my sight. I will early destroy all the wicked of the land; that I may cut off all wicked doers from the city of the Lord."

David's first public act after his anointing was one in which we see both chivalry and policy united. He sent a message of thanks to the men of Jabesh-gilead for their noble conduct in rescuing the bodies of Saul and his sons from dishonor; and while invoking the blessing of God upon them, he delicately intimated to them that his brethren of Judah had made him their king. No doubt his regard for the memory of Jonathan had something to do with the sending of this message; yet I suppose that this noble motive was slightly alloyed by the anticipation that those who received it would be forward to tender to him their allegiance. But if that hope entered at all into his calculations, it was doomed to disappointment, for the men of Jabesh made no response. Perhaps they remembered to David's disadvantage his recent sojourn among the Philistines, and were suspicious of one who had, in their view, so compromised himself with their enemies; or perhaps the influence of Ishbosheth and Abner, who were in their immediate neighborhood, added to their own feeling of attachment to the house of Saul for what he had done for them, kept them from giving any heed to the overtures of David; in any case, nothing came out of this politic "bid" of David's for their support.

So, for at least five and a half years, if we have been right in our interpretation of the tenth and eleventh verses of the second chapter of 2 Samuel, David lived in the city of Hebron in peace. During this period, thinking probably, like other Eastern chiefs, that his greatness as a ruler would be estimated by the number of his wives, he added four to those whom he had already wedded. Among these was Maachah, the daughter of Talmai, king of Geshur, one of the tribes on whom he had inflicted such cruelty while he sojourned at Ziklag. This alliance, besides being a case of polygamy, which is always prolific in unhappiness, was a flagrant violation of the divine command, which forbade the Israelites to intermarry with the people of the land; and let it be noted here, that from this concubinage came Absalom, whose after-history so wrung the heart of David, and made him feel "how sharper than a serpent's tooth it is to have a thankless child." God's law, whether physical or spiritual, whether positive or moral, can not be contravened with impunity. A man's sin will, sooner or later, find him out; and he may rest assured that, in some way or other, God will bring it to his remembrance.

But David's peace at Hebron was not to remain unbroken; for, after conquering those whom we have already named, Abner, in whose hands Ishbosheth seems to have been little else than a weak tool, advanced to attack David. The rival armies confronted each other at Gibeon. They attempted to settle their differences, at first, by a kind of duel between two companies of twelve men; but when these had slain each other, a fierce battle ensued, in which Abner and his host were defeated and put to flight. The army of David was commanded by his nephew Joab, who here for the first time appears in the history, and who was supported by his brothers Abishai and Asahel. The last-mentioned of these warlike brothers was distinguished by his fleetness of foot, and in the pursuit of the retreating enemy he pressed sore upon Abner, evidently bent on securing his destruction. But conscious of his own strength, and perhaps also knowing something of the implacable disposition of Joab, Abner desired to spare his pursuer, and urged him to return. When, however, this advice was disregarded, he put Asahel to death; and the sight of his body, as he lay covered with blood, robbed victory of its glory in the eyes of David's soldiers, and filled the heart of Joab with a terrible purpose of revenge, which he carried out in the most deceitful manner at a later day.

The war thus begun between the house of David and the house of Saul lasted a long time; but when it was seen that the former was continually gaining the advantage, the people of the land, weary of the strife, and longing for the blessings of peace, began to incline to the side of the stronger, and spoke of putting David on the throne. Seeing this, Abner, with the instinct of a cunning, selfish, and unprincipled man, prepared to save himself by going over to the ranks of David, and taking the kingdom of Ishbosheth with him. A pretext was soon found for carrying out his design; for when Ishbosheth faulted him for claiming one of his father's concubines, which in Eastern etiquette was the next thing to claiming the throne itself, he became indignant, and swore this angry oath: "So do God to Abner, and more also, except, as the Lord hath sworn to David, even so I do to him; to translate the kingdom from the house of Saul, and to set up the throne of David over Israel and over Judah, from Dan even to Beersheba." What a depth of wickedness does this reveal! He knew all the while that he was fighting not against David only, but against God. Why, then, did he fight against him so long? Because he judged it best for his

## HEBRON AND JERUSALEM.

own interests so to do. And why does he propose to join David now? Because his pride has been wounded, and he thinks he can make good terms with David for his future eminence. Thus he had no regard to God all through. He thought only for himself, and his introduction of Jehovah's name into his asseveration is the most sickening profanity.

When he opened up negotiations with David for the transfer of the kingdom, the son of Jesse did not show himself over-eager to respond. He, too, had his dignity to consult, and he declared that he could not enter into a league with him until he had sent unto him Michal, the daughter of Saul, whom he had first wedded. A man who had already six wives had no great need for a seventh, and we do not suppose that there was much affection for Michal remaining in David's heart. Still, she had been wrongfully taken from him, and the giving of her to another was a grievous and deliberate insult offered to him by Saul, for which it was natural that he should now desire some sort of apology. Moreover, the making of such a request to Abner would be an admirable test of his sincerity; and so, when it was at once complied with, he declared his readiness to enter into negotiations with him. Thereupon, after communicating with the elders of Israel and with his kinsmen of the tribe of Benjamin, Abner went to Hebron, accompanied by twenty men; and in the absence of Joab and Abishai, he was hospitably entertained by David, and dismissed with many tokens of good-will.

When Joab returned, and discovered how Abner had been treated, he became furious; and after bitterly inveighing against the simplicity of David for allowing himself to be duped by so cunning a diplomatist as Abner, he sent after him, decoyed him back by a false message, and deceitfully slew him, under the pretense of desiring to have a private conference with him.

This cold-blooded deed must be branded with the deepest condemnation; Joab violated what was equivalent to a flag of truce; and though some may remind us of the old law of blood-revenge, and affirm that, under the Mosaic institute, Joab, as the next of kin to Asahel, had a perfect right to do as he did, there are two things which go to bar this plea; for Asahel was slain in battle, and Hebron was a city of refuge, in which Abner's life ought to have been respected, until at least he had been tried by the elders. Hence this act of Joab was not only cruelly treacherous, but also a flagrant violation of the law of God. David was greatly afflicted by it, and took every means, short of putting Joab to death, to show that he had no hand whatever in its instigation. He proclaimed a public mourning for Abner, and went himself to the funeral, making lamentation over him with a song, which has been here preserved, and mourning yet more deeply for what he calls his own helplessness, for thus he speaks: "I am this day weak, though anointed king; and these men the sons of Zeruiah be too hard for me: the Lord shall reward the doer of evil according to his wickedness."

But David was weak, not so much because Joab was strong, as because he himself shrank from doing what he knew to be right in the case. Had he put Joab to death, public opinion would have sustained him in the execution of justice; and even if it had not, he would have had the inward witness that he was doing his duty to the state. For a magistrate to be weak, is to be wicked. He is set to administer and execute the law without fear or favor; and whensoever he swerves from justice from either cause, he is a traitor at once to God and to the commonwealth. "Weak!" this is not to speak like a man, not to say a king. Oh, what suffering—may I not even say what sin?—David might have saved himself from, if he had only thus early rid himself of the tyrannic and overbearing presence of Joab! I wonder if in afterdays, when his soul was vexed and chafed by the conduct of his unscrupulous nephew, David ever thought of his sinful weakness in this moment of emergency. He spared the serpent, only to be himself stung by it at last.

Abner's death took away the solitary pillar on which the kingdom of Ishbosheth rested; and two of his servants, thinking thereby to serve themselves, slew him, and took the news to David, who did with them as before he had done with the Amalekite who professed to have slain Saul. And now, every obstacle to his full royalty having been removed, he was waited upon by the elders of Israel, who requested him to become their king.

The circumstances connected with his coronation are too remarkable to be passed lightly by. The assembly was not one of the elders of Israel alone, though they appear to have been the spokesmen on the occasion, but it was virtually an aggregate gathering of the nation. The particular numbers present from each tribe are given in the book of Chronicles (1 Chron. xii., 23-40), from which we learn that Judah, Simeon, Levi, Benjamin, and in fact all the tribes, were present in force, with the single exception of Issachar, which sent only two hundred men; but they made up in influence for their smallness in number; for they are described as "men that had understanding of the times, to know what Israel ought to do." The entire number present was two hundred and eighty thousand; and it is most important that we should observe the ground on which they rest their choice of David, the ceremony that was observed in connection with his coronation, and the rejoicings that were made over it. "Behold," they say, "we are thy bone and thy flesh." He was no alien who had come across some narrow ocean channel, or some lofty mountain chain, to conquer them for himself. "Also in time past, when Saul was king over us, thou wast he that leddest out and broughtest in Israel." They had not forgotten the day when he overthrew the giant in the Valley of Elah; nor had they lost sight of the fact that the only really brilliant portion of Saul's reign was that in which David was by his side. They added, "and the Lord said to thee, Thou shalt feed my people Israel, and thou shalt be captain over Israel." But why should they thus refer to God's choice of David? I answer, for two reasons. First: because, although they had known all along that David had been fore-appointed to the throne, they had yet been struggling against that arrangement; and so, it was fitting now that they should express their repentance, and declare their readiness to receive him in God's name, and as from God's hand. Second: because they wished to remind him and themselves that the real king of their nation was Jehovah, and that he and they alike were under allegiance to him. This reference to the will of the Lord, too, will enable us to understand what is meant when it is said that "King David made a league with them in Hebron, before the Lord." He pledged himself, both to the people and to God, to rule in accordance with the principles which had already been laid down by Jehovah for the administration of the national affairs.

It is a mistake, therefore, to suppose that the Jewish monarchy was an absolute and unconstitutional one. On the contrary, there were in it the highest securities—on the one hand, for the liberties of the people; and on the other, for the prerogative of the king. They chose him, it is true, but they also pledged themselves to obey him so long as he ruled in accordance with the divine law. He was their ruler, but his authority was recognized only in so far as it was confirmed and regulated by the divine statute-book. Thus both he and they recognized God as the real sovereign of the nation; and so long, at least, as David sat on the throne, the theocracy was a reality, and not a mere name. In this, indeed, as we have more than once observed, we have one great fundamental difference between the administration of Saul and that of David. Saul accepted the monarchy, designing to make it as absolute and autocratic as that of other kings; but David counted himself only an under-shepherd, and desired to regulate his conduct as a ruler by the commands of God. The perception of this feature in his character gave the people great confidence in him, and formed, we may be sure, one reason for their joy on this memorable occasion; for, as soon as the anointing was over, they began a feast which lasted for three days, and which is thus described by the sacred historian: "There they were with David three days, eating and drinking: for their brethren had prepared for them. Moreover, they that were nigh them, even unto Issachar and Zebulon and Naphtali, brought bread on asses, and on camels, and on mules, and on oxen, and meat, meal, cakes of figs, and bunches of raisins, and wine, and oil, and oxen, and sheep abundantly: for there was joy in Israel."*

Nor are we to suppose that this joy was only a social thing. It had a religious element in it also; and it was probably on this occasion, when Levites and priests, together with the princes of the tribes, and the men of war from every quarter were assembled once more under one ruler in whom they all had confidence, that the Psalmist composed and sang that song of degrees which is so familiar to us all: "Behold, how good and how pleasant it is for brethren to dwell together in unity! It is like the precious ointment upon the head, that ran down upon the beard, even Aaron's beard: that went down to the skirts of his garments; as the dew of Hermon, and as the dew that descended upon the mountains of Zion: for there the Lord commanded the blessing, even life for evermore."†

---

* 1 Chron. xii., 39, 40.　　　　　† Psa. cxxxiii.

Thus, in the thirty-eighth year of his age, while he was yet in the prime and vigor of his manhood, and with all the experience which the trials of his early years had given him, David was seated upon the throne of the united kingdom of Israel, amidst the rejoicings of the people, and with every token of the favor of his God.

His first care as a monarch was to obtain a suitable capital; and whether he was directed by the special guidance of the Holy Spirit, or whether he was left solely to his own judgment regarding it, we can not but admire the wisdom of the arrangement which he made, especially when we contrast it with the short-sighted policy of Saul in reference to the same matter. The son of Kish set up his court in his native town of Gibeah, a place of no intrinsic importance, and bearing reproach among the people as having been the scene of one of the foulest outrages ever committed in the land. Moreover, it was within the territory of his own tribe of Benjamin, and his preference for it was apt to provoke the jealousy of the others. David, however, proceeded upon other and more statesman-like principles. He would not continue in Hebron. No doubt that city was equally sacred to all the people, from its connection with their common father Abraham, but it had been recognized as the special capital of Judah; and if David had remained in it, some overzealous partisan of Judah might have said that the other tribes had been merely annexed to or absorbed in the little kingdom which for seven years and a half had its seat of government there. Hence, just as in our own times, Victor Emanuel, when he was called to the throne of a united Italy, removed his capital first from Turin to Florence, and afterward from Florence to Rome, feeling that it was due to the other portions of his people that he should be no longer a mere Sardinian or Tuscan prince, so David wisely considered that a regard to the feelings of the other tribes demanded that some other city than Hebron should be chosen as the metropolis.

But in determining what place should be selected, many difficulties would present themselves. Bethlehem, though dearer to him than all other cities, could not be thought of; and if he had gone into the territory of any other tribe than his own, he might have been liable to the imputation of partiality, and might have provoked jealousy throughout eleven-twelfths of his dominions. In these circumstances, the easiest solution of the difficulty would be to get hold of some place of requisite strength and importance not presently identified with any of the tribes, and in the acquirement of which all of them might have a share. Such a place was the fortress of Zion, held by the tribe of the Jebusites, whom, up to this time, no army had been able to dislodge. Visible as it was from the heights of his native Bethlehem, it must have been perfectly familiar to him, and perhaps the conquest of it had been one of the fondest aspirations of his youth. It was situated at the extreme verge of the territory of Judah, where it abutted on that of Benjamin, and belonged, properly speaking, to neither. As we learn from incidental notices in the books of Joshua and Judges, both of these tribes had attempted its conquest without success. The men of Judah, baffled in their effort, had retired to Hebron; and the men of Benjamin, with all their prowess, were able to take only the lower city, and, leaving the Jebusites undisturbed in their fortress, were compelled to settle down side by side with a people whom they had only partially overcome.

Here, therefore, was a place eligible in every respect to be his capital; so, taking advantage of the enthusiasm which his coronation had evoked, David led his army to Jerusalem. But the Jebusites, strong in the confidence which they felt in the natural impregnability of their position, laughed him to scorn, saying to him, "Except thou take away the blind and the lame, thou shalt not come in hither." Different explanations have been given of these words. Kitto and some others understand "the blind and the lame" to mean idols of brass which the Jebusites brought forth and put upon the walls, and explain the taking away of the blind and lame, hated of David's soul, as the destruction of these idols. This, however, seems to me to be a cumbrous and improbable interpretation, and I much prefer that which is given by Keil, who translates the words thus: "Thou wilt not come in, but the blind and the lame will drive thee away." The Jebusites so thoroughly relied on the strength of their citadel, surrounded as it was on three sides by deep ravines, that they mockingly said the blind and the lame would be a sufficient garrison to repel David's assaults.

But, roused by their scorn, he gave forth his order in words which, though susceptible of different translations, may be rendered thus: "Every one who smites the Jebusites, let him hurl over the precipice both the lame and the blind, who are hateful to David's soul;" that is to say, let there be no quarter. Furthermore, in order to stimulate his men to the uttermost, he offered the post of commander-in-chief to the captain who should first lead his troops into the citadel. The prize was won by Joab, somewhat, we may suppose, to David's mortification; for it is not unlikely that he had hoped, by the means which he had taken, to promote some less unscrupulous man to that honorable position, without seeming to insult his nephew.

Out of this siege there arose this proverb, "The blind and the lame shall not come into the house." This expression is generally taken to mean that these classes were excluded from the Temple, but for that assertion we have no proof, and it is hard to see what this proverb could have to do with the Temple, which was not at that time in existence. The true explanation seems to be, "The blind and the lame are there—let him enter the place if he can:" a proverb which came to be current in regard to any fortress that was reputed to be impregnable.

Thus David took the stronghold of Zion, and began forthwith to lay the foundations of that city, whose history ever since, so thrilling in its incidents, and so checkered in its vicissitudes, is full of deepest interest to every thoughtful and intelligent soul. Beautiful for situation, it was to become the joy of the whole land as the site of the Temple which "Jehovah had chosen to place his name there." Surrounded by bulwarks, crowned with towers, it might have seemed secure from all attack; yet Babylonians, Asmoneans, Romans, Saracens, Crusaders, Turks, all have in turn besieged it. Still, these dreadful sieges give it not its chief renown. As we pronounce its name, we almost forget all other things connected with it, while we remember that He walked its streets who came to earth for us men and for our salvation; that in the immediate neighborhood of its walls he endured the terrible agony of Gethsemane; and that within sight of its gates he poured out his soul unto death, when he made his soul an offering for sin. To this city the heart of the Jew in every land yet fondly turns: and its name, recalling to the Christian the memory of his Lord, is at the same time associated with his hope of heaven—that grand mother-city of the children of God—the New Jerusalem.

But I must not dwell on such alluring themes. Only as we stand here and see how first the fortress of Zion was taken by the prowess of David's troops, we may have some idea of the statesmanship of the man who out of all other sites chose this, so formidable in its strength, so stately in its situation, and so beautiful in its surroundings, for the capital of his realm. The instinct of the warrior, the sagacity of the ruler, and the genius of the poet, are all apparent in his selection of this compact yet strong and queenly site for the metropolis of the land.

And now, gathering up the lessons of this evening's lecture, let us note how, when God has some great work for a man to do, he prepares him for it, by the discipline of his providence. Not all at once did David pass from the shepherd life of Bethlehem to the throne of Jerusalem. There was a long, and weary, and trying road to be traversed by him after his anointing by Samuel, before he reached the lofty elevation for which he was designated and consecrated by the prophet's oil. He was not cradled in luxury, nor dandled in affluence, but his character was hardened by trial, and his judgment was matured by frequently recurring emergency. From the very first, indeed, he was "prudent in matters," but such a history as his could not but stimulate and sharpen his natural abilities. His military genius, which was destined yet to show itself on many a glorious field as he extended his dominion "from sea to sea, and from the river to the ends of the land," had been quickened and developed by his experiences in the long war with the house of Saul; and his knowledge of human nature, an acquirement so needful for one who was to be a ruler of men, had been increased by his dealing with his followers in the hold, and with his enemies in diplomacy; while, best of all, his confidence in God had been strengthened by his manifold trials, in and through which he had been sustained by the divine grace, and out of which he had been delivered by the divine hand.

All these things, though perhaps he knew not of it at the time, were disciplining him for the work which he was afterward to accomplish, while his lesser reign at Hebron gave him an opportunity for forming within him those lofty purposes which he sought in later days to carry out. His early difficulties stimulated his inventiveness and strengthened his resolutions. And his after-reign was only the more glorious because of the hardness which, in his younger days, he had to endure.

But it is not different yet. Success is not usually a sudden thing, or, if it be so, it is not a wholesome thing. Generally speaking, it is a matter of time, and trial, and diligence, and study. The heat of the conservatory, which brings the flower rapidly to maturity, does also nurse it into weakness, so that its beauty is only short-lived; but the plant that grows in the open air is strengthened while it grows, and is able to withstand even the biting winter's cold. Resistance is necessary to the development of power; and the greatest misfortune that can befall a youth is to have no difficulties whatever with which to contend. It is by overmastering obstacles that a man's character is mainly made. Hence, let no one be discouraged who is called in early life to struggle with adversity. He is thereby only making himself for his future life-work. I am confident that there is no one here who has arrived at middle age, who does not now recognize that, though he knew not of it at the time, he was, under Providence, preparing himself by his early wrestlings with difficulty, and, most of all, when the difficulty was the greatest, for the particular position which he is now occupying. Not in a day, nor in a year, nor in many years, do we reach the throne of our individual power, the sphere of our personal and peculiar labor. We graduate up to it through trial, and each new difficulty surmounted is not only a new step in the ladder upward, but also a new qualification for the work that is before us. Courage, then, my young brother; though every thing may seem to be against you, hold on; for if you be only sure that God is for you (and he will be for you if you will be for him), you will at length attain to the throne for which he has designed you, and the crown for which he has anointed you. His plan of your life will not fail, and when you see it all you will recognize its wisdom.

Nor does this principle hold merely of the early part of our earthly life as related to the later. It will be illustrated also in our earthly life as connected with our heavenly. If we be Christ's, it is no doubt true that he is preparing a place for each of us; but it is just as true that, through the discipline of our daily difficulties, he is preparing each of us for his own particular place, and the characters which we are forming here will find their appropriate employment and development in the work which in heaven will be assigned to us. This at once explains our frequent trials, and gives us strength to undergo them; and just as through his wanderings and warfares, his Adullam experiences and his Hebron monarchy, David was fitted for his Jerusalem reign; so, by our cares and losses, our disappointments and our sorrows, our hopes deferred and our labors abundant, we shall each be fitted for his own peculiar post in the New Jerusalem above. Thus, by the leverage of this principle we lift our earthly lives up to the very level of heaven itself; and every experience through which we are passing now, becomes a preparation for our eternal royalty at Christ's right hand.

But let us note, finally, the similarity, and yet the dissimilarity, of the kingdom of David to that of Christ. It was in connection with David's position that the Messiah was first spoken of in prophecy as a king. David's power, small in its beginnings, waxed greater and greater, until it became supreme, and united all the tribes under its benignant protection. So it has been with that of Christ. The outlaw in the cave of Adullam was not so contemptible in the eyes of his fellow-countryman as He was who was "despised and rejected of men;" and the followers of David, consisting as they did of those who were in debt, and those who were discontented, and those who were in distress, were not so unlikely to overcome their enemies, and lead their master to his throne, as the fishermen of Galilee were to gain the world's ear, and advance the cause of their ascended Lord. Yet, as the house of David waxed stronger and stronger, while the house of Saul waxed weaker and weaker, so the kingdom of Christ has still gone on advancing, in the face of every resistance, while that of Satan has continually receded before it. We may not think so as we compare the condition of both from day to day. Yet if we will but widen our investigation, and compare century with century, we shall see all along these nineteen cycles a clear and steady progress, indicating final triumph.

In one thing, however, the parallel fails. David's advance was made with the sword, that of the kingdom of Christ is made with the power of love and truth. He is the Prince of Peace, and his victories are gained over the errors, the prejudices, the selfishness, and the sins of men. Bloodless in their character, they are beneficent in their results; and as he advances to his final conquest, his course will be marked with blessings, and his progress will be attended with rejoicing. Not yet, indeed, do we behold the nations of the world united in the acknowledgment of his allegiance, and ready for his coronation. But the day is coming when he shall reign in every heart, and over every land—a day that shall bring greater joy to the world than Hebron saw when, the miseries of intestine war having been removed, David was anointed over Israel. "Thy kingdom come," O Christ! "Come forth out of thy royal chamber, thou prince of all the kings of the earth." Draw the hearts of men everywhere to thyself by the attraction of thy love. Come, and bring with thee the Sabbath of the world. Come, and let thy coronation-day be ushered in with the song of myriad voices—

> "Bring forth the royal diadem
> And crown him Lord of all."

## XII.

### THE BRINGING UP OF THE ARK.

2 SAMUEL v., 11–vi., 23 ; 1 CHRONICLES xiii., 1–xvi., 23.

AFTER David had established himself in Jerusalem, two things were needed to make it the capital of the nation. These were, that it should possess a palace for himself; and that it should be the abode of the ark of the covenant, over which hovered continually the visible symbol of Jehovah's presence. As I have repeatedly remarked, the distinguishing peculiarity of David as a king was that he recognized in the most loyal manner the higher royalty of God, and regarded himself as a mere human vice-regent. Had he been content to build only an official residence for himself, Jerusalem would have been no more than the city of David; but in a theocracy it was necessary also that the metropolis should be the city of God; and so, in that spirit of patriotic piety for which he was so remarkable, David set himself at once as earnestly to prepare a place for the reception of the ark, as to erect a habitation for himself. Entering into a league with Hiram, king of Tyre, he caused to be built for himself a splendid cedar palace, with the questionable addition of a harem. Yet amidst all this magnificence he did not forget to acknowledge the goodness of Him from whom all his greatness came, for it was most probably in connection with his taking possession of his palace that he wrote and sang the 30th Psalm, which bears the following title: "A Psalm and Song at the dedication of the house of David." If in minor things a man's true self comes most clearly out, then in this domestic ode we may see something of what David was at home, and may learn how in every thing he acknowledged God. After having gone over his new abode, accompanied, as we may suppose, by all the members of his household, he gathered them together in some convenient chamber, or in the open court round which his palace was built, and sang with them this Psalm, in which we know not whether to admire more the pathetic allusions to the sufferings of the past, or the holy resolutions in regard to the conduct of the future: "I will extol thee, O Lord; for thou hast lifted me up, and hast not made my foes to rejoice over me. O Lord my God, I cried unto thee, and thou hast healed me. O Lord, thou hast brought up my soul from the grave: thou hast kept me alive, that I should not go down to the pit. Sing unto the Lord, O ye saints of his, and give thanks at the remembrance of his holiness. For his anger endureth but a moment; in his favor is life: weeping may endure for a night, but joy cometh in the morning. And in my prosperity I said, I shall never be moved. Lord, by thy favor thou hast made my mountain to stand strong: thou didst hide thy face, and I was troubled. I cried to thee, O Lord; and unto the Lord I made supplication. What profit is there in my blood, when I go down to the pit? Shall the dust praise thee? shall it declare thy truth? Hear, O Lord, and have mercy upon me: Lord, be thou my helper. Thou hast turned for me my mourning into dancing: thou hast put off my sackcloth, and girded me with gladness; to the end that my glory may sing praise to thee, and not be silent. O Lord my God, I will give thanks unto thee forever."

If we contrast the spirit which breathes through these lines with that which animated Nebuchadnezzar, when he said, "Is not this great Babylon that I have built for the house of the kingdom, by the might of my power and for the honor of my majesty?" we shall see more clearly into the piety of David's heart, while at the same time we may all learn how our joy and prosperity may be consecrated and turned into a means of honoring Jehovah. Elegant mansions, costly furniture, art treasures, and extensive possessions will do no harm to those who, as they survey them all, can turn to God, and say, "Thou hast girded us with gladness, to the end that our glory may sing praise to thee and not be silent. O Lord our God, we will give thanks unto thee forever." But if these earthly glories turn our heads, and puff us up with stupid self-conceit, or lead us to boast of ourselves and to despise others, then we have built our house upon the edge of a volcano, whose first eruption may send us to a degradation deeper than that of him who wandered forth among the oxen, and ate the grass of the fields.

Before David could turn his attention to the removal of the ark, however, he had to encounter and overcome the Philistines. That warlike people could not regard his establishment on the throne of Israel and his occupation of Jerusalem with indifference. So long as he held his court at Hebron, he was too insignificant to be attacked by them; but now that he had humiliated the Jebusites, and settled himself in their reputedly impregnable fortress, they felt it needful, for the maintenance of their national supremacy, to take the field against him, with all the forces at their command. Their chosen battle-field on this occasion was the Valley of Rephaim, or "the giants," a broad and fertile plain about a mile in length, which was the southern entrance into Jerusalem, and which extended northward, terminating in a narrow ridge of rocks, which breaks abruptly into the ravine of Hinnom. After inquiring at the sacred oracle what he should do, David led his troops into "the hold;" that is, either into the region of his sojourning during his war with Saul, or into some other place of great natural strength, from which he could repel the invaders. Here he had a signal victory over the enemy, whom he drove before him as with

the irresistible might of an overflowing flood. But he took
no credit to himself for his success, for, in a spirit of gratitude and humility, he commemorated the victory by calling
the name of the place Baal-perazim; saying also, "God hath
broken in upon mine enemies by mine hand like the breaking forth of waters." In this engagement, probably with
the view of stimulating the courage and inspiring the confidence of their troops, the Philistine leaders had brought their
idols into the field; but David, having taken them with the
other booty, caused them to be burned—a proof, on the one
hand, of his pious determination to acknowledge Jehovah
alone as divine, and a manifestation, on the other, of the
helplessness of the heathen divinities, who could not deliver
themselves, much less those who trusted in them, from the
conqueror's hands.

In spite, however, of this defeat, both of their gods and of
themselves, the Philistines, some months afterward, renewed
the contest. Again they encamped in Rephaim; again David inquired of the Lord, and was directed to take such measures as resulted in their complete disorganization. He was
commanded to come upon them from the rear by making a
circuitous march, and was cautioned to take his stand at a
certain spot until, by "the sound of going in the tops of
the mulberry-trees," the signal should be given to advance.
All this being carefully observed by him, his sudden appearance created such a panic in the Philistian host that they
arose and fled, and were smitten by their pursuers all the
way from Seba until the entrance into their own city of
Gaza.

We can not but be struck, in this narrative, with the humble piety of David in asking guidance from the Lord, and
with his willingness implicitly to obey the commands which
he received. Nor can we fail to observe the clear and ex-
plicit nature of the answers which he received from the Urim

and Thummim. The ancient heathens had their oracles in connection with the temples in which they worshiped their divinities; but the responses given at these places to those who consulted them were generally expressed so ambiguously that no great guidance was given by them, and they could not be falsified by any event. Thus it is on record that when Crœsus inquired of Apollo what would be the result of his attacking the Persians, the answer was that, by doing so, "he should overthrow a great army"—a reply which would have been appropriate either to the destruction of the Persian army, or, as in the event it happened to be, to that of his own. When again Pyrrhus, the king of Epirus, asked what was to be the issue of his war with the Romans, the response was given in words which might mean either, "I say that thou, the son of Eacus, art able to conquer the Romans," or "I say that the Romans are able to conquer thee, the son of Eacus." But here, in the replies given by the sacred breastplate, there is no obscurity. Every thing is definite and clear, and David could have no hesitation as to his duty in each case. Of course, there is not now any such means of obtaining the unerring guidance of God as David then enjoyed, in so far as the contingencies of our daily lives are concerned; but still, in answer to prayer, God will lead us in the right way, provided only we unfeignedly commit ourselves to him, and willingly accept his direction step by step. Here is the warrant on which every one of us is entitled to proceed: "If any of you lack wisdom, let him ask of God, that giveth to all men liberally, and upbraideth not, and it shall be given him." Let us, therefore, use the Bible and the throne of grace as David employed the Urim and Thummim, and we may depend upon it that, even as "the sound of a going in the tops of the mulberry-trees" indicated to him when he was to advance, there will be something, either within ourselves, or in the arrangement of God's providence external to us, which shall point out to us what course we are to follow, and when we are to enter upon it.

And now, having overcome his enemies for the time, David had leisure to devote to the bringing up of the ark of the covenant. That, as every one knows, was the sacred chest, overshadowed by the golden cherubim, which usually stood in the Holy of Holies of the Tabernacle, and which contained in it a copy of the law of Moses; the golden pot of manna, which was preserved as a memorial of the wilderness; and the rod of Aaron, which blossomed, and which was kept as a proof of the divine appointment of Aaron and his sons to the priestly office. The lid of this chest was the mercy-seat, and was year by year sprinkled with the blood of atonement, when on the great Day of Atonement the high-priest went in before the Lord. Its proper place was in the innermost chamber of the Tabernacle; but at this period of the history of Israel, religious matters were in the greatest confusion, arising out of the folly of which, many years before, the elders of the people had been guilty,* when they carried the ark with them to the field of battle. They trusted in the symbol, rather than in Jehovah, whose the symbol was, and as a consequence they were defeated, and the ark was taken by the Philistines, who put it into the Temple of Dagon; thence, however, owing to the fall of the image of their idol before it, they had it speedily removed; but wherever they took it, troubles and diseases broke out, which they traced to its presence, and so they sent it back to Israel in a singular manner, of which a full account is given in the sixth chapter of 1 Samuel. It was ultimately received by the men of Kirjath-jearim, a city on the boundary line between the territories of Judah and Benjamin; and Eleazar, the son of Abinadab, was set apart for the purpose of attending to it there. In that city,

---

\* 1 Sam. iv., 3.

therefore, all these years during the ministry of Samuel, and the reigns of Saul and Ishbosheth, the ark had remained; while the Tabernacle continued at Shiloh, or perhaps, for a portion of the time, at Nob. But this was not all; for while the Tabernacle was in one city, and the ark in another, there were also two high-priests—Zadok at Shiloh, who was of the elder line of the sons of Aaron, which had hitherto adhered to the house of Saul; and Abiathar, the sole survivor of the Nob massacre, who had fled to David with the Urim and Thummim when he was in the cave. Now, in seeking to bring order out of all this confusion, David, acting perhaps under the divine direction, left the Tabernacle untouched, but wished to bring the ark to Jerusalem, where he had prepared a temporary tent (probably after the pattern of the original one), in which it might remain until the cherished purpose of his heart should be accomplished, and a permanent temple erected for its abode. Furthermore, he retained the two high-priests as of co ordinate dignity, thereby binding both of them to himself without exciting the jealousy of either.

When he had determined to bring up the ark, he gathered together thirty thousand chosen men, and went in state to the ancient city in which it had so long been kept; but a sad and awful occurrence struck terror into all their hearts, and led to the postponement of the formal entrance of the sacred symbol into Jerusalem. Ignoring the command that the sacred chest should be borne only on the shoulders of the priests, the two sons of Abinadab put it on a new cart, and when they came to a place which was known as the threshing-floor of Nachon, as the cart shook violently, Uzzah, one of the sons of Abinadab, put forth his hand upon the ark to steady it, and was at once struck dead. Whether this was caused by the immediate outflashing of the divine power, or, as some believe, by a bolt of lightning in the midst of a thunder-storm which they suppose was raging at the time, the event was by them all connected with the touching of the ark by Uzzah, and they were filled with dismay. Harps, cornets, cymbals, psalteries, and timbrels were silenced, and David, in sore distress at what had taken place, caused them to carry the sacred thing into the house of Obed-edom the Gittite, which happened to be at hand; while, in memory of the stroke with which they had been visited, he named the place Perez-uzzah, "the Breach of Uzzah."

Leaving for the present out of view the purpose that was to be subserved by this judgment, we may note the different degrees of punishment by which in different cases the profanation of the ark was visited. The Philistines, whose sin was ignorance, were smitten only with disease; the men of Beth-shemesh who looked into the ark, Levites though they were, were smitten with death, because they ought to have known the law of God upon the matter; and now again Uzzah is stricken down, because ignorance, where knowledge ought to have been possessed, is no extenuation of guilt.

But though thus sadly interrupted in the carrying out of his purpose, David would not give it up; for learning, three months afterward, that God had greatly blessed, in some visible manner, the household of Obed-edom, in whose dwelling the ark was placed, he set out again to bring it to Jerusalem. But this time, the book of the law having doubtless been most carefully searched for directions, every thing was done decently and in order. It was a great and memorable day in Israel; and as David had composed many special odes for the occasion, we may perhaps give you the most vivid idea of the whole proceedings, by making our narrative little more than a statement of the particular order in which we suppose that these hymns were sung.

Let it be premised, however, that on this day, as on all the high festival occasions afterward, both in the Tabernacle and the Temple, the service of song was conducted solely by the

Levites. They were the holy tribe; and just as the high-priest offered in the room of the people the sacrifices of burnt-offering and atonement, so the Levites offered in the stead of the tribes the sacrifice of praise. We do not, indeed, hear any thing of music as a portion of the worship of Jehovah until the times of David; but "it is not improbable that the Levites all along had practiced music, and that some musical service was part of the worship of the Tabernacle; for, unless this supposition be made, it is inconceivable that a body of trained singers and musicians should be found ready for an occasion like that on which they made their first appearance."[*] No doubt, at the school of the prophets at Ramah, music formed part of the regular exercises of the students; and David's own skill and taste in that exquisite art must have enabled him to make perfect arrangements for this great festival, even as they enabled him afterward to make permanent regulations for the conduct of "the service of song in the house of the Lord."

From the narrative in the fifteenth chapter of the First Book of Chronicles, we learn that, in addition to the elders of Israel (each of whom, as on the day of the coronation, would be accompanied by a delegation from his tribe), and the captains over thousands, there were present nine hundred and sixty-two priests and Levites. From these last would be taken a sufficient number to relieve each other in carrying, by turns, the ark of the covenant, and then the rest would be told off for the musical service. The singing was accompanied by the sound of instruments, the performers on which were placed under the direction of skilled leaders. Thus Heman, Asaph, and Ethan were appointed to conduct the cymbals of brass; Zechariah, and Aziel, and Shemiramoth, and Jehiel, and Unni, and Eliab, and Maaseiah, and

---

[*] Smith's "Dictionary," article MUSIC.

Benaiah were set over those who played on psalteries on Alamoth, that is, on the higher notes; Mattithiah, and Elipheleh, and Mikneiah, and Obed-edom, and Jeiel, and Azaziah were put over those who sounded the harps on the Sheminith, that is, on the eighth, which, I suppose, may mean the lower octave; while others were to blow with the trumpets before the ark. It was thus a great processional oratorio, the route being somewhat less than nine miles in length, for that was the distance between Kirjath-jearim and Jerusalem. When the company had been marshaled, and were starting from Jerusalem, I conjecture that, with the judgment that fell on Uzzah still in the minds of all, the Levites broke forth, in solemn tones, with the beautiful 15th Psalm: "Lord, who shall abide in thy tabernacle? who shall dwell in thy holy hill? He that walketh uprightly, and worketh righteousness, and speaketh the truth in his heart. He that backbiteth not with his tongue, nor doeth evil to his neighbor, nor taketh up a reproach against his neighbor. In whose eyes a vile person is contemned: but he honoreth them that fear the Lord. He that sweareth to his own hurt, and changeth not. He that putteth not out his money to usury, nor taketh reward against the innocent. He that doeth these things shall never be moved." When they came to the house of Obed-edom, and while arrangements were being made for the removal from it of the ark, they sang the opening verses of the 132d Psalm, as if to deprecate a repetition of the calamity which had formerly saddened all their hearts: "Lord, remember David, and all his afflictions: how he sware unto the Lord, and vowed unto the mighty God of Jacob; surely I will not come into the tabernacle of my house, nor go up into my bed; I will not give sleep to mine eyes, or slumber to mine eyelids, until I find out a place for the Lord, a habitation for the mighty God of Jacob. Lo, we heard of it at Ephratah; we found it in the fields of the wood," *i.e.*, at Kirjath-jearim. Then, as the priests appointed for the purpose went into the house for the ark, they sang by themselves these words: "We will go into his tabernacles: we will worship at his footstool." As they emerged, bearing the sacred burden on their shoulders, and while they took the first six paces in their march, their brethren resumed the strain, and sang, "Arise, O Lord, into thy rest; thou, and the ark of thy strength. Let thy priests be clothed with righteousness; and let thy saints shout for joy. For thy servant David's sake turn not away the face of thine anointed. The Lord hath sworn in truth unto David; he will not turn from it; of the fruit of thy body will I set upon thy throne. If thy children will keep my covenant and my testimony that I shall teach them, their children shall also sit upon thy throne for evermore. For the Lord hath chosen Zion; he hath desired it for his habitation. This is my rest forever: here will I dwell; for I have desired it. I will abundantly bless her provision: I will satisfy her poor with bread. I will also clothe her priests with salvation: and her saints shall shout aloud for joy. There will I make the horn of David to bud: I have ordained a lamp for mine anointed. His enemies will I clothe with shame: but upon himself shall his crown flourish." At this point the procession halted, while a double sacrifice was offered unto the Lord; and such was the elation of feeling among them all, that the king, clothed for the time in a linen ephod like the priests, is said to have danced before the Lord.

But now again the march is renewed. At the sound of the trumpet they that bare the ark advanced, and the singers, accompanied by the instruments of music, raised the old wilderness watch-word, "Let God arise, let his enemies be scattered," and continued at intervals to sing appropriate strophes of that grand processional hymn, the 68th Psalm. It is too long to be quoted entire; but if you will carefully study it for yourselves, you will easily be able to divide it into its separate portions, and will discover how appropriate it was to the occasion which called it forth. What could be finer than the following strain, which we give in the spirited metrical version of an intimate friend and brother in the ministry?

"O God, when thou didst march of old before thy people's face,
 And led their way, by cloud and flame, through the great wilderness,
Earth shook; the heavens before thee dropped, on Sinai tremors fell,
Before the presence of the Lord, the God of Israel.
Lord, thou thy weary heritage didst cheer with plenteous rain:
Thy congregation dwelt therein; their poor thou didst sustain.
God gave the word: anon the land rings with the joyful sound;
Great was the host of herald tongues that published it around.
Kings fled, with all their bannered state, they bore themselves afar,
And she that dwelt at home did share the trophies of the war:
Now may ye rise and clothe yourselves in splendor manifold,
Like doves whose wings are silver-bright, whose plumes are burnished gold.
The land, when God had crushed the kings, with scattered bones was white;
It glistened like the crown of snow on Salmon's crested height:
God's hill is high as Bashan's hill; why leap ye, hills of pride?
This Zion is the hill where God forever will abide.
God's cherub chariots, myriad-fold; come flaming from afar;
And, as on Sinai, God is there, as in a victor's car.
Thou hast ascended, armed with gifts, and captor captive led,
And thou with men, rebellious men, dost deign thy tent to spread.
Bless'd be the Lord, salvation's Lord, who lifts our load of woe;
Whose daily bounties, rich and free, in volumed fullness flow;
For God, he is salvation's God, and each successive breath
We owe to him whose hand doth cast the die of life and death.
Praise God, ye kingdoms of the earth, high be his name extolled,
Who rides upon the heaven of heavens, whose splendors were of old.
Forth comes his voice, a mighty voice; what strength his frown enshrouds!
His majesty o'er Israel shines, his strength is in the clouds.
O God! from out thy holy place, how dread thy terrors gleam,
Where thou art in thy glory throned, between the cherubim.

Thou to thy people givest strength, and mak'st them safely dwell;
Then be thy name forever bless'd, thou God of Israel.*

When they drew near to Jerusalem they sung the 24th Psalm, which is, perhaps, the most artistic in its structure of all those to which we have referred. It is antiphonal in its nature, and was evidently designed to be sung by chorus answering to chorus. Perhaps no more striking idea of the method of its execution on this occasion can be given than that which is presented in the following description, by Dr. Kitto: "The chief musician, who seems to have been the king himself, appears to have begun the sacred lay with a solemn and sonorous recital of these sentences, 'The earth is the Lord's, and the fullness thereof; the world, and they that dwell therein. For he hath founded it upon the seas, and established it upon the floods.' The chorus of vocal music appears then to have taken up the song, and sung the same words in a more tuneful and elaborate manner; and the instruments fell in with them, raising the mighty declaration to heaven. We may presume that the chorus then divided, each singing in their turns, and both joining at the close, 'For he hath founded it upon the seas, and established it upon the floods.' This part of the music may be supposed to have lasted until the procession reached the foot of Zion, or came in sight of it, which, from the nature of the inclosed site, can not be till one comes quite near to it. Then the king must be supposed to have stepped forth and begun again, in a solemn and earnest tone, 'Who shall ascend into the hill of the Lord? or who shall stand in his holy place?' to which the first chorus responds, 'He that hath clean hands, and a pure heart; who hath not lifted up his soul unto vanity, nor sworn deceitfully.' And then the second

---

* "Sacred Lyrics," by John Guthrie, M.A., Glasgow, p. 170.

## The Bringing up of the Ark.

chorus gives its reply, 'He shall receive the blessing from the Lord, and righteousness from the God of his salvation.' This part of the song may, in like manner, be supposed to have lasted till they reached the gate of the city, when the king began again in this grand and exalted strain, 'Lift up your heads, O ye gates; and be ye lifted up, ye everlasting doors; and the King of glory shall come in;' which would be repeated then, in the same way as before, by the general chorus. The persons having charge of the gates ask, 'Who is this King of glory?' to which the first chorus answers, 'It is Jehovah, strong and mighty: Jehovah, mighty in battle;' which the second chorus then repeats in like manner as before, closing with the grand refrain, 'He is the King of glory: He is the King of glory.' We must now suppose the instruments to take up the same notes, and continue sounding them to the entrance of the Tabernacle (or tent) which David had prepared. There the king again begins: 'Lift up your heads, O ye gates; and be ye lifted up, ye everlasting doors; and the King of glory shall come in.' This is followed and answered as before—all closing by the instruments sounding, and the people shouting, 'He is the King of glory.'"*

One can not call up thus before the eye of his imagination such a scene as this, without having his heart stirred to its very depths; and we do not wonder that the effects produced upon the actual spectators were of the most thrilling character; nor are we surprised that the greatest poets in our own language, such as Milton and Young, have appropriated these very words, as the most sublime they could find, to describe the procession of the heavenly hosts; the one, in his delineation of the Son returning from the work of creation; the other, in an attempt to describe the glories of the Redeemer's ascension from Mount Olivet.†

---

\* Kitto's "Daily Bible Illustrations," vol. iii., pp. 385, 386.

† Milton's "Paradise Lost," Book vii.; Young's "Night Thoughts," Night iv.

But amidst all these applications of the words of David, we must not forget another, and perhaps the most important of all. The ark symbolized Christ in his peace-giving presence, and the Tabernacle is an emblem of the human heart, in which he desires to dwell. Even now he may be standing and knocking at the door of some heart here. He who is the King of glory, and mighty in battle, is asking an entrance, where he well might force his way. But he condescends to plead for admission. Oh, let him not plead in vain! Open unto him, that you may know what that blessed promise means: "If any man hear my voice and open the door, I will come in to him, and will sup with him, and he with me."

At the close of the singing of the 24th Psalm, the curtains of the tent were folded back, and, amidst the reverent silence of the assembled thousands, the ark was put in its appointed place. Thereafter, as the joyful conclusion of the glad and sacred services, David gave to Asaph and his brethren, that they might sing it with every proper accompaniment, that song which we have preserved in the sixteenth chapter of the First Book of Chronicles, and which seems to be a combination of portions taken from the 105th, 96th, and 106th Psalms. Then he offered more burnt-offerings and peace-offerings before the Lord; and having concluded the ceremony by blessing the people in the name of the Lord, he most generously distributed refreshments among them all. So ended this auspicious day. "All the people departed, every one to his own home; and David returned to bless his house." Only one thing occurred to mar his happiness. After he entered his palace, Michal, the daughter of Saul, who had never much sympathy with the devotional side of David's nature, taunted him with scorn for his dancing before the ark, and sneered at him as if he had been one of the vain fellows that were altogether regardless of propriety. But the only result was to widen the breach which already

## The Bringing up of the Ark.

existed between them, and to consign her to the perpetual isolation of widowhood, while she was still in name a wife.

Two practical lessons are all that space will now permit me to enforce.

Observe, then, in the first place, as here illustrated, the majesty of the divine holiness. When Uzzah touched the ark, he was smitten with death. Many have wondered at the apparent severity of the punishment; but when you examine into the matter minutely, you will see that the divine procedure here harmonizes with the general principle of God's operations as observed in similar instances. The law commanded that the ark should be carried on the shoulders of the priests, and Uzzah and all the people ought to have known that. Hence this judgment—for judgment it undoubtedly was—was a mark of God's displeasure for irreverence, and was designed to put them all on their guard. The whole Tabernacle service appears to have been arranged with the view of intensifying the idea of God's holiness in the minds of the people, and leading them up to the truth that they could, as sinners, approach him only through sacrifice. To keep these two things constantly before the people, they were not allowed to come near the sacred place where the symbol of Jehovah's presence dwelt; and those whose business took them into the sanctuary had to be specially set apart for the purpose; while the high-priest was permitted to go into the Holy of Holies only once a year, and then only when he carried with him the blood of sacrifice. Hence, any interference with the arrangements which converged toward the teachings of these important truths was solemnly guarded against; and at the outset of every new period of the history of Israel, some warning was given to keep them from irreverence: Nadab and Abihu perished in the wilderness; Uzzah here was struck down at the inauguration of a new era in the Jewish worship; and Ananias and

Sapphira were punished in the same way in the early infancy of the Christian Church.

Now the connection of this latter case with that of Uzzah here will show you how we in these days can be guilty of Uzzah's sin. The Corinthians were guilty of it when, forgetting the sacred character of the Lord's Supper, they became intoxicated at the table of the Lord; and we shall be guilty of it if, with hearts estranged from God, and lives which are inconsistent with his Word, we presume to connect ourselves with his Church, and take part in the management of its affairs. David, therefore, rightly read the meaning of the breach of Uzzah when, in addition to rectifying his error by putting the ark on the shoulders of the priests, he sang these words: "Who shall ascend into the hill of the Lord? or who shall stand in his holy place? He that hath clean hands and a pure heart;" and unless we who are members of the Church have this character, we shall be guilty of Uzzah's sin. But how shall we get such a character? Only by living union to the Lord Jesus Christ, who offered himself in sacrifice to God for us. In and through him we may approach God with acceptance, and, sprinkled with his blood, we may have no fear of any catastrophe. Beautiful here, in connection with the majesty of God's holiness, and the necessity of atonement, if sinners would safely approach him, is the lesson of the cherubim in the Word of God. We first meet these symbols (for whether we see them in the form of living creatures, or in that of artificial figures, they are still symbols), guarding the tree of life, and keeping back our sinful parents from approaching it; we next meet them over the mercy-seat, where they are looking down with satisfaction on the blood of the victim; we behold them next in Isaiah's vision, "Crying, Holy, holy, holy, is the Lord of hosts;" and we observe one of them taking a live coal from the altar—mark, the altar, which tells of sacrifice—and purifying therewith the prophet's lips; we come upon them next in the vision of Ezekiel, where they are the guardians of the mystic wheels, which indicate, in the minds of many, the providence of God among the nations; and we behold them for the last time in the Apocalypse of John, where they call again, "Holy, holy, holy, Lord God Almighty;" but where there is a throne, with a lamb upon it, as if it had been slain; and beside the throne four-and-twenty seats, occupied by elders, representing the tribes of the redeemed. Now observe how the Apocalypse, with its paradise regained, stands in contrast to Genesis, with its paradise lost. In Genesis, the cherubim, guarding God's holiness, are warding men away; in the Apocalypse, the cherubim—still, as before, zealous for the divine holiness, for they make that the burden of their song—are complacent on-lookers, while the elders are seated on either side of the throne. Why is this? because on the throne itself there is the Lamb of God who was slain from the foundation of the world, and who in the days of his flesh bore the sins of men. Here is explained the mystery of the mercy-seat, over which, with its drops of blood annually renewed, the cherubim stood with folded wings, and on which they looked with such satisfied gaze. "Jesus Christ is the propitiation for our sins, and not for ours only, but for the sins of the whole world." If, therefore, we would approach Jehovah acceptably, if we would not provoke his judgments upon us, if we would secure our peace with him, we must sprinkle ourselves with this blood of atonement; that is, we must believingly appropriate to ourselves the benefits and blessings which Christ has secured for us by his sacrificial death. While, again, if we would be fitted for the service of the Lord, we must, Isaiah-like, have our lips purged by sacrificial fire. We have nothing to fear from God if we approach him in the right way; we have every thing to fear from him if we approach him in the wrong way. Let us, therefore, come "by that new and living way which Jesus hath consecrated for us, that is to say, his flesh; and having a high-priest over the house of God, let us draw near with a true heart, in full assurance of faith, having our hearts sprinkled from an evil conscience, and our bodies washed with pure water."

Finally: let us learn from the conduct of David in retiring to bless his house, that public religious services should not be allowed by us to interfere with the discharge of the duties of family religion. After such a day as that which we have attempted to describe, David might have imagined that he had a good excuse for omitting all domestic worship; but it rather seemed that the devotions of the day gave him new zest for the exercises of the family altar. And this is what always ought to be. It is to be feared, however, that many among us content themselves with a mere go-to-meeting piety, and seem to believe that religion consists in a round of public religious services. They attend all manner of holy convocations. You see them at every important devotional meeting you take part in. But they rarely enter the closet; they never bless their houses; and their lives are just as selfish and unspiritual as are those of multitudes who make no profession of attachment to Jesus whatever. I do not make light of the ordinances of God's worship; on the contrary, I believe them to be most serviceable in feeding the fire of piety within the heart. But what I mean to say is, that piety does not consist in attending on these means of grace, and that our engagement in public services must never be made an excuse by us for the neglect of household duties. "Why did you not come to church last night," said one working-man to another, on a Monday morning; "our minister was preaching a third sermon on the duty of family religion; why did you not come?" "Because," was the reply, "I was at home doing it." I would like to see not less earnestness in attendance upon the regular ordinances of the sanctuary, but more of this "at home doing it." Have you family worship in your dwelling? Oh, if you have not, you know not what a privilege you are depriving yourself of! It is a great means of promoting family peace and domestic prosperity. Try it, and you will find that God will deal well with you through it, as of old he dealt with Obed-edom when the ark was in his house. Try it at once. Begin to-night. Never mind, though you may falter in your first utterances. There is much power in broken prayers. Go, therefore, from this house of privilege to the family altar, and lay thereon a grateful offering. It will bind the members of your household together by a cord of spiritual and indissoluble union. It will elevate your home-life into a miniature of that of heaven. It will give you a foretaste of the blessedness of those who form the family above.

## XIII.

### *NATHAN'S MESSAGE.*

#### 2 SAMUEL vii.; ix.

WITH great pomp and gladness, the ark of the covenant had been brought to Jerusalem, but David was not yet satisfied; for it had been placed in a mere temporary tent, and his great desire was to erect a splendid temple for its permanent abode. Hence, before he was well established in his own cedar palace, he sent for Nathan the prophet, who now for the first time appears in the narrative, and intimated to him his purpose in these words: "See now, I dwell in a house of cedar, but the ark of God dwelleth within curtains." The sentiment underlying these words was in the highest degree honorable to David. They indicate that he felt it to be a moral anomaly, if not a species of dishonesty, that he should look so well after his own personal comfort and regal dignity, while yet the house of God was but a tent. It were well, in these days, that we all shared these convictions, for we are too apt to lavish our wealth exclusively upon our own enjoyment and indulgence, forgetful of the higher claims which God and his cause have upon us. I say not, indeed, that it is wrong for a man to take such a position in society as his riches warrant him to assume, or that there is sin in spending money on our residences, or in surrounding ourselves with the treasures of human wisdom in books, or the triumphs of human art in pictures or statuary; but I do say that our gifts to the cause of God ought to be at least abreast of our expenditure for these other things; and that if we so cripple ourselves by our extravagance on house, or dress, or luxuries, as to render it impossible for us to do any thing for the promotion of the Gospel abroad, or for the instruction of the ignorant at home, we are "verily guilty concerning our brethren," and before our God. The principle here acknowledged by David is a thoroughly sound one, and though he was discouraged from applying it in the particular way on which he had set his heart, we must not suppose that his feelings, as expressed to Nathan, were wrong. On the contrary, the spiritual instinct in him was true, and God declared that "it was well that it was in his heart." Now what was this principle? It was this, that in proportion as we increase our expenditure upon ourselves for the comforts and the elegancies of life, we ought to increase our offerings to God for the carrying on of works of faith and labors of love among our fellowmen. If we can afford to enter a larger dwelling, we ought to make ourselves afford to add proportionately to our contributions for all good objects. If we allow ourselves to gratify our taste in the purchase of a new picture or a new book, we should feel impelled to do just so much more for the gratification of the impulse of Christian benevolence. The value of this principle, when rightly understood, and conscientiously carried out, will be very great. It will act in two ways. On the one hand, it will keep us from hampering ourselves in our benevolence by personal extravagance, and so be a check on that tendency to luxury which is manifested even in many Christian households. On the other hand, it will impel us to add to our gifts to the Lord Jesus Christ; since every time we do any thing for ourselves there will be a new call made upon us to do more for him. The world's maxim is, "Be just before you are generous;" and, indeed, it would be well if the world's own votaries always acted thereon, for it is very easy to be benevolent with other people's money. But the Christian's maxim ought to be, "Make your generosity a matter of justice." Be just to God, as good stewards of his manifold bounties; and whenever you increase your doings for yourselves, be sure that you proportionately increase your doings for him. There is no harm in your cedar palace, provided only the erection of that stimulate you to do more than ever for Christ. I am the more particular to put the matter thus, because, from a mistaken zeal for the Lord, many have taken up a position regarding it which is flagrantly unjust. They do not hesitate to blame Christian men for dwelling in fine houses, and surrounding themselves with beautiful objects, while so many poor people are starving for want of food, and so many ignorant ones are perishing for lack of knowledge, and this altogether irrespective of the fact that some who do live in cedar houses are among the most benevolent in the land. But where is this to end? Are we all to go back to the cheerless, carpetless, comfortless houses of hundreds of years ago? or are we to be content with the blanket and the wigwam of the Indian, and give all else to benevolence? Nay. The Lord does not blame David here for building his cedar palace. On the contrary, I believe he was as glad to see David in it, as a modern father is to visit his son in the comfortable home which his industry and integrity have secured for him. God does not want us to go in threadbare attire, and live in cold and ugly apartments. He loves to see his stewards comfortable. But while he rejoices in our comfort, he desires that we should share it with others. If I were to go to a wealthy man's house, and, after surveying his paintings and his plate, his carriage and his horses, and all the other accessories' of refinement around him, I should say, "To what purpose is this waste? Ought not all these things to be sold and given to the poor?" I should feel as if somehow the meanness of Judas had got into my heart, and I should not hope to do him any good; but if, conceding to him that God delights in his comfort and rejoices in his happiness, I should unfold to him this principle, that the enjoyment of so many good things carries with it the obligation to do just so much the more for Christ, I should expect to make some impression upon him. There may be those here tonight who have done much more for themselves than others could honestly attempt. Let me ask them to consider that their larger measure of enjoyment involves in it the duty of doing just so much the more, for the furtherance of the Gospel and the welfare of their fellow-men. Let me beg them to press this question to their consciences: "Am I doing as much more than others for Christ as I am doing for myself?" And if they can not conscientiously say "Yes," then let me beseech them to do less for themselves, that they may do more for him.

When Nathan heard David's proposal, which would be, of course, much more fully explained to him than it is in the simple summary of the conversation given in the history, he answered, "Go, do all that is in thine heart; for the Lord is with thee." This, however, was only his own individual opinion, in which he gave expression, as a good man would naturally do, to the feelings of gratification with which he had heard of the royal intention. But during the subsequent night, God gave him a special message to the king, which, while preventing him from undertaking the building of the Temple, yet contained in it predictions of greatest interest, not only to himself, but to all nations. I need not go over it in detail. Let it suffice that I indicate what I regard to be its meaning, premising that for the view which I present I am indebted to the suggestive comments of Keil upon the passage.

The first part of the announcement virtually amounts to this: "Thou shalt not build an house for me, but I, who selected thee when thou wast following the sheep, will build thee an house, and then thy son shall rear an house for my name." Nor is this a mere play upon words, as at first sight it might appear to be. It refers to the fact that, up to this time, David's kingdom was not thoroughly established, and draws from that the inference that God's ark was not yet to exchange the Tabernacle, which was the symbol of unsettled abode, for the Temple, which was the emblem of permanent residence. "As long as the quiet and full possession of the land of Canaan was disputed by their enemies round about, even the dwelling-place of their God could not assume any other form than that of a wanderer's tent. The kingdom of God in Israel first acquired its rest and consolidation through the efforts of David, when God had made all his foes subject to him, and had established his throne firmly, that is, had assured to his descendants the possession of the kingdom for all future time. And it was this which ushered in the time for the building of a stationary house as a dwelling for the name of the Lord. The conquest of the citadel of Zion, and the elevation of that fortress into the palace of the king, was the commencement of the establishment of the kingdom,"* but only the commencement, for many foes had yet to be encountered and overcome. Till they were subdued, then, the Temple should not be built; for the tent, or symbol of pilgrimage, would not be laid aside by God for his ark until it had been first made clearly evident that the people among whom that ark was to reside were themselves permanently established in the land which had been given them. This permanent establishment David, aided by Jehovah, was to make good, and then his son would rear the Temple, in token of the perpetuity of the kingdom and dynasty which he was to found. In the version given in the

---

* Keil and Delitzsch, "Biblical Commentary on the Books of Samuel," p. 344.

book of Samuel, no personal reason is assigned why David was not to build the Temple, but, from his own words on his death-bed, we learn that he was forbidden to do what was in his heart, "because he was a man of war and had shed blood." Perhaps this was founded on the sacredness of blood as a symbol, of which so much is made under the old covenant; but possibly Keil may be right when he sees, even in these words, a confirmation of the interpretation which I have just given, and takes them to indicate that, so long as wars were necessary or inevitable for David, they were practical proofs that his kingdom and government were not yet established. Besides, the Temple, as a symbol of God's kingdom, was to shadow forth its peace as well as its permanence, and for that reason not David the warrior, but Solomon the peaceful, was its appropriate builder.

The second portion of Nathan's message, extending from the twelfth to the sixteenth verse, gives a more precise account of the manner in which God would build his servant's house, and has a clear reference to Solomon and his descendants. In this aspect of the prophecy, it was fulfilled when God kept the kingdom for Solomon in spite of the plots of his brother Adonijah, when Solomon built the Temple, and also, alas! when Solomon sinned by idolatry, and entailed upon Rehoboam the loss of the ten tribes. Thus God "chastened him with the rod of men, and with the stripes of the children of men;" but inasmuch as he and his descendants were continued on the throne of Judah, these other words were verified: "My mercy shall not depart away from him, as I took it from Saul, whom I put away before thee."

But while the primary reference of this prediction to Solomon and his immediate descendants is unmistakable, it must be evident even to the least thoughtful reader, that "a greater than Solomon is here." Thrice it is alleged that the throne of David's kingdom should be established forever; and we may not seek to reduce these words to the popular notion of a long, indefinite period. We must take them in an absolute sense, as they are understood in the 89th Psalm, where there is a clear reference to this prophecy, and where the expression is thus paraphrased. "His seed also will I make to endure forever, and his throne as the days of heaven." Now, as Keil remarks, "The posterity of David could only last forever by running out in a person who lives forever, that is, by culminating in the Messiah, who lives forever, and of whose kingdom there is no end."\*

Thus we reach a new landmark in the development of Messianic prophecy in the Old Testament. The promised deliverer is spoken of first as "the seed of the woman;" then as the seed of Abraham; then as the child of Isaac; then as the son of Jacob; and then as the Shiloh of the tribe of Judah. Now, out of that tribe the family of David is designated as that in which he was to appear; while with this description of his lineage there is conjoined the information that he was to found a kingdom which should be universal in its extent, and eternal in its duration. Thus, in the course of the ages, that first Edenic prediction, so nebulous and indistinct, acquired definiteness and precision, until at length, when the fullness of the time was come, there converged toward Jesus of Nazareth so many lines of prophetic proof, that he could be at once identified as the promised Redeemer.

But the connection of a prediction of the Messiah with a message to David, regarding the building of the Temple, illustrates another peculiarity by which many Old Testament prophecies are distinguished. While some of these ancient

---

\* Keil and Delitzsch, "Biblical Commentary on the Books of Samuel," p. 347.

## NATHAN'S MESSAGE. 237

oracles stand out clearly from the circumstances and the times in which they were given, and refer simply and alone to Christ, there are others which, while pointing ultimately to him, yet do so through and in connection with the position and history of those to whom they were originally addressed. Now of this latter class the prediction on which I have been remarking is an example. David was himself, in his official position and dignity as king, a prophecy of the Messiah. Hence predictions which had a primary reference to him as a king, and to his house as a dynasty, had through him an allusion to the Messiah, and were thoroughly fulfilled only in Christ. When, however, we interpret all such oracles, both of the type and of the antetype, we are not putting upon them a double sense. The truth rather is, that he to whom they were first given sustained a double character, and we find that the one meaning of the predictions holds true of him in both characters. It is, therefore, utterly impossible to exhaust the meaning of such a prophecy as this before us, or such a Psalm as the second, without going through David to David's son, who was also David's Lord. Indeed, from some of David's own expressions here, and especially from some of his words in the 2d, 89th, and 110th Psalms, which all reduplicate on this message of Nathan's, it would almost seem that he himself had some idea of its ultimate reference. Perhaps we may apply to him the words of Peter to the prophets generally, and say, " that he searched what, or what manner of time, the Spirit of Christ did signify when it testified beforehand the sufferings of Christ, and the glory that should follow." But, however that may be, and whether or not he had in connection with this promise any prevision of the Redeemer, we can not but feel that there are expressions here which, true in a subsidiary sense of David, can only be said to be fully verified in Jesus Christ.

But now, leaving the significance of the prophecy itself,

we must attend to the manner in which it was received by David. At the first, perhaps, there might be a pang of disappointment in his heart, when he was told so decisively that he was not to be the builder of the Temple, for this had been the one great desire of his soul; and it is not easy for one in a moment to reconcile himself to another arrangement of his life than that which he had planned for himself. We think of the author who, having been kept by one interruption after another from the great work to which he meant to give his life, is at last fairly in sight of its being undertaken by him, and then, overtaken by weakness, is compelled to leave it unattempted. We think of the statesman who has fought his way through the jealousies, and envyings, and depreciations of rivals into the front, and who seems just about to lay his hand upon the helm of the commonwealth, when God in his providence breaks him down with disease, and bids him step aside that another may go before him. We think of the President who had safely piloted his country through the rapids of a terrible civil war, and was just about to reconstruct on a broader and more stable foundation a reunited nation, when he was stricken down, and the life that was shaping itself into a finished pillar became, to human view, only a broken shaft. And as these and similar disarrangements of earthly plans come up before us, bringing with them their appropriate feelings, we may be apt to imagine that when David saw the hope of his life cut off in a moment, he would be plunged into the deepest dejection. But if, even for an instant, such an emotion existed in his breast, it was speedily subdued, and he was not only resigned to the determination of God, but also jubilant and grateful for the divine goodness. Nor is it difficult to account for this; for he sought to build the Temple, not for his own glory, but for that of Jehovah. In desiring to rear a majestic house for God's dwelling-place and worship, he was actuated by no vulgar craving for fame, like that which impelled Erostratus to set fire to the Ephesian Diana's fane; he wished to honor Jehovah; and if God preferred that he should be honored by him in another way, who was he that he should question the wisdom of his choice? Moreover, he was assured that the Temple should be built, and that was, in his estimation, a greater thing than that *he* should build it. Furthermore, the Lord had been graciously pleased to speak to him of the royal house which he was to found, and of the kingdom rising out of his own which was to last forever; and in the contemplation of these wondrous things he forgot his personal predilections, and was dumb with amazement at the divine regard for him, taking refuge in God's omniscience as a guarantee that his silence would not be misunderstood. "What can David say more unto thee? for thou, Lord God, knowest thy servant." Then, when he could find speech again, he used it to magnify God's name, and to turn the promises which he had just received into prayers. "And now, O Lord God, the word that thou hast spoken concerning thy servant, establish it forever, and do as thou hast said." "Let it please thee to bless the house of thy servant, that it may continue forever before thee: for thou, O Lord God, hast spoken it: and with thy blessing let the house of thy servant be blessed forever." Thus faith ever produces humility, gratitude, and prayer—humility at the thought that God has been so good to the believer; gratitude at the remembrance of the goodness promised; and prayer that the promise may be fulfilled. To some, indeed, it may seem that the two former are more natural results of faith than the latter, since, if the faith be strong, it might be expected to leave God to himself, without making any request to him on the subject. But they who think thus know little of the workings of the filial heart. Your child does not refrain from asking because you have made him a promise;

nay, rather, just because of your promise, he asks all the more. And if it be thus with our faith in a human father, we may not wonder that it is so also with our confidence in the promises made to us by our Father who is in heaven. When Mary of Nazareth was told that to her was reserved the highest honor of womanhood, it was thus she made reply to Gabriel: "Behold the handmaid of the Lord; be it unto me according to thy word," thereby uniting the sublimest faith and prayer in one. And we then only truly believe God's promise when we take it and turn it into a petition. Let us profit, then, from such examples; and when we come upon some gracious word, let us pause over it, and transmute it into supplication. Is it written "I, even I, am he that blotteth out thy transgressions for mine own sake, and will not remember thy sins," let us while we read make this response: "For thy name's sake, O Lord, pardon mine iniquity, for it is great." Is it written, "A new heart also will I give you, and a new spirit will I put within you," let us while we read make this request: "Create in me a clean heart, O God; and renew a right spirit within me." Is it written, "I will put my Spirit within you?" let us while we read raise this supplication: "Be it unto me according to thy word." But why need I enlarge? You can scarcely read a page of the Scriptures without coming upon some exceeding great and precious promise; be it yours, therefore, to pause over each, and let your faith in it blossom into a prayer for it. This will be the true responsive reading of the sacred Scriptures, wherein there shall be not merely the answering of voice to voice among men, but the responding of your heart to God. Happy they in whose souls there is thus a continually recurring amen to the benedictions of the Lord!

In the chapter which follows God's message to David through Nathan, and the account of David's reception of it, we have a general summary of the wars of David, not presented in the order in which they occurred, but gathered up into one aggregate account; and at the close we have an enumeration of the members of what in modern phrase would be called his cabinet. Both of these, however, we shall meanwhile omit, reserving them for our next discourse, which shall be devoted to an account of the national administration of David. And we conclude now with a brief reference to his treatment of Mephibosheth, the son of Jonathan.

Considering the devoted friendship between David and Jonathan, and the solemn league into which they entered with each other, we are apt to think that David was very tardy in seeking to carry out the weighty obligations under which he lay. And if he had been really aware that a son of Jonathan was in existence, we should have been disposed to blame him very much for neglecting the child of his noble and disinterested friend; but, from what appears in the narrative here, taken in connection with the incidents of Mephibosheth's early life, we are led to conclude that he was ignorant of his existence up till the time when he made the inquiry of which an account is here given. Referring to the fourth chapter of 2d Samuel, fourth verse, we learn that when Jonathan was slain Mephibosheth was only five years old. Now, for six years before that date David had not been at the court of Saul. Probably, therefore, he had never heard of the birth of Jonathan's son, and the events which occurred after the battle of Gilboa were of such a nature as to render it all but impossible for him to hear much concerning Mephibosheth. He was living at Gibeah with his nurse when news of the death of his father arrived. When she heard what had happened, she hastened to take him to a place of safety; but, in her trepidation, she either let him fall, or stumbled and fell with him, and in consequence of the injuries which he thus received he was a cripple for life. After his escape from Gibeah he was taken to the other side of the

Jordan, and brought up in the house of Machir, at Lo-debar, in Gilead, where he was discovered by Ziba, a servant of the house of Saul, whom David employed for the purpose of bringing him to court. When Mephibosheth came to Jerusalem, David caused him to be reinstated in the family inheritance of Saul, and, committing its management to Ziba as steward, with instructions to bring the returns at stated times to his master, he retained Mephibosheth himself at Jerusalem, and reserved for him a place of honor at his own table. Not every king would thus have honored the heir of the dynasty which he had dispossessed; but David remembered Jonathan and believed God. The memory of his former friend bound him to Mephibosheth; and his belief in the promise of God through Nathan kept him from all fear of being dispossessed of his throne.

In bringing our review of this important portion of the sacred narrative to a close, I restrict myself to one particular line of remark. We have seen that David was himself a prophecy of Christ. It follows from that, therefore, that the Temple which he so desired to build is a prophecy of the Church. With all its grandeur under Solomon, that stately building was, after all, only a type of that more glorious spiritual fabric which is "built upon the foundation of the apostles and prophets, Jesus Christ himself being the chief cornerstone, in whom all the building, fitly framed together, groweth into an holy temple in the Lord." Now, in the erection of this living temple we may all take part. When by faith in Jesus Christ we become united to him, and receive the Holy Spirit into our hearts, we, as it were, build ourselves, or, in another aspect of it, are built by God, as living stones into that glorious edifice which Jehovah through the ages is rearing for his own eternal abode. When, again, by our instrumentality, either directly in the efforts which we put forth at home, or indirectly through the labors of those whom we sustain abroad, we work for the conversion of others, we are engaged as under-builders on the same spiritual edifice. David would have counted it the highest privilege of his life if he had been permitted to build the Temple on Moriah; and even after the prohibition came by the mouth of Nathan, it was the joy of his latter years to collect materials wherewith Solomon, his son, might raise a house worthy of Jehovah's worship. Nay, more, in the days of Solomon himself, after the gorgeous structure had been raised, every one who had done any thing, however small, in the way of helping on its erection, was invested with a peculiar honor in the eyes of his fellow-countrymen. As the Psalm expresses it: "A man was famous according as he had lifted axes upon the thick trees." But a higher privilege, and a more lasting renown, will be the portion of him who assists in the most humble capacity in the uprearing of that Church which is to be "for a habitation of God through the Spirit." "They that be wise shall shine as the brightness of the firmament, and they that turn many to righteousness as the stars for ever and ever." Shall this honor, my hearer, be thine? What art thou doing now for the building of the spiritual temple of the Lord of Hosts? Let me beseech thee to build for eternity, by building here. Only beware how thou buildest, for "if any man build upon this foundation gold, silver, precious stones, wood, hay, stubble; every man's work shall be made manifest: for the day shall declare it, because it shall be revealed by fire; and the fire shall try every man's work of what sort it is." Remember this also, that if we would build acceptably at this temple, we must sacredly preserve our own holiness of heart and purity of life. It is recorded of Sir Christopher Wren, that, having heard that some of the workmen engaged in the erection of St. Paul's Cathedral, London, had been guilty of profane swearing, he caused it to be posted all round the works that if any one should be heard taking the name of

God in vain, he should be instantly dismissed; because he considered it an impious thing that any such practices should be indulged in by those who were building a house of God. But if so much care was taken by that great man, that those who were working on a material structure should hallow God's name on their lips, should not we who seek to build up the Church of Christ itself endeavor always to honor God in our hearts? They who are engaged in church work, or missionary effort, should be men of peace, of holiness, of love themselves; for if they are not distinguished by these characteristics, they will do more harm than good to others, and they will draw down punishment upon themselves; for "if any man defile the temple of God, him shall God destroy." Here, then, is the order of our exhortations: first build your own selves into this temple by faith in Jesus Christ; thereafter seek to build others into it also by your efforts, your contributions, and your prayers; and all the while that you are working thus, see that ye keep yourselves unspotted from the world, "for the temple of God is holy, which temple are ye. Know ye not that your bodies are the members of Christ? Shall ye, then, take the members of Christ and make them instruments of uncleanness? God forbid! Know ye not that your body is the temple of the Holy Ghost which is in you, which ye have of God, and ye are not your own? for ye are bought with a price: therefore glorify God in your body, and in your spirit, which are God's."

## XIV.

### DAVID'S ADMINISTRATION.

2 SAMUEL viii., 15.

IN the minds of most readers of the Bible, the name of David, king of Israel, is associated mainly with military prowess, poetic genius, and personal piety; and only on the rarest occasions do we hear any reference made to his administrative ability. Yet in this last quality he was, at least, as remarkable as in any one of the others which we have named; and great injustice is done to him if we leave out of view the eminent services which he rendered to his country by the exercise of his governmental and organizing faculties. It has happened thus with the son of Jesse, as with many others, that the showier and more dashing talents which he possessed have eclipsed, or cast into the shade, his other less ostentatious, but, in their own places, equally valuable characteristics. It may help us, therefore, to a correct estimate of his public and official career, as well as prove in itself a most interesting study, if we devote a short while to an inquiry into the manner in which he arranged and administered the affairs of the nation. In prosecuting our investigations, we shall avail ourselves of the details which are very fully given in various portions of the books of Samuel, the Kings, and the Chronicles, acknowledging our obligations throughout to the labors of Dean Stanley, Dr. Blaikie, Dr. Kitto, and others, in this department; and we shall fail to produce in your minds the conviction at which we have ourselves arrived, if we do not lead you to conclude that more than Charlemagne did for Europe, or Alfred for England, David accomplished for the tribes of Israel.

We shall commence our review by setting before you the military organization of the country. This may be divided into three branches: first, the regular standing army; second, the king's own body-guard; and, third, the order of military knighthood, if so we may call it, which he established at his court. As regards the regular army, we find that there were in the land two hundred and eighty-eight thousand men enrolled as soldiers. These unitedly composed what was called the host. Now there were two evils to be guarded against in reference to this large body of troops. On the one hand, the maintenance of an army of such magnitude, if it had been kept constantly under arms, would have seriously drained the resources of the country, both by the positive expense which would have been incurred in supporting it, and by the withdrawal of so many able-bodied men from those agricultural pursuits, on the fruits of which the people mainly depended. On the other hand, if all these soldiers had been called out at one time, and brought to one central place for drill, the outlying boundaries of the land would have been left, for the mean while, undefended. But both of these dangers were obviated by the plan which David adopted, and of which a minute account is given in 1 Chronicles xxvii., where we have a register of "the children of Israel after their number—to wit, the chief fathers and captains of thousands and hundreds, and their officers that served the king in any matter of the courses, which came in and went out month by month throughout all the months of the year, of every course were twenty-and-four thousand." From this account it appears that the army was divided into twelve portions, each of which had its own month of service. Over each of those divisions, as we may call them, there was one general officer, under whom were captains of thousands, whose bands, again, were subdivided into hundreds, each of which was led by an officer, corresponding somewhat to the

## David's Administration.

Roman centurion of after days. Over the host as commander-in-chief was Joab, the son of Zeruiah.

In addition to this national army, there was the king's body-guard, generally supposed to be identical with those who in 2 Samuel viii., 18, are styled the Cherethites and the Pelethites. Dean Stanley and others are of opinion that those who composed this royal brigade (equivalent almost to what, in Great Britain, are denominated the household troops), were mostly foreigners; and they remind us of the analogous instances of the Swiss Guard, who stood so true to Louis XVI. at the French Revolution, and the guard of honor of the Pope at the present day. But there does not appear to me to be sufficient reason for adopting such a view, since the commander-in-chief of these troops was Benaiah, the son of Jehoiada, of the family of the priests; and so far as we can discover from the record, David, at this time at least, and up to the era of his great transgression, was secure in the affection and confidence of his subjects, and did not need the adventitious and, to his people, almost insulting aid of strangers.

Besides these two kinds of forces, and as furnishing a reward of honor for those who had distinguished themselves in any signal manner, David appears to have founded a military order analogous to that of knighthood in more recent times. The members of this body are called "worthies," or "mighty men," and a list of them, together with a rehearsal of some of their most illustrious deeds, is given in 2 Samuel xxiii., and 1 Chronicles xi. Stanley, following in this instance the German author Ewald, attributes the special form which this order took, to the circumstances of David, when he was in the cave of Adullam. He says that, as there were six hundred men in the hold, that number was preserved as the limit to which the order was restricted. It became subdivided into three large bands of two hundred each, and thirty small bands of twenty each. The small bands were commanded by thirty officers, one for each band, and these officers formed the thirty worthies, or mighty men; and the three large bands were commanded by three officers, who together formed the three; while the whole were under one chief, the captain of the mighty men. This reckoning, however, gives only thirty-four as the total of the worthies, whereas in 2 Samuel xxiii. the aggregate number is thirty-seven. Moreover, there seems to be a distinction in the same chapter between the first three and another three, who, while very honorable, had not attained to the valor of the first; and for this distinction the subdivision of Stanley fails to find a place. Perhaps, therefore, assuming the basis of six hundred to be correct, we may modify Ewald's arrangement thus, so as to bring it into harmony with the number thirty-seven. The six hundred, we may suppose, were divided into six bands of one hundred, as well as into twenty of thirty each. Over the senior portion of the band, amounting to three companies of one hundred each, there were the first three; over the junior portion of the band, composed of other three companies of one hundred each, were the second three; and then, over all, there was the captain of the mighties, who was Jashobeam, the Hachmonite. The captain of each band formed one of the band, and must be reckoned with it in making up the numbers.

The deeds of the worthies, specified in the chapters to which I have been referring, are mostly such as in a rude and barbarous age are rewarded by badges of distinction; and those who sneer at the record of them here must bear in mind that even in this boasted age, and in countries which claim to be enlightened, the honors of knighthood and the peerage are frequently bestowed upon no higher grounds. The day has not yet fully arrived for the recognition of the nobility of holiness and love. True, in these latter years we

## DAVID'S ADMINISTRATION.

may have made some advancement toward it, but it is as yet in Messiah's kingdom alone that distinction is conferred for works of faith, and holiness, and love. This is the grand foundation-difference between the typical kingdom of David and that of Christ, which is its antetype; and we must never allow ourselves to lose sight of it while we are considering either the one or the other. David's kingdom was founded and maintained by military power, and it was fitting, therefore, that its honors should be bestowed on martial heroes for daring deeds upon the field of battle. Christ's kingdom is founded on righteousness and love, and to those who cry to him for honor he makes this reply, pointing to Gethsemane and Calvary the while: "Are ye able to drink of the cup that I shall drink of, and to be baptized with the baptism that I am baptized with?" But of this more anon.

We pass now to the civil administration of the son of Jesse; and here it will appear that he exerted himself most earnestly to improve the courts of justice, the educational institutions, the domestic comfort, and the commercial prosperity of the country. He gave new vitality to the old tribal arrangements; for (as we learn from 1 Chronicles xxvii.), he set thirteen princes over as many different districts. What the judicial functions of these princes exactly were does not appear, but probably they corresponded very nearly to those of the lord lieutenants of counties in Great Britain, with this difference, that they belonged, *ex officio*, to the general council or senate of the nation, which was summoned on all occasions of emergency or importance. Thus, when David formally handed over the crown to Solomon, we read (1 Chronicles xxviii., 1) that he assembled all the princes of Israel. Over and above these princes, he distributed (1 Chronicles xxiii., 4) six thousand Levites over the land as officers and judges. Of these nearly one-half were settled among the tribes east of the Jordan, perhaps because.

from their distance from the seat of government, these tribes were more in need of superintendence than the rest. They were sent out, as we read, "for every matter pertaining to God and the king;" but it would be a mistake to suppose that they had to do merely with judicial trials. The Levites generally were the health officers of the nation. They would, therefore, look after all sanitary arrangements, and take order that the minute injunctions of the Mosaic law in this department were fully obeyed. They had to do, also, with the healing art, and formed, in fact, a medical board over the land; while again, if we bear in mind that the people were by them to be made acquainted with the law of their God, and that their sacred books were well-nigh the only books at that time in existence among them, we may not be far wrong in regarding these Levites, or a portion of them, as set over the education of the community, and responsible for the department of public instruction. In any case, I think there is good warrant for the assertion of Dr. Blaikie, when he says that "infinitely more was done for the education and enlightenment of the people than was ever attempted or dreamed of in any Eastern country. It is nowhere said whether Samuel's schools received a special share of attention; but the deep interest David must have taken in Samuel's plans, and his early acquaintance with their blessed effects, leave little room to doubt that these institutions were carefully fostered, and owed to David a share of that vitality which they continued to exhibit in the days of Elijah and Elisha."* In addition to what this writer has advanced, I would remark that the pre-eminence attained by Solomon in all the branches of education is, to my mind, an evidence of the advanced condition of the nation generally

---

\* Blaikie's "David, King of Israel: the Divine Plan, and Lessons of his Life," p. 201.

## DAVID'S ADMINISTRATION.

in this department; since, unless a good foundation of elementary knowledge had been imparted to the youth of the land as a whole, it is hardly possible to account for the appearance of such a man as Solomon in that age. No doubt he was endowed with preternatural wisdom. But this, as is usual in the economy of Providence, would be ingrafted upon a high degree of ordinary culture; and the question forces itself upon the historical student, Who were his tutors, and who taught them? You do not find the loftiest mountains rising isolatedly from the centre of some great plain. The highest summits are never solitary peaks. They belong usually to some great chain, and are merely the loftiest elevations in a country, the general character of which is mountainous; and in the same way the greatest scholars appear, not among an ignorant people, but among those who have a high average of education, and in countries where a good substratum of instruction is enjoyed even by the common average of the community. The historian, Froude, has put this thought admirably when he says, "No great general ever arose out of a nation of cowards; no great statesman or philosopher out of a nation of fools; no great artist out of a nation of materialists; no great dramatist, except when the drama was the passion of the people. Greatness is never more than the highest degree of an excellence which prevails widely round it, and forms the environment in which it grows."* Now, if these views be correct, the rise of Solomon, who was so conspicuous for his intellectual culture and scientific attainments, may be regarded as a proof that in the reign of David, and more particularly, perhaps, in the zenith of his administration, education was extensively diffused, and earnestly fostered by him among the tribes.

But David did much, also, to promote the domestic com-

---

* "History of England," vol. i., p. 74.

fort of the people. It was said of Augustus that he found Rome brick, and that he left it marble; and a similar testimony as to Paris was borne to the late Emperor of the French, by all who knew that capital as it was before he so transformed and beautified it. Something of the same kind has to be said also of David. Up till his time, the inhabitants of Canaan dwelt in places which might perhaps be better called huts than houses. But when he took possession of Jerusalem, he not only strengthened its fortifications, but he also built the city of David, and, conspicuous therein, a stately palace for himself; nay, he introduced from Tyre artificers in wood, and brass, and stone, and so adorned his capital that men could sing concerning it, "Beautiful for situation, the joy of the whole earth, is mount Zion, on the sides of the north, the city of the great King." "Walk about Zion, and go round about her: tell the towers thereof. Mark ye well her bulwarks, consider her palaces; that ye may tell it to the generation following."

But besides the influence of all this on domestic architecture, not in Jerusalem alone, but over the whole country, the prosecution of such labors tended largely to develop commerce. The land over which he ruled was principally pastoral and agricultural. It produced more food than the population needed. But by the introduction of builders from Tyre, and the importation of timber from Lebanon, there was furnished an outlet for their superfluous provisions, while the general comfort of the people was advanced. This kind of trade prepared the way for the farther development of commerce under Solomon, whose ships went to India, and, as there is reason to believe, also to China; while it knit the Hirams and their successors in close alliance to David and his sons, and inaugurated an interchange of commercial commodities between Jerusalem and Tyre, which we find in existence even in the days of the Christian apostles.* Then

---

* See Acts xii . 20.

again, on the principle of letting nothing be lost, David seems to have put the waste lands under extensive cultivation. He had, as we learn from 1 Chronicles xxvii., 25, "storehouses in the fields, in the cities, and in the villages, and in the castles;" he had a regular staff of men who did "the work of the field for the tillage of the ground." He had superintendents over the vineyards and wine-cellars, and over the olive and sycamore trees, together with the oil which they produced. There were men over the herds in Sharon and in the valleys of Shaphat, as well as over the camels and asses. Thus, as Blaikie has remarked, "Many a hill, under his able management, would become encircled with vine-clad terraces, and many a plain formerly abandoned to sterility would rejoice and blossom as the rose. The king's example, too, spreading to smaller proprietors, now blessed with peace and freedom, would effect a revolution in the agriculture of the land."* Hence the military glory of David's life was not its highest distinction, and we may warrantably enough regard him as the inaugurator of an internal civil administration which, for thoroughness and efficiency, surpassed every thing which up to his day any country on the face of the earth, with the single exception of Egypt, had enjoyed.

It is time, however, that we looked to the arrangements which David made in ecclesiastical matters; but before we enumerate them, we must have a clear idea of the position in which he stood. He was not merely the king. He was, at the same time, a prophet as really as either Gad or Nathan; and as we saw, at the great festival of the bringing up of the ark, he arrayed himself in the linen ephod of the priests, and took part in the offering of sacrifice. Hence, while the ultimate reference of the 110th Psalm is undeniably to the Mes-

---

* Blaikie's "David, King of Israel: the Divine Plan, and Lessons of his Life." p. 202.

siah, its primary application may well enough have been to David, who was in some sense a second Melchizedek — a priest among kings, and a king among priests. It was, therefore, by virtue of the union of these three offices in himself, that he was entitled to take upon him the regulation of the Tabernacle service, and the setting in order of those things which in the days of Saul had been too generally neglected, and allowed to fall into the greatest confusion. As we saw before, the seat of the Tabernacle was at Nob, or perhaps (as an incidental allusion in 1 Chronicles xvi., 39, would seem to imply) at Gibeon; but the ark, which was the glory of the Tabernacle, was not there. That had been for a long time at Kirjath-jearim; but David brought it to Jerusalem, thereby making that city the ecclesiastical as well as judicial centre of the land. He did not, however, suppress the services at the Tabernacle, but left Zadok to superintend them, continuing him as co-ordinate priest by the side of Abiathar, and allowing the seat of the ancient Tabernacle to sink by degrees into the obscurity which ultimately enveloped it. While, however, he did not positively demolish the former Tabernacle, he devoted special attention to the arrangement of the services in the new sacred tent at Jerusalem. These, of course, had to be performed by the priests and Levites. The special functions of the former were to offer sacrifices, to burn incense, and to change the shew-bread; the peculiar duties of the latter were to perform the lower office of attending to the outward fabric, and, in general, to do all that was required to make the public worship of God excellent in character, decorous in arrangement, and reverent in spirit. But the Levites had now so increased in numbers, and there were so many belonging to the priestly family of Aaron, that it was needful to make some orderly division of the work among them.

In seeking to meet this necessity, David adopted a plan

## DAVID'S ADMINISTRATION.

similar to that which he had introduced into the army, and arranged the priests into twenty-four courses, giving to each its order by lot; and we find that this arrangement continued in the days of Zacharias, the father of John the Baptist. "Each course served a week alternately, under a subordinate prefect; and in the time of Zacharias, at least, the duties of each individual seem to have been determined by lot; but all attended at the great festivals."* Of the Levites, who numbered thirty-eight thousand men of thirty years old and upward, six thousand were, as we have already seen, told off as officers and judges, and allocated to different districts over the land; twenty-four thousand were appointed to set forward the work of the Lord, and four thousand were porters; while the remaining four thousand were appointed to praise the Lord, with the accompaniment of instruments of music. These, however, were not all ordinarily needed at one and the same time, so he divided them also into courses, of which we have a minute account in 1 Chronicles xxiii.; and there also we have the following most interesting record of his motive in all this proceeding (verses 25–32): "For David said, The Lord God of Israel hath given rest unto his people, that they may dwell in Jerusalem forever: and also unto the Levites: they shall no more carry the tabernacle, nor any vessels of it for the service thereof. For by the last words of David the Levites were numbered from twenty years old and above: because their office was to wait on the sons of Aaron for the service of the house of the Lord, in the courts, and in the chambers, and in the purifying of all holy things, and the work of the service of the house of God; both for the shew-bread, and for the fine flour for meat-offering, and for the unleavened cakes, and for that which is baked in the pan, and for that which is fried, and for all

---

* Kitto's "Cyclopædia," article PRIEST.

manner of measure and size; and to stand every morning to thank and praise the Lord, and likewise at even; and to offer all burnt-sacrifices unto the Lord in the sabbaths, in the new moons, and on the set feasts, by number, according to the order commanded unto them, continually before the Lord: and that they should keep the charge of the tabernacle of the congregation, and the charge of the holy place, and the charge of the sons of Aaron their brethren, in the service of the house of the Lord."

The arrangements for the musical part of the service were particularly elaborate, and the twenty-fifth chapter of 1 Chronicles is devoted to their enumeration. The prime leaders—the first three—were Asaph, Heman, and Jeduthun; and under these—each superintended by a son of one or other of them, as the lot appointed—were twenty-four bands of twelve each, who are described as "instructed in the songs of the Lord, and cunning in them." Nay, more, there were, besides these, three daughters of Heman, who, like their brothers, were skilled in the psaltery, the cymbal, and the harp. Under these twenty-four bands of twelve each, were arranged twenty-four courses, taken by lot from the four thousand. Thus, as a regular thing, only a twenty-fourth part of these musicians would be about the Tabernacle service at one time; but as they all came in alternate courses, the efficiency of each course would be maintained; so that on great occasions—as, for example, at the annual national festivals—when they were all engaged, the effect produced must have been at once most artistic and overpowering.

Two things, however, have to be borne in mind about these musical services. The first is that they were performed in the open air. The court of the Tabernacle, as afterward of the Temple, had no covering overhead. Hence the high service of a Jewish festival-day would resemble nothing so much as an oratorio in the open air, when the mingled harmony of human voices and instruments of music must have filled the Valley of Jehoshaphat, and floated, in subdued and solemn tones, over the slopes of Olivet. The second thing about these services is, that only the Levites were authorized to take part in them. Praise, as I have formerly remarked, was regarded as a sacrifice to God, just as really as the meat-offering and drink-offering, and only those who belonged to the holy tribe of Levi were competent to offer it. They presented it in the stead of the people, and as their consecrated representatives. Now this vicarious character of the Tabernacle praise is that which has been done away in the Gospel Church; for, through faith in Jesus Christ, we are all priests and Levites, consecrated, by the anointing of the Holy Ghost, for the offering of spiritual sacrifices. Hence, says Peter, "Ye are a royal priesthood, a holy nation, a peculiar people, that ye should show forth the praises of Him, who hath called you out of darkness into his marvelous light;" and to the same effect the author of the Epistle to the Hebrews has said, "By him, therefore, let us offer the sacrifice of praise to God continually, that is, the fruit of our lips, giving thanks to his name." The little child may join in the hymn now, as well as the trained singer, provided only he have a loving and believing heart, and there is no restriction of any part of worship in the Church of Christ to any order or class of men in it. But if while praise was thus vicarious, it was deemed of so much importance, and so much attention was devoted to the attainment of excellence in it, ought we to allow it to sink into a subordinate position, now that it is the common privilege of all believers? Why should not all our Christian congregations become as skillful in the rendering of "the songs of the Lord" as these four thousand Levites were? Nay, may not every congregation be instructed by the method of organization which David here inaugurated? What is to hinder us, for example, from dividing ourselves as a church into twelve, or, say, twenty-four musical courses, under appropriate leaders, each course in rotation being responsible for the leading of psalmody for a certain time, and all maintaining a constant aggregate weekly practice, so that on the Lord's Day, as we gather together here, we shall be just one well-trained and thoroughly organized choir, raising such a chorus of jubilant praise as shall be, in some degree, worthy of the priceless blessings for which we give God thanks? What is to hinder this? again I ask. We want, in the first place, some organizing David, who shall consecrate himself to this work as thoroughly as the King of Israel did of old. But we want even more than that, the spirit of Levitical consecration in the heart of every worshiper. Ah! if we but remembered that, as Christians, we are anointed by God's Spirit for his peculiar service, and if we did only faintly realize that the praise of the sanctuary was a portion of that service to which we have been thus set apart, we should be more willing to give the time and attention which are needful to qualify ourselves for it. We have fallen into the grievous mistake of supposing that the music of the sanctuary is for human ears, more than for the ear of God; and in seeking to please men by it, we have allowed devotion almost to disappear from it. Nay, we have thereby come even to displease men by it; for it is here, as in so many other things, they who seek human appreciation and applause as the main end invariably, in the long run, lose that which they so desired; while they, who think mainly and especially of doing honor to God, do at the last receive also the respect of men. When, in our praise, we can merge all thought of self in the eager, earnest effort to please God; when, feeling that we are singing to God, we try to give him of our best; then, also, the ears of men will be turned toward us, and the hymns of the service will, because they are the sincere expression of our hearts, produce the most salutary impressions on those who hear them, and will be as much a means of edification and conversion as the prayers or the discourse. The life of the good man, who is thinking only of serving God, has often been the means of converting a soul; and the song of a devout Christian, who has been singing only to give expression to his own feelings, has not unfrequently carried the truth to the soul of him who heard it. When, therefore, we have such singing in our churches, we shall hear people say, "I was converted by the singing of such and such a hymn," just as often as we shall have them saying, "I was awakened by such and such a sermon " for, as the holy Herbert has said,

> "A verse may find him who a sermon flies,
> And turn delight into a sacrifice."

I have dwelt more largely on David's administration, military, civil, and ecclesiastical, than may appear to you to have been either necessary or profitable; but my apology must be, that I wished in a single discourse to dispose of the whole matter, so that we may not require to turn aside from other and more important things to refer to it again. For the same reason, let me in one sentence epitomize the victories of David as they are referred to in the eighth chapter of 2 Samuel. They were over the Philistines, over the Moabites, over the King of Zobah, in the direction of the river Euphrates, a campaign in which he encountered the Syrians, and took and garrisoned Damascus. He likewise grappled with and overcame the Ammonites, because of a deliberate insult which they offered to his ambassadors, whom he sent on a visit of condolence to the king after the death of his father. He also overcame the Amalekites, and took and garrisoned Edom. To the war with the Ammonites we shall have occasion to refer again, when we treat of the darkest spot in David's history; meanwhile let it be noted that the 60th Psalm was probably written during the war with Edom, when some reverse had been sustained; and perhaps we do not err if we date the 20th Psalm at this warlike era of David's life. By these victories he greatly extended the boundaries of the land, while in Jerusalem he strengthened himself by gathering around him, as the members of his cabinet, the wisest and most eminent men of the nation.

I close with two practical considerations suggested by this whole subject.

Let us see here the intimate connection between religion, and the intellectual enlightenment and social prosperity of a nation. David was a man of God, eagerly anxious in all things to know the Divine will and do it. He regarded his position on the throne as a trust which had been given to him, for the welfare of his people and for the glory of Jehovah; and the result of his conscientious endeavors to act up to his responsibilities was that educational, social, and religious regeneration which to-night we have been considering. But this is no solitary instance. Similar results followed the religious earnestness of Hezekiah and Josiah, in Old Testament ages; and in modern times, the nations which have been blessed with Christian rulers have ever led the van in all the nobler characteristics of civilization and prosperity. When an African prince sent a courteous message to the Queen of England, asking, "What is the secret of England's greatness?" she sent him a copy of the sacred Scriptures, with the reply, "This is the secret of England's greatness." And if one should put a similar question in regard to this great republic, he might be correctly answered in a similar manner; for the character of the Pilgrim Fathers, which was made by their faith in the Bible, and their devotion to the Lord Jesus Christ, has stamped itself indelibly on this Western land; yea, as it seems to me, in spite of certain recent occurrences, it is to-day more conspicuous in the regulation of national affairs than ever. But much yet remains to be accomplished; and if we would have a prosperity worthy of the name, it must, as in the case of Israel under David, be rooted in religion. It may seem strange, indeed, that in a republic I should seek to enforce this lesson from the character of a king in a monarchy; but when you regard it rightly, the practical point of my remarks will only become the more sharp and incisive, for here the sovereign is the people; and so their character is even more intimately related to the country's prosperity than is that of a king in a monarchy. They give the tone to their representatives; and as water can not rise above its level, so the morality and patriotism of the members of our Legislatures and Congress will not be above that of the people who elect them. If we wish to purge away all remaining corruptions, and to take a place among the nations which shall be at once pure and permanent, we must seek to bring the sovereign people under the influence of the religion of Jesus. This is the salt which will at once purify and preserve the State. Hence, while utterly repudiating all sympathy with what is called a national establishment of religion, we ought as patriots, no less than as Christians, to seek to have the people thoroughly Christianized. The Gospel is the grand reformer. The home missionary on our frontier, the city missionary in our streets and lanes, the humble Christian worker in all departments of benevolent activity, will do more, in the long run, to purify our legislatures than any number of political agitators; for while the latter are seeking merely to destroy evils, the former are laboring to form character, as that alone can be formed to holiness and integrity, by trust in God and obedience to Jesus Christ. No nation, monarchical or republican, has ever stood, unless it has been founded on the moral excellence of the people. The Roman republic became an easy prey to the ambitious grasp of Cæsar, when the virtues of its ancient worthies gave place to luxury, lasciviousness, and dishonesty; and the repeated failures of France in modern times to rise to the responsibility of self-government have been due to the absence among the people of those solid qualities which religion fosters, and the presence in the midst of them of every vilest sort of abomination. Let us be instructed by such melancholy instances, and improve the opportunity which God has given us, by seeking to form the character of the people on the basis of the Word of God. No law upon the statute-book, no formal insertion of the name of Deity in the Constitution, will make a nation Christian; nothing can do that but the Christianity of the people themselves; and every man who is laboring to make the masses Christian is in the highest and the purest sense a patriot. Let each citizen-king be animated with the public-spiritedness and deep religious fervor which the Gospel produces; and then "all nations shall call us blessed, for we shall be a delightsome land."

Finally: let us take note of the principle on which the honors of the kingdom of Christ are distributed, as distinguished from that on which David proceeded, in the founding of his order of merit. The men whom he exalted were warriors, who had done daring deeds upon the field of battle. Of one it is told that "he slew eight hundred at one time;" of another it is said that "he smote the Philistines until his hand was weary, and clave unto his sword;" of another, that "he lifted up his spear against three hundred, and slew them." Nor would I seek to disparage such deeds; for when war becomes a necessity, as it sometimes does, every man's heart glows with admiration of such dauntless courage. But there is a nobler heroism even than that—the heroism of love; and this it is that Jesus evermore delights to honor. To "drink of his cup," and to be "baptized with his baptism," is the road to this renown, and it is to be won, not by destroying men's lives, but by saving them, if need be, even by the sacrifice of our own. The field on which this heroism is to be shown is that of daily life, and the insignia of this knighthood—not withering and perishable like those of earth, but enduring as immortality itself—may be gained even by the lowliest follower of the Lamb. He who in his own character shall approximate the nearest to the Lord, he who, in his self-sacrificing devotion to the salvation of men, shall come the closest to the death of Christ upon the cross, shall be the greatest; while the humble believer who gives a cup of cold water to a disciple in the name of a disciple shall in no wise be forgotten. This is the law of the kingdom, as sanctioned and illustrated by the example of the King himself.

> "For He before whose sceptre
>   The nations rise or fall,
> Who gives no least commandment
>   But come to pass it shall,
> Said that he who would be greatest
>   Should be servant unto all.
>
> "And in conflict with the evils
>   Which his bright creation mars,
> Laid he not aside the sceptre
>   Which can reach to all the stars?
> Of the service which he rendered—
>   See on his hand the scars!"

Forth, then, my hearers, and seek this deathless honor. You may find opportunities of winning it, at every corner of the streets, in every home, in any place. Lift up the fallen; comfort the mourner; relieve the destitute; remember the forgotten; nurse the sick; wipe the death-damp from the brow of the sufferer in his last agony; tell the ignorant of Jesus, and sacrifice yourself, if need be, for the good of others. So shall you win a place in the peerage of the skies, and obtain honorable mention among the worthies of the celestial kingdom.

## XV.

### *THE GREAT TRANSGRESSION.*

#### 2 SAMUEL xi., 27.

NOT without the deepest reluctance do I compel myself to-night to make public allusion to the great blemish of David's career. Willingly would I have passed it over in silence, or attempted, like Noah's sons, to go backward and drop over it the mantle of concealment. But to have done that would only have been to leave out of the Psalmist's history its most solemn lesson, while it would have rendered all but unintelligible to you the appalling calamities that came upon him in his later days. Hence, I can see no way of evading the consideration of this painful subject, and my earnest prayer is that the God of purity may so guide me that I shall speak only words of wisdom.

The details of the matter are so fully given in the narrative, that I need not enter upon them. I shall, therefore, keeping our own spiritual profit in view, endeavor to set before you the precursors of David's fall, the aggravations of his sin, the penitence he manifested, the forgiveness he received, and the consequences which flowed from his iniquity.

Let us look, first, at the precursors of David's fall. You never find in a man's history such a sin as this was, without discovering that certain things have gone before which help to explain its commission. You will generally discover that a variety of circumstances combined to put him into a state of heart which was, if I may so express it, just ready for receiving and yielding to the temptation by which he was assailed. At another time the evil suggestion would have been at once repelled; but then, in consequence of certain foregoing things, he had so weakened himself, that he yielded almost without a struggle. This, at least, appears to have been the case with David; and it may greatly help to stir us up to watchfulness, if we can find out how such a man as he undoubtedly was, came to fall so easy a prey to the great Tempter.

Now, in searching for an answer to this inquiry, let us note, in the first place, that for a long course of years he had enjoyed, virtually, unbroken prosperity. Ever since he had come to the throne of united Israel, things seem to have gone well with him. He had hardly known what it was, as a warrior, to suffer a defeat; or, as a monarch, to endure unpopularity and the antagonism of his people. But all this was highly dangerous to him; for the influence of such an experience, even on the best of men, is to weaken their spiritual character, and make them more tolerant of evil both in themselves and others. Like Moab, David during these years had not been "emptied from vessel to vessel," and so he had "settled upon his lees." "Because he had no changes," his will became more feeble, his conscience weaker, and his whole nature less sensitive to sin.

Again, let it be observed that this sad episode occurred during a period of idleness. The army, with which he should have been, was at Rabbah, seeking to consummate the destruction of Ammon, which in a former campaign had been begun; "but David tarried still at Jerusalem." This was hardly like the warrior-king. It seemed almost as if effeminacy was beginning in him, and he was preferring, for no good reason which one can see, the luxury of the palace to the hardship and peril of the camp. Besides this, in the absence of his mighty men, he would be deprived of his usual companions, and left very much to himself. Hence it is natural to suppose that he was living, just then, an aimless, idle, and luxurious life, and was consequently peculiarly open to the suggestions of the adversary. Satan tempts other men; but the idle man tempts Satan, and very soon the evil one finds him something to do.

Once more let it be noted, that when at such a time Satan comes to a man, he makes his appeal to that particular part of his nature where passion is strongest and principle is weakest. Now in David what that was might be very easily discovered. From an early period of his career, he had been especially susceptible in the very matter in which now he fell. This is evident from his marriage of Abigail, and also from the great latitude which he allowed himself, after his settlement in Jerusalem, in respect to his harem. Polygamy, though not forbidden by the Mosaic law, was regulated and discouraged; but David proceeded as if it had been a perfectly warrantable and legitimate thing, and this conduct on his part undoubtedly tended to weaken his impression of the sanctity of marriage. That sense of delicacy and chastity, which has such a purifying and preserving influence on the life, could not flourish side by side with the polygamy in which he permitted himself; and so, though he thought not of it at the time, his taking of many wives to himself prepared the way for the revolting iniquity which he committed.*
Here, then, in the moral weakness which constant prosperity had created, in the opportunity which idleness afforded to temptation, and in the blunted sensibility which polygamy had superinduced, we see how David was so easily overcome.

---

* It is a strong verification of this view of the case that, as indeed Blaikie has remarked ("David, King of Israel: the Divine Plan, and Lessons of his Life," p. 145), while, in the confession of the 51st Psalm, "he specifies the sin of blood-guiltiness, and seems to have been overwhelmed with a sense of his meanness, injustice, and selfishness, there is no special allusion to the sin of adultery, and no special indication of that sin pressing heavy on his conscience."

But let us turn now to look at the aggravations by which this iniquity was accompanied. No one great sin ever stands alone. Either other sins of less apparent enormity have led up to it, or additional transgressions have been committed for the purpose of concealing it from public view. This last was true in the present instance; for, after having unsuccessfully attempted, in the meanest possible manner, to use Uriah himself for the purpose of hiding the consequences of his iniquity, David wrote that diabolical letter to Joab, which, though it was virtually Uriah's death-warrant, he asked the victim to deliver with his own hand. Alas! alas! "how are the mighty fallen!" Is this the man according to God's own heart? The time was when, in tenderness of conscience, he upbraided himself for cutting off the skirt of Saul's robe; but here he is compassing the destruction of one of the bravest and most devoted of his own officers. One might have thought that his very application to the cunning, treacherous, and unscrupulous Joab might have roused the torpid moral sense of David, for there was nothing in common between them, at least so far as David's better nature was concerned; but in the present instance, it was Joab's very wickedness that commended him to the king as the most fitting instrument for carrying out his infamous design. Nay, perhaps the fact that Joab was there may have suggested to him this particular method of getting rid of the Hittite, for "oft the sight of means to do ill deeds makes ill deeds done;" and so it may well have been that David is reaping here the pestilential fruits of his sparing Joab, when justice demanded his execution for the murder of Abner. In any case, here is David, whom God had honored and blessed, who had every thing that was necessary to comfort and happiness, and who had reached a time of life when he could no longer plead either the inexperience or the passion of youth, betrayed into all this terrible wickedness. The sin which was committed in the moment of passion prepares the way for the premeditated villainy of murder; for murder the slaughter of Uriah was, just as really as if David himself had stabbed him under the fifth rib. "Lord, what is man?" If this be true, who among us is safe if he should remit his watchfulness for but a single hour?

But it may be asked, How can you account for such enormous iniquity in such a man as we have seen that David was? To this I answer, that we may explain it by the absence for the time being of that restraining influence which his better nature was wont to exercise over his life. Passion had dethroned conscience; and then, owing to the intensity of his character, and the general greatness of the man, his sins became as much blacker than those of others as his good qualities were greater than theirs. In every good man there are still two natures striving for the mastery. "The flesh lusteth against the spirit, and the spirit against the flesh." The new nature is generally in the ascendant, but sometimes the old evil nature will re-assert its supremacy, and the effect of this temporary revolution will be determined by the temperament and characteristics of the individual. Now there are some men in whom every thing is on a large scale. When their good nature is uppermost, they overtop all others in holiness; but if, unhappily, they should be thrown off their guard, and the old man should gain the mastery, some dreadful wickedness may be expected. This is all the more likely to be the case if the quality of intensity be added to their greatness; for a man with such a temperament is never any thing by half. But it was just thus with David. He was a man of great intensity and pre-eminent energy. He was in every respect above ordinary men; and so when, for the time, the fleshly nature was the stronger within him, the sins which he committed were as much greater than those of common men, as in other cir cumstances his excellencies were nobler than theirs. We often make great mistakes in judging of the characters of others, because we ignore all these considerations; and many well-conducted persons among us get great credit for their good moral character, while the truth is that they are blameless not so much because they have higher-toned principle than others, as because they have feeble, timid natures, that are too cautious or too weak to let them go very far either into holiness or into sin. But David was not one of these. Every thing about him was intense; and hence, when he sinned, he did it in such a way as to make well-nigh the most hardened shudder. In all this, observe, I am not extenuating David's guilt. It is one thing to explain, it is another thing to excuse. A man of David's nature ought to be more peculiarly on his guard than other men. The express train, dashing along at furious speed, will do more mischief if it runs off the line than the slow-going horse-car in our city streets. Every one understands that; but every one demands, in consequence, that the driver of the one shall be proportionately more watchful than that of the other. Now with such a nature as David had, and knew that he had, he ought to have been supremely on his guard, while again the privileges which he had received from God rendered it both easy and practicable for him to be vigilant. To sum up all, then, taking David's nature as it is here set before us, I can perfectly well understand how, when he sinned, he sinned so terribly; while having regard to his privileges and position, his sin appears to be utterly inexcusable. Nothing can be said either in its vindication or extenuation. From first to last, it illustrates the climax of the apostle; and as we trace its course we call it "earthly, sensual, devilish." May the analysis of it at this time lead us to keep a good outlook, so that we may not go down upon the rocks on which he struck.

But now let us look briefly at his penitence. This was a long time in making its appearance. For at least a year, if not more, David carried on his conscience, unconfessed and unforgiven, the burden of these heinous iniquities. During that time Uriah had been slain; he had added Bath-sheba to the number of his wives; the child of guilt and shame had been born; and yet there was no token of sorrow or regret about the king; nay, perhaps, during that time he had even continued the formal observance of God's worship, both in the sacred tent and in his household; but there was no acknowledgment of his transgression. It must not be supposed, however, that he was quite happy. On the contrary, he must have been ill at ease, and there are not wanting indications that he was really miserable; for the campaign against Rabbah, of which we have the record in the twelfth chapter of 2 Samuel, must be held as having occurred before Nathan's visit to him; and in his conduct in connection with that siege there are evidences that there was some irritating thing within him which disturbed his usual magnanimity of disposition. Thus, in ordinary circumstances, when he received the message of Joab, asking him to come and take the city in person, the chivalrous spirit of the king would have prompted him to say that he who had so efficiently conducted the expedition thus far should not be robbed by him of the honor of bringing it to a successful issue; but as it was, the enterprise promised him an opportunity for a time of escaping from himself, and he probably went thither in the maddest of all attempts, that, namely, of outrunning a guilty conscience. Then, in his treatment of the fallen foe, we trace the haughty and vindictive spirit of one who was suffering from some hidden remorse. Nothing will make the temper so sour, or the heart so cruel, as a conscience ill at ease; hence, when we read that he put the people under saws and under harrows of iron, and made them to pass through the brick-kiln, we instinctively understand that the inner gnawing of remorse had made him for the time dead to the promptings of generosity, and disposed him to the commission of the most capricious cruelty. But this condition of heart was not to be perpetual. "The thing that David had done displeased the Lord;" and just because, in spite of all he had done, he was one of the Lord's own, he must be brought to a better mind. This was accomplished by the visit of Nathan, and the bold, manly application which he made to the king himself of the exquisite parable of the ewe lamb. On that parable we dare hardly presume to offer a remark. It is so finished in its beauty, so admirable in its construction, so perfect in its adaptation to the end which the divine messenger had in view, as to stand out incomparably the finest thing of its kind which the Old Testament contains. We can picture to ourselves the interview. Nathan, passing through the palace of cedar, leaves warriors and statesmen in the outer chamber, and, with a heart heavy with the burden of the Lord, enters the royal closet. He tells his touching story with simple pathos, his voice, mayhap, quivering with emotion, as he says, "It grew up together with him, and with his children; it did eat of his own meat, and drank of his own cup, and lay in his bosom, and was unto him as a daughter." Then, with an eye flashing with honest indignation, he speaks of the rich man's unfeeling covetousness and cruelty; and ere he has well ceased, the king, in the impatience of his anger, exclaims, "As the Lord liveth, the man that hath done this thing shall surely die: and he shall restore the lamb fourfold, because he did this thing, and because he had no pity." Then, with the faithful directness of a man of God, the prophet makes reply, "Thou art the man." In a moment David sees all that he had done; and as one article after another of Nathan's solemn indictment falls upon his ear, he acknowledges the truth of each, until, humbled to the very dust, he cries, in severest agony, "I have sinned against the Lord."

It may seem to some, that a penitence thus suddenly produced could be neither very deep nor very thorough. But to those who think thus, three things must be said.

First: an impression may be produced in a moment which will remain indelible. We have heard, for example, of one who, as he was traveling in an Alpine region at midnight, saw for an instant, by the brilliancy of a flash of lightning, that he was in such a position that another step would have been over a fearful precipice, and the effect upon him was that he started back and waited for the morning dawn. Now such a flash of lightning into the darkness of David's soul, this "Thou art the man," of Nathan's, was to him. It revealed to him, by its momentary brilliance, the full aggravation of his iniquity. He did not need or desire a second sight of it. That was enough to stir him up to hatred of his sin, and of himself.

But, second: we must, in connection with this narrative, read the Psalms to which David's penitence gave birth, namely, the 51st and the 32d; and if these are not the genuine utterances of a passionate sincerity, where shall we find that quality in any literature? Admirably has Chandler said of the 51st Psalm: "The heart appears in every line; and the bitter anguish of a wounded conscience discovers itself by the most natural and convincing symbols. Let but the Psalm be read without prejudice, and with a view only to collect the real sentiments expressed in it, and the disposition of heart that appears throughout the whole of it, and no man of candor, I am confident, will ever suspect that it was the dictate of hypocrisy, or could be penned from any other motive but a strong conviction of the heinousness of his offense, and the earnest desire of God's forgiveness, and being restrained from the commission of the like transgressions for

## THE GREAT TRANSGRESSION. 273

the future."* But lest the testimony of this author should be accounted as partial, let me put before you another of a different sort. Voltaire once attempted to burlesque this Psalm, and what was the result? While carefully perusing it, that he might familiarize himself with the train of sentiment which he designed to caricature, he became so oppressed and overawed by its solemn devotional tone, that he threw down the pen and fell back half senseless on his couch, in an agony of remorse. This is told as an undoubted fact by Dr. Leander Van Ess. Hence we can not but admit the depth and fervor of the penitence out of which such a prayer arose; and though the 32d Psalm is more jubilant in its tone, as referring to forgiveness in actual possession, the very gladness which it expresses is a witness to the sadness for sin which had gone before.

Furthermore, as another evidence of the genuineness of David's repentance, we point to the words of Nathan, "The Lord also hath put away thy sin," and ask if the prophet, as Jehovah's representative, would have said any thing like that, if the penitence of David had been insincere. On the whole, therefore, while we mourn over the grievous iniquity of which David was guilty, let us be thankful that we have, along with the record of his sin, the account of his repentance—a repentance, let us say, as much more intense than that of ordinary men as his sin was more heinous. There was no attempt at self-vindication; there was no plea in palliation; there was nothing but the frank confession, "I acknowledge my transgression;" "I have sinned;" "My sin is ever before me." Nor was it the shame of his iniquity before men, or the fear of the punishment which he had incurred, that distressed him. His deepest anguish was that he had displeased the Lord: "Against thee, thee only, have I sinned, and done

---

* Chandler's "Life of David," p. 427.

this evil in thy sight." This was the burden of his confession, and the earnest longing of his soul was expressed in these words: "Restore unto me the joy of thy salvation." It were well that these considerations were more frequently remembered. Many make a mock at David's sin, who say nothing of his repentance. It is enough for them to read in one place that he was the man according to God's own heart, and in another that he committed these great sins, and forthwith they turn the battery of their scorn on the religion of the Bible. But all such procedure is unreasonable. David did not sin because he was the man according to God's own heart, but in spite of his being so; while if he had not been in the main a godly man he would have remained in his sin, and would have taken no step of any sort to acknowledge his guilt, or to raise himself from the degradation into which he had fallen. What, really, is the distinction between the people of God and the wicked on the earth? Is it that the one class commit no sins, while the other fall into iniquity? No; the godly man does sin. No one will be more ready to acknowledge that than himself. The difference, therefore, is not there. It lies in this: that when the child of God falls into sin, he rises out of it and leaves it, and cries to God for pardon, purity, and help; but when the ungodly man falls into sin, he continues in it, and delights in it, as does the sow in her wallowing in the mire. It is a poor, shallow philosophy, therefore, that sneers at such a history as this of David; nay, it is worse even than that: it is the very spirit of Satan, rejoicing, as it does, in the iniquity of others. On this point, however, I gladly avail myself of the language of a powerful writer, not usually considered to have any very strong bias in favor of the Scriptural views of men and things —I mean Thomas Carlyle. "Faults!" says this author, in his "Lecture on the Hero as Prophet;" "the greatest of faults, I should say, is to be conscious of none. Readers of the Bible, above all, one would think, might know better. Who is called there the man according to God's own heart? David, the Hebrew king, had fallen into sins enough; blackest crimes; there was no want of sins. And thereupon unbelievers sneer and ask, 'Is this your man according to God's heart?' The sneer, I must say, seems to me but a shallow one. What are faults? what are the outward details of a life, if the inner secret of it—the remorse, temptations, true, often-baffled, never-ending struggle of it—be forgotten? 'It is not in man that walketh to direct his steps.' Of all acts, is not, for a man, repentance the most divine? The deadliest sin, I say, were that same supercilious consciousness of no sin. That is death. The heart so conscious is divorced from sincerity, humility, and fact—is dead. It is pure, as dead, dry sand is pure. David's life and history, as written for us in those Psalms of his, I consider to be the truest emblem ever given of a man's moral progress and warfare here below. All earnest souls will ever discern in it the faithful struggle of an earnest human soul toward what is good and best. Struggle often baffled sore, baffled down into entire wreck, yet a struggle never ended; ever with tears, repentance, true, unconquerable purpose begun anew. Poor human nature! Is not a man's walking in truth always that—'a succession of falls?' Man can do no other. In this wild element of a life, he has to struggle upward: now fallen, now abased; and ever with tears, repentance, and bleeding heart, he has to rise again, struggle again, still onward. That his struggle be a faithful, unconquerable one, that is the question of questions."

We have now to look, very briefly, at the consequences of this trespass, as they developed themselves in David's after-history and that of his family. One sin destroyeth much good, and terrible evils sprung out of this iniquity. True, David received forgiveness, but forgiveness does not arrest

the consequences of the deeds which we have committed.
It does not prevent the operation of the natural law whereby sin works ever toward misery and retribution. It restricts the punishment of iniquity, in the case of the forgiven one, to the present life; but within that limit the consequences of sin, even to a child of God, as David was, are often very dreadful. What a series of tragedies is comprised in the history of David, from this point on till his death! all of them, too, more or less immediately connected with this sin. First, there is the death of Bath-sheba's child; then there comes back upon him, in an intenser form, his own wickedness, as we see his guilt repeated in the sin of Amnon, and his murder by the hand of Absalom; then there is the rebellion of Absalom, which never could have gained any headway in the land without the adherence to it of Ahithophel; and he, as I shall hope to show you afterward, was the grandfather of Bath-sheba; so that the very strength of the revolt, which so nearly hurled David from his throne, came as a direct result of the wickedness which to-night we have been considering; then there was the death of Absalom, inflicted by Joab, who, from this point on, becomes more arrogant and overbearing than ever, because he is conscious that, in the possession of the secret of the manner of Uriah's death, he has his sovereign thoroughly in his power; then, last of all, there came another revolt to disturb the peacefulness of David's death-bed, and to give a sad significance to his latest words, "Though my house be not so with God." Most awfully were Nathan's words fulfilled: "Now, therefore, the sword shall not depart from thine house." These are the sheaves of that harvest of sorrow which David reaped from the field whereon he sowed "to the flesh." But sadder even than these desolating things is the change which, from this point, we observe in David himself. Henceforth he is no longer the man he was. He goes about

crushed in spirit, humiliated before his people, and degraded even in his own estimation. The nobler features of his character seem to have become eclipsed; and infirmities of temper, weakness of will, and even dimness of judgment, begin to appear. The spring of his life seems to have gone. The elasticity and bound of his character are seen no more. He trusts, indeed, in God to the last, but it is not with the joyful confidence of one who is rich in the consciousness of his father's complacency, but rather with the dull and heavy grasp of one who knows that he has deeply wounded his father's heart. "Alas! for him," says Kitto, "the bird which once rose to heights unattained before by mortal wing, filling the air with its joyful songs, now lies, with maimed wing, upon the ground, pouring forth its doleful cries to God."*

We can not read such a history as that which we have been considering to-night, without remarking on the honesty of the biographies which the Word of God contains. The sacred writers draw no veil over the errors and imperfections of those whom they describe. They tell of the falsehood of Abraham; the cunning selfishness of Jacob; the petulant hastiness of Moses; the weakness of Aaron; the vacillation of Peter; and the sharp contention between Paul and Barnabas, with the same unvarnished truthfulness as they describe the excellences for which these great men were remarkable; and the same historian who records that David was called the "man according to God's own heart," relates also this terrible story of wickedness; while, at the same time, there is no attempt at extenuation or excuse. Have we not in all this a corroboration of the inspiration of the sacred penman? And when, as in the instance of our Lord Jesus Christ, they set before us a pure and perfect life, with as little attempt at elaboration, and as little effort at exaggeration

---

* "Daily Bible Illustrations," vol. iii., p. 431.

as there is of apology in the case before us, may we not conclude that in both they are painting simply and only from reality? There was only one man who could be described as "holy, harmless, undefiled, and separate from sinners," and He was more than man. "Cease ye from man, whose breath is in his nostrils; for wherein is he to be accounted of?" This is the exclamation which rises from our lips, as we ponder over this biography. "The best of men are but men at the best," and need equally with others to be washed in the fountain which has been opened for sin and for uncleanness.

But we must not overlook the practical purpose which the record of the sins of good men was designed to serve. "Whatsoever was written aforetime was written for our learning;" and even the dullest scholar can be at no loss to discover the moral of such a history as that of David's fall. It bids us be continually on our guard, lest we enter into temptation; for if even a David fell so fearfully, who among us can be secure? Here was a man of pre-eminent ability, of great piety, and of extensive usefulness, and yet he was guilty of most revolting sin. Surely the practical inference is, "Let him that thinketh he standeth take heed lest he fall." No station in society, no eminence in the church, no excellence in character, no mere inspiration of genius, can keep a man from sin; nay, not even the gift of divine inspiration can preserve its possessor from a fall. Nothing can do that but the grace of God working in him through prayer, and persevering watchfulness. I say persevering watchfulness, for our vigilance must be continued so long as life on earth shall last.

We often speak of youth as the most dangerous time of life; and indeed, when one has regard to the new nature which begins to assert itself in the opening years of manhood; to the inexperience with which those who are at that stage of existence are characterized; and to the self-sufficiency by which, for the most part, they are distinguished, it would be difficult to exaggerate the dangers which, especially in our great cities, beset the years of youth. But that is not the only dangerous time. It might often seem as if we believed that it was; and for a hundred lectures addressed to young men, there is hardly one delivered to those in middle life, or who are verging toward the period of old age. Yet, if we take the Word of God for our guide, it would almost appear as if these latter stages of existence were more trying and dangerous even than that of youth. This at least is true, that the saddest moral catastrophes of which the Bible tells occurred in the history of men who were no longer young. Noah and Lot were far from youth when they fell before the influence of strong drink; and Demas was not by any means a "novice" when he forsook Paul, "having loved this present world." So David here was past the mid-time of his days when he committed these great transgressions. Moreover, against these instances we have those of Joseph, of Moses, and of Daniel, who in the opening time of life stood true to duty and to God. I say not these things, however, to make young men less watchful, but to make men in middle life, and all through life, continue vigilant. So long as we are in the world, we are in an enemy's country; and if we are not particularly on our guard, we shall be sure to suffer. The world is full of defilement; and in passing through it we must gather our garments tightly round us, if we would keep ourselves unspotted from it. Even Paul could say that he "kept his body under, bringing it into subjection, lest that by any means, having preached to others, he should be a castaway;" and if all this self-control and vigilance was necessary for him, how much more for us! Watch, therefore, lest ye enter into temptation. Give no parley to the tempter. Make a covenant with your eyes, that they will not look upon iniquity, and realizing at all times the peril in which you stand, clothe yourselves in the panoply of God. But watching alone will not suffice. "Watch and pray," the Saviour said; not watch, and then pray; not pray, and then watch; but watch and pray at once. While the eye is eagerly searching out the danger, let the heart at the same time be sending up the earnest supplication, "Hold thou up my goings in thy path, that my footsteps slip not." Thus shall we be kept in safety, until at length we enter into that land where our purity and our reward shall be alike indestructible.

But while David's sin forbids any saint to presume on his infallibility, his reception by God, when he returned to him in penitence, equally forbids any backslider to despair. If after such iniquity he was so graciously received, and had from Nathan the assurance that "the Lord had put away his sin," surely any one may return, and find forgiveness from the Lord. Is there any one here to-night who is carrying on his conscience the load of unforgiven sin? He may be looking back to the time when, in his father's home, he bent his knees in prayer to God; or to the days when, in the Sunday-school, he loved to labor among the children for Christ; or to the years wherein he used to enjoy sweet seasons of communion at the table of the Lord; and as in thought he contrasts these with the depths to which he has fallen, he may be tempted to say, "There is no hope for me; I have been too ungrateful and abandoned to be forgiven." Let such an one hear the voice that comes to-night from David's history, saying to him, "Return!" "Let the wicked forsake his way, and the unrighteous man his thoughts: and let him return unto the Lord, and he will have mercy upon him; and to our God, for he will abundantly pardon." Let him ponder well the 51st Psalm, pouring his own soul into its confessions and petitions, and soon light will break in upon his soul, like the sunbeam from behind a cloud, and he will be made to sing

## The Great Transgression. 281

the joyful strain with which the 32d Psalm opens. "Blessed is he whose transgression is forgiven, whose sin is covered. Blessed is the man unto whom the Lord imputeth not iniquity, and in whose spirit there is no guile." Thus, though the fall of David has undeniably caused many to blaspheme, it may prove a warning to many, so that they shall stand upright, and may save from the depths of utter despair those who remember that, aggravated as his guilt was, he was received back into the favor of God when he cried to him in penitential sincerity for forgiving mercy.

Finally: we can not but note "what an evil thing and a bitter it is to forsake the Lord." Recall for a moment to your recollection the consequences of David's sins. Behold how, by reproducing themselves in darker and intenser forms, these iniquities of his returned upon his head. He caused the death of Uriah, and the sword departed not from his house all his after-days; he was guilty of impurity, and his son Amnon bettered the example which his father set: he committed murder; Absalom committed fratricide: he rebelled against the Lord; Absalom rebelled against himself; and all this, though the sins themselves were forgiven. But if this were the case with pardoned iniquities, what must it be with those which are unforgiven? If this were the retribution of the present life, what must be that of the life that is to come, to those who have felt no penitence, and asked no mercy? Oh, my friends, will you continue to live in such a way as to draw down eternal misery upon your heads? Do not, I beseech you, that abominable thing which God hates. Come now, if you have never come before, and seek for pardon and regeneration through Jesus Christ our Lord. Let the time past of your lives be sufficient "to have wrought the will of the flesh." Begin now to live for God. "Be it known unto you, men and brethren, that through Jesus Christ is preached unto you the forgiveness of sins; but beware, lest that come upon you which is spoken of in the prophets: 'Behold, ye despisers, and wonder, and perish; for I work a work in your days, a work which ye shall in no wise believe, though a man declare it unto you.'" "Knowing the terror of the Lord," we would persuade you now to embrace the salvation which he has provided. Why will ye rush upon destruction, with this great deliverance in your offer?

## XVI.

### THE BEREAVEMENT.

2 SAMUEL xii., 15–23.

THE penal consequences of David's sin took the form of family trials and national troubles, and were of such a nature as to wring his heart with the severest anguish, not only by their own bitterness, but also, and perhaps especially, by the vividness with which they brought back upon his conscience the remembrance of his own iniquity. To-night we shall restrict ourselves to the first of his domestic sorrows, and seek to draw from its consideration such lessons as shall prove both wholesome and instructive.

After his pointed and impressive exhortation to the king, and his parting words of tender consolation, conveying in them the assurance of the Divine forgiveness, Nathan withdrew from the palace. He had performed a difficult and delicate duty with signal wisdom; he had succeeded in arousing the conscience of David without forfeiting his friendship; he had been able, in a spirit of love to the monarch, to preserve his fidelity to the monarch's God; and now, with a heart heaving with an emotion that resembled the after-swell which a storm always leaves behind, he retired, we may believe, to pray to his heavenly Master for the poor spirit-stricken penitent whom he had left in such distress. To the same God, we may be sure, David himself repaired; and perhaps it was just then, in the first access of his deep self-abasement and shame, that he wrote that Psalm which has come weeping down through the centuries, and been in them all the liturgy of repenting sinners. Begin ning with a cry for mercy, he makes the most unqualified acknowledgment of his sin; and realizing more than he had ever done before the deep depravity of heart which his transgression revealed, he makes this earnest request, "Create in me a clean heart, O God, and renew a right spirit within me." He longs for a restoration of the joy of salvation, and at last, as if his prayer had been already answered, he concludes with a strain of chastened joy, which seems to me like the sunshine streaming through the departing shower, and forming to the eye the many-colored bow of ancient promise.

In this spirit, probably, David came forth from his closet with deep humility indeed, yet with the fond anticipation of coming brightness. But not long was he permitted to be at rest. Nathan's last words to him had a forecast of evil, as well as an assurance of pardon. Here they are: "The Lord also hath put away thy sin; thou shalt not die. Howbeit, because by this deed thou hast given great occasion to the enemies of the Lord to blaspheme, the child also that is born unto thee shall surely die." Speedily was this prediction fulfilled. "The Lord struck the child." Not that there was any miracle here; but with startling suddenness some one of those ailments to which little ones are so liable came upon him, and he was very sick. Tender-hearted to a fault, and dotingly fond at all times of his children, David was greatly distressed by this event. The light which had begun to play upon his countenance disappeared, and he was filled with the deepest grief. Nor is it difficult to account for this. The sufferings of an infant are always most saddening to witness. The helpless look of the little patient; the pitiful wail; the labored breathing; the constant restlessness; all combine to make the spectacle of its anguish most affecting to any beholder: how much more to those who call him their own? Nor is this all. In the case of little children, we are well-nigh powerless to relieve them. They can not tell us how they feel. We are largely in the dark as to the meaning of the symptoms that appear; and medical science, always a matter of considerable uncertainty, is peculiarly experimental in infantile diseases. Hence the agony of a parent beside a dying infant's cot. Each pleading look of the upturned eye goes like a dart to the mother's heart, while the convulsive start or tremor sends a thrill of anguish through the father's frame. But over and above these natural and ordinary causes of sorrow for an infant's sufferings, there were in David's case certain peculiar ingredients of bitterness. Nathan had specially connected all the pangs of his child with his own sin. It is a mystery that any infant, innocent as it is of actual transgression, should suffer at all; and sometimes the dark shadow which that mystery projects may increase the sadness of the afflicted parent. But in David's case, whatever mystery there might be about the question why the child was made to suffer for his guilt, there was none about the fact. Nathan had made that perfectly plain to him. Hence every quiver of pain the infant gave would be a new needle-point thrust into his own conscience, stinging him with sharpest remorse. For seven days this illness lasted, and David betook himself to his old solace: he prayed to God; yea, he "fasted, and went in, and lay all night upon the earth." We like to read these words, for they tell us that David, though an erring son of God, was yet a son. A godless man would have been driven farther from Jehovah by these troubles, and might have been led to make proclamation of his utter atheism; but David went to God. The more heavily he felt the rod, the nearer he crept to him who used it. He fled from God to God. He hid himself from God in God. This shows that his sin was out of the usual course of his nature. It was like the deflection of the needle, due to certain causes, which at the time he permitted to have influence over him; but, these causes removed, his old polarity of soul returned, and in his time of trouble he called on Jehovah. This was his habit. Repeatedly in his Psalms has he employed language which clearly indicates that God was regarded by him as a strong rock, whereunto, in time of trial, he continually resorted. Thus we have him saying, on one occasion, of his enemies: "For my love they are my adversaries: but I give myself unto prayer;" and again, "From the end of the earth will I cry unto thee, when my heart is overwhelmed: lead me to the rock that is higher than I."

It does not seem that any one of his Psalms was composed on this occasion, yet there are in some of them strains which might well enough have arisen from the recollection of his experiences in connection with this infant's death. Such, for example, are these: "O Lord, rebuke me not in thine anger, neither chasten me in thy hot displeasure! Have mercy upon me, O Lord; for I am weak. O Lord, heal me; for my bones are vexed. My soul is also sore vexed: but thou, O Lord, how long? Return, O Lord, deliver my soul: oh! save me for thy mercies' sake."\* But not for himself alone did he thus make supplication. He besought God for the child. Here is a great boldness of faith and of request, which startles us almost by its importunity. Had not Nathan said the child should surely die? yet here David pleads for his life, saying, "Who can tell whether God will be gracious to me, that the child may live?" Why is this? Was it because David did not believe Nathan's words? No, but because he had unbounded faith in the efficacy of prayer; and though in the present instance the specific object which he asked was denied him, we must not suppose that it was so because his prayer was displeasing to God; for just a similar prayer offered by Hezekiah, after his death was solemnly

---

\* Psa. vi., 1-4.

foretold by Isaiah, was the means of lengthening out his days by fifteen years. So, too, after Jonah's unqualified proclamation of Nineveh's destruction, the inhabitants rose and betook themselves to prayer, saying, just like David here, "Who can tell if God will turn and repent, and turn away from his fierce anger, that we perish not?" and their cry was heard. Hence we dare not say that David was wrong in making this request. And we can only marvel at the faith and child-like regard for God which the making of it evinced. Modern men of science make great difficulty about offering prayer, the granting of which seems to go against the physical laws of God's universe. But these ancient suppliants felt no such difficulty. They were not afraid even to pray against the coming of that which God had affirmed would come. Not even moral difficulties stood in their way. And they were right, for there is always this "Who can tell;" and there is, besides, in God the fatherly heart to which no real son of his can ever make appeal entirely in vain.

The child died, and the servants of the king, with a real delicacy of heart, and with genuine consideration for his feelings, were afraid to tell him that all was over. But they need not have been so timid; for, though exceedingly honorable to them, the fear lest the knowledge of the child's death should thoroughly unman the king, proceeded from ignorance of his true character. He knew that in the case of an infant, when death comes, the time for fasting and grieving is over, and so he arose and washed, and anointed himself, and went into the house of God and worshiped; "then he came to his own house; and when he required, they set bread before him, and he did eat." Astonished at his behavior, his servants asked for an explanation. He gave this noble answer, evidencing at once the strength of his character and the firmness of his faith in the future life: "While the child was yet alive, I fasted and wept: for I said, Who can tell whether

God will be gracious to me, that the child may live? But now he is dead, wherefore should I fast? can I bring him back again? I shall go to him, but he shall not return to me." Here was true resignation. Here was strong faith. Here was a holy and a glorious hope—alike for the living and the dead—and in the assurance of future and eternal reunion before the throne he was comforted.

For when the royal mourner says, "I shall go to him," we must not so empty his words of all meaning as to suppose that he refers simply to the grave. What comfort was there in the mere idea of having his body laid beside the dust of his infant? That was not a "going to him" in any sense that could give the least satisfaction to his afflicted heart. Hence his language implies far more than that, and intimates that he had a firm conviction of his child's continued existence and present happiness; while at the same time he cherished for himself the hope of entering in due season into the enjoyment of similar felicity. David's resignation, therefore, was not a mere stoical submission to the inevitable, still less was it a stolid insensibility; but it was the result of his persuasion of the happiness of his departed child, and of his humble hope of joining him therein. Like Paul Gerhardt, the prince of German hymnologists, he might have sung:

> "Oh that I could but watch afar,
>   And hearken but a while
> To that sweet song that hath no jar,
>   And see his heavenly smile,
> As he doth praise the holy God
> Who made him pure for that abode;
> In tears of joy full well I know
> This burdened heart would overflow!
>
> "And I should say, Stay there, my son,
>   My wild laments are o'er;

> Oh well for thee that thou hast won:
>   I call thee back no more!
> But come, thou fiery chariot, come,
> And bear me swiftly to that home
> Where he with many a loved one dwells,
> And evermore of gladness tells.
>
> "Then be it as my Father wills,
>   I will not weep for thee:
> Thou livest, joy thy spirit fills,
>   Pure sunshine thou dost see—
> The sunshine of eternal rest:
> Abide, my son, where thou art blest:
> I with our friends will onward fare,
> And, when God wills, shall find thee there."

I can not pass from this subject without endeavoring, while our interest is still fresh in it, to embody its practical teaching in a few particulars. Notice, then, in the first place, that the illness and death of little children may be intimately connected with the conduct and spiritual history of the parents. No doubt they belong to a tainted race, and come into the world with the sentence hanging over them, "Dust thou art, and unto dust shalt thou return." But, over and above the evidence which their death furnishes of their connection with Adam, we see from the case before us, that it may also be in some way or other caused or connected with the character of their immediate parents. Far be it from me to say, that whenever infants die, there must have been some foregoing iniquity in father or mother to cause it, like as it was in the history before us. It is not for man to assume the prerogative of God, and positively assert in any case what Nathan, as God's prophet, asserted here. But still, God's providence is conducted on moral principles, and the death of infants is one way in which he may either visit parents with the penal consequences of their sin, or lead them to thoughtfulness, and quicken their spiritual life. And when such events occur in our own family history, it becomes us to look well into our own hearts and see if we can discover what God's design in the dispensation is. It may be that we have been allowing the things of this world to usurp too large a portion of our attention, or to intrude into the sacred domain of the heart, where God alone should reign ; and he takes this plan to arrest us, and compel us to face eternity, with its infinitely momentous things. Perhaps we may have been permitting ourselves to become enslaved by some degrading habit, flattering ourselves all the while that there is no guilt in it, and that when we please we can break away from it ; and he sends the death-angel for our little one, as he sent Nathan to David, to stir our consciences into activity, to show ourselves to us, to awaken us to penitence, and to bring us back to the paths of purity and of liberty. Or, yet again, we may be ourselves unconverted, and, as the surest means of engaging our hearts to heavenly things, God takes the little one who is the light of our eyes to heaven. Very touchingly is this view presented in the life of Sandy Robertson, by Dr. Guthrie, in " Lost and Found." This poor boy, who had been reclaimed by means of the ragged school, was lying dying, and was greatly concerned about his godless mother. He often implored her to seek the kingdom of heaven ; and one day telling Dr. Guthrie of a visit paid to him by the Rev. James Robertson, of Newington, whose conversation and prayers he much enjoyed, he said, "'Oh, how nice he spoke to my mother! On going away, he said to her, 'Now, before I go, I will tell you a story. There was a man that had a flock of sheep, which he wished to remove from one field to another, and better pasture. There was one sheep refused to go, and ran hither and thither. The man did not stop to follow that sheep, to drive and force it through the gate. No, but he took her lamb and laid it in his bosom, and carried it in his arms, and the sheep followed her bleating lamb, and was soon safe and happy in the sweet, rich pasture.'" So it has often been, and the words of the prophet have had a new verification, "A little child shall lead them." But why need I enlarge here? As with afflictions of other kinds, the death of infants may have a corrective, a restorative, or a preventive power on the parents and other members of the family to which they belong, and so their sufferings have in them not a little of that vicarious element which, in a unique and mysterious degree, distinguished the sufferings and death of Christ. Hence, so far from saying, when a little one is removed, "Oh, it is only a child," there are elements about such a dispensation which ought to lead us to look upon it as peculiarly solemn, carrying in it most needful discipline and most salutary influence.

But, in the second place, we learn from this touching episode in David's life, that the surest solace under the affliction and death of infants is in God. David prayed, and though the life of the child was not given to his tearful entreaties, it would be a mistake to suppose that his supplication was unanswered. The reply came in the shape of that strength which enabled him to become at once so calm, and that faith which helped him to manifest such thorough resignation. It would neither have been good for David himself, nor for the people over whom he ruled, if his prayer had been literally granted. Hence, in that form in which he presented his petition, it was refused; but it was good for him to draw near to God for all that, and when we see him going up with such composure to the house of God, we learn that he had not prayed in vain. His tears of weakness had brought down God's strength. His earnest cry had received an answer similar to that vouchsafed to the repeated prayer of Paul: "My grace is sufficient for thee. My strength is made perfect in weakness." Oh, what should we do in times of family distress, if we could not lay our case before the

Lord? Blessed solace of prayer! the tumult of the spirit is hushed by thy soothing influence; and if we could be cast where prayer is stifled, and supplication impossible, that were to our miserable souls the very centre of hell. In all trials, therefore, and especially in the dark hour of family bereavement, let us repair to "the mercy-seat."

Finally, we may learn from David's words here, that we may cherish the most unwavering assurance of the salvation of those who die in infancy. Even in the comparative darkness of the Jewish dispensation, the Psalmist had the fullest persuasion of the eternal welfare of his baby-boy; and, under the Gospel economy, there are many things revealed which tend to make the doctrine of infant salvation perfectly indubitable. Not to refer to the fact that, as they have committed no actual transgressions, little children do not personally deserve condemnation, and may, therefore, presumably be regarded as included in the provisions of the covenant of grace, there are certain things which to my mind place the doctrine to which I refer beyond all question.

In the first place, there seems to me a moral impossibility involved in the very thought of infants being consigned to perdition. For what are the elements in the punishment of the lost? So far as we know, they are these two, memory and conscience. But in an infant conscience is virtually non-existent. Moral agency and responsibility have not yet been developed, and so there can be no such thing to it as remorse.

Again: memory has nothing of guilt in an infant's life to recall, and so it seems to me to be utterly impossible to connect retribution of any sort in the other world with those who have been taken from the present in the stage of infancy.

But, in the second place, there are positive indications

that infants are included in the work of Christ. I grant at once that there is no one passage which in so many words makes the assertion that all who die in infancy are eternally saved; but then we may not wonder at the absence of such a declaration, since it would have been liable to great abuse; and we do not need to regret that we have it not, because there are many passages which very clearly imply it. Thus Jesus said of infants, "Of such is the kingdom of heaven." This does not mean only, as some would have us to believe, that the kingdom of heaven consists of persons resembling little children. The word translated "of such" has evidently a definite reference to children themselves, and has elsewhere been employed in that way by the Saviour himself. Thus, when he says, "The hour cometh, and now is, when the true worshipers shall worship the Father in spirit and in truth: for the Father seeketh such to worship him," he clearly means, the Father seeketh these to worship him. I might quote others to the like effect, but that will suffice to show that the phrase "Of such is the kingdom of heaven," is equivalent to "Of these is the kingdom of heaven." This view of the matter is confirmed by the fact that the Saviour gives these words as a reason for his taking up little children into his arms; for if the ground of his procedure were simply that the adult subjects of the kingdom of heaven are child-like, the same sort of reason might have led him to take up lambs in his arms and to bless them; inasmuch as the adult members of his kingdom should resemble lambs in some respects just as really as they should resemble children in others. Some, however, would interpret the words on which I am now commenting by these others, uttered by Jesus on another occasion: "Verily I say unto you, whosoever shall not receive the kingdom of God as a little child, he shall not enter therein;" as if that expression implied "with a child-like disposition;" but that is not the construction of the words. Let the ellipsis be supplied, and then it will be seen that even this expression bears out our view, for it reads thus: "Whosoever shall not receive the kingdom of heaven as a little child receives it;" and this confirms our interpretation of the other passage. But some may allege that the phrase "the kingdom of heaven" does not refer to future glory, but to Christ's kingdom upon earth; and to these we reply: True, it does refer to Christ's kingdom upon earth, but it does so only because that is a province of the one great kingdom which, having Him as its head, stretches into eternity. That it refers to the kingdom on earth, is our warrant for receiving little children into the Church below; and that it refers to the kingdom in heaven—for the kingdoms are but one—is the ground of our hope in the salvation of little children eternally.

Then, passing from the domain of argument, we may affirm that the whole tone and spirit of the Gospel favors the idea of infant salvation. The Saviour was peculiarly tender to the little ones. It was foretold regarding him that he should carry the lambs in his bosom; and the infinite sufficiency of his grand atonement would seem to me shorn of half of its glory, if it were not available for little children. Let us, therefore, take to ourselves, without let or abatement of any sort, the rich consolation which this doctrine affords. Let the bereaved parents among us dry our tears. As the good Archbishop Leighton has it, "Our children have but gone an hour or two sooner to bed, as children used to do, and we are undressing to follow; and the more we put off the love of this present world, and all things superfluous beforehand, we shall have the less to do when we lie down."

Let us consider to whom they have gone. They have been taken to the arms of Jesus, and to the bright glory of the heavenly state. Nothing now can mar their felicity, or dim the lustre of their joy, or damp the ardor of their song; and could they speak to us from their abode of bliss, they would say to us, "Weep not for us, but weep for yourselves, that you are not here to share our happiness."

Let us consider from what they have been taken. They have been removed from earth, with its pains and privations, its sufferings and sorrows. Looking back upon our own checkered histories, could we contemplate without a feeling of grief the idea of our children passing through such trials as those which have met us in the world? Would we wish that their hearts should be wrung as ours have been by the harshness of an unfeeling world, or by the ingratitude of those whom they had served? Nay, in view of the pang of our bereavement, would we wish that a similar sorrow should be theirs? Yet does not their continuance in the world involve in it the endurance of all these things? and ought it not, therefore, to be a matter of thankfulness that they have reached heaven without having tasted the full bitterness of this world's woes? Above all, can we contemplate the spiritual dangers with which the world is environed, and not feel grateful that our departed little ones are now eternally safe from them? Let us think of the temptations that have beset us, and of the dreadful battles which we have had with them; and how near we were to being conquered by them, and then let us say if in this view we can feel otherwise than glad that they have gained the victory without the perils and hardships of the fight. Perhaps, had they been exposed to these dangers, they would have fallen before them; perhaps, had they lived, they would have grown up only to fill our hearts with sadness, and to bring our heads with sorrow to the grave; but all this is now impossible, for they are safe with Jesus. It is hard to part with our children, but the death of our little ones is not the heaviest calamity that could befall us. A living cross is heavier than a dead one. And the sadness of David's soul over this little one was as nothing, in comparison with the agony that rent his heart when Absalom chased him from his palace, and went down into a hopeless tomb.

Let us consider, again, for what our little ones have been taken. Perhaps we have been wandering away from Christ, and he has taken this way to bring us back. Perhaps we have never known him, and he has taken this way of introducing himself to us, coming to us as he did to his followers of old, over the very waves of our trouble, and saying to us, "It is I, be not afraid." Perhaps some other member of our family was to be led through this affliction to the Lord, and thus one little one was taken from us for a season, that both might abide with us forever in the heavenly land. And if this should be so, can we, dare we repine?

Let us consider, finally, how this bereavement over which we mourn will appear to us when we come to die ourselves. I have seen mothers and fathers not a few at that solemn hour, but never one have I heard expressing anxiety for the little children who had gone before them. The great concern, then, was for those they were leaving behind. The Lord thus is afflicting us now, that our sorrow may be mitigated at the last. Let us think of these things, and then the bereavement of our little ones will seem to be, as it in reality is, a token of love, and not of anger.

"Oh, not in cruelty, not in wrath,
 The reaper came that day;
'Twas an angel visited the green earth
 And took the flowers away."

But the appropriation to ourselves of all these consolations implies that we are ourselves journeying heavenward. David says, "I shall go to him!" Bereaved parents, are you advancing toward heaven? If you are not, then none of these comforts are yours. Your little ones shall indeed be saved, but you yourselves shall never be reunited to them. A great gulf shall be eternally fixed between you and the home which they have entered. Must this be so? You remember how you felt when you laid them in the tomb, and how, for the time, you were stirred up to think of God and Christ; but these emotions are gone now, and you are worse than ever, yea, living in folly and sin. Let the memory of your departed little ones this night stir you into religious earnestness.

Years ago, when I was leaving my Liverpool home to fulfill an engagement in the city of Glasgow, the last sight on which my eye rested was that of my little daughter at the window in her grandmother's arms. As the carriage drove me away, she waved her hand in fond and laughing glee, and many a time during my railway ride the pleasant vision came up before my memory, and filled my heart with joy. I never saw her again! The next morning a telegram stunned me with the tidings of her death; and now that earthly glimpse of her has been idealized and glorified, and it seems to me as if God had set her in the window of heaven to beckon me upward to my eternal home. I would not give that memory for all the gold of earth. I would not part with the inspiration that it stirs within me for all that the world could bestow. But, my bereaved friends, is it not true of you also, that God has made heaven more attractive to you by reason of the presence of your little ones in it? Will you not yield yourselves to the influence of this celestial magnetism? See how their angel hands are beckoning you upward; hark how the very song they used to sing with infant voice comes floating down into your ears:

> "Come to this happy land,
> Come, come away!"

Oh, do not resist the appeal, but give yourselves henceforth unreservedly to Jesus, and make this your prayer:

> "Lord God the Spirit! purify
> My thoughts, bind fast my life to thee;
> So shall I meet my babes on high,
> Though they may not return to me."*

---

* I can not forbear referring here to a work on this subject, which is a perfect treasure-house of consolation to those who have suffered from this domestic sorrow. It is out of sight the best book of the kind which I have ever seen. The title is "Words of Comfort for Parents bereaved of Little Children." Edited by William Logan: New York, Carter Brothers.

## XVII.

### *THE REVOLT OF ABSALOM.*

2 SAMUEL xiii., 1-16; xiv.

WITH the birth of Bath-sheba's second son, a gleam of gladness seems to have shone in upon David's house. The prophet Nathan intimated that the child was an object of God's peculiar affection, and in the names which the king bestowed upon him we may see some indications of returning happiness, for he called him Solomon, *the peaceful,* and Jedidiah, *the beloved of the Lord.* But the dark cloud of retribution still hovered over the palace, and ere long there flashed from it such lightning bolts of judgment as humbled the monarch in the dust, and tended to bring his gray hairs with sorrow to the grave. The particulars are detailed with painful minuteness in the chapters which now lie before us; but, without entering upon them all, it will be enough that we indicate the more important of them, and draw from them the lessons for the teaching of which the harrowing history has been here preserved.

The physical beauty which distinguished the sons of Jesse seems in David's family to have specially descended to his children by Maacah, the daughter of Talmai, the heathen King of Geshur; for it is recorded of Absalom that "in all Israel there was none so much to be praised for his beauty; from the sole of his foot even to the crown of his head there was no blemish in him;" and of his sister Tamar it is said that she was fair to look upon. Unfortunately for her, this personal attractiveness made her the object of an unholy passion on the part of her half-brother Amnon, who, having accomplished his purpose, aided by the diabolical assistance of an unprincipled man, who seems to have been permanently connected with the court, turned her away dishonored from his door. Just then, with ashes on her head, and her garments rent, and crying bitterly, she was met by her brother Absalom, who, discovering the reason of her sorrow, counseled her to silence, and took her to his own home, where she remained desolate. Of course a scandal of this sort was sure to be talked about, and tidings of it came at length to David's ear. He was very wroth; but that was not all. His heart must have been deeply distressed by the knowledge of his son's great wickedness, while yet the consciousness of his own similar iniquity kept him from publicly punishing him for his crime. The penalty of this transgression, according to the Mosaic law, was death; yet, if that were by him to be insisted on in the case of his son, where would he be himself? So, weak from the consciousness of his own trespass, he was constrained to take no notice of this revolting crime, though we may be sure that he must have keenly felt the anguish of soul which every right-hearted parent experiences in seeing the wrong-doing of his children.

The inaction of David, however, only stirred up Absalom the more resolutely to seek revenge; for, since her father took no notice of such a deed, it devolved on him, as the full brother of Tamar, to espouse her cause. Nor need we wonder that he should have been indignant at the treatment to which she had been subjected. We should have thought less of him if he had continued to be as friendly with Amnon as before. But though Oriental custom may be pleaded in extenuation of his after-conduct, to which we have a parallel in that of Simeon and Levi, in circumstances very similar to those before us, yet he had no right, under the Mosaic institute, to take the law into his own hands, still less to execute it in so cunning and revengeful a spirit as that which he evinced. It seems that he had a sheep-farm at Baal-hazor, and at the end of two years he invited all the king's sons to the great festival of the sheep-shearing. He wished David also to be present, but the monarch declined. And when he desired that Amnon should be permitted to go, the king at first demurred, fearing the consequences; but at length, won by the entreaties of his favorite son, and under the influence of that fatal irresolution which marked his treatment of his children in later years, he gave a reluctant consent. The result might have been foreseen. Amidst the dissipation of the feast, the servants of Absalom, instigated by their master, slew Amnon, and the fratricide fled for refuge to the court of his grandfather at Geshur, while messengers hurried to Jerusalem with the tidings of his treacherous deed. "And it came to pass that behold the king's sons came, and lifted up their voice and wept: and the king also and all his servants wept very sore." Yes:

> Sorrow tracketh wrong,
> As echo follows song.
> On! on! on! on!

"Verily there is a God that judgeth in the earth." And in the ordering of his providence, not less than in the statements of his Word, we see that sin can not go unpunished. Here is another sheaf of that bitter harvest of corruption that David was made to reap from the field wherein he sowed to the flesh. His lovely and beloved daughter made desolate; his eldest son murdered amidst the revelry of a drunken banquet; and Absalom, the pride of his palace and the darling of his heart, the murderer, self-exiled from his father's house and from his native land. How true it is that "the way of transgressors is hard."

For three long years Absalom remained at Geshur. During this interval David's grief for Amnon abated, but his heart went out in longing after Absalom. He did not recall him to his court indeed, for that would have been equivalent to saying that the deed of which he had been guilty was of a trifling character; but, as the after events indicate, he would have been glad of any pretext which, without seeming to outrage justice, would have enabled him to bring him back. This state of feeling he could not hide from his intimate associates, and Joab, seeking at once to serve David and Absalom, concocted a plan by which the latter was recalled. He sent a wise woman from Tekoah in before the king, with a feigned case of difficulty, which in some of its leading features bore a striking resemblance to his own position in regard to Absalom; and, in the course of the prosecution of her suit, David's suspicions were so aroused that he said, "Is not the hand of Joab with thee in all this?" Her answer revealed the whole scheme, and the issue was that Joab was sent to Geshur to bring Absalom back to Jerusalem. Not yet, however, was David fully reconciled to his son; for when the youth came to the holy city, David said, "Let him turn to his own house, and let him not see my face."

This state of matters lasted for two years more, when, Absalom's patience being exhausted, he sent for Joab. The captain of the host thought proper twice to disregard his urgent entreaty; and this proceeding so exasperated Absalom that he ordered his servants to set one of Joab's barley-fields on fire. This act of destruction, as he had foreseen, brought Joab forthwith; and in reply to his indignant question, "Wherefore have thy servants set my field on fire?" Absalom answered, "Behold, I sent unto thee, saying, Come hither, that I may send thee to the king, to say, Wherefore am I come from Geshur? it had been good for me to have been there still: now, therefore, let me see the king's face; and if there be any iniquity in me, let him kill me."

It is difficult, at first sight, to account for the conduct of

Joab here; for, after he had earnestly exerted himself to procure Absalom's recall, it appears strange that he should have been so indifferent to the position which the young man was made by his father to occupy. But we find the explanation in the fact that in this, as in all other things, the crafty and unscrupulous warrior was seeking only to promote his own interests. He had obtained a great ascendency over David by his complicity in the murder of Uriah, and by making the monarch believe that he was indispensable to him. Now he desired to gain a similar power over Absalom. This, however, could only be done by laying him under some great obligation. Hence he probably kept away from the young man, with the view of getting him to come humbly to him as a suppliant, asking the favor of his intercession with the king. But the burning of his field let him see that Absalom was made of sterner stuff; and so, in order that he might not provoke his vengeance, he was led to do for him, by a sort of compulsion, that which he had intended to do only when he was urgently entreated for it as for a great kindness. By his influence with David, he easily effected a reconciliation between father and son; but, on the side of the son at least, it was but a hollow thing, after all; for, from the moment of his restoration to the royal favor, on during the space of four years, Absalom was engaged in making preparations for that revolt which at one time threatened to bring the reign of David to an ignominious end.

Civil war is always a terrible calamity; but when the standard of rebellion is raised by a son against his father, we have about the most painful form of strife of which this earth can be the scene. It is sad to have an enemy of one who has been formerly a friend; but that he whom we have fondled in our arms and nestled in our bosom, and whose first lisping utterances have been in the attempt to call us father, should live to be at deadly feud with us, and to attempt our destruction—this is misery indeed; and in seeking to realize the anguish of David at this time, we think of the saying which the great dramatist has put into the mouth of the old British king: "How sharper than a serpent's tooth it is to have a thankless child;" or of those lines of another poet, which he penned in quite another connection, but which are equally appropriate here:

> "So the struck eagle stretch'd upon the plain,
> No more through rolling clouds to soar again,
> View'd his own feather on the fatal dart,
> And wing'd the shaft that quiver'd in his heart;
> Keen were his pangs, but keener far to feel
> He nursed the pinion which impelled the steel;
> While the same plumage that had warm'd his nest,
> Drank the last life-drop of his bleeding breast."

In entering upon the particulars of this sad episode in David's life, there are two questions which suggest themselves to the thoughtful reader of the narrative, and as the settlement of these will greatly help us to understand the whole matter, we may very appropriately now consider them. They are these—first: How came Absalom to think of rebelling against his father at all? and, second: How came his revolt to gather strength so rapidly as to cause David to leave Jerusalem, and to prove so nearly successful? In regard to the first of these questions, it is easy to see that there was much in David's treatment of Absalom, looked at from his son's point of view, to cause alienation and to provoke antagonism. We are allowed in the narrative to see how all along the king's heart had gone out after Absalom; but the youth himself knew nothing of that. He might have heard that Joab had to resort to schemes of a roundabout description in order to procure his recall, and he certainly must have felt that there was no cordial reception given him.

Now while, in one sense, this conduct on David's part was a sort of homage to public justice, yet in another it was neither right nor politic. It was not right; for, on the one hand, if Absalom had committed a crime, he ought to have been punished for it; and on the other, if there was ground for his recall from banishment, there was also ground for receiving him at court. It was not politic; for it could not but put Absalom into a position of antagonism to his father, and the fretting impatience of these two years was but the bitter bud out of which at length ripened the rebellion of which we are to speak.

Again, Absalom would regard himself as the rightful heir to his father's throne. Amnon, the eldest son, to whom, in conformity with all Eastern notions, it should have descended, was dead. Chileab, the second, seems to have been dead also; at least, his name drops completely out of the history. Absalom came next, and perhaps in ordinary circumstances he might have been content to wait for his father's death before urging his claim; but certain things at court would incite him to take immediate steps to further his own interests. He saw that the influence of Bath-sheba was paramount. He knew that Solomon was the favorite son; and the declaration of Nathan that he, the peaceable, was to succeed his father could not be unknown to him. Hence he would conclude that, if he was ever to be king, it could only be by some such sudden and immediate *coup d'état* as that which he actually attempted. Putting these things together, then, and remembering, besides, that there was no spark of religious principle in the breast of Absalom, we may have some understanding of the feelings by which he was stirred, and the motives by which he was actuated in raising the standard of revolt against his father.

It is equally easy to account for the rapidity with which the disaffection spread, and the strength which the rebellion gained. Absalom had great personal attractions. This may seem a matter of small moment, but, in reality, it had an immense effect. Even such a one as Samuel was not proof against the influence of a man's outward appearance, and we need not marvel, therefore, that the common people of the land should be specially drawn to one whose beauty was proverbial. In modern times we know that the personal attractions of the Young Pretender, in 1745, drew perhaps as many to his army as did the cause which he represented; and young and handsome as Absalom was, he was quite likely to be, simply on that account, the idol of the army, and the darling of the populace. Add to this, that he was the only one of David's sons who, on the mother's side, was of royal lineage; and to a people who are so moved by considerations like these as the Orientals, this must have given additional weight to his claims. Nor, on the other side, must we forget that David was no longer the man he was when the people rallied with enthusiasm around him. Age had begun to tell upon him; and sadder far than that, from the era of his great trespass, he had been broken-hearted and melancholy. To his people generally he would appear as a retired, moody old man. The spring of his life was gone. He took little interest in public affairs, and, in particular, he neglected that most important of all the duties of an Eastern ruler, the sitting in the gate to hear those appeals which his subjects made to his personal decision.

It has been supposed, indeed, that during the four years of Absalom's preparations David was suffering from disease to such an extent that he was prevented from taking his place as aforetime in the administration of justice; and certainly there are some expressions in the 41st Psalm, belonging to this era of his life, which can be most naturally interpreted on that hypothesis. But however we may account for it, the fact is clear that David had largely disappeared from the public eye, and that he had ceased, to a great extent, to take interest in the duties of his office. Furthermore, the people knew of his great trespass, and this brought even the good features of his character into contempt. They saw him devoting himself to retirement, and giving almost his entire attention to religious duties, while, perhaps, they heard occasionally of his great purpose of building a temple, and of the efforts which he was making in the collection of materials for it, and they ridiculed him as "an old hypocrite." They did not know or believe in the sincerity of his repentance, and so they held him up to scorn. Had he been a worthless rake, making no pretensions to religion, they would not have objected to him; or had he been a devout man, with a blameless reputation, they would have been compelled to respect him; but, knowing his sin, and seeing his devotion, they simply despised him. That this is no exaggerated description, seems clear from certain expressions in the 69th Psalm, which is generally understood to belong to this period of David's life. There we find him writing, "When I wept, and chastened my soul with fasting, that was to my reproach. I made sackcloth also my garment; and I became a proverb to them. They that sit in the gate speak against me; and I was the song of the drunkards." Now, presuming all this to be true, we can see how the people, and especially those nearest the king in Jerusalem, were in a manner prepared for a change in the sovereignty of the nation. But the bad points in David's character and administration were yet further darkened by the contrast which was suggested by the conduct of Absalom. Over against the seclusion of his father, the people—and especially the West-End tradesmen, if there were any such in those days—would set the state of Absalom; and as they saw him riding forth in his chariot, with fifty men preceding him, they would say, "That is something like a king; but as for David, we might as well have no court, for any thing we see of him." Again, over against David's neglect of the administration of justice, they would put Absalom's assiduous attention to the matters brought before him, and his affable, frank, and conciliatory manner to all strangers; while his insidious ejaculation, "O that I were made judge in the land, that every man which hath any suit or cause might come to me and I would do him justice," could not but produce the effects which it was intended to accomplish. Hence we can understand how Absalom stole the hearts of the men of Israel. But it was stealing for all that; and though, in the hands of God, he was the instrument through whom chastisement was inflicted upon David, we shall yet see that a terrible retribution fell upon himself.

The method which he took for inaugurating his revolt was characterized by the cunning that seems to have been inherent in his nature. He sent spies through all the tribes, instructing them, at a given signal, to proclaim him king. Then, feigning that he had a religious vow which took him to Hebron, he went thither with two hundred men, and set up his standard in the city of Abraham, where first his father had received the crown of Judah. From Hebron he sent to Giloh for Ahithophel, one of his father's counselors, who seems to have known of the plot, and to have gone from Jerusalem to his own city of Giloh, in order to be within Absalom's call. This man, though his name signifies "the brother of foolishness," was in great repute for wisdom, and men went to consult him almost as they went to the oracle of God. By comparing 2 Samuel xi., 3, where it is said that Bath-sheba was the daughter of Eliam, with 2 Samuel xxiii., 34, where it is recorded that Eliam was the son of Ahithophel the Gilonite, and connecting these with the fact that Uriah and Eliam were comrades, both belonging to the order of the worthies, we get the interesting result that

## THE REVOLT OF ABSALOM. 309

Ahithophel was the grandfather of Bath-sheba. And from this the inference seems inevitable, that his defection to Absalom was caused by the displeasure which he felt at the wrong done ten years before to the wife of Uriah.*

Thus the strength of Absalom's conspiracy is seen to be a direct result of David's great transgression. Ahithophel's name was in itself almost a guarantee of Absalom's success. And we may judge of the importance which was attached to him, not only from the prayer offered by David when he heard of his treachery, and the commission which he gave to Hushai to counteract his advice, but also from the plaintive wail which he makes over him in the 41st Psalm: "Yea, mine own familiar friend, in whom I trusted, which did eat of my bread, hath lifted up his heel against me." And again, more strikingly, in the 55th Psalm: "For it was not an enemy that reproached me; then I could have borne it: neither was it he that hated me that did magnify himself against me; then I would have hid myself from him: but it was thou, a man mine equal, my guide, and mine acquaintance. We took sweet counsel together, and walked unto the house of God in company."

Evil tidings fly swiftly. So a messenger soon brought news to David of Absalom's procedure, and the king at once resolved to leave Jerusalem. This determination was probably taken by him because there were not sufficient troops to garrison the city, or because he had no confidence in the inhabitants that they would be faithful to him; and the story of his departure from his palace is here told with a beauty and a pathos which are perfectly unapproachable. He left ten of his concubines behind to look after the house, and went on, as it is said, to a place that is far off; or rath-

---

* See, on this point, Blunt's "Sciptural Coincidences," p. 136; also "Biblical Studies," by E. H. Plumtre, p. 97.

er, as it might be rendered, to "the house far off"—the last house, probably, in the city. Here the sorrowful procession was marshaled. His faithful body-guard went first; then the remnant of his band of six hundred; then his servants. Among those beside him he saw Ittai the Gittite; and struck, perhaps, with the fact that an alien should be faithful to him when his own son was false, he besought him to return; but the soldier nobly replied, in words which he as nobly redeemed, "As the Lord liveth, and as my lord the king liveth, surely in what place my lord the king shall be, whether in death or life, even there also will thy servant be." And so they went on—out down into the valley and across the Kedron—while a loud, long wail ascended from the weeping multitude. At this point they were met by Zadok the high-priest, and by the Levites who, coming from the sacred tent, had brought with them the ark of the covenant of the Lord, while Abiathar stood waiting till the people had gone out of the city. But David's piety was not of that superstitious sort which clung to the ark as if it had been a talisman. To him it was but the symbol of God's covenant love, which was equally sure to him wherever he might be; so he said, in words which the most callous can not read without emotion, "Carry back the ark of God into the city: if I shall find favor in the eyes of the Lord, he will bring me again, and show me both it and his habitation: but if he thus say, I have no delight in thee; behold, here am I, let him do to me as seemeth good unto him." But the faith of David was equaled only by his prudence; for he counseled the priests to return to the city, and to send him tidings of what should be decided by Absalom, by the hands of their sons, Jonathan and Ahimaaz. So, having dismissed them, they went on up the Mount of Olives, the king with his feet bare, and his head covered, weeping as he went, and the whole company following his example.

## The Revolt of Absalom.

Now for the first time, as it would seem, he was informed of Ahithophel's falling away to Absalom; and just as he had breathed the prayer, "O Lord, I pray thee, turn the counsel of Ahithophel into foolishness," Hushai, the Archite, made his appearance, with his coat rent, and earth upon his head. This man was also one of David's privy councilors, and his coming at this particular juncture, immediately after the monarch had heard of Ahithophel's treachery, seems to have suggested to him that he was a fitting instrument for counteracting the influence of that astute man. Hence he said to him, "If thou passest on with me, then thou shalt be a burden unto me: but if thou return to the city, and say unto Absalom, I will be thy servant, O king; as I have been thy father's servant hitherto, so will I now also be thy servant: then mayest thou for me defeat the counsel of Ahithophel. And hast thou not there with thee Zadok and Abiathar the priests? therefore it shall be, that what thing soever thou shalt hear out of the king's house, thou shall tell it to Zadok and Abiathar the priests. Behold, they have there with them their two sons, Ahimaaz, Zadok's son, and Jonathan, Abiathar's son; and by them ye shall send unto me every thing that ye can hear." In the midst of such piety and resignation, it is strange to find David asking his friend thus to act a dishonest part, and play the spy. We are not called to vindicate his conduct. The Scriptures simply record it; and we must not suppose that every thing here is approved which is not directly, and in so many words, condemned. But we may say two things by way of debarring hasty judgment here.

First—and I am using now the words of Professor Plumtre: "Slowly in the character of any people; more slowly still in that of any Eastern people; most slowly of all, perhaps, in that of Israel, have men risen to the excellence of veracity. We must not think that the king's religion was a hypocrisy because it did not bear at once the fruit of the spotless honor and unswerving truth which mark the highest forms of Christian goodness. The Christian Church herself has to notice many like inconsistencies among her crowned martyrs."*

Second: let us not forget what those means are by which, even in these modern days, with all our Christian loftiness of character, we seek to countermine and check political rebellion. Some years ago, while I was a resident in Liverpool, there was great talk of Fenianism. We heard of plots for the taking of the ancient city of Chester, and the burning of ships in our own docks. How did we hear of them? By spies, who feigned themselves Fenians for the time! and the man whose astuteness made these discoveries through means of Hushai-like instruments was rewarded by being made a companion of the Most Honorable Order of the Bath! Observe, I do not vindicate either David or these modern officers. I simply state the facts, and beg to say, that if men, with the New Testament in their hands, can do such things, we ought to be tender in our treatment of David here. When they reached the top of the hill, and had commenced the descent on the opposite side, Ziba, the servant of Mephibosheth, met them, bringing supplies, and making, at the same time, a false accusation of treason against his master. David, not seeing the trap which had been so cunningly laid for him, unsuspiciously fell into it, and gave to Ziba as a gift all the land which he had been farming for Mephibosheth. We may have more to say of this when Mephibosheth comes to speak for himself. Meanwhile, let us move forward with the sorrowful company.

The path was along a ridge which had a deep ravine beneath it, and another ridge of a similar sort rising on the op-

---

* "Biblical Studies," p. 102.

posite side; and as they went forward on their side, a wicked man of the house of Saul made his appearance on the other, and, keeping abreast of them the while, heaped curses, such as only an Oriental can utter, on the head of David. He cried, "Come out, come out, thou bloody man, and thou man of Belial: the Lord hath returned upon thee all the blood of the house of Saul, in whose stead thou hast reigned; and the Lord hath delivered the kingdom into the hand of Absalom thy son: and, behold, thou art taken in thy mischief, because thou art a bloody man." Nor was he content with uttering maledictions; he cast stones at David and his servants across the gorge, and made every manifestation of implacable enmity and malignity. Abishai, the brother of Joab, was greatly provoked by his procedure, and sought permission to slay him; but David, with an expression of querulousness which shows how keenly he felt the ascendency which Joab and his brother had obtained over him, said, "So let him curse, because the Lord hath said unto him, Curse David. Who shall then say, Wherefore hast thou done so?" Then, in language which lets us see how bitterly he felt Absalom's treason, and how all other troubles were swallowed up in that one great sorrow, he added, "Behold, my son, which came forth of my bowels, seeketh my life: how much more now may this Benjamite do it? let him alone, and let him curse; for the Lord hath bidden him. It may be that the Lord will look upon mine affliction, and that the Lord will requite me good for his cursing this day." So they set forward, and came at length to the Valley of the Jordan, where they tarried to refresh themselves. In all probability it was morning when they left the palace, and the shades of evening had closed over them before they had safely settled their encampment; but through the darkness with which they were enveloped the book of Psalms permits us to see, and from it we learn somewhat of the monarch's feelings after that trying and fatiguing day; for even the most rationalistic interpreters connect with the events which we are reviewing those calm and trustful hymns, the one for the evening and the other for the morning, which stand fourth and third in the Psalter. Let us, then, listen a while at the door of the royal tent, that we may hear with what pious thoughts and earnest prayers he shutteth in that doleful day: "Hear me when I call, O God of my righteousness: thou hast enlarged me when I was in distress; have mercy upon me, and hear my prayer. O ye sons of men, how long will ye turn my glory into shame? how long will ye love vanity, and seek after leasing? But know that the Lord hath set apart him that is godly for himself: the Lord will hear when I call unto him. Stand in awe, and sin not: commune with your own heart upon your bed, and be still. Offer the sacrifices of righteousness, and put your trust in the Lord. There be many that say, Who will show us any good? Lord, lift thou up the light of thy countenance upon us. Thou hast put gladness in my heart, more than in the time that their corn and their wine increased. I will both lay me down in peace, and sleep: for thou, Lord, only makest me dwell in safety." Then, as the light of the morning breaks, the harp is again tuned, and heart and voice accompany it, as thus he sings: "Lord, how are they increased that trouble me! Many are they that rise up against me. Many there be which say of my soul, There is no help for him in God. But thou, O Lord, art a shield for me; my glory, and the lifter up of mine head. I cried unto the Lord with my voice, and he heard me out of his holy hill. I laid me down and slept; I awaked; for the Lord sustained me. I will not be afraid of ten thousands of people, that have set themselves against me round about. Arise, O Lord; save me, O my God: for thou hast smitten all mine enemies upon the cheek-bone; thou hast broken the teeth of the ungodly. Salvation belongeth unto the Lord: thy blessing is upon thy people."

Richter, as quoted by Carlyle, has said, "The canary-bird sings sweeter the longer it has been trained in a darkened cage."* Oh, what rich melody comes from David's heart in the day when God has darkened the cage for him! It is in times of trial that he comes most brightly out; and at no season are we more impressed with his piety, his genius, his sincerity, than when we hear him solace his troubled soul with song. The notes of the nightingale, whensoever heard, must be ever sweet, but they are sweetest far when they come trilling through the darkness; and for the same reason we count these companion hymns as among the finest David ever wrote. At this point we must for the present leave him. Let us stay only to carry with us some valuable lessons.

In the first place, we may learn from this whole narrative what ruinous consequences must ever flow from the ignoring or violation of God's laws for the household. Though David regulated his public administration by the will of God, yet, in his family matters, he seems to have disregarded the plain indications of Jehovah's mind, contained even in the books of Moses. For though polygamy was in certain circumstances permitted, still the whole spirit of the precepts of the Pentateuch was to discourage it, and to sustain the primeval appointment that one man should be the husband of one wife; and when David set that law at naught, he could not look for any thing else than domestic discord. The family of each wife became a separate party in the State, and their homes became hot-beds of intrigue, faction, and all manner of annoyance. But this was not the only point wherein David violated God's ordinance of the family. He was shamefully indulgent to his children. It might be said of him as of Eli, "That his sons made themselves vile, and he restrained them not." Had he dealt rightly with Amnon,

---

\* See the Essay on Burns, in Carlyle's miscellaneous writings.

Absalom's fratricide, and all the evils which it drew in its train might have been avoided. And even after the guilt of his eldest born, if he had firmly adhered to his first refusal to allow Amnon to go to the sheep-shearing at his brother's farm, the evil might still have been eluded. But with that fatal easiness of temper which characterized his treatment of his children, he yielded to Absalom's entreaties, and the result was the tragedy which is here described. It may be said, indeed, that his discipline of Absalom was firm; but that was hardly the case, for he never really brought matters to a point even with him; and his recalling him from exile, while yet he did not see him, though it may seem to have been an indication of strength of principle, was in truth a token of weakness. He feared to push things to an issue. He had not the courage to deal with a judicial hand with Absalom, and so, while his treatment of him did not satisfy the claims of justice, it only the more thoroughly alienated the son from the father.

The whole history is thus fraught with richest lessons to parents. It is a warning against over-indulgence, and neglect of discipline. No doubt there are evils in the other extreme, and we must be cautious lest we provoke our "children to wrath" by over-sternness; yet in the family there must be government, and the parent who does not secure the allegiance and obedience of his child, is as really violating the fifth commandment as is the child who disobeys and dishonors him. There is a happy rule of love, and a willing subjection of respect, which it ought to be every parent's ambition to exercise and receive, and miserable is the household from which these are absent! In saying all this, I do not in the least degree excuse David's children for their conduct. On the contrary, it was godless and heartless in the extremest degree. Let no son, therefore, shelter himself under my words for dishonoring his father, or disobeying his mother; since, no matter what a parent's faults may be, a parent is a parent still, and ought to have a place in the holy of holies in the heart of every child.

In the second place, we may learn from this whole subject that, if parents would have thorough discipline in their homes, they must be pure and holy themselves. David's weakness in the matters which have been before us sprung out of his wickedness. His conscience made him a coward. He was afraid to bring the law into force against his children, lest its sword should descend also on his own head. Alas! in how many homes in these days is the disobedience of the children due to the conscious sinfulness of the parents. How can a drunken and profane father, or an extravagant, proud, and worldly mother, hope to receive the respect of children? or how can they enforce, in the case of their families, laws which they are themselves continually violating? Example is better than precept; and where consciously a bad example is set, either the precept will not be enforced, or its enforcement will provoke the child into more bitter antagonism and rebellion.

In the third place, we may learn from this story to put a right estimate on personal beauty. It does not indicate spiritual loveliness, for Absalom was far from being as attractive in character as he was in appearance. It is a gift from God, hence we are not to despise it. We may honor it for his sake. If we have it not ourselves, we are not to envy those who possess it; while, if we do possess it, the case of Tamar bids us be on our guard lest it should prove either a temptation to others or a snare to ourselves. Alas! how many have been brought by it, through their own folly, into a deeper than Tamar's disgrace, because with them it has been a voluntary thing.

Finally: we may contrast David's conduct toward Absalom here with that of God toward the sinner. The wise woman of Tekoah had referred to God in these beautiful words: "For we must needs die, and are as water spilled on the ground, which can not be gathered up again; neither doth God respect any person; yet doth he devise means that his banished be not expelled from him." But in the case of God and the sinner there are several things present which we look in vain for in that of David with Absalom.

First of all, in recalling the sinner, God has devised means by which his law is fully satisfied for human guilt; but David had no proper satisfaction to the law for Absalom's guilt. The means which God has employed for honoring his justice while bringing back the banished sinner are well known to you all. They are the mission, and work, and sacrifice of Jesus, who for the sinner has "magnified God's law, and made it honorable." Hence, in connection with that atonement, God is seen to be a just God, and a Saviour; yea, he declares his righteousness even in the very act of remitting the believer's sin.

In the second place, while David refused to see the face of the returned Absalom, God welcomes every penitent to his heart, and accepts him as righteous in his sight for the sake of Jesus, in whom he believes. What a welcome the father gave, in the parable, to the returning prodigal! but that is nothing to the welcome given by God to the repenting sinner. Do not fear, then, oh sinner, to repair to him. He will receive you for Christ's sake. He will retain you in his favor, and he will never let you perish. Is it not written, "Him that cometh unto me I will in no wise cast out?"

In the third place, as the result of all this on the part of God, the sinner's nature is changed, so that instead of being, as formerly, alienated in heart from God, he loves him, and desires to please him. Absalom, as we saw, was fretted and exasperated by his father's treatment of him; and very probably the rebellion which he attempted was plotted during these two years when he was not permitted to look upon his father's face. But the forgiven sinner's heart is melted by God's love; and through the grace of the Holy Spirit he is changed from a rebel into a friend. Oh, the rich grace "of highest God!" Sinner, behold here the way of life! Ye banished ones, return; and God will give you welcome. Come, with the prodigal's resolution and confession. Come as you are. Come now. And your return will gladden every heart in heaven, and strike a thrill through every note in the chorus of the skies; while God himself, with benignant love, shall say, "This, my son, was dead, and is alive again; he was lost, and is found."

## XVIII.

### *ABSALOM'S DEFEAT AND DEATH.*

#### 2 SAMUEL xvi., 15; xix.

LEAVING David and his weary followers to rest themselves in the Valley of the Jordan, let us return to Jerusalem, and mark the progress of the rebellion there. On the arrival of Absalom at the Holy City, whither he had come from Hebron with Ahithophel and the whole band of his adherents, he was met by Hushai, who saluted him as king, and offered him his allegiance. Evidently this was more than Absalom had expected. The character of the Archite stood so high for integrity and fidelity, that the rebel had not dared to hope for his assistance; so, scarcely knowing what to make of his protestations and homage, he said to him, partly in bantering welcome, and partly also in suspicion, "Is this thy kindness to thy friend? why wentest thou not with thy friend?" But if he had entertained any misgivings upon the subject, the reply of Hushai set them all at rest; so he joyfully received him into the ranks of his followers, and installed him among his privy councilors.

His first act in Jerusalem was to take public possession of his father's harem. By this most abominable procedure he not only unconsciously fulfilled the prediction of Nathan,* but also committed himself, in the most offensive and insulting manner, to irreconcilable hostility against his father. The offense was one which no monarch could forgive; and the readiness with which he committed it was, therefore, a

---

\* 2 Samuel xii.. 11.

proclamation of war to "the bitter end." It was like throwing away the scabbard after having drawn the sword, or like burning the boats after having crossed the river. It effectually cut off all possibility of retreating from the course on which he had entered, and showed that he was determined to come to no terms with David. Nor can we fail to see the motive by which Ahithophel was actuated in advising Absalom to commit this iniquity. For one thing, it would stimulate all who flocked round the rebel standard to fiercer energy in the effort to make their cause successful, inasmuch as they would fight with the feeling that they had nothing to hope for from their adversary but destruction. For another, it was the course which was most likely to secure Ahithophel's own safety. Knowing well David's foolish fondness for his children, he was thoroughly persuaded that, in the event of the rebellion being crushed, he would be sure to become reconciled to his son. In such a case, Ahithophel also knew that he would be the victim on whose head the royal vengeance would first and most especially fall. Hence he took care to provide against such an issue, by setting Absalom on a course which, in all Eastern countries, makes reconciliation impossible.

Meanwhile the people of the city took note of all this, and, seeing men of such acknowledged ability as Ahithophel and Hushai among the principal supporters of Absalom, they easily transferred their allegiance to the newly-recognized king, the rather, perhaps, that the flight of David had seemed to them a virtual abdication of the throne, or, at all events, an indication that he had no confidence in the loyalty of the inhabitants of his capital. In any case, they were quite ready, if not eager, to welcome Absalom as their king. The fickleness of popular favor has passed into a proverb; and the scenes which were witnessed in Great Britain at the eras of the Commonwealth, the Restoration, and the Revolution, may help us to understand what took place at Jerusalem in the case before us. Besides, as one has suggestively asked, "Were not these Jews the ancestors of those who, centuries later, cried, at one time, 'Hosanna!' and at another, 'Crucify him!' in reference to a nobler prince than the son of Jesse?"

Soon after coming to Jerusalem, Absalom seems to have called together what we might term a council, to determine the course which the campaign was to take. At this meeting, Ahithophel, as being by common consent the ablest man, was first asked to declare his opinion. In reply, he offered to set out in immediate pursuit of David with twelve thousand men, calculating that he would come upon the king and his band, "weary and weak-handed;" and that, overawed by superior numbers, his followers would take to flight, and leave the aged monarch to his fate. This, he believed, would end the war, since after the death of David, and finding they had nothing left to fight for, his adherents would return to Jerusalem, and give in their allegiance to Absalom as his rightful heir.

This plan was worthy of Ahithophel's reputation. If it had been energetically followed, it would have been completely successful, and would have changed the entire color and complexion of Jewish history. But there was one at that council-board whom Absalom had not summoned, for "God had appointed to defeat the wise counsel of Ahithophel;" and therefore, though it was well received at first, it was afterward rejected, yet so as to make manifest the unfettered moral freedom of all concerned. Absalom, wishing to view the matter from every side, called on Hushai to give his advice; and such was the impression produced by him, that his proposition was unanimously adopted. The Archite had a difficult game to play; and we may well believe that, when Ahithophel's scheme was propounded to him, his heart misgave him for his aged king. But he proved equal to the

## Absalom's Defeat and Death.

occasion; for, assuming the air and manner of a true friend of Absalom, he so magnified the difficulties in the way of the execution of his rival's proposal as to prepare the way for the acceptance of that which he suggested, and which he described in a style so winning and rhetorical as completely to captivate all his hearers. Reminding them of the prowess of David and his worthies, and picturing to their imagination the fierceness with which they would fight if they were brought to bay in some rocky retreat, and the panic which they might create in the ranks of Absalom by some sudden sally, he advised that the prince should tarry at Jerusalem until an army had been gathered from the whole country, and that thereafter he should take the field against his father, who would then become an easy prey, whether they met him in the open country, or had to besiege him in a fortified town.

Every one can see that, in a strategic point of view, this plan was infinitely inferior to Ahithophel's; but the manner in which it was expounded, and perhaps, also, the glory which it promised to Absalom in placing him at the head of such an army as Hushai had described, so charmed the prince and the members of the assembly, that they at once decided to follow it. This determination drove Ahithophel from the council-chamber in moody indignation. But whither was he now to go? After what had occurred in the harem, David would never consent to receive him again; neither could he now have pleasure in the service of Absalom. So, deeming that life had nothing more of honor or enjoyment in store for him, "he saddled his ass, and arose, and gat him home to his house, to his city, and put his household in order, and hanged himself."

This is the first recorded case of deliberate suicide. Saul, already mortally wounded on the battle-field, fell upon his sword, but this is the earliest instance in history of premeditated self-murder; and the feelings which led to it, and which we can easily analyze, were very similar to those which have impelled many in our own times to commit the same awful iniquity. Chief among them was wounded pride. He who had been so long to his fellow-men like the oracle of God, could not survive the humiliation of having Hushai's advice preferred to his own. Then, besides this, there was the conviction that Absalom's cause was now hopelessly ruined. He foresaw that the following of Hushai's counsel would give David time to collect his forces, as indeed the Archite meant it should. But he knew also that this was all that David needed for the recovery of his throne; and as, in such an event, he would be the first victim of the monarch's indignation, he determined to deprive David of the satisfaction of putting him to death by himself anticipating his doom. Perhaps, also, there was a mingling of remorse with those other emotions of pride. He had left a master who loved and valued him, who, indeed, regarded him as his equal and guide, and he had transferred his services to one who, as he now discovered, had not the wisdom to appreciate his worth, but preferred the gaudy glitter of empty rhetoric to the substantial wisdom of unadorned speech. This contrast, thus forced upon him, might awaken his conscience to the value of the friendship which he had forfeited when he turned against David, until at length remorse and shame so overwhelmed him, that, like a deeper traitor, of whom he was only the feeble prototype, he could not endure life, and hurried himself into eternity. It never occurred to him to ask, "If I can not face David, how shall I look upon Jehovah? If I can not endure the accusations of conscience, how shall I stand before the judgment-seat of God?"

Just about the time that Ahithophel was leaving Jerusalem, with the dark resolve of self-destruction maturing in his heart, a female servant was sent by Zadok and Abiathar to the well of En-rogel, near which their two sons, Jonathan

## Absalom's Defeat and Death. 325

and Ahimaaz, were concealed. Hushai had told the high-priests the issue of the council, and they had commissioned this young woman to convey his message to their sons, that they might carry it to David. The fountain of En-rogel was only a little way out of the city. Its name signifies the *well of treading*, and indicates that it was frequented by those who were engaged in the washing of clothes—a work which then, as occasionally yet in the Highlands of Scotland, was performed by treading with the feet rather than by rubbing with the hands. It was also restricted to women. Hence, as the presence of a female servant in that neighborhood would excite no suspicion, we can understand how such a messenger was sent on such an important commission.

Having received the message, the two young men set out at once for the Valley of the Jordan; but, in spite of all the precautions which had been taken to insure secrecy, they were seen by a lad, who, guessing their errand, went and told Absalom. The rebel prince immediately sent his servants in pursuit of them; but discovering that they were chased, the youths held forward fleetly as far as Bahurim, where they found a singular hiding-place in the court of a house. Fixing themselves on the side of an open well, the woman of the house put over its mouth a covering, on which she spread ground corn, so that there was nothing to indicate their presence; and when Absalom's servants came asking after them, she turned away suspicion by an equivocal answer, which evinced the readiness of her wit no less than the kindness of her heart: "They be gone over the brook of water."

After escaping from this danger the couriers pushed on until they came to David's encampment, where they delivered their message. "Arise, and pass quickly over the water: for thus hath Ahithophel counseled against you." It may appear strange that no mention was made by these young men of Hushai's own counsel, and of the fact that it had been preferred to that of Ahithophel. But we must bear in mind that we have here only the merest outline of what was actually said; and even if no reference was made by the messengers to the actual decision of the council, it is conceivable that this silence may have been suggested by Hushai himself, who may have been afraid that, even after all that had occurred to the contrary, Ahithophel's counsel might yet be followed. In any case, he seems to have wished that David should at once make for a place of safety; so, on the night following his receipt of the message, the monarch and all his company passed over Jordan, and halted not until they entered Mahanaim.

The town called by this name was built upon a spot hallowed by its connection with Jacob's history. There the angels of God met the patriarch; and perhaps, as the old story rose to David's recollection, the strains of his own Psalm would come to his lips to strengthen his faith and revive his courage: "The angel of the Lord encampeth round about them that fear him and delivereth them." Mahanaim lay within the territory of Gad, and near the line by which it was separated from that of Manasseh. It was a city of considerable importance, for Ishbosheth had made it his capital during his seven and a half years' reign over Israel. It was evidently a fortified place, and that, together with the fact that it was a city of the Levites, who were always faithful to him, may have induced David to make it his head-quarters. But, whatever considerations may have moved him to choose it, he had no reason to repent of his selection, for he was soon surrounded by kind and generous friends. In particular, three principal men in that region are named as having brought to him and his men seasonable and abundant supplies. These were Shobi, the son of Nahash, of Rabbah, of the children of Ammon: Machir, the son of Ammiel, of Lo-debar; and Barzillai, the Gileadite, of Rogelim; and we can not pass them without staying a few moments to note some interesting particulars regarding them. Shobi belonged to Rabbah, of the children of Ammon: now, when we remember how, about ten years before, David had taken that city, and subjected its defenders to unwonted cruelties, we may be disposed to wonder that any one from it should have been so ready to render assistance to the fugitive king in the day of his calamity. But Nahash, the father of Shobi, had been, apparently, a valued friend of David's; and though the insult which he had received from Hanun had provoked him to make war upon the Ammonites, nothing is more likely than that, after the campaign was over, he appointed Shobi as a kind of viceroy over Rabbah; thus displacing Hanun, and binding Shobi to him by the strongest ties of interest and gratitude. If this were so, we have a thorough explanation of the fact that the richest supplies in David's extremity came from these Ammonites, with whom, in former times, he had waged fiercest war.

Machir, the son of Ammiel, had been the host and guardian of Mephibosheth, and so could not but be attracted to David for his kindness to the disabled son of Jonathan. Some have supposed, indeed, that there was even a closer connection between him and David. It happens that in 1 Samuel xi., 3, Bath-sheba is styled the daughter of Eliam; and in 1 Chronicles iii., 5, she is called the daughter of Ammiel. The two names, Eliam and Ammiel, are identical in meaning, and seem to be used interchangeably; and from a comparison of these two texts, some, among whom is Professor Plumtre, draw the inference that Machir was the brother of Bath-sheba. This, however, would necessitate the further inference that Ammiel was the grandson of Ahithophel—a consideration which has escaped the notice of the professor, and which, in my judgment, renders it quite improbable that there was any relationship such as that which he has sought to establish between Machir and Bath-sheba, since it is difficult to explain how Ahithophel should be of Giloh, and his grandson of Gilead. As for good old Barzillai, the heart is drawn out toward him with peculiar tenderness. He was a beautiful specimen of a venerable chief, whose kindness of heart was equaled only by his contentedness of spirit; and he stands out before us with vivid, life-like distinctness, as one of the most interesting characters in this thrilling history. He appears only on another occasion; yet we feel as if we knew him thoroughly, and loved him dearly. His old age was beautiful exceedingly, and it is delightful to see how at a time of life when, usually, men take a closer grip of worldly things, and become more selfish and illiberal, he was ready to give of his best to David in the hour of his extremity.

We know not how long Absalom took to collect his forces, but at the earliest moment after the muster he went forth with them across the Jordan. He missed Joab, on whom, perhaps, he had been counting, but who had preferred to follow his father. This, however, did not disconcert him, for he found a suitable substitute for the crafty son of Zeruiah in Amasa, the son of Abigail, whose fitness for the post is seen in the fact that, after the restoration, David made him his own captain instead of Joab. Absalom's forces were encamped in the land of Gilead, and David, around whom, by this time, a large army had collected, hastened to give him battle. With the old martial fire stirring within him, he divided his troops into three divisions, under Joab, Abishai, and Ittai, and declared his intention of leading them in person. This, however, his loving followers would not allow, for on his life their cause depended, and they would not hear of his running the risk of the battle-field. Reluctantly he yielded to their importunity, and, relieved of the responsibility of leadership, his mind seems to have occupied itself with

Absalom, over whom he yearned with wounded but yet tender affection. When his troops left Mahanaim, he took his station at the side of the gate; and as rank after rank deployed before him, he gave, with quivering voice and tearful eye, his orders thus: "Deal gently, for my sake, with the young man, even with Absalom."

The scene of the battle was in what is called, for what reason does not appear, "the wood of Ephraim," and victory crowned the loyal army of the brave old king. Better disciplined and better led than the hastily mustered forces of Absalom, the soldiers of David broke the ranks of their enemies, and sent them to seek for shelter in the forests which are abundant on the eastern borders of Jordan. Here they were so entangled that they were easily overcome. Nor did Absalom escape; for, as he rode through the thicket, his head (not his hair, as is generally supposed) was caught in the thick boughs of a tree; and his mule running from beneath him, he was left hanging "between the heaven and the earth." In this position he was seen by a young man of David's army, who told Joab of the circumstance; and the general, blaming the youth for not having slain him, hastened forward with ten of his troopers, who surrounded the tree, while with his own hand he pierced the heart of Absalom with three darts. Then, deeming the campaign ended, he blew the trumpet as the signal for recall; and taking the body of Absalom, he cast it into a pit, and raised over it a heap of stones like to those which used to be formed over the graves of grievous malefactors.

What a different tomb was this from that stately mausoleum which, in his pride of heart, and with the desire of perpetuating his name, he had reared for himself in the king's dale! And as we stand to throw one stone upon his cairn, we can not help exclaiming, How different his death had been if his life had been but worthier! Had he chosen the path of filial love and reverence, and sought to walk in morality and devout submission to the will of God, he might have blessed his own age, and left an example that might have won the admiration and imitation of succeeding generations; but as it is, he is held up here to the execration of humanity as the incarnation of filial ingratitude, and the impersonation of revenge in its foulest and most unnatural shape. Combining in his career the guilt of Reuben with the sin of Cain, he added to it a parricidal treachery all his own; and having broken every law, both of the family and the State, he so put himself beyond the pale of human mercy, that we can not fail to see a fitness in the fate that overtook him. We undertake not to justify Joab for his disregard of David's tender injunction, yet none the less must we recognize the righteous retribution of which, in this instance, he was the executioner. The disobedient son, under the Mosaic law, was to be stoned to death; and in the heap that was added to the original cairn by the successive generations of his countrymen as they pronounced curses on his memory, we see a monumental beacon that marks forever the dangerous reef whereon he made shipwreck of his soul.

But how was the news to be broken to his father? Ahimaaz offered to be the bearer of the tidings. But Joab would not intrust him with the commission, and preferred to send one Cushi, most probably an Ethiopian servant, with the message. This, however, did not satisfy the high-priest's son; so, extorting a permission from the captain of the host, the fleet courier ran, and arrived first at the gate of Mahanaim, where a scene occurred which lets us see far into the unfathomed depths of a true parent's heart. Fastened and almost fascinated to the spot, the king is still in the same place in which he had parted from his troops in the early morning. All day long he has been waiting for intelligence; and as he has sat watching there, his throne, his crown, his kingdom, all have been forgotten in his eager concern for Absalom. He is not now the king, so much is he the father. When the swift-footed Ahimaaz comes with tidings of victory, they are all unheeded as the question rises, "Is the young man Absalom safe?" And when Cushi makes his appearance, the inquiry still is, "Is the young man Absalom safe?" Then, as the full truth comes out, every thing else is swallowed up in the torrent of that emotion which, sweeping gratitude, and submission, and even faith in God before it for the time, bears him up to the chamber over the gate, where he cries, with a great and exceeding bitter cry, "O my son Absalom! my son, my son Absalom! would God I had died for thee, O Absalom, my son, my son!" There are griefs, as well as joys, with which a stranger may not intermeddle; let us shut the chamber door and withdraw, leaving the royal mourner a while in the sanctity of his sore sorrow, while we seek to glean from the narrative the solemn lessons which it teaches.

From the issue of the council-meeting, we may see how, in perfect harmony with the free agency of men, and even through that free agency, God fulfills his purposes. Before Absalom called his friends together, it was appointed by God to turn the counsel of Ahithophel to foolishness; and that appointment was carried out, while yet no violence was done to the will of any person, and no countenance given to the fraud and hypocrisy of Hushai. Thus God maketh the cunning and craft of men, as well as their wrath, to praise, and the remainder thereof he restrains. How he accomplishes this, we know not. We only see the two extremes: the first, in his own appointment herein revealed; the second, in the men's consciousness of perfect freedom to do as they chose; but the intermediate process, the manner in which the Divine appointment accomplished its fulfillment through moral agents, baffles us to comprehend. Still the mystery of the mode does not alter the certainty of the fact that it is thus God carries on his moral government of the world. We see numerous illustrations of it everywhere. Even in the narrative over which we have now come it has another exemplification in that, while Absalom was the instrument in fulfilling Nathan's prophecies about his father, he was yet, as a free agent, held responsible for the sin which he committed in so doing, and was punished with righteous retribution. So it is always. God is working now in the affairs of individual men, just as really and truly as he was working here in those of David. The only difference is, that in this inspired history his hand is everywhere acknowledged, while we too frequently ignore his agency. Let us seek to have a firmer faith in the doctrine of a particular providence, and in the fact that all things are controlled and overruled by God for the carrying forward of his great appointments, while yet we recognize as fully our own liberty and responsibility. "There are many devices in a man's heart; nevertheless the counsel of the Lord, that shall stand." "The Lord bringeth the counsel of the heathen to naught, he maketh the devices of the people of none effect." "The counsel of the Lord standeth forever, the thoughts of his heart to all generations."

In the record of Ahithophel's suicide we see how foolish even the wisest of men may be in spiritual matters. This astute counselor, who was reputed as the oracle of God, has forethought enough to set his household in order before he dies; yet he has not sufficient prudence to forecast what shall be after death, and arrange for that. Had he considered "that undiscovered country from whose bourne no traveler returns," he had never been guilty of this great iniquity. Had he thought on how he was to meet his God, he would not have rushed unsent for into the Eternal Presence, red-handed with his own murder. We wonder at his infatuation. We marvel at his inconsistency. Yet are there not many among ourselves guilty of a like folly? We may not meditate suicide indeed — God forbid that we ever should; but we have set our households in order; we have arranged our business and our property, so that if we were taken from the earth those dependent on us would be spared all unnecessary trouble and expense; we have made our wills, and done every thing that we think needful in that regard, and we have done well therein; so well, that if any have not made these arrangements, they ought to make them forthwith. Yet have we done no more? What about our souls? We are about to enter upon the unseen; we are soon to stand " naked and open before the eyes of Him with whom we have to do;" we have the awful eternity before us, with the certainty that we must spend its cycles either in unmitigated misery or in purest enjoyment; and what provision have we made for that? Oh! if, having arranged our temporal matters, we leave uncared for the higher concerns of our spirits, are we not guilty of the folly of Ahithophel here? and may it not be said to us at last, "This ought ye to have done, and not to have left the other undone." Say not to me there is time enough to arrange all that; you know not what an hour may bring forth. Make haste, therefore, and delay not to commit your soul to him who alone is able to keep it "against that day."

From the grief of David here, the parents among us may see how needful it is that they should not, by the influence either of their training or example, injure the character of their children. Many things indeed entered into that bitter cup which David was made to drink in the chamber over Mahanaim's gate. There was the natural sorrow of a parent in the loss of a child whom he had once loved most passionately, and whom he still yearned after, though he had ceased to be worthy of his affection. There was also the hopelessness of this dreadful separation between him and his boy. When the infant of Bath-sheba died, he could say, "I shall go to him;" but on this occasion there is no such comforting assurance. Absalom's sun had gone down in thickest darkness; no one ray of hope remained to relieve the gloom of his father's heart; and none but those who have been called to mourn in similar circumstances can tell how bitter is a grief like that.

But worse than either of these ingredients in this cup of anguish would be, as I think, the consciousness in David's heart, that if he had himself been all he ought to have been, his son might not thus have perished. Was there no connection between his own great trespass and Absalom's iniquity? If he had been less foolishly indulgent, Absalom might never have rebelled. Nay, if he had been wiser, even after Absalom's fratricidal guilt, probably he had not stung him into revolt. Such thoughts and questionings as these, would, I doubt not, intensify the sadness of the Psalmist in this trying hour; and it becomes every parent among us to see that in his training of his children, and in his life before them, there is nothing that may tend to ruin them. David now professes, and I believe with truth, to desire that he had died for Absalom; but that was a vain wish. He ought to have lived more for Absalom. He ought, by his own character, to have taught him to love holiness, or, at all events, he ought to have seen that there was nothing in his own conduct to encourage his son in wickedness or to provoke him to wrath; and then, though Absalom had made shipwreck, he might have had the consolation that he had done his utmost to prevent such a catastrophe.

In this connection I can not help recalling an incident in the life of James Stirling, well known as the first temperance missionary in Scotland. James was a drunkard up to his sixtieth year ; but then he was, through the abstinence movement, rescued from his danger, and "plucked as a brand out of the burning!" Out of gratitude for his deliverance, he gave himself for the next twenty years of his life to the advocacy of the Temperance cause, traveling over the length and breadth of Scotland, helping to save men from the curse of strong drink. On one of these journeys, when he arrived at Aberdeen, he met with one of his sons, who, taking after his father's early example, had become a drunkard, and was at that time a soldier. The two had a long and interesting talk in the evening, and old James thought the youth was doing better ; but in the morning he was sent for in great haste, and hurrying to the place, wondering much what the message meant, he was shown—oh horror!—the body of his son, who had committed suicide during the night. Who may describe the anguish of that father's heart as David's wail was wrung out of him, while he appended this of his own: Had I been a sober man all my life, this might never have occurred.*

Parents, will you ponder the lesson which this incident suggests? Do not contribute to the ruin of your children by any indiscretion, or inconsistency, or sin of yours. In a report of the Liverpool Observatory I once read this statement, as a reason why ship-masters ought to have their chronometers daily compared with the true time, and their variations rated: "The error of a second a day may in the course of a voyage sink a ship." So it is here: the variation of our conduct from the sacred standard, if statedly persevered in by us before our children, may not only be the means of our own destruction, but may ruin them eternally. What a solemn thought is that! God keep us from doing thus fatal injury to those whom we most dearly love!

---

* See "The Gloaming of Life," by Rev. Alex. Wallace, D.D., Glasgow.

Finally: the fate of Absalom may be a warning to the careless youth among us. Divine laws will not be ignored with impunity. You may not thrust your hand into the flames, and imagine that God will work a miracle to save it from being burned; you may not leap over a precipice, and expect that God will so counteract the law of gravitation as to preserve you from falling. But just as preposterous is it to expect that, if you live in daily contempt of God's moral commands, you will escape his punishment. The retribution may seem long in coming; but it will come, and the delay will only make it heavier when it falls. Be on your guard, then, dear young friends, against this defiance of the Almighty, and seek your true safety in obeying God's precepts. A great philosopher was in the habit of saying that "to command Nature we must obey her;" and every mechanic and man of science knows that this is true. By obeying natural laws, we may command the power of nature, which is only the physical power of God, and use it in our service. We yoke steam to our chariots by obeying God's laws in regard to steam; we send the lightning on our messages by obeying God's laws in reference to electricity. But this is true also spiritually. We can only have God's blessing, and command God's grace, by obeying his moral laws. If we disobey them, we shall be destroyed; if we obey them, he will be our helper and our strength. Your great security, then, is in obedience to God; and this is his prime command, that "you should believe on his Son whom he hath sent." Seek your happiness in the service of the Lord, so that when parents, kinsmen, or friends may ask, "Is the young man safe?" the answer may be, "The eternal God is his refuge, and underneath are the everlasting arms."

Let me beseech you, by every consideration, to take this wise and prudent course. For your own sakes, I would urge you to listen to my entreating voice, that so you may secure true success in life, peace at death, and happiness throughout eternity. For your parents' sake, I implore you to follow the course which I have now indicated; for the sake of the meek, loving mother, who nightly watched you long ago, and who still prays for you in the far-away home; for your father's sake, that venerable man who, in your boyhood's days, so reverently took down the "big ha' Bible," and read to you from its sacred page around the evening altar; yea, higher still, for your Saviour's sake, who weeps over the sinful city wherein you dwell, as he wept over doomed Jerusalem: by all that is dear and sacred; by all that is noble, and great, and glorious, and divine; by the measureless duration of eternity, and the transcendent happiness of yonder heaven, I beseech you to seek your safety midst the battle of life in the protection of your Saviour. And if these considerations have no weight with you, look once more at that royal mourner pacing his room in agony; hear his deep groans; mark his heavy sobs, such as can come only from the big, bursting heart of a weeping man; behold how, drop by drop, the tears course adown his cheeks, and fall heavily upon the floor. Tell me: would you like your father, your mother, your sister, your brother, to bewail you thus? Oh, if you would spare those near and dear to you this terrible, this life-long sorrow; if, in the transit of your spirit to its own place, you would not hear borne upon the breeze the echo of this hopeless cry, "Would God I had died for thee!" then turn from this time forth to Jesus, and give yourself to his holy keeping, through faith in him and obedience to his laws.

## XIX.

### *THE RESTORATION OF DAVID TO HIS THRONE.*

#### 2 Samuel xix.; xx.

THE passionate grief of David over Absalom changed the glory of victory into gloom, and so affected his troops as they returned to Mahanaim, that "they gat them by stealth unto the city, as people being ashamed steal away when they flee in battle." This was only natural, and what, in the circumstances, might have been expected; for while, so far as Absalom was concerned, we can well account for and sympathize with the bitterness of his father's sorrow, yet looked at from the army's point of view, it could not but seem as if the monarch had failed to appreciate the magnitude of the risk his soldiers had run, or to estimate the value of the services which they had rendered. They had periled their lives in their devotion to his cause; they had, by their promptitude and prowess, ended the rebellion in the very first battle; and when they might have hoped to be met with congratulations and loaded with honors, the king is invisible, and nothing is heard from him but the echo of his unceasing cry, "O my son Absalom! O Absalom, my son, my son!" We can not wonder, therefore, that they were disappointed and dissatisfied, and that their feelings should have found vent in the stinging reproach of Joab: "Thou hast shamed this day the faces of all thy servants, which this day have saved thy life, and the lives of thy sons and of thy daughters, and the lives of thy wives, and the lives of thy concubines; in that thou lovest thine enemies, and hatest thy friends. For thou hast declared this day, that thou regardest neither princes nor servants: for this day I perceive, that if Absalom had lived, and all we had died this day, then it had pleased thee well."

Something like this needed to be said; but perhaps Joab was not the best man to say it, and certainly he did not say it in the most tender and considerate manner. He might have shown a little more sympathy with the king in his hour of trouble. He might have remembered that, though David had recovered his kingdom, he had also lost a son, and that, too, in circumstances of the most sorrowful character. He might have made some allowance for the conflict of emotions which was going on within him; and while stirring him up to "go forth and show himself to the people," he might also have said something to soothe and calm the agitation of his spirit. But Joab could touch nothing with a velvet hand. Rough, violent, and callous himself, he could not understand the sensitiveness of another; hence, while doing a very proper thing, he did it in so harsh and dictatorial a manner, that the king, even while yielding to his entreaty, chafed more than ever under the yoke of Zeruiah's sons, and registered a resolution to free himself from their domination as soon as it might be practicable.

Some, indeed, may suppose that the sternness of Joab here was assumed, in order the better to rouse David to the danger which anew he was incurring; and if any choose to adopt that view, I have no objection to offer, save this, that, from my reading of his character, it does not seem ever to have required any effort on Joab's part to be hard and unfeeling; but whatever may be said about the way in which he gave it, this must be plainly conceded, that his advice was not offered a moment too soon, for the troops were rapidly disbanding, and by-and-by the confidence and affection of the people would have been entirely alienated. When, however, they heard that the king was again sitting in the gate, they speedily returned; and as they looked upon his pale, haggard, grief-worn countenance, their hearts, true to the deepest instincts of our nature, would be drawn to him even more than if he had met them with every token of unmingled gladness.

But though he had thus regained the attachment of his troops, and quenched the fire of rebellion which at one time looked so threatening, David still remained at Mahanaim, and took no steps to return to Jerusalem. He had been called to the throne at first by the choice of the people, as well as by the designation of Jehovah, and he would not move in the direction of resuming his regal dignity until, in some form or other, the desire of the tribes had been indicated to him. Hence it was with satisfaction that he heard how, almost everywhere throughout the land, the inhabitants were saying one to another, "Why speak ye not a word of bringing the king back?"

But there was one unaccountable exception to this general expression of returning allegiance. The people of Judah were silent. Probably they felt that they had been more deeply committed to the revolt of Absalom than others, inasmuch as he had first unfurled his banner at Hebron; perhaps, also, they were ashamed of the part which the inhabitants of Jerusalem had played in the rebellion, and possibly they might be afraid that David might visit their perfidy with severe punishment. But, in any case, their silence was very painful to the king; and not willing that his own tribe, who had first called him to the honor of royalty, should be backward now, he sent a message to Zadok and Abiathar, begging them to say to the elders of Judah, "Why are ye the last to bring the king back to his house? seeing the speech of all Israel is come to the king, even to his house. Ye are my brethren. Ye are my bones and my flesh: wherefore then are ye the last to bring back the king?" And lest there should be

## The Restoration of David to his Throne. 341

any fear of vengeance on his part, he signifies his intention to elevate Amasa, who had been the captain of Absalom's army, to the post of commander-in-chief, instead of Joab. This message had the desired effect: "It bowed the heart of all the men of Judah, even as the heart of one man;" so that they not only invited the king back, but also came to Gilgal, that they might meet him and bring him again to his palace.

In all this procedure, however, David was not actuated by his usual sagacity; and the result of his apparent preference of Judah over the other tribes not only provoked another rebellion after his return to Jerusalem, but also prepared the way for the division of the kingdom, which took place in the days of his grandson, Rehoboam. It was quite right in the king to tarry at Mahanaim until he was asked to return in state to Jerusalem; it was natural, also, that when his own tribe was backward, he should stimulate it to activity; but he ought to have sent a similar message to the elders of all the tribes, acknowledging their forwardness to move in his interests; and when the men of Judah came to Gilgal, to make a public "progress" with him from that city to Jerusalem, he should have insisted upon waiting until the other tribes were represented, as they had been on the day when first he assumed the throne over undivided Israel. As it was, however, we can not but see how he wounded the self-respect of the other tribes, by making it appear that the invitation of the men of Judah was of more consequence to him than that of all the others put together; and so he made a wedge, which, though it proved ineffectual in the hands of Sheba, the son of Bichri, needed only the hammer-stroke of the sterner and more subtle Jeroboam to divide Israel from Judah in perpetual separation. But while we mark the lack of forethought indicated by David here, we must not violate the order of the narrative by introducing out of its place the rebellion of Sheba.

Along with the men of Judah, and accompanied by a thousand men of Benjamin, came Shimei of Bahurim, and Ziba, the steward of Mephibosheth, to whom David had so hastily transferred all his master's property. The latter was in great state, surrounded by his fifteen sons, and attended by twenty slaves. As soon as David landed from the ferry-boat which bore him over the river, Shimei came near to make a humble confession of his guilt in cursing the king, and to request forgiveness. Abishai was again forward with his offer to put the mean-spirited and unfeeling man to death. In the eye of the brother of Joab, all this confession of iniquity, and expression of zeal in being the first of "all the house of Joseph to go down to meet the king," was but a piece of sickening hypocrisy; and perhaps he was right, for in general the men who are loudest in curses are themselves cringing wretches, who will swallow all their formerly professed principles, and eat in all their strongest utterances, if only they may save their lives and property. But the day of David's restoration was not to be stained by any deed of blood, however righteously it might have been shed. Amnesty was to be everywhere proclaimed. So, with his usual querulous expression of impatience at Abishai's interference, David said, "What have I to do with you, ye sons of Zeruiah, that ye should this day be adversaries unto me? Shall there any man be put to death this day in Israel? for do not I know that I am this day king over Israel?" So Shimei was reprieved; and the king sware that he, at least, would not put him to death—a piece of weakness of which at a later day he saw reason to repent.

After he had safely passed the Jordan, the venerable Barzillai approached to bid him farewell. With touching earnestness, which shows how deeply he had been moved by his great kindness, the king besought him to accompany him to Jerusalem, and take his place as one whom he would delight

## The Restoration of David to his Throne. 343

to honor at the royal table; but the aged chief, who realized that he had already one foot in the grave, and who was not willing to barter the happiness of his homely life, and the prospect of being buried in the sepulchre of his fathers, for all the glitter of a court, even when such a one as David was at its head, delicately declined the invitation for himself; yet, that he might not seem rudely to repel that which was offered in real gratitude, he commended his son Chimham to the favor of his sovereign; and it is gratifying to know that David was specially attentive to the old man's request; for not only did Chimham eat at the royal table, but he obtained a portion of David's patrimonial possession near to Bethlehem. This, at least, is the most natural explanation of the fact that in the days of Jeremiah we find mention made of a locality near to Bethlehem which was even then know as the habitation of Chimham.* Nor is this the only referece to Barzillai in the later history of the nation; for at the return from the Babylonish captivity, it came out that one of Barzillai's daughters married a Levite, whose descendants, some of whom were even then in the land, out of regard to the faithful old chief, called themselves "The children of Barzillai."†

Less satisfactory in every point of view was David's treatment of the good Mephibosheth, who came to meet him with every token of respect and affection. From the day of the king's departure from his capital, the son of Jonathan had neither dressed his feet, nor trimmed his beard, nor washed his clothes; and now, having doubtless heard of Ziba's perfidy, he approached his father's friend, and his own benefactor, with mingled feelings of satisfaction and regret—satisfaction that David had returned to his throne in safety, regret that he had innocently fallen under the royal suspicion.

---

* Jeremiah xli., 17.  † Nehemiah vii., 63.

When David saw him, he asked, in an upbraiding tone, "Wherefore wentest not thou with me, Mephibosheth?" and he answered, "My lord, O king, my servant deceived me: for thy servant said, I will saddle me an ass, that I may ride thereon, and go to the king; because thy servant is lame. And he hath slandered thy servant unto my lord the king; but my lord the king is as an angel of God: do therefore, what is good in thine eyes. For all of my father's house were but dead men before my lord the king: yet didst thou set thy servant among them that did eat at thine own table. What right therefore have I yet to cry any more unto the king?"

This is, indeed, a very different story from that which Ziba told on the memorable day of David's flight, and some have supposed that it was untrue, grounding their opinion on the fact that David did not restore all his lands to Mephibosheth, but said, "Thou and Ziba divide the land." To maintain this view, however, seems to me to be a vindication of David at the expense of truth and justice, since the words of Mephibosheth bear upon them the stamp of the most thorough ingenuousness; and besides, it is not Mephibosheth, but the sacred chronicler himself, who tells us of the honest mourning of the poor cripple over his patron's calamity. Ziba had tried to make it appear that Mephibosheth was expecting to gain for himself the kingdom, in the confusion caused by Absalom. But, as Mr. Groves has said: "When the circumstances on both sides are weighed, there seems to be no escape from the conclusion that Mephibosheth had been faithful all through. He could have had nothing to hope for from the revolution, for Absalom had made no such vow to Jonathan as that into which David had entered; so from the success of Absalom, he could expect no benefit. Neither could he, a poor, nervous, timid cripple, seriously entertain the idea that the people would prefer him as their ruler to Absalom, who was the handsomest, the readiest, and the most popular man in the country. Moreover, his story is consistent throughout. Decrepit as he was, he could not but be dependent upon his servant; and it is quite conceivable that Ziba, who had nothing to lose, but every thing to gain, by his perfidy, should, when ordered to make ready the ass for Mephibosheth, start away after David himself, and leave his master in helplessness and misery behind. Besides, presuming that he had been thus outwitted, he had no subsequent opportunity of going out to David."*

We have already seen how difficult it was, even for such fleet couriers as Jonathan and Ahimaaz, to make their way in safety to the king; how hopeless, therefore, must it have seemed to a lame man like Mephibosheth! Thus, having lost the first opportunity of joining David by the treachery of Ziba, he had been compelled to remain in the city; but he did all that, in the circumstances, he could have done. He went into deep mourning for his patron; and so soon as it was safe for him to make his appearance, he came out to meet the king—not, observe, making an humble confession and earnest prayer for forgiveness, like the cringing Shimei, but in the conscious integrity of one who felt that he had been cruelly maligned. But, more than this, David himself appears to have been convinced of his innocence, for he revokes half of the grant that he had made to Ziba; and he does it with such symptoms of impatience as betoken that he was ill at ease in regard to the whole business, and did not care to have any further reference made to it.

Every one knows that when he has been entrapped into the doing of an ungenerous or unjust thing, there springs up in him an irritation at himself, which is apt to betray itself in hastiness of speech and manner quite similar to that man-

---

\* Smith's "Dictionary," art. MEPHIBOSHETH.

ifested by David here when he says, "Why speakest thou any more of thy matters? I have said, Thou and Ziba divide the land." But both the temper and the decision were unworthy of David. Why should he vent on Mephibosheth the indignation which ought to have been directed against Ziba for deceiving him, and against himself for falling so easily into Ziba's snare? Moreover, why should he pronounce a judgment which on the very face of it was unjust?

Some, indeed, in their zeal for David's reputation here, will have it that he was simply restoring the original grant, which they affirm was bestowed on the condition that Ziba was to till the land, and give half the proceeds to Mephibosheth; but this defense of the king is evidently untenable, since, from the reply of Mephibosheth, it is clear that something was taken by Ziba which he had not enjoyed before. Why should the cripple have said, "Yea, let him take all," if something had not been taken from him which Ziba had not hitherto possessed? Hence, however reluctantly, we are compelled to come to the conclusion that David here behaved himself most unroyally, and gave a decision which was a manifest compromise, and that, too, in a matter of justice, where no such compromise ought to have been admissible. If Mephibosheth spake the truth, the whole of his estate should have been restored; if Ziba's statement had been correct, no part of it should have been returned; but as it was, the king, in his weak desire to please all parties, did a grievous injustice to one who was perhaps more sincerely attached to him than any inmate of his palace, and who ought to have been specially beloved by him for his father's sake. Oh, this trimming and time-serving, this desire of peace at any price, this political expediency and wise diplomacy, which seeks above and beyond all things to keep all sweet, how much it has darkened the reputation even of good men, and retarded the onward march of morality and religion!

Ziba was, it may be, a man of influence in the party that yet called itself by the name of Saul; so, though David was probably inwardly convinced of his unprincipled character, he thought that he could not afford to offend him; or perhaps, from a weak desire that no one should be punished on the joyful day of his restoration, he lets him go free, not thinking that thereby he is deeply wounding the most sensitive heart of Mephibosheth in its holiest spot. True, indeed, that noble spirit made this touching reply: "Yea, let him take all, forasmuch as my lord the king is come again in peace unto his own house." But it is just a soul capable of such noble self-denial that feels most keenly the sting of any suspicion of its love or fidelity; and as no further reference is made to him in the sacred narrative, especially as David gives no charge concerning him to Solomon at his death, eight years later, it is not unlikely that he did not long survive the grief and pain that Ziba's treachery had caused him.

All this while David and the men of Judah seem to have been on the way between Jordan and Gilgal; and when they arrived at that city, an angry altercation rose between the members of the royal tribe and those of the others who happened to be present. The men of Israel, as those connected with the ten tribes begin already to be called, were indignant at the proceedings of the men of Judah. They alleged that their brethren had stolen away the king; and their irritation was not allayed, but rather increased, by the fact that the men of Judah assigned their near relationship to David as their reason for the prominence which they had assumed; for they replied with vehemence, "We have ten parts in the king, and we have also more right in David than ye: why then did ye despise us, that our advice should not be first had in bringing back our king?" The men of Judah answered with yet greater warmth; and in the midst of the controversy, a Benjamite, Sheba by name, blew once more the trumpet of revolt, raising the shout, "To your tents, O Israel." This act of his was the spark which, falling on the already excited multitude, kindled them into rebellion; so the Israelites gathered around Sheba, while the men of Judah, cleaving to the king, carried him in safety to Jerusalem, where, having first marked his displeasure at the guilt of his concubines with Absalom by consigning them to a living widowhood, he immediately took steps for the crushing of the new insurrection. Passing over Joab, who had hitherto been commander of the forces, he commissioned Amasa to lead his troops against the enemy. But whether that officer, so recently in rebellion against David, had not yet gained the confidence of the king's forces, so that they were slow in gathering round him, or whether he was secretly in sympathy with Sheba's revolt, and, really wishing it success, put off time to give it strength, does not appear. In any case, he tarried longer than the time appointed; and David, fearing that the rebellion might become even more formidable than Absalom's, commissioned Abishai to head his troops, and pursue Sheba before he could intrench himself within a walled city.

It is observable that all through this affair there is a studied slight of Joab; yet that unscrupulous leader saw his opportunity; for, taking rank under his brother, he went out along with the king's body-guard and all the mighty men; and meeting Amasa at the great stone in Gibeon, he slew him in the same cold-blooded and treacherous fashion as he had formerly dispatched Abner. On that occasion, however, he had the pretext of avenging the death of his brother; this time the deed was one of envy and jealousy. He could not endure that any one should supersede him in the post which he had so long filled, and, with the kiss of pretended friendship on his lip, he smote his adversary with such vehemence that the blood stained "his own girdle that was upon his loins, and his shoes that were upon his feet." This horrible murder brought the men of David's army to a stand. Not until the body of Amasa was removed from their path and covered with a cloth, would they consent to move forward. Thereafter Joab assumed the command, and followed Sheba to Abel of Beth-maachah, a town of some importance in the north of Palestine, in the territory of the tribe of Naphtali. Here he prevailed on a wise woman, whose influence was great over the inhabitants, to procure the death of Sheba; and having received evidence that the traitor had been executed, he blew the trumpet, recalling his men, and returned to Jerusalem to tell David that the rebellion was at an end. The news, we may be sure, was more welcome than the messenger who carried it; for thus again, in spite of his determination to the contrary, he had been laid under deep obligation to Joab, whose ascendency over him had so chafed his spirit during his entire reign. There was nothing said by the king about the murder of Amasa, but David's silence would be to Joab more expressive even than speech; and we know how keenly he felt his nephew's cruelty by the allusions which he made to it on his death-bed, and the commands which he gave to Solomon concerning him.

But now, leaving this record of blood, let us turn and look at the Psalms which have been generally regarded as belonging to the era of Absalom's rebellion. Already we have referred to the beautiful morning and evening hymns, so expressive of calm confidence in God, which David composed, as is commonly believed, in connection with his flight from Jerusalem, and which are numbered 4th and 3d in our Psalter; but there are others which must in no wise be overlooked. Indeed, as we have before seen, a time of affliction is ever, in David's case, a most prolific time in spiritual song. It is the stroke that brings sound from the lyre; and when the soul-harp is rightly strung, the touch of God's chastening hand will ever draw from it the sweetest music.

We are not surprised, therefore, to find that many Psalms are traced to the circumstances and experiences of David during his son's revolt; and a brief allusion to them, while yet the incidents of the narrative are fresh in our recollection, may help us to understand their character better than we have done before. The 5th Psalm, which is much akin in tone and sentiment to that which precedes, may well enough have been written on the same occasion; and it is interesting to note how, amidst the excitement of his flight, and the plottings and counterplottings of the time, he preserves the calm composure of confidence in God. "But as for me, I will come into thy house in the multitude of thy mercy: and in thy fear will I worship toward thy holy temple. Lead me, O Lord, in thy righteousness because of mine enemies; make thy way straight before my face;" and again: "Let all those that put their trust in thee rejoice: let them ever shout for joy, because thou defendest them." "For thou, Lord, wilt bless the righteous; with favor wilt thou compass him as with a shield." To the same trying hour belongs the 143d Psalm, which, read in the light of the history, becomes full of touching beauty and devout pathos. Remembering the connection between his sin and his calamities, he begs God not to enter into judgment with him, because in his sight no flesh living could be justified; then, plaintively describing the evil done to him by his enemies, he falls back on the memory of former times, and encouraged by the tokens of God's mercy which he had then received, he says, "I stretch forth my hands unto thee: my soul thirsteth after thee, as a thirsty land." Thereafter, in a strain of earnest supplication, he calls for help, saying, "Hear me speedily, O Lord; my spirit faileth: hide not thy face

## THE RESTORATION OF DAVID TO HIS THRONE. 351

from me, lest I be like unto them that go down into the pit. Cause me to hear thy loving-kindness in the morning; for in thee do I trust: cause me to know the way wherein I should walk; for I lift up my soul unto thee."

After he had heard of Ahithophel's treachery, he wrote, most probably, the 41st, and 55th, and 69th Psalms, which agree in these three particulars, viz., in the mournful description which he gives of his case, and the plaintive wail he utters over the treachery of his former friend; in the calm trustfulness with which he leaves his cause with God; and in the prayers which he offers for the punishment and destruction of his enemies. Indeed, this last particular has given great perplexity to commentators, and "the cursing Psalms," as they are scornfully called, are everywhere held up as evidences of the revengeful spirit of David. But they who do so seriously mistake; for, in the first place, that they were not uttered in a spirit of revenge, is evident from the disposition of David all through the history. How meekly he bore Shimei's curses; how magnanimously he refrained from punishing in the day of his victory! Indeed, if we have had any fault to find with him at this time, it has been because he shrank from the execution of what we should have regarded as needful justice. Hence, having regard to the mood of the monarch as indicated by the facts of the history, we can not suppose that the Psalms then written were dictated by a vindictive or personally revengeful spirit.

Again, we must remember that David was the anointed of the Lord, and that rebellion against him was treason against Jehovah. As I have often before said in these discourses, the Lord was the true King of Israel, and David reigned by his appointment. All, therefore, who rebelled against him were guilty of treason against the Lord, and were not his personal enemies, but the enemies of the Most High. Hence his prayer for their punishment was a prayer that God would vindicate the honor of his moral government by showing his justice in their chastisement. But Paul prayed after that fashion, as well as David, and no one will accuse him of acting unworthily of the Gospel. Has he not written thus: "Alexander the coppersmith did me much evil. The Lord reward him according to his works?" and do we not find that the sternest denunciations of judgment against God's enemies came from the lips of the meek and holy Jesus himself? Hence we have no difficulty about these Psalms, more than about any other passages of Scripture which declare that God is set for the destruction of the wicked, and for the maintenance of truth and righteousness; for, as Dr. Alexander has said, "Whatever it is right for God to do in judgment may be properly enough asked from God in prayer by his people, provided only they ask it from a regard to God's honor and glory, and not out of personal resentment."*

Another feature of these Ahithophel Psalms must be specially alluded to. They are all Messianic, and are quoted or referred to by the writers of the New Testament as predictions which had their complete fulfillment in the betrayal and crucifixion of the Lord. Nor need we marvel at this: for David was a typical person; and in singing of his own calamities, the Holy Ghost so guided his spirit that he employed language which, though in a lower sense appropriate to himself, does yet find its highest significance in Jesus. Whensoever, therefore, we sing them now, we can not but feel that a greater than David is here.

During his sojourn at Mahanaim, ere yet he had been invited back to Jerusalem, it is not unlikely that he composed and sang the 42d and 43d Psalms, and perhaps also the 84th, all of which refer to the privation which he experienced in being cut off from God's sanctuary. We saw that when his

---

* Commentary on the Psalms, by J. A. Alexander, D.D.

infant was taken from him, he went first to the house of God to worship; and in the sad days which succeeded the death of Absalom he must often have lamented that he was unable to approach the place where God peculiarly dwelt, and he might have said, "As the hart panteth after the water-brooks, so panteth my soul after thee, O God. My soul thirsteth for God, for the living God: when shall I come and appear before God?" If we are right in assigning this date to that beautiful ode, what new significance is thereby given to the words, "Deep calleth unto deep at the noise of thy water-spouts: all thy waves and thy billows are gone over me." Could we have a better description than that of the agony in the chamber over Mahanaim's gate? or could we have a finer calm after that stormful experience than that presented by the very next words: "Yet the Lord will command his loving-kindness in the day-time, and in the night his song shall be with me, and my prayer unto the God of my life?" while the recurring refrain comes with its soothing cadence, and hushes the soul to peace: "Why art thou cast down, O my soul? and why art thou disquieted within me? hope thou in God: for I shall yet praise him, who is the health of my countenance, and my God." The 84th is similar; and as the lack of a blessing makes us value it the more, we can well understand how the good man sings, "A day in thy courts is better than a thousand. I had rather be a door-keeper in the house of my God, than to dwell in the tents of wickedness." The 144th Psalm, also, is held by many to belong to this era, and was most probably written after the entire suppression of Absalom's rebellion, and of the revolt of Sheba, which followed so close upon it. He makes public thanksgiving to God for his deliverance; and after dwelling minutely on the various elements of national prosperity, which he earnestly supplicates for his country, he concludes in a fine spirit of patriotism, ripening into piety,

"Happy is that people, that is in such a case: yea, happy is that people, whose God is the Lord."

Willingly would I have lingered longer over these sacred lyrics, which acquire for us such new pathos when we place them in the setting of the history out of which they sprung, but I must forbear. Let me conclude, as usual, by gleaning a few practical lessons from the incidents which have this evening been before our attention.

Let us learn, in the first place, from Barzillai's answer to the king, to test the allurements of the world by the question, "How long have I to live?" The venerable chief felt that the life of the court was not for one like him, who had already one foot in the grave; and with a combination of wisdom and courtesy which is far from common, he determined to remain in his old home, and, after a brief season, to be buried in the sepulchre of his fathers. Now, though we may not have reached the age of fourscore years, there is much in his question which can not fail to be suggestive to every one of us. The longest life is but brief, after all.

Can we afford, then, to fritter away our hours in idleness, or to waste them in riot and dissipation? Even if we were sure that we should live to be of the age of Methusaleh, it would still be criminal in us to allow our time to pass unimproved; but how much more is this the case, when the utmost limit of our days is fourscore years, and the average duration of life much shorter? Is it not true that, for any thing we know, many among us may be to-night much nearer death than was Barzillai when he spake thus pensively to David? and yet what are we doing with our days and nights? What have we to show for the years of the past; and what preparation have we made for eternity? If we were to be here forever; if we were not moral and accountable beings; or if the present state of existence were not given to us to settle our eternal destiny, we might have some excuse for devoting our entire energies to the making of money, or to the indulgence of appetite, or to the eager chase after the bubble reputation, which too often bursts in the hand that grasps it. But as it is, have we any word expressive enough to describe the folly of the man who is shutting his eyes to the future life, and is taking no means whatever to train his soul for everlasting fellowship with God? "Art is long, and life is brief," was the motto of the old masters as they painted those great works which have made their names illustrious. They felt that their moments were too precious to be wasted in trifling or in sin, and they gave themselves entirely to that labor which has made their works the models and the inspiration of artists in all succeeding ages. But what is the work of the painter in comparison with that which God has given each man to do, "the working out of his own salvation with fear and trembling;" the reproducing, not in colors on canvas, but in living deeds of holiness and benevolence, of the likeness of Jesus Christ; the chiseling out, not in cold marble, but in warm and breathing manhood, of a Christian character? That is a work great enough for all our energies, and needing the labor of every hour of every day of our lives.

Shall we, then, abstract ourselves from this glorious life-aim, and give ourselves to frivolity, dissipation, and iniquity? "How long have we to live," that we should squander thus not merely the days that are passing over us, but the eternity of holy happiness which God has offered us in Christ, and which can only be secured by faithful obedience to him here? Let the time past of our lives suffice for all of us "to have wrought the will of the Gentiles." From this night let us begin anew. Let us, finding pardon through the Redeemer's atonement, and regeneration by the power of the Holy Ghost, go forward from this hour, to consecrate all our powers, resources, and opportunities, and every hour of ev ery day, to the grand ambition of "attaining the measure of the stature of the perfect man in Christ Jesus." And when any one seeks to tempt us from this holy quest, let us reply, "Life is too short for the work I have on hand. I am doing a great work, and I can not come down. Why should the work cease while I leave it and come down to you?"

But we may learn also, from the bearing of Mephibosheth, how to be meek under a false accusation. We have the deepest sympathy for the son of Jonathan in the circumstances in which here he was placed, and we can not help feeling that David was not acting like his usual self when he pronounced his hasty decision regarding him. He had forgotten at the moment all that he had owed to his early friend. He had lost sight, for the time, of his loving covenant by the stone Ezel, when the two heroes wept so long upon each other's necks. Even if Mephibosheth had been guilty of all that Ziba had laid to his charge, the memory of Jonathan might have pleaded for forgiveness; but when, as I think I have satisfactorily shown, the crippled prince was really innocent, David's treatment of him was in a marked degree ungenerous. Yet how nobly Mephibosheth behaves! He does not care for his own interests. He seeks no revenge on Ziba. It is enough for him that the king has come to his own again. He is even content to be under suspicion, if but David may be prosperous. How beautiful is all this! It reminds us of his father's nobleness in giving up all claim to the throne, and being willing to be David's subordinate; and in similar circumstances we may imitate his demeanor with advantage.

We need not expect to pass through the world without being sometimes falsely accused, and wrongfully treated. He who can not err has said to his followers, "Woe unto you when all men speak well of you;" and we have reason to fear that there is something defective in us, or amiss with us, if every body is on our side. Only let us see that, when we are accused, we are accused falsely; and that, when we do suffer, we suffer wrongfully, for Christ's sake; and then we may take it not only patiently, but joyfully. It will be right and proper for us, like Mephibosheth here, to give the true version of affairs; but if after that injustice should come upon us, let us bear it meekly, remembering Him who " when he was reviled, reviled not again, and who when he suffered, threatened not, but committed himself to him that judgeth righteously." He who is always standing on his own vindication, and insisting on having himself put right, will do himself and the cause more harm than good. Let him be still, and God will vindicate him. If men will not take his word, let him wait until God proves his truthfulness. The Christian has always his court of appeal in heaven, and God will vindicate him at length. Let him even consent to be defrauded, therefore, rather than insist on what would be only justice. God will take care of him; "for curses, like chickens, come home to roost," and false accusations, like the boomerang, go back to the hand by which they have been flung.

From the Psalms which were written by David in this crisis of his history, we may learn how precious a solace communion with God is to the believer in the time of trial. We have repeatedly seen how, in days of calamity and darkness, it was the habit of David's soul to fall back into the arms of Jehovah. At other times he might forget the Lord, but in his hours of trouble, he was driven for shelter beneath the shadow of the almighty wings; ay, even when, on an occasion like this, he could not but feel that his miseries were the consequences of his own sins, he came, in humble penitence and confidence, to Jehovah, and was "in no wise cast out."

I do not know if there be, even in the Word of God itself,

a more precious manifestation of the magnanimous mercy of Jehovah to the penitent believer than that which is furnished by his treatment of David at this time. Consider what this man has done; think that all the evils which he is now enduring are the results of his own aggravated transgression; yet behold how God soothes, sustains, and restores him; so that he can sing, "Why art thou cast down, O my soul? and why art thou disquieted within me? hope thou in God: for I shall yet praise him, who is the health of my countenance, and my God." Who dares to say after this that the Lord is a hard master, or an austere one? Or who needs despair, after such an exhibition of his grace as this? Is there a backslider here to-night, who, in the thickening of calamities around him, is made to remember his iniquities, and to groan under the burden of his guilt, let him return unto the Lord like David, and he will be received as David was. It is as true now as it was of old, that "he giveth songs in the night," and, amidst the manifold music of this harmonious universe, there is none so sweet in the ear of Jehovah as the nightingale song that comes trilling from a penitent heart in the midnight of its tribulation. It is but natural for the prosperous soul to sing when, like the lark, it is soaring up to the very gate of heaven; but when the spirit is in darkness, and finds peace in penitence and trust, the gush of music that comes welling up from its depths is more than natural—it is a triumph of grace; and as such is ever sweeter in the ears of God. "The broken spirit is to him a pleasing sacrifice." Will no repentant one offer such a sacrifice to him to-night? And thou, tempest-tossed and distracted brother, whose trials have well-nigh overwhelmed thee, though thou canst not trace them to any particular cause, take heart from David's experience. He who sustained the Psalmist will never fail thee, nor forsake thee. The sure anchorage on which David rode out even this terrific storm will hold thee safe. Cheer thee, then, for God is with thee ; and when the gale is ended, and life's voyage over, thou shalt be with him.

In the English Channel there is a beneficent light-house, which for more than a century has braved the storms of winter. Many and many a time for days together, as the waves broke completely over it, it has not been seen from the shore, and men almost feared that it had been swept away; but when the storm was down, there it stood still, throwing its light across the waters, because it is not only founded on, but built into, the rock. Like that noble tower, my brother, thou art built *upon, and into*, the Rock of Ages. Thou art so one with him as to be a part of himself; and let the hurricane howl its loudest, and the waves dash with their fiercest might, no real harm can come to thee. They must sweep him away if they would ingulf thee; and no storm of passion, or persecution, or treachery, or antagonism of any kind can shake his everlasting foundations.

Well might David sing when he was upheld by such a God; and if but we had faith in him, we too might bid defiance to the allied powers of earth and hell. "Lord, increase our faith!" and then our power, our purity, and our peace shall grow in like proportion. "Lord, increase our faith!" and then,

> "Though troubles rise, and terrors frown,
>   And days of darkness fall,
> Through thee, all dangers we'll defy,
>   And more than conquer all."

## XX.

### *FAMINE AND PESTILENCE*

2 SAMUEL xxii.; xxiv.

AFTER David's restoration to the throne, Palestine was desolated by a famine which lasted for three years. From the peculiar character of our climate, we can scarcely realize the magnitude of such a calamity, which was probably caused by drought; but the description given of a similar visitation in the days of Elijah, as well as the accounts which have been given within the last few years, of the terrible sufferings which were endured from the same cause by the inhabitants of Orissa and Rajpootana, may help us somewhat to understand what an Eastern famine is. During these weary years no rain had fallen to refresh the thirsty land; no fields had waved with rich luxuriance; no barn-yards had been filled with stores of grain. The shouting of the vintage, the song of the reaper, and the mirth of harvest-home had not been heard in the land, and want had stamped each human countenance with its sharp, deep die. Many of the inhabitants had perished, and everywhere were weeping widows wringing their hands in despair, and orphaned children mourning for parents whom they would see no more.

In the midst of this wide-spread desolation, the people thought of God; and David was only representing their deep yearning of heart when he went to inquire of the Lord what was the cause of the terrible calamity which had come upon them. A proud philosophy, in these modern days, would say that all this was the merest superstition; inasmuch as all such things as famine and pestilence make their appearance in accordance with natural laws, and have no connection with the moral character of a community; while prayer for their removal, being a virtual request that God should interfere with the operation of these laws and work a miracle in their suspension, must ever be in vain. But there are things deeper and truer than any such philosophy, and among these I place the spiritual instincts of the human heart. Why is it, we are disposed to ask, that in almost all languages pestilence has been called by a name which—like our own word plague, which means a stroke—directly points to God's agency in its appearance? and whence comes it that, when a people is enduring such a calamity, there is a general thought of God among them, and their resolution becomes that of Jeremiah: "Let us search, and try our ways, and turn again unto the Lord?" Do not these things, and others like them, point to the fact that, by the mystic intuitions of the soul, God is recognized in all such visitations? and while we take into account the laws of external nature, shall we refuse to pay regard to the nature that is within us? Besides, this assertion of the supremacy of law, which is so characteristic of some schools of philosophy, is, after all, a virtual atheism. For if we admit that there is a personal God, and that he is in any real sense the moral governor of mankind, the conclusion is irresistible, that he regulates the occurrences of the physical universe with a view to the moral training of his human creatures. How he does so, while yet the order of the physical universe is maintained, we can not explain; that he does so, must be admitted by us frankly, unless we make his providence a nonentity, and his personal existence a delusion. As Isaac Taylor has remarked, "This is, in fact, the great miracle of providence, that no miracles are needed to accomplish its purposes." It is all very well to say that there can be no true *nexus* between a moral evil and a physical calamity, and I grant at once that there is no such immediate sequence in such a case, as there is between a physical cause and a physical effect; but there is a very real connection for all that. The disobedience of your child does not cause the infliction of punishment on him by you in the same way that the falling of a spark on gunpowder causes an explosion. But there is a very intimate relationship between the two, notwithstanding; and it is a relationship established by the moral character of the parental government. Now, the connection between men's disobedience and God's infliction of chastisement upon them through his physical laws is of a similar sort. Nor let any one say that moral evil should be visited only with a punishment that shall tell only on the moral part of man's nature. We reach the moral through the physical. The punishment, to tell upon the individual, must be inflicted where it will be most felt; and just as the parent seeks to benefit his child morally, by inflicting on him some physical suffering, so God, in his government of the world, checks the sins of men by sending upon communities the physical calamities of pestilence, famine, and the like. I do not deny, of course, that these calamities come through the ordinary operation of law; what I affirm is, that *these laws have been so adjusted by the Divine Governor of the world, that through them, and without any miraculous interference with them, he visits moral evil with physical chastisement;* and so it is not superstition, but rather the truest piety and the highest philosophy, which leads a people, under such a visitation as that of famine, to turn to Jehovah, saying, "Show us wherefore thou contendest with us."

These general principles will hold in any country and in any age, but they had special force among the Jews, from the fact that the sanctions of the covenant, in terms of which they held the land of promise, were mainly temporal and physical. The blessings promised as the reward of their obedience were principally such as could be enjoyed on

## Famine and Pestilence. 363

earth, and the penalties set forth as the consequences of their disobedience were chiefly physical calamities. I would be slow, indeed, to allege that, in the sanctions of the old covenant, there was no allusion whatever to the future state; but, speaking generally, I would repeat that the promises and threatenings of the Mosaic economy had special and primary reference to earthly things. This is seen all through the history of the Jewish nation; but it comes out with peculiar prominence in the terms of the covenant itself, as these are given in the twenty-seventh and twenty-eighth chapters of the book of Deuteronomy, where, among many similar promises, we find this, conditioned on the obedience of the people. "The Lord shall make thee plenteous in goods, in the fruit of thy body, and in the fruit of thy cattle, and in the fruit of thy ground, in the land which the Lord sware unto thy fathers to give thee. The Lord shall open unto thee his good treasure, the heaven to give the rain unto thy land in his season, and to bless all the work of thine hand." In like manner, among the threatenings denounced against their unfaithfulness, these words occur: "Thy heaven that is over thy head shall be brass, and the earth that is under thee shall be iron. The Lord shall make the rain of thy land powder and dust: from heaven shall it come down upon thee, until thou be destroyed." Now there is nothing of miraculous intervention with nature's laws hinted at in all this, for when these blessings and chastisements did come, they came in the ordinary course of nature; but with such statements as these in the book of their law, it was not only natural, but right, for David and the people to look for a spiritual cause for all their sufferings, and to inquire why such a prolonged famine had come upon them.

But while it is comparatively easy to vindicate David's procedure in inquiring of the Lord from the sneers of a proud and really atheistic philosophy, the reply which he received from the sacred oracle, and the action which he took thereon, introduce new questions whose solution is attended with much greater difficulty. The Lord answered, "It is for Saul, and for his bloody house, because he slew the Gibeonites." The name of this people brings up the old story of the deception which their fathers played on Joshua and the tribes when they were taking possession of the land of Canaan. Disguising themselves with old garments and clouty shoes, and taking old sacks upon their asses, and wine-bottles, old and rent and bound up, they came to Joshua at Gilgal; and making it appear that they had traveled a long distance, they desired to form a league with him. The unsuspicious leader fell into the trap which they had laid for him; and though the discovery of their craftiness naturally provoked the people, the princes counseled that they should be faithful to their oath, saying, "We have sworn unto them by the Lord God of Israel: now therefore we may not touch them. This we will do to them; we will even let them live, lest wrath be on us, because of the oath which we sware unto them. And the princes said unto them, Let them live; but let them be hewers of wood and drawers of water unto all the congregation." This proposal was agreed to; and thus it happened that, though they belonged to the guilty race of the Amorites, these Gibeonites lived for four hundred years among the tribes of Israel, in peaceful servitude and uncomplaining submission. But Saul, for some reason or other, conceived an aversion to them, and set himself to accomplish their extermination.

Perhaps in one of those spasmodic fits of religious enthusiasm to which we saw he was so liable, he may have imagined that zeal for the honor of God required him to root out the Gibeonites from the land, or more probably he desired to get possession of their lands for himself and his favorites; but in any case, in dealing thus with the men of Gibeon, he distinctly violated—without any justifiable reason—the covenant made with them by Joshua. We have no mention, in the history of Saul, of this raid made by him upon the Gibeonites, and we hear of it now for the first time after he had been dead and buried for thirty years. But let no one think it strange that the penalty should come thus, in famine, upon an entire nation, after a new generation had sprung up. For a nation's history is a unit; and as there can be no such thing as retribution of a nation in the future state, it follows that if punishment for national sins is to be inflicted at all, it must fall in the subsequent earthly history of the nation that committed them. The generation which was alive in France at the eras of the massacre of St. Bartholomew and the revocation of the Edict of Nantes, was a different one from that which lived at the time of the first Revolution; yet in the events of the latter, with its Reign of Terror and rivers of blood, we have the undoubted consequences of the former. Many generations have come and gone in Spain since the days of Philip and the great Armada, yet we can not doubt that the miserable condition of that land for more than a century—a condition out of which its inhabitants find it hard even now to emerge—was due to the sins of those who knew not the day of their visitation, and suppressed the Protestantism which, but for the Inquisition, would have arisen among them, and enabled them to lead the van of European progress. The English occupants of India in 1857 were not the same as those who, under Clive, and Hastings, and others, so unrighteously obtained possession of large portions of that empire; nay, they were in many instances men of another order and a nobler nature; yet upon these, ay, even upon the heads of sainted missionaries who repudiated and condemned the cruelty and craft of the first invaders, the terrible Nemesis of the mutiny did fall. Hence there is nothing out of keeping with God's usual procedure, in the fact that forty years after a national sin had been committed by Israel under Saul, the punishment came, and fell upon a generation different from that which had been guilty of the wrong. Though the generation was different, the nation was the same. God is indeed "a jealous God, visiting the iniquities of the fathers upon the children unto the third and fourth generation."

It may be asked, however, why should such chastisement come upon the tribes of Israel for Saul's massacre of the Gibeonites, rather than for his murder of the priests of Nob? and perhaps a satisfactory answer may be found in the following considerations: First, the people did not sympathize with Saul in his attack upon the priests, but were so dreadfully shocked by his impiety that none save Doeg, the alien Edomite, could be found to carry his murderous order on that occasion into execution. In regard to the Gibeonites, however, as Saul is here said to have slain them "in his zeal to the children of Israel and Judah," it seems likely that the people generally were on his side, and aiders and abettors in his crime, if not, indeed, the first suggesters of it. Second, it is probable that even at the moment of the famine, the people, or at least some portion of them, were actually enjoying the fruits of the destruction of the Gibeonites. This, at least, is the opinion of Dr. Kitto,* indorsed and adopted by Dr. Blaikie; and it is presumably correct. You remember that when Saul saw David's party growing strong in the land, he said to his courtiers, "Hear now, ye Benjamites, will the son of Jesse give every one of you fields and vineyards, and make you captains of hundreds and captains of thousands?" Now this implies that he had made such gifts to some, if not to all of them. But where did he get these fields and vineyards? They could not be part of his

---

* "Daily Bible Readings," vol. iii., p. 479.

patrimonial possession, for that was too small to be parceled out among his followers; neither could they be allotments of territory taken from the Philistines, or other enemies of Israel, for his success against them was never so great as to enable him to enrich any one with its spoils. But in the eviction or destruction of the Gibeonites, now mentioned for the first time, we may perhaps conjecture that Saul found the means for making the gifts to which, in the words already quoted, he so boastfully alludes. One of the towns of the Gibeonites was in Judah, and three of them in Benjamin; and out of these and the surrounding districts the son of Kish might make provision for his favorites. The fact that the Gibeonites were not an integral portion of the chosen people, might furnish him with a pretext for attacking them; while the hope of gain would silence all the scruples of his followers, and induce them to make common cause with their king against their defenseless dependents. Now if these conjectures be correct, they will explain not only why punishment came upon the land for the slaughter of the Gibeonites, and not for that of the priests, but also why, in the expiation demanded by the Gibeonites, the victims were chosen from the house of Saul.

But this selection of victims by the Gibeonites suggests another of the singular difficulties of this narrative. Why was the form of expiation for this sin of Saul's referred by David to the Gibeonites, and not directly to God, who had indicated the sin for which the famine was a visitation? The answer to this question must be sought in the old Eastern custom of blood-revenge. When murder had been committed, the nearest of kin to the murdered person was empowered to put the murderer to death wherever he might find him; and if the murderer himself was not killed by the nearest of kin then living, the right descended to the next generation, and the son of the one might kill the son of the other; nay, the obligation held for many generations, and was never relaxed until the offender himself, or, if he was dead, his representative, had paid the fatal ransom. By the Mosaic law this custom was regulated, and some of its most objectionable features removed through the provision of the cities of refuge; but among the Gibeonites, who did not hold themselves bound by Jewish law, the ancient practice appears to have been maintained in all its original stringency. Hence, knowing that no real removal of their grievance was possible without appealing to them, David inquired what they demanded as a satisfaction, and their answer, while indicating that they were willing to restrict themselves within narrow limits, also declared that within these limits they were perfectly inexorable, and would accept of no pecuniary ransom. They had a claim on the whole nation, but they would confine themselves to the family of Saul; and so they replied, "The man that consumed us, and that devised against us, that we should be destroyed from remaining in any of the coasts of Israel, let seven men of his sons be delivered unto us, and we will hang them up unto the Lord in Gibeah of Saul, whom the Lord did choose." With a sad heart we may be sure David said, "I will give them." Then came the painful work of selecting the victims. Of course Mephibosheth and his household were saved, for David remembered his covenant with Jonathan; but he took two of the sons of Rizpah, that one of Saul's concubines concerning whom the dispute arose between Ishbosheth and Abner, and also five sons of Merab, the eldest daughter of Saul, who had been wedded to Adriel, the son of Barzillai, the Meholathite, one whom we must carefully distinguish from the venerable chief of Rogelim, whose kindness David had so warmly appreciated. Bitter must have been the anguish of the homes on which this dire calamity alighted; nor may we attempt to depict the agony of the parents, as their loved ones were torn from their embrace and given up to death. Suffice it to say that the Gibeonites put them to death, and hung their bodies on gibbets on the hill of Gibeah, that place having been selected because it was the head-quarters of the house of Saul.

But not unattended were these seven dismal scaffolds; for day and night, through long weeks, a female form flitted to and fro among them, lavishing special care upon the bodies of the two sons of Saul; and as we see the haggard Rizpah, with her lean and bony hands, scaring away the ravens by day and the wild beasts by night, our hearts are filled with pity for her sonless desolation. What a deep fountain is a mother's heart! With a love stronger than death, she cared for no privations; she feared no dangers; she heeded no hardships, if only she might save the bodies of her sons from desecration! Such passionate devotion must have moved every heart; and when David heard of it, he took steps to secure decent burial for the bodies of those whom the Gibeonites had slain; and while engaged in this office of kindness, he bethought himself of the bones of Saul and Jonathan, which he caused to be exhumed from their resting-place at Jabesh, and to be interred in the family sepulchre of Kish. Then, this atonement having been made, the rain descended, in token that God was entreated for the land.

I have refrained from any remark on the character of this whole transaction, because, from our ignorance of Eastern customs generally, and especially of that rude form of justice prevalent among the Orientals called blood-revenge, we are, to a great extent, incapacitated from pronouncing judgment upon it. Evidently, however, the whole thing was regarded by David, by the Gibeonites, and by the members of Saul's family themselves, as a judicial affair. We read of no vindictive violence on the part of the Gibeonites in the manner in which the victims were put to death; we hear of no resistance to their demands on the side of the family of Saul;

and we see in David's demeanor all through a kind of constraint, which indicates that he went through with it only with the deepest reluctance, and under a sense of the strongest obligation. Indeed, the entire negotiation bears a resemblance to the extradition of criminals by one country to another, that they may be dealt with according to the laws of the realm in which their crime was committed, the only difference being that here the descendants of the criminals were held to be their representatives, and dealt with as if they had themselves committed the evil deed; whereas in our modern times, the criminal himself can alone be made amenable to the law. This difference, however, arises from the peculiar custom to which I have adverted, and the fact that, after the execution of Saul's descendants, God was entreated for the land, appears conclusive that their death was regarded by him as a public vindication of that justice which Saul had outraged by his attack upon the Gibeonites.

After this sore famine, the land of Israel was again exposed to the evils of war. David's old enemies, the Philistines, took the field against him once more, having in their ranks some men of gigantic stature and great strength, belonging to the family of Goliath. One of these, by name Ishbi-benob, pressed so sore against the king in a hand-to-hand encounter, that, but for the interference of Abishai, David would have been slain. The old courage was in him still, but the old strength was gone; so his army besought him not to run such risk again, and prevailed on him not to take the field in person any more; but they did not fight the less bravely because their chief was not with them, for in one or two decisive encounters the Philistines seem to have been entirely subdued. Yet David's troubles did not end with the defeat of his enemies, for a sore pestilence came upon the land, which cut off seventy thousand of the inhabitants. The account of this visitation, indeed, is not given until the twenty-fourth chapter of 2 Samuel, but it will be more convenient to introduce it here, and I shall attempt in my summary of the recorded facts to weave together the two narratives of Samuel and the Chronicles.

For some reason not given, but most probably because of the pride of the people in their national greatness, God was displeased with Israel, and the punishment came in connection with the command of David to number Israel and Judah. In the one account we are told that God moved David to give this command; in the other, it is alleged that Satan stood up against Israel, and provoked David to number the people. But the meaning is that God permitted Satan thus to move David, in order that through his act an opportunity might arise for the punishment of Israel's sin. The command of David was not sinful in itself, but became so, from the spirit of pride and vainglory out of which it originated, and which was shared with him by the people over whom he ruled. The law provided for the taking of a census of the population, but in connection with the enumeration, and probably to check the disposition to boasting which it was likely to evoke, it enacted thus (Exod. xxx., 12): "When thou takest the sum of the children of Israel after their number, then shall they give every man a ransom for his soul unto the Lord, when thou numberest them; that there be no plague among them, when thou numberest them. This they shall give, every one that passeth among them that are numbered, half a shekel after the shekel of the sanctuary: a half-shekel shall be the offering of the Lord." Now we have no record of the making of this offering here, and Josephus affirms that, in the neglect of this offering, we have the occasion of the pestilence that followed — a suggestion which may well enough be correct, especially when we reflect that the omission of this acknowledgment of God may be regarded as indicating the presence of that spirit of vain glory which God designed to punish and repress. In this matter Joab, strangely enough, seems to have been wiser than David, for he not only protested against the taking of the census, but, after he was commanded to carry it out, he undertook it with undisguised reluctance, and (as we learn from 1 Chron. xxi., 6) left it unfinished, by declining to take the numbers of the tribes of Levi and Benjamin. Indeed, it is affirmed that "the king's word was abominable unto him." Nay, more, David himself appears to have shrunk from adding up the total, for it is recorded (1 Chron. xxvii., 23) that he did not take "the number of them from twenty years old and under: because the Lord had said he would increase Israel like to the stars of the heavens." Thus this census was never finished; and it is solemnly said, "Neither was the number put in the account of the Chronicles of king David." First among the things that hindered it there came a deep feeling of compunction into David's own heart. This was followed by a frank acknowledgment of his guilt to God, and an earnest appeal for mercy. Then the prophet Gad appeared, offering him, in God's name, a choice of three calamities—famine, pestilence, or war, and saying to him, "Advise now, and see what answer I shall return to him that sent me." With devout wisdom and simple trust, David put himself and his people into Jehovah's hand, using these memorable words, "Let us fall now into the hand of the Lord; for his mercies are great: and let me not fall into the hand of man."

So the pestilence came—a plague, a black death, a cholera, or other form of dreadful epidemic. In the midst of its ravages David set out, as it would seem, to inquire of the Lord at the old Tabernacle at Gibeon;* but when he got as far as the summit of Moriah, then occupied as a threshing-floor by Araunah, or Ornan, a chief among the Jebu-

---

\* 1 Chron. xxi., 28–30.

sites, he was met by a solemn vision. He beheld the angel of the Lord standing between heaven and earth, having a drawn sword in his hand, which was stretched over Jerusalem. This at once arrested his progress, and he, and they who were with him, fell upon their faces, while he cried out, in lowly lamentation: "Is it not I that commanded the people to be numbered? even I it is that have sinned and done evil indeed; but as for these sheep, what have they done? let thine hand, I pray thee, O Lord my God, be on me, and on my father's house; but not on thy people, that they should be plagued." In answer to this fervent appeal, Gad was commissioned to say to David, "Go up, rear an altar unto the Lord in the threshing-floor of Araunah the Jebusite." In obedience to this injunction, the king went forward to negotiate with the Jebusite for the purchase of the place; and though the generous chief offered to make it a gift, together with oxen for the sacrifice, and his threshing implements for the fire, David would not accept them, saying, "Nay; but I will surely buy it of thee at a price: neither will I offer burnt-offerings unto the Lord my God of that which doth cost me nothing." So giving him, according to the one account, fifty shekels of silver, and according to the other, six hundred shekels of gold, by weight, he offered burnt-offerings and peace-offerings, and the plague was stayed, while the site was marked off as the spot whereon at length Solomon his son was to erect that stately Temple, the materials for the building of which he had been himself so long collecting. Very interesting was this colloquy between the two princes. "It was," as Stanley beautifully says, "the meeting of two ages. Araunah, as he yields that spot, is the last of the Canaanites; the last of that stern old race that we discern in any individual form and character. David, as he raises that altar, is the close harbinger of the reign of Solomon—the founder of a new institution which another was to complete;"* and through all the ages of the world's history the place itself was to be enshrined as the most sacred and interesting spot on the surface of the earth. In reviewing the portion of history now before our notice, there are two or three points of practical and present importance which demand attention.

In the first place, here let us be on our guard against national perfidy. Saul and his people attempted the destruction or expatriation of the Gibeonites, a poor tribe, who were willing to purchase a peaceful existence by the discharge of the most menial duties; and as the result, forty years after the land was desolated by famine, and five of Saul's descendants were demanded for the vindication of public justice.

As I have been repeating this history, I doubt not that your minds have been engaged in drawing the parallel between the relation of Saul to the Gibeonites and that of our own nation to those two races whose condition and destiny seem to be so bound up with our own. I enter not now into any minute analysis of our dealings with the African race on the one hand, and the Indian on the other; neither do I presume to say on which side the blame has to be laid; but I do affirm that this old record has—especially for us now—a lesson of most solemn warning. Let us be careful to maintain inviolate all treaty obligations. Let us deal with these tribes in a spirit of honesty and kindness, not forbearing to punish acts of deliberate treachery, yet eagerly abstaining from all wanton cruelty. Otherwise, we may be sure that we shall entail upon ourselves most serious evils. The God of the Gibeonites is the God of the Indians and Africans as well. Ah, how many Rizpahs did the war consign to sonless sorrow, as they mourned over those who were the victims of wrongs which they had no hand in commit-

---

* "Jewish Church," vol. ii., p. 135.

ting! And is there not now one widow in the land, mourning over a husband who fell the victim of a treachery which the cruelty of others had provoked?* It is the old, old story, and nothing can prevent its recurrence but the introduction of the new principle of the Gospel of Christ, whose watchwords are love, and righteousness, and peace.

In the second place, let us be on our guard against national pride. David's numbering of the people was but the occasion of the pestilence which wrought such havoc in the land. "An anterior sin, shared alike by king and people, was the primary cause of the plague."† Now it is, as we have said, most natural to suppose that this sin was pride. As Nebuchadnezzar drew down upon himself a terrible punishment by cherishing the spirit which found utterance in these words: "Is not this great Babylon which I have built by the might of my power and for the honor of my majesty?" so the Israelites, as they looked upon their extensive territory, and thought upon their enemies all thoroughly subdued, gave way to vainglory, and forgot to give God the praise. But is there nothing like this among ourselves? We talk of our national pre-eminence in wealth, in liberty, and in extent of territory. We speak of our vessels sailing over every ocean, and trafficking in every harbor; and while all this may be done in a spirit of humility and devout gratitude to God, is there nothing like Nebuchadnezzar's vainglory in the utterances upon this subject which come so roundly from the lips of our popular orators, and which are given forth by our daily and periodical press? In sober truth, our greatness is but the measure of our responsibility, and the perception of its magnitude ought only to impel us the more earnestly to pray to God for grace to do the work

---

\* These words were written only a few days after the murder of General Canby by the Indians.
† Wright's "David," p. 348.

which the very greatness of our privileges has laid upon us. What have we that we have not received? Who hath made us to differ from others? Instead, therefore, of sounding a trumpet before us to proclaim our greatness, let us seek to turn that greatness to account in the service of God, and the promotion of the welfare of the human race. Let our watchword be, "Not unto us, O Lord, not unto us, but unto thy name give glory, for thy mercy and thy truth's sake;" and never let us forget the prophet's words, "The lofty looks of man shall be humbled, and the haughtiness of men shall be bowed down; and the Lord alone shall be exalted in that day."

We have here, in the third place, an illustration of the necessity of an expiation for sin. The plague was stayed in connection with the offering of sacrifice; and as we read the record, we can not forget how the Son of David made himself a sacrifice in the immediate neighborhood of this same spot, in order that the plague of sin might be removed from human hearts, and his believing people restored to the health of holiness. The voice of the entire Old Testament on this subject is, "Without shedding of blood there can be no remission;" and all its altars are but like so many finger-posts pointing down through the ages to Messiah, and having on them this inscription, "Behold the Lamb of God which taketh away the sin of the world!" It was not possible for the blood of bulls and of goats to take away sin, but these offerings foreshadowed a sacrifice of richer blood and nobler name than themselves, and now in Christ we have the reality which they prefigured. They were offered, year by year, continually; this needed to be offered only once: they were animals inferior to man; he was the eternal, only-begotten Son of God in human nature; and so when he rose from the tomb of Joseph, it was demonstrated to all that he had finished transgression and made an end of sin. Till he appeared, the avenging angel stood between earth and heaven, having his sword stretched out over the human race; but when he died, that sword was sheathed forever in his own breast. And as the lightning conductor saves the building by satisfying the electric law, and drawing the heavenly fire down upon itself, he saved sinners by attracting in upon himself, and away from them, the penalty of their transgressions. Here, then, in Christ crucified is the sinner's hope. "Look unto him and be saved;" for he is able to save unto the uttermost all that come unto God by him.

Let us learn, finally, that a sincere sacrifice is always one that costs us something. David would not offer burnt-offerings of that which cost him nothing, and it would be well if every professed follower of Jesus acted on the same principle. Whatever we lay upon God's altar should cost us something. Are we laboring in the ministry of the Gospel? then the offering which we make to God in the pulpit should be purchased by study, and ought not to be the rash and hasty utterance of unpremeditated speech. Are we teachers in the Sunday-school? then the lesson which we give our scholars should be given at the cost of prayerful preparation, and ought not to be the empty talk of those who have never looked at the subject until they have met their pupils in the class. Are we asked to contribute to a good cause? then the gift which we put into the offering-box should be something that has cost us some effort or self-denial to obtain, and not simply the overflow of a full cup which we can give without feeling that we are giving at all. Are we asked to labor in some enterprise of benevolence? then we are not to plead that we can not do so without breaking in upon our ease and enjoyment, but we are to take a part of these and use them in the service of the Lord. Yea, what need I more? Is not the Christian's whole life, in its loftiest view, a sacrifice to Christ? Let us see, then, that we make it a costly sacrifice. Let us grudge no labor; let us spare no pains; let us spare no self-denial, if only we may keep ourselves unspotted from the world, and make our lives a fitting acknowledgment of the obligation under which we lie to him "who gave himself for us!" What purity, what love, what self-denial, what activity our lives would manifest, if, looking upon them as sacrifices to God, we should apply to them the words of David, "I will not offer burnt-offerings unto the Lord my God of that which doth cost me nothing." There will not be wanting those, indeed, to say, as we break our precious vase, and pour our costly ointment on the Saviour's head, "To what purpose is this waste?" But only love can fully interpret love; and he who made his greatest sacrifice for us will rightly understand and thoroughly appreciate our offering. There is nothing wasted that is expended upon him. Let us seek, therefore, to cultivate this grace of self-sacrifice, not only that we may honor him, but that we ourselves may enter into the full meaning of the precious words, "It is more blessed to give than to receive." "Every man, according as he purposeth in his heart, so let him give; not grudgingly, nor of necessity; for God loveth a cheerful giver. And God is able to make all grace abound toward you, that ye always having all sufficiency in all things, may abound to every good work."

> "Love still delights to bring her best,
> And where love is, that offering evermore is blest."

## XXI.

### *EVEN-SONG.*

#### 2 SAMUEL xxii.

THE harp of David was his constant companion. When in his early days he followed the sheep upon the slopes of Bethlehem, he beguiled the weary hours with the music of its notes. At the court of Saul he charmed away the evil spirit from that monarch's breast by its soothing strains; and in all the vicissitudes of his checkered life, his hand, responsive to his heart, drew from his lyre appropriate music, while his voice accompanied its sounds in words which, even apart from the divine inspiration that pervaded them, "the world will not willingly let die." In the cave of Adullam, in the wilderness of Judah, at the court of Achish, and in the Valley of the Jordan, on that dismal day when he fled from his capital, before the rebellious Absalom, we have seen how he solaced himself with sacred song; and in the deeper darkness in which he was enveloped by his own shameful sin, he proved that the contrite heart, when swept by the fingers of Jehovah's love, gives forth ever the most thrilling tones.

Nor was it only in times of trial that the Psalmist struck his harp. His joys, as well as his sorrows, found utterance in song; and when he brought up the ark to Jerusalem, or returned in triumph from some long campaign, he signalized the occasion by a gladsome ode of thanksgiving and praise. Hence we do not wonder that, when he had been delivered from all his enemies, and was enjoying a season of repose in the evening twilight of his life, he gave expression to his feelings in the words of this Psalm. His "May of life had fallen now into the sere and yellow leaf." The snows of seventy winters had fallen on his head, but his heart was as fresh, his imagination as brilliant, and his piety as fervent as ever; so, as he looked back on the way by which the Lord had led him, and recounted all the deliverances which God had wrought for him, he took his harp once more, and sang to its loved music this Psalm, which for faith, for fervor, for sublimity, and for devout thankfulness, is second to none of his productions.

We have not hitherto gone very minutely into any of his Psalms, and have contented ourselves with indicating in a general way the historical occasions on which some of them were composed, and pointing out the new significance which they acquire when read in the light of the circumstances out of which they sprung; but as the inspired chronicler has incorporated this one in the narrative, and means us to regard it as David's "even-song," chanted by him on the retrospect of his life's changeful day, we may profitably spend a short time in a survey of its contents.

With a considerable number of minor variations, the ode before us is reproduced as the eighteenth in the book of Psalms, and it has been said by some that the one is an incorrect copy of the other. But to me it rather seems that in the book of Samuel we have it in the form in which at first the monarch sung it in his closet, as a personal outburst of gratitude to God; while in the Psalter we have it revised and adapted to public worship, for the general use of the tribes, and so, appropriately addressed to the chief musician. This view is rendered more probable by the fact that we have other cases of a similar sort in the book of Psalms, as, for example, the 14th, the 53d, and the closing strain of the 40th, which is nearly identical with the 70th. We believe, therefore, that for reasons which have not been explained, David prepared a twofold form of this magnificent production; and so, treating the two as separate and independent, we content ourselves with noting the fact that there are variations between them, without attempting either to point out, or to account for, each particular discrepancy.

The mention of Saul in the title does not indicate that the Psalm was composed in David's early life, but rather that, even though thirty years had gone since his persecution by the son of Kish, the deliverances which he then experienced had not faded from his memory, but still stood out before him as the greatest mercies which he had ever received. We are prone to forget past favors. The benefactors of our youth are not always remembered in our after-years; and in the crowd and conflict of events in our later history, we have too often little thought to spare, and few thanks to express, for our early mercies. We do not enough consider that, in mounting the ladder of life, it is often more difficult to set our foot on the first round than to take any single step thereafter; and, therefore, that those who aided us in the beginning have given us by far the most effectual assistance. But it was not so with David, for as he sits here looking back on his career, his first conflicts seem still his greatest; and much as he blessed God for after-kindness, he places high above all the other favors which he had received his deliverance out of the hand of Saul. Nor may we neglect to note that in all this David is but the representative of the believer in Jesus; for, no matter how many or how great the mercies which he experiences, the first grand "crowning mercy" of salvation from the guilt and pollution of iniquity ever comes uppermost; and to every song of praise which he sings he adds some such doxology as that of John: "Unto him that loved us, and washed us from our sins in his own blood, and hath made us kings and priests unto God and his Father, to him be glory and dominion for ever and ever. Amen."

## DAVID, KING OF ISRAEL.

The Psalm may be divided into five distinct though unequal parts. There is, first, an introduction extending to the end of the fourth verse, and giving a general indication of the character of the ode; there is, second, a highly figurative and sublime description of the dangers in which he had been involved, and the deliverance which God had wrought for him: this comprises verses 5–20; there is, third, an exposition of that principle of the divine administration in accordance with which he had been delivered: this is contained in verses 21–29; there is, fourth, a recapitulation in more simple terms of God's doings on his behalf: this includes verses 30–49; there is, finally, the closing stanza, in which he gathers up the expression of his gratitude into one full chorus of praise, and looks down the long vista of ages to the far-off days of the Messiah.

In the introductory portion of the ode David sets forth what God had been to him, and there are two things which specially claim attention in his words. The first is the number and variety of the terms which he employs to describe the protection which God afforded him; and the second is the emphatic personal manner in which he speaks.

He seems to have a difficulty in finding any one word which would adequately express all that Jehovah had been to him, so he heaps one term upon another, calling him "a rock, a fortress, a deliverer, a shield, a high tower, a horn, a refuge, and a Saviour." This is no vain repetition, neither is it a straining after effect, like that of the young orator who piles epithet upon epithet, weakening only where he meant to strengthen; but it is an attempt to describe, from many sides, that which he felt could not be fully shown from any single stand-point. He means to say, that for every sort of peril in which he had been placed, God had been a protection appropriate thereto. As if he had said, "those whom God intends to succor and defend are not only safe against one kind of dangers, but are, as it were, surrounded by impregnable ramparts on all sides; so that, should a thousand deaths be presented to their view, they ought not to be afraid even at this formidable array." Nor is this many-sided description of God's protection without its value to us; for though we may have proved his power to help us in one way, we are apt to fall into despair when some new danger threatens us; and therefore it is re-assuring to have David's testimony to the fact, that those whom God shields are incased all round, and will have perfect protection in every emergency. But numerous as are the figures under which God's help is here brought before us, each of them is preceded by the emphatic appropriating "my."* It is remarkable that when the soul is either very deeply sunk in sorrow, or very highly elevated in joy, its language is thoroughly personal. All vague generalities and commonplace phraseology are swept away, and the heart speaks for itself. It will allow no stranger to intermeddle either with its gladness or its grief; but it becomes intensely personal, and deals only in the singular number. The hymn of Hannah and the magnificat of Mary are illustrations in point; and in the epistles of Paul, although the apostle often uses the plural number in the course of his argument, yet when he ascends to the higher region of experience, he drops the we and the our, and it is then, "I thank God, through Jesus Christ my Lord; I live; yet not I, but Christ liveth in me." Nowhere, however, does this personali-

---

* In my early boyhood, after having heard a sermon in which the preacher dwelt much on "the appropriating act of faith," I asked my father what he meant by that expression. He gave me the same reply which had been given him by his mother to the same inquiry, when he was a lad, viz., "Take your Bible, and underscore all the 'mys,' the 'mines,' and the 'mes' you come upon, and you will soon discover what appropriation is." It is the focusing of all that God is upon yourself, even as the lens concentrates the sun's rays upon one bright, burning spot.

ty of earnestness more frequently appear than in the Psalms of David; and in the firm appropriation which he here makes of God to himself we see how necessary to spiritual happiness it is that we should be able to call God our own. A fortress is threatening and terrible to all who are outside of it; but it is, just because of that, only the more safe to those who are within it; and only when we believingly appropriate God as our own do we enter into the divine fortress and enjoy his protection. So long as we are unreconciled to him, his glorious attributes, his infinite resources, his boundless might appear arrayed against us; but when, through faith in Jesus Christ, we enter into covenant with him, all these are on our side, and we are enabled to sing, "Behold God is my salvation." Mark, *is* our salvation; that is a higher thing than to say God works out our salvation. He stands between us and every evil; and because we are Christ's, and Christ is his, we can say with truth that all things, however frowning they may look, are ours. My hearer, have you said unto the Lord, thou art my God? Is he thy salvation? Remember that he is not and can not be the salvation of any one until the soul of the individual believingly appropriates him. Take him thus to thy heart; give him thus thy hand, and thou art safe forever.

In the second portion of the Psalm, extending from the fifth to the twentieth verse, the inspired poet describes his perils and his deliverances, depicting "by the sublimest expressions and loftiest terms the majesty of God, and the awful manner in which he came to his assistance, saved him from his enemies, and extricated him from all his difficulties, namely, by arming, as it were, the elements of heaven against them, and sending a dreadful storm of thunder, lightning, hail, rain, and tempestuous wind to discomfit and destroy them. In this description there is every circumstance of horror that can be mentioned; the sentiments and images are grand beyond description, the words lofty and expressive, and God is introduced in a manner worthy of his majesty, encompassed with all the powers of nature as his attendants, and as the instruments of his vengeance to execute his purposes in the salvation of David and the destruction of his enemies."\* He speaks of his sufferings in this wise: "The waves of death compassed me, the floods of ungodly men made me afraid. The sorrows of Hades compassed me about, the snares of death were laid for me in anticipation." And when we remember his hair-breadth escape from the javelin of Saul, and the many occasions in which he was imperiled by the machinations of his enemies, we may not say that he exaggerates; but through them all his solace was in prayer. "In my distress I called upon the Lord, and cried unto my God: he heard my voice out of his temple, and my cry came before him, even into his ears." The good man's refuge is ever at the mercy-seat. Though every way seem shut against him, the way to God is always open, and when he can get near to Jehovah he is safe; for then he links himself to omnipotence, and God's faithfulness is pledged to give him succor. Very deeply was this felt by David in all his calamities, and he did not cry to God in vain; for he sent him deliverance in such signal ways that it was made perfectly evident that his salvation was of the Lord. The delineation of his deliverance here is in a strain of the most highly-wrought imagery, borrowed from the description of Jehovah's descent on Sinai; and such is the inherent sublimity of his words, that even the most meagre translations of them catch somewhat of their grandeur. The old version of Sternhold and Hopkins ceases to be doggerel, and becomes classic here; and as we read the lines,

---

\* "A Critical History of the Life of David," by S. Chandler, D.D., p. 366.

> "On cherub and on cherubim
> Full royally he rode,
> And on the wings of mighty winds
> Came flying all abroad,"

we have before us a conception the most sublime that ever entered into human imagination.* We must remember, however, that all this is poetic, and not historic. David does not mean to say that these portents actually accompanied God's descent to his assistance. The simple truth is, that no miracles were wrought on David's account, but still his deliverance was as much God's doing as if he had come down with all the glory of Sinai in his defense; and the discomfiture of his enemies was as complete as if Jehovah of hosts had marshaled the armies which marched forth to meet them; so that, as the result of all, he makes this acknowledgment, "He brought me forth into a large place; he delivered me, because he delighted in me."

This last phrase, "He delighted in me," fitly introduces the next division of the Psalm, which sets forth the harmony of David's deliverance with the general principle of the divine administration. There is a retributive element in God's moral government. The Saviour himself has said, "With what measure ye mete it shall be measured to you again;" and David here asserts that God deals with men according to the principles on which men themselves act toward each other. To the merciful, God is merciful; to the upright, he is upright; to the pure, he is pure; and to the froward, he is froward. This last term, indeed, must not be held as denoting that God is ever in himself froward, but that in his providential government of men, the individual who is froward is met with the frowardness of another; or

---

* See an interesting paper on this verse, and the imitations of it by modern poets, in Henry Kirke White's "Remains," p. 294.

if this be not strong enough as an interpretation, we must hold the words as equivalent to the declaration made elsewhere, that "he taketh the wise in their own craftiness, and that he causes men to fall themselves into the pit which they have digged for others." The general principle is this, that God is on the side of right, and that if men conscientiously adhere to that which they know to be their duty, he will, in the long run, "bring forth their righteousness as the light, and their judgment as the noonday." Now, in the main David did this, so far, at least, as his public administration and public enemies were concerned. I speak not now of his character before God; for so viewed, he was far from perfect; but as he stood related to his subjects and his enemies, he was distinguished by integrity and uprightness. He was not dishonestly seeking his own ends. He was only following God's leadings, and the men who were opposed to him were his enemies, just because he was so conspicuously the servant and the friend of God. The words of Mr. Spurgeon here are well worthy of quotation: "Albeit the dispensations of divine grace are to the fullest degree sovereign and irrespective of human merit, yet in the dealings of Providence there is often discernible a rule of justice by which the injured are avenged and the righteous ultimately triumph. David's early troubles arose from the wicked malice of envious Saul, who, no doubt, prosecuted his persecutions under cover of charges brought against the character of the man after God's own heart. These charges David declares to have been utterly false, and asserts that he possessed a grace-given righteousness which the Lord had graciously rewarded in defiance of all his calumniators. Before God, the man after God's own heart was a humble sinner; but before his slanderers he could, with unblushing face, speak of the cleanness of his hands and the righteousness of his life. He knows little of the sanctifying power of

divine grace who is not, at the bar of human equity, able to plead innocence. There is no self-righteousness in an honest man knowing that he is honest, nor even in his believing that God rewarded him in Providence because of his honesty, for such is often a most evident matter of fact. It is not at all an opposition to the doctrine of salvation by grace, and no sort of evidence of a Pharisaic spirit, when a gracious man, having been slandered, stoutly maintains his own integrity and vigorously defends his character. A godly man has a clear conscience, and knows himself to be upright. Is he to deny his own consciousness, and to despise the work of the Holy Ghost by hypocritically making himself worse than he is? A godly man prizes his integrity very highly, or else he could not be a godly man at all; and is he to be called proud because he will not readily lose the jewel of a reputable character? A godly man can see that in divine Providence uprightness and truth are, in the long run, sure to bring their own reward; may he not, when he sees that reward bestowed in his own case, praise the Lord for it? Yea, rather, must he not show forth the faithfulness and goodness of his God? This cluster of expressions, therefore, must be read as the song of a good conscience after having safely outridden a storm of obloquy, persecution, and abuse; and then there will be no fear of our upbraiding the writer as one who sets too high a price upon his own moral character."\*
The principle underlying this section of the Psalm is the same as that which has been expanded into the 37th and 73d odes in our Psalter, and must never be lost sight of by any of us. It is "unto the upright" that "light ariseth in the darkness," and it is he whose heart is established, and who shall not be afraid until he shall see his desire upon his enemies. Or, more simply still, even in the present life

---

\* Spurgeon's "Treasury of David," vol. i., pp. 272, 273.

there is a retributive element in God's moral government, and men shall be done by as they do.

From the thirtieth verse on till the close of the forty-ninth we have a virtual recapitulation, only in simpler phrase and in more detail, of the deliverances which David had experienced; and it is interesting to note all through this section of the ode—indeed, I may say, throughout the entire Psalm —the writer's recognition of God's hand in every thing. There had been many human agents employed in working for him, but here he makes mention of God alone. In the succeeding chapter the historian gives us a list of David's thirty-seven mighty men, and recounts some of their most valiant deeds; and, as the honors which their monarch conferred upon them conclusively show, he was not ungrateful to them for their fidelity, but his highest praise, and his devoutest thanks went to the God who wrought in and through them for his anointed's sake. Herein the Psalmist has left us an example worthy of our imitation. We see the visible instrument, but we forget all too often the invisible Author of all our mercies; and in these days especially, when men make so much of physical laws, we are apt to hide God behind the operations which he is himself carrying on; and while admiring the harmony and order of the universe, we have no song of praise to Him who upholds it all. Let us be on our guard against all this. It might perhaps be too much to say, with Wordsworth, that one would "rather be a pagan, suckled in a creed outworn," than one of those who believe that the world is governed by laws without a lawgiver. But to me there is no atheism more revolting than that of the man, be he philosopher or not, who takes all his mercies as things of course, ground out to him daily by the mill of ceaseless law, and who has no song of gratitude to sing to Him " of whom, and to whom, and through whom are all things."

But while in these verses we have this recognition of God

in all things everywhere apparent, there are specially three attributes of God himself which are prominently mentioned in them. The first is his faithfulness, as set forth in the expression, "The word of the Lord is tried." The term "tried" denotes generally "put to the test;" but here it has involved in it the additional idea that the trial has been satisfactorily passed. Before they are considered fit for actual service on shipboard, anchors, chains, and cables are subjected to such a strain as shall give those who employ them confidence to use them in any emergency; and when some great engineering work is finished, a railway viaduct, for example, it is tested by some rigid trial before it is opened for public traffic. Now, David's life had been, in some sense, such a trial of the Word of God. By his struggles, his sorrows, his emergencies, yea, even by his sins, he had been, as it were, put forth to show how great a strain the promises of God could bear; and so at the close of his career he says: "The Word of the Lord is tried. It has stood firm with me in all my conflicts and calamities, and despite all my sins; therefore let no one despair. That which has been so solid beneath the weight even of my sinful tread, will support any one who trustfully ventures on it for himself." Thus interpreted, these words of David are an exact parallel to the testimony of Paul, when he says:* "This is a faithful saying, and worthy of all acceptation, that Christ Jesus came into the world to save sinners; of whom I am chief" (or first). "Howbeit for this cause I obtained mercy, that in me first" (that is, first not in the order of time, but first in the degree of guilt—a sinner of the first rank—an A1 sinner) "Jesus Christ might show forth all long-suffering, for a pattern to them, which should hereafter believe on him to life everlasting." What an encouragement, therefore, is there here to every one to rest in faith upon the

---

* 1 Timothy i., 15, 16.

promise of Jehovah! No matter though we may have been sinners of as deep a dye as Paul—murderers, blasphemers, persecutors; no matter though we may have been backsliders of as dark a character as David—adulterers, liars, murderers, yet if even "from thence we seek the Lord, we shall find him, if we seek him with all our hearts." He who received them will not spurn us away from him. The promise which upheld them will support us. The welcome which was given to them will not be withheld from us, for is it not written, "Him that cometh unto me, I will in no wise cast out?" This Word has been tried and proved in different ages of the Church, now by an Augustine, and now by a Luther; now by a Bunyan, and now by a Newton; but never, perhaps, was it put to so great a strain as when the malefactor on the cross cried at the very warning of the twelfth hour to Jesus, "Lord, remember me when thou comest into thy kingdom!" Let the answer which then came, "To-day shalt thou be with me in paradise," encourage thee, oh sinner, to put it to the proof now for thyself, and thou shalt be another trophy of the Redeemer's power to save, another witness bearer to the faithfulness of God in the keeping of his gracious promise.

The second quality of the divine character to which special prominence is given in these verses is the gentleness of God. It comes out in these words: "Thy gentleness hath made me great." This expression is to me the gem of the Psalm. I am never weary of recurring to it. As in looking on a spacious landscape, every feature of which is beautiful, the eye finds itself at length resting with supreme satisfaction on some one object of surpassing loveliness within it; or, as in listening to a piece of music, all of which is inspiriting, the ear catches up some specially bewitching strain, which we keep humming over to ourselves in all our intervals of labor; so, after we have read this whole Psalm, we come back again and again to this delightful phrase. It falls upon the ear as if with the soft breathings of an æolian harp, and amidst the jewels which shine out of this Book of Truth, there is not one that sparkles with a radiance so divine as this, "Thy gentleness hath made me great!" It is indeed the very heart and centre of the cross of Christ. David felt that God's kindness to him, in his weakness, his waywardness, his very wantonness of sin, had lifted him up to the external greatness of his throne, and had built up in him the internal greatness of his character.

But what did he know of this quality of Jehovah's heart, compared with that of it which has been revealed to us in the work of Christ, and in our calling into and training in the Christian life? While we lay helplessly condemned beneath the sentence of his law, God came to us, not with Sinai's terror, but with tender love. "He that might the vantage best have took, found out the remedy." And while his sternness might have driven us from him, or moved us to strive against him, we have willingly yielded to the attraction of his gentleness. Go read the record of the Saviour's dealings with the woman at the well, with the woman that was a sinner, with the self-satisfied Nicodemus, and with the publican Zaccheus, and see how much his gentleness did in making them truly great. Nay, look back on your own experience, and bear witness to those around you, how his love "drew you, and you followed on," willingly surrendering yourselves to its divine attraction. Nor is this all. Even when we have been suffering under his hand, or have been wandering from his way, how much of gentleness has he manifested in our very chastisement. He has "stayed his rough wind, in the day of his east wind;" and if, like the eagle with her young, he has "stirred our nest" and pushed us out of it, we have scarcely remembered the roughness of that discipline, when we have found ourselves upborne on the ample wings of his grace, to loftier attainments in holiness than otherwise we could have reached. All along the pathways by which he has led us, we have met manifestations of his gentleness : it has been the background of our very trials, and as the mother soothes her broken-hearted and dispirited child by the loving ministrations of her tender hand, until he has forgotten his sorrow in the sunshine of her affection, so God has been with us, "gentle as a nurse cherishing her children." He has borne with us as none other could have done; and by that "method of indirectness" which the mother knows so well how to practice with her wayward boy, he has led us by a way which we knew not, and kept us attached —not by any outward bond, but by the inner tie of endearing affection—to himself. I have heard one tell, with ringing laughter, how once in a storm at sea, when danger was anticipated, a great overgrown man, not used to prayer, and remembering only the hymn of his childhood, flung himself upon his knees, and cried,

> "Gentle Jesus, meek and mild,
> Look upon a little child!"

But, after all, are we not all, even the oldest among us, children still, and is not this still the most endearing epithet of Jesus to every one of us—"gentle Jesus." I beseech you, therefore, brethren, by the gentleness of Christ, that ye present yourselves now unto him, and so receive from him the greatness of present holiness and future immortality. Every day we live we are receiving new proofs of his tender love to us; but when we have passed through the veil, and stand in heaven's own light, looking back upon all the ways in which our God has dealt with us, we shall understand this phrase more fully than we ever can on earth; and as we cast our crowns before the throne, our adoring homage to him who sits thereon will find its appropriate expression in these blessed words: "Thy gentleness hath made me great!"

The third divine attribute to which prominence is here given is the eternity of God. It comes out in these words: "The Lord liveth, and blessed be my rock; and let the God of my salvation be exalted." A certain sense of solitariness grows upon a man as he becomes older. Those who were venerable in his youthful days, and to whom he looked for counsel, are one by one carried to the tomb. The companions of his early manhood fall at his side. He comes at length to a time when he does not care to make many new friends; and when he reaches the limit of three-score years and ten, he begins to feel himself almost a stranger, even in the place where he has spent his life. Perhaps a king, more than most other men, will realize this experience. The poet has spoken of "the lonely glory of a throne." The monarch has no equals, and, from the nature of the case, can have few confidants and counselors, except such as are venerable for age. But as his reign wears on, one after another of these early friends are taken away; and as each is removed, he is apt to think that a part of himself has been withdrawn from him. Thus loneliness steals over him, and he comes at length to be, like Moses among the tribes, the solitary survivor of a buried generation. Something like this, I doubt not, was felt by David as he advanced into old age. Samuel was gone; Jonathan was no more; Ahithophel had proved a traitor; Joab had become a thorn in his side; but there was One always true, and it was with no ordinary emotion, we may be sure, that out of his earthly solitude he sang of his fidelity and deathlessness: "The Lord liveth, and blessed be my rock, and exalted be the God of my salvation." Let the aged among us fall back on this assurance, and find their solace in the companionship of the Most High. He hath said, "I will never leave thee nor forsake thee."

The last strain of this remarkable Psalm gathers into one inference of gratitude all the argument of the ode: "Therefore I will give thanks unto thee, O Lord;" and looking forward to the permanence of his song, and its acceptance by the Gentiles as a portion of their daily psalmody, he adds, "among the Gentiles." Then, calling to mind Nathan's prediction of the eternity of his kingdom, he concludes with these words: "He is the tower of salvation for his king: and sheweth mercy unto his anointed, unto David and to his seed for evermore." Thus, rising out of David's personal history, this ode, like many others, ascends at length to David's Lord, of whom, in the "perspective of prophecy," the singer caught a glimpse ere yet he laid aside his harp.

I have taken merely the most cursory glance at the structure of this sublime poem. Let me commend it to your careful study in the retirement of the closet, and meanwhile let me suggest two practical lessons from this whole subject.

Let us learn, then, to thank God for our mercies and deliverances. When the crisis of some great agony is on us, there are no words which leap so readily to our lips as these: "God help me!" At such times we feel shut up to go to God, and we engage our friends to pray to him on our behalf. But when the danger is past and the suffering is gone, how seldom we think of Him on whom, while they lasted, we called so passionately for relief. Of the ten lepers whom Jesus cleansed, only one returned to give him thanks.

We despise the conduct of the French infidel who, while the storm was threatening to submerge the vessel in which he sailed, was on his knees in trembling prayer; but when the gale was over, ridiculed his own fear as cowardice, and laughed at his own prayer as superstition. But are we so much better ourselves? Where is our thanksgiving for God's free mercy, which, in answer to our prayers, he has so frequently shown us? In the time of pestilence the churches will be crowded with eager suppliants that the plague may be removed; but when the disease has gone, you will have only the merest handful to hold a day of thanksgiving. It is not always thus, indeed; and when true gratitude is manifested it moves us intensely, even from its very rarity. One case of this description, at the close of the cotton famine in Lancashire, England, stirred the whole British nation to its depths. It was in the town of Staleybridge, which for many months had been suffering the deepest distress. All those weary weeks its factories had been silent, and its tall chimneys smokeless; and its operatives, all their savings gone, were reduced to a want which they bore with the most heroic endurance. At length the war was ended, and a consignment of cotton came to the town. Hastening to the railway dépôt, the men unyoked the horses from the first wagon, and drew it themselves into the court-yard of one of the factories. Soon an immense crowd surrounded it, and the tears filled the eyes of the multitude as they gazed upon it, for it meant employment, and employment meant bread. Just then, while all were deeply moved, one solitary voice began to sing the grand old doxology, "Praise God, from whom all blessings flow," and in a moment every one in the vast assemblage joined in, while on the gaunt and famine-stricken cheeks of faces upturned to heaven the big tears kept coursing down. Often has that simple strain been sung in most inspiring circumstances, but never with more depth of feeling or more fervor of gratitude than on that occasion. But why should our gratitude be confined to rare seasons? The true thanksgiving is thanksliving. The noblest doxology is a holy life. Let us aim, my brethren, to translate into conduct the words of this sublime Psalm; let us make each his own life a hymn of praise, according to the poet's advice:

> "Be good, my child, and let who will be clever—
> Do noble deeds, not dream them all day long;
> And so make life, death, and that vast forever
> One grand deep song."*

Finally, let us learn from the experience of God's goodness in the past, and trust to him for the present and the future. "The Lord's aye to the fore," said a good Scotchwoman in her day of trial; and by this faith she was upheld. "The best of all is, God is with us," said John Wesley, as he was dying; and by this trust he was supported as he passed within the veil. David had many experiences of God's faithfulness, and so he could go calmly forward, saying, "God lives, blessed be my rock; and let the God of my salvation be exalted." Let us follow his example, and "remember the days of old." The Lord is now just what he was when he delivered us in the past. He loves us as tenderly as he did then. He is as near us as he was then. And he will deliver us once more. Oliver Heywood, one of the English Puritan ministers who was ejected in 1662 by the odious Act of Uniformity, has related a touching anecdote which may impress the lesson on which I now insist more forcibly than any words of mine. He tells of a mother who, when one child was taken from her, calmly bowed to the trial, and said, "God lives, blessed be my rock; and let the God of my salvation be exalted." Another child was removed by death, and still she sang as before, "God lives." But at length her beloved husband was stricken down, and she seemed to sink into the very depths of despair. As she sat wringing her hands in anguish, a little child, whom God had spared to her, came to her knee and said, "Mother, is God dead?" "God dead, my child! What do you mean?" "When brother and sister were taken away, you said, 'God lives;' but now that father is no more,

---

* Charles Kingsley.

you sit and weep, and never say a word about God; so I thought he must be dead too." "No, my child, God is not dead; and he has sent you to rebuke the unbelief of my heart. He liveth; yes, he liveth! and I will still cling to him. 'Blessed be his name, and let the God of my salvation be exalted.'" God liveth! Let that be the sheet-anchor of your heart, and it will hold you in the fiercest hurricane.

## XXII.

### *THE CORONATION OF SOLOMON.*

1 KINGS i.; 1 CHRONICLES xxviii.; xxix.

DAVID was now a feeble old man. The silver cord was beginning to be loosed, and the golden bowl was breaking. The grasshopper had become a burden, and desire had failed. The days had come when, in regard to all mere earthly joys, he said, "I have no pleasure in them." He was waiting patiently for his change, having his comfort cared for and his wants supplied by a beautiful Shunammite maiden, who had been carefully selected for the purpose. Surely, now, the storms of his life are ended, and he will have a smooth sea as he glides into the eternal haven. So we might have reckoned; but still the dark retribution of his evil deed was following him; and ere he fell asleep in death, the words of Nathan, "The sword shall never depart from thine house," were to have another fulfillment. Adonijah, his fourth son, whom he had pampered and petted by the weakest indulgence, impatient for his father's death, and eager to obtain his crown, entered into a well-concerted plan to secure the object of his ambition. Let the parents before me take note of this, and mark the folly of permitting their children to go unrestrained into wickedness, or to obtain without control every capricious desire. David "had never displeased Adonijah at any time in saying, Why hast thou done so?" And now behold the result, as the monarch's old age is saddened by the revolt of another of his sons against his authority. Indiscriminate indulgence of a son will only issue in his open rebellion against his father. We may pamper our children into wrath, as well as provoke them to it; and he is no true lover either of himself or of his son who does not seek to govern him by affectionate restraint. There must be discipline in the home, else the issue will be sorrow. The rule must not be that of the despot, indeed, else the end will also be disastrous; but there must be rule—only let the hand of firmness wear ever the glove of love.

After the example of Absalom, Adonijah set up a great establishment, and rode about in a chariot drawn by horses magnificently caparisoned, and preceded by fifty heralds. Among his adherents were Joab, the captain of the host, and Abiathar the priest. We do not wonder at the defection of the crafty son of Zeruiah, for David had made him feel in many ways that he was weary of his arrogant and overbearing demeanor; and he knew that he had little or nothing to hope for from Solomon if he should come to the throne. But it is not so easy to account for Abiathar's desertion. He had been with David in the cave of Adullam, had been the companion of his vicissitudes for more than thirty years, and had done noble service during Absalom's revolt; and it is with the deepest sorrow that we see him now among those who are taking advantage of the monarch's weakness to put a creature of their own upon the throne. Mr. Blunt* supposes, and with some show of probability, that in the later years of his reign David had in some way shown his preference for Zadok over Abiathar, and that in jealousy of his rival, whom David had favored, we have the key of his connection with Adonijah's rebellion. But whatever might be his secret reason for his treasonable conduct, he would be at no loss for pretexts by which to vindicate it both to himself and others. He might allege that Adonijah was the eldest

---

\* Blunt's "Scriptural Coincidences," pp. 153-157.

surviving son of David; and that, as he was in the mid-time of his days, and not, like Solomon, a mere youth, many dangers to the State might be escaped by seating him upon the throne. But God had already indicated, in the most solemn manner, that Solomon was to be his father's successor; and any attempt to give the kingdom to another was not only rebellion against David, but treason against Jehovah.

On this ground, therefore, as well as on that of personal devotion to the aged king, the revolt of Adonijah was opposed by Nathan, by Zadok, by Benaiah, the son of Jehoiada, and by the great majority of the mighty men whom David had honored for their valor in his service. Against such weighty adversaries one would have supposed that Adonijah might have despaired of success; but perhaps he imagined that Joab and his army would prove more than a match for any force that could be arrayed against him. In any case, he acted with the greatest promptitude, and went out with his followers to the well En-rogel, near to which Jonathan and Ahimaaz had been concealed on the day of the king's flight from Jerusalem. Here he made a great feast, and was already rejoicing in the success which he imagined he had achieved, when he found himself unexpectedly checkmated and defeated; for Nathan, having heard of his doings, had gone immediately to Bath-sheba, and sent her into the royal closet to inform the king of what was going on. While she was yet speaking to him, Nathan himself, according to previous agreement with her, came in and confirmed her words; whereupon, after assuring Bath-sheba with an oath that the throne should be given to Solomon, David gave such orders to Nathan, Zadok, and Jehoiada, as showed that even in the smouldering ashes of the old man something of the ancient fire still lived. He bade them set Solomon upon the white mule of state, and lead him through the city to Gihon, where Zadok should anoint him king in

Jehovah's name. This done, he commanded that the trumpet should be blown before him, and the shout raised, "God save King Solomon!" Thereafter they were to bring him back to the palace and seat him on the throne, that all might know that he had appointed him to be ruler over Israel.

These injunctions were obeyed to the letter, and the result was that the popular enthusiasm was evoked to the utmost; for the people "piped with pipes, and rejoiced with great joy, and the earth rent with the sound of them." The echo of their shouting broke in upon the mirth of Adonijah's feast at En-rogel, and provoked from Joab the question, "Wherefore is this noise of the city being in an uproar?" which Jonathan, the son of Abiathar, came just in time to answer. He told all that we have recounted, adding, as a new incident, that the servants of the king had gone to congratulate him upon Solomon's appointment, saying to him, "God make the name of Solomon better than thy name, and make his throne greater than thy throne;" and receiving for answer, "Blessed be the Lord God of Israel, which hath given one to sit on my throne this day, mine eyes even seeing it." These tidings at once disconcerted the followers of Adonijah, so that they fled every man to his home, while the prince himself sought refuge in the Tabernacle, and laying hold upon the horns of the altar, said, "Let King Solomon swear unto me to-day that he will not slay his servant with the sword." Wisely, however, Solomon declined to fetter himself with any oath, but simply said, "If he will show himself a worthy man, there shall not a hair of him fall to the earth: but if wickedness shall be found in him, he shall die."

So ended this day of trouble, and rebuke, and blasphemy; but, satisfactory as the conclusion was, so far as Solomon was concerned, something more was needed before he could be regarded unchallengeably as his father's successor. As

## THE CORONATION OF SOLOMON.

we have repeatedly seen, the constitution of the kingdom of Israel required not only that the monarch should be designated by Jehovah and anointed by the priest, but also that he should be publicly recognized and accepted by the tribes, or their properly authorized representatives. Thus, a considerable time after his anointing by Samuel, Saul was chosen by the people; and many years intervened between David's designation at Bethlehem and his election to the throne, first of Judah at Hebron, and afterward of the twelve tribes at Jerusalem. Until, therefore, the assembly of the representatives of the people had ratified and, as it were, repeated the deed of Zadok, Solomon was not, in all respects, the king. Hence, some time after the event which we have just described, when David had gained so much strength that he could undergo the fatigue of a long day in the open air, he summoned "all the princes of Israel, the princes of the tribes, and the captains of the companies that ministered to the king by course, and the captains over the thousands, and captains over the hundreds, and the stewards over all the substance and possession of the king, and of his sons, with the officers, and with the mighty men, and with all the valiant men, unto Jerusalem." It was a solemn occasion, like to that on which Moses had taken farewell of the tribes whom he had led through the wilderness, or that on which Joshua had given his parting exhortation to the people whom he had settled in Canaan; or that on which Samuel had formally laid aside his functions and handed over the sovereignty to Saul.

Deep must have been the feelings of David's heart as he presided for the last time over the assembly of the people; and with mingled emotions they must have looked on the fragile form of him who had been so long identified with their national history, and on the intelligent countenance of the youth at his side, who was so soon to add new lustre to their renown. With tender affection, David addressed them as his brethren and his people (1 Chron. xxviii., 2), and unfolded to them the cherished purpose of his heart to build a temple to Jehovah, together with the message which he had received from Nathan in regard to it. Then, turning to the blushing youth beside him, he said, "And thou, Solomon my son, know thou the God of thy father, and serve him with a perfect heart and with a willing mind: for the Lord searcheth all hearts, and understandeth all the imaginations of the thoughts: if thou seek him, he will be found of thee; but if thou forsake him, he will cast thee off forever. Take heed now; for the Lord hath chosen thee to build a house for the sanctuary: be strong, and do it."

After this he gave him the plans which he had already prepared, by divine direction, of "the porch, and of the houses thereof, and of the treasuries thereof, and of the upper chambers thereof, and of the inner parlors thereof, and of the place of the mercy-seat, and the pattern of all that he had by the Spirit, of the courts of the house of the Lord, and of all the chambers round about," and a list of the things which he had already consecrated for the purpose. Then he brought forth the gold which he had accumulated for the various articles which the Temple required; and when the spectators had recovered from the amazement which the sight of such treasures must have produced, he renewed his charge to his son, saying, "Be strong and of good courage, and do it: fear not, nor be dismayed, for the Lord God, even my God, will be with thee; he will not fail thee, nor forsake thee, until thou hast finished all the work for the service of the house of the Lord." But Solomon was not the only party concerned; so, turning to the congregation, David commended his son to their confidence and care, detailing still more of the preparations which he had made for the great work which he wished to be performed, and beseeching them to do their best, since "the palace was not for man, but for God." Nay, as he was their God, as well as the God of their king, it was meet that they also should be sharers with him in the honor and the privilege of carrying forward this holy undertaking; so he made an appeal to them in this heart-searching question: "Who then is willing to consecrate his service this day unto the Lord?" The response was liberal and enthusiastic; for the people, catching the holy infection of the royal self-sacrifice, laid upon the altar "of gold five thousand talents and ten thousand drams, and of silver ten thousand talents, and of brass eighteen thousand talents, and one hundred thousand talents of iron," while those who had precious stones generously devoted them to the sacred enterprise. It was a gladsome day; a time of holy privilege highly prized; a season of precious opportunity thoroughly improved; an era of revived spiritual life, leading to unreserved consecration of soul and substance to the Lord. The hearts alike of king and people were opened to receive God's blessing, and in the receiving they gave out their own incense of gratitude, even as the flower, when it unfolds its petals to the morning sunbeam, does, by the very unfolding, give forth its fragrance to the air around. But it is ever thus. He who knows and feels that he is receiving is then and thereby led to give out of his heart's gratitude to God; and, looking at once to the origin and the issue of this great national revival of religion, we regard it as the grandest scene in David's whole career.

As sometimes the setting sun gilds the western sky, and makes of the very clouds which had obscured the afternoon a bank of burnished gold, giving thereby a glory to the heavens which in the absence of the clouds could never be produced, so this last public appearance of the aged monarch fringes with a golden border even the dark passages of his life, and borrows, too, from them a frame-work of blackness which, by its very contrast, brings out more vividly the brightness of the departing luminary. The clouds had been very dark, but the sun had been behind them all the while; and now, ere he goes down beneath the west, he has broken through them and partially dispersed them, and men recognize once more his greatness. We see now the "one increasing purpose" which ran through all his life. We understand now why he was so eager in amassing treasure, and so active in adding spoil to spoil; for as the student, on his return from college, lays reverently in his mother's lap the prizes which he has toiled night and day to win, so David here places devoutly on Jehovah's altar all that he had gained throughout his earthly career, saying, virtually, "For thee I won them, and to thee I give them." Even as he laid them there, indeed, they were wet with his penitential tears over the great transgression of his life. Still he laid them there; and he who forgave the iniquity of his sin accepted the gift he brought.

Such an assembly, crowned with such an offering to God, could not separate without an act of special worship, and who so fit to lead the devotions in speech as he who had led them in the worship of liberal offerings? So, taking his place before the people, David blessed the Lord in language as affecting as it is sublime, as tender as it is true. I can not resist the impulse to repeat it here: "Blessed be thou, Lord God of Israel our father, for ever and ever. Thine, O Lord, is the greatness, and the power, and the glory, and the victory, and the majesty: for all that is in the heaven and in the earth is thine; thine is the kingdom, O Lord, and thou art exalted as head above all. Both riches and honor come of thee, and thou reignest over all; and in thine hand is power and might;-and in thine hand it is to make great, and to give strength unto all. Now therefore, our God, we thank thee, and praise thy glorious name. But who am I, and what is my people, that we should be able to offer so willingly after this sort? for all things come of thee, and of thine own have we given thee. For we are strangers before thee, and sojourners, as were all our fathers: our days on the earth are as a shadow, and there is none abiding. O Lord our God, all this store that we have prepared to build thee a house for thine holy name cometh of thine hand, and is all thine own. I know also, my God, that thou triest the heart, and hast pleasure in uprightness. As for me, in the uprightness of mine heart I have willingly offered all these things: and now have I seen with joy thy people, which are present here, to offer willingly unto thee. O Lord God of Abraham, Isaac, and of Israel, our fathers, keep this forever in the imagination of the thoughts of the heart of thy people, and prepare their heart unto thee: and give unto Solomon my son a perfect heart, to keep thy commandments, thy testimonies, and thy statutes, and to do all these things, and to build the palace, for the which I have made provision." This prayer was followed by a sacrificial feast, after which Solomon was anointed for the second time as the accepted monarch of the tribes of Israel.

But this public service was probably not the only thing connected with Solomon's anointing, for after the assembly had dispersed, and the aged king had retired to his chamber, it is not unlikely that he took his harp once more, and sang to its strains that wondrous Messiah-psalm which, rising from the circumstances of his son, looks down through all the ages to the final triumph of the Redeemer's kingdom. I refer to the 72d Psalm; and as we read it now, in the light of the events which I have recounted, we can not but feel a new interest in it, and derive new inspiration from it. I can not go fully into its consideration, but must content myself with giving the briefest summary of its substance. Beginning with the description of a king who, blessed with Jehovah's judgments, should "judge his people with righteousness and his poor with judgment," he passes to the benignity of his sway. "He shall come down like rain upon the mown grass: as showers that water the earth." Then he asserts the universality of his dominion: "His dominion shall be from sea to sea, and from the river unto the ends of the earth;" and the perpetuity of his reign: "His name shall endure forever: his name shall be continued as long as the sun: and men shall be blessed in him: all nations shall call him blessed." The conclusion is a grand outburst of praise, which seems almost to anticipate the hallelujahs of the skies. "Blessed be the Lord God, the God of Israel, who only doeth wondrous things. And blessed be his glorious name forever: and let the whole earth be filled with his glory. Amen and Amen." Little wonder that as men read this glowing ode, they say, "A greater than Solomon is here." This is emphatically the missionary Psalm, and it were well if, every time we sang it, our hearts would expand into the noble liberality manifested by the king and the people of Israel on the day by which it was probably occasioned; for what is the cause of missions but the building of a nobler temple than that which Solomon reared—a temple, the stones of which are living souls; the incense of which is the love of holy hearts, and the praises of which are the songs of the redeemed?

Let me make this thought the centre of the practical remarks with which my exposition must conclude. Observe, then, in the first place, the work to which God has called us in the world. It is that of building a temple for his abode. The edifice for which David made such magnificent preparations, and which Solomon reared in splendor, was, after all, only a typical structure. That which was outward came first, and afterward that which is spiritual. In the New Testament, indeed, the figure of the temple is employed with a threefold reference. Sometimes it is used to signify the body of the Saviour himself, as when he said to the Jews, "Destroy this temple, and in three days I will raise it up again." Sometimes it is applied to the body of the believer, as when Paul says, "Know ye not that your body is the temple of the Holy Ghost which is in you, which ye have of God?" But more usually it is employed to describe the spiritual church which our Lord Jesus Christ has founded in the world. The Lord himself is the foundation of this holy edifice, according as Paul has said, "Other foundation can no man lay than that is laid, which is Jesus Christ." Believers are the stones of which it is composed, as Peter has written: "Ye also as living stones are built up a spiritual house;" and Paul again has affirmed, "In whom ye also are builded together for a habitation of God through the Spirit." Apostles, evangelists, ministers, missionaries, and active Christian workers are the builders engaged in its erection, for Paul has called himself "a wise master-builder," and urges others to enthusiasm in the great undertaking; while at the same time he bids every man "take heed how he buildeth thereupon."

This, then, is the work which is committed to our care as Christians—the building *in* of believing souls to this great living edifice, which we call the Christian Church; or, in simpler and less figurative phraseology, the conversion of human souls, and the formation in them of a holy character; and it will be completed only when the prophecy shall be fulfilled, that "the earth shall be filled with the knowledge of the Lord as the waters cover the sea." I have said this is our work, and yet in another sense, and from another side, it is the work of God himself; but it is his work, carried on, in, and through our consecration of ourselves to its performance, "for we are laborers together with God." And what a work it is! There is an interest deep and peculiar in taking the stones from the quarry, and hewing them into shape, and polishing them into shining smoothness, and placing them in their courses one above another, until at length the house is finished for a royal palace, or a temple of worship. But what is that, after all, to the delight which is felt, or the enthusiasm which is awakened, as we dig up human souls from the quarry of sin, or ignorance, or degradation, and, through the processes of a loving and holy education prepare them for their places in this living temple! What marble so precious as a human soul! what granite so indestructible as an immortal spirit! what beauty so rare as that of a character which is moulded and fashioned after the pattern of the Redeemer himself! And it is given to us to work with such valuable and imperishable materials for the adornment of that stately structure which is "built upon the foundation of the apostles and prophets, Jesus Christ himself being the chief corner-stone." What an exalted honor, but what a solemn responsibility! Let us not loiter at our holy enterprise, but day by day let us labor on with untiring earnestness, until, when evening comes, we shall be greeted with the "well-done" of him who is the architect and is to be the inhabitant of the temple itself. My hearer, hast thou builded in yet even one living stone into this holy fane?

Observe, in the second place, that it is not given to any one man, or to any single generation, to finish this glorious structure. David gathered the materials, and Solomon built the house. So, many of those who were present on the joyful occasion which we have described might also be spectators on the gladsome day of the consecration, when the mystic cloud descended and filled the newly-finished Temple. But with the Church of Christ it is different. That has been in process of erection for centuries, and it is not completed yet. In this respect it resembles not so much the sacred building that crowned the height of Moriah as one of these mediæval cathedrals on which many successive generations labored, and which to-day remain as the result of many hundred years of toil. "Other men have labored" on it, and "we are entered upon their labors." The architect is one; the builders are multitudinous, belonging to every age and nation. It is but a small portion of it we can hope to rear at best, therefore let us employ every moment of our time, and let us make our part worthy of the workmanship of our illustrious predecessors. It is ours to carry forward a building on which Paul, and John, and Augustine, and Chrysostom, and Luther, and Calvin, and Knox, and Edwards, and Wesley, and Whitefield spent their strength and showed their skill. Let us not dishonor their workmanship, but let us strive so to do our portion that those who may come after us shall be stimulated by our example, as we have been by that of those who have gone before us.

Observe, again, the principles by which we should be animated in prosecuting this work. "The palace is not for man, but for God." What we do for him, therefore, should be of our best, the more especially as every thing which we have has come from him. Every day we are receiving new favors from his hands; and behind and above all the rest there is the unspeakable gift of his Son. Let us do as we may, therefore, it is still true that "of his own we give to him;" for if we lay our hearts upon his altar, it is he who has produced within us the holy impulse of self-consecration; and if we bring our offering of silver and gold to him, we are but giving to him that which is already his, since in the sense of absolute possession he is the sole proprietor of the universe, and we are only the hands by which for the time he holds that wealth which we so fondly call our own. To adopt the New Testament words, "We are stewards of the manifold bounty of God;" and if we had a right idea of our duty, we would seek to use every thing which we have for him. Now he desires us specially to build this spiritual house for his own abode. Shall we not, then, gratefully, lovingly, and liberally obey his command? Moreover, this house will be his eternal habitation. The Temple of Solomon is no more, and the stateliest cathedral must one day crumble into dust; but this spiritual edifice abides, and shall be the temple of the skies. In threading our way through the streets of some ancient city—such, for example, as the Cowgate and Canongate of Edinburgh—we mark the strange devices graven above the portals of the houses, which indicate that in former days they were the habitations of nobility; and here and there we come upon some quaint mottoes, such as this, "My trust is in the Lord;" or this, "Be merciful to me, O God," which render it probable that the dwellings on which they are engraved were first erected by those "who feared the Lord and thought upon his name." But now they are for the most part the homes of the guilty and the vile, and wickedness is holding riot in the chambers which architecture originally reared for the habitations of rank or the homes of piety. One can not visit these places as they are to-day without thinking of the transitoriness of all earthly things, and wondering whether, if the first builder had foreseen the base uses to which his house would be ultimately turned, he would have bestowed so much pains on its erection, or adorned it with such exquisite products of the sculptor's skill. But there is no danger of such a deterioration in the house—composed of human souls—which Christian men are rearing for a habitation of God through the Spirit. The Lord shall be the eternal inhabitant, and the beauty and the grandeur of his palace shall be as immortal as he is himself. It was the boast of the Grecian artist that he painted for eternity, and yet his works have all but disappeared already; but they who engage in the service of Christ and succeed in bringing souls to him, are building literally for eternity. Their work shall abide. Time that changes all things else will not eat into these spiritual walls, and eternity itself shall see no decay in this fabric of the ages. It will need all time for its completion, indeed, but then it will last through eternity; and so, if we wish to put forth our efforts where they will be most permanently effective, we will devote them to labor on this palace for the King of kings.

Once more, let us reflect that the progress of this spiritual edifice, thus honoring to God, is also inseparably associated with the happiness of men. Recall for a moment the words of the 72d Psalm, which, though applicable primarily to the influence of the Prince of Peace as a ruler, may be translated into harmony with this great temple-building. "Men shall be blessed in him, and all nations shall call him blessed;" that is to say, in proportion as souls are brought to Jesus and built into this spiritual fabric, the purity, the prosperity, and the progress of mankind shall advance. Does any one doubt this? Let him look around! To what do we owe our liberties, our privileges, and our proud position among the nations of the earth? Is it not to the degree in which the Gospel of Christ has leavened the land? The Christianity of the nation is the nation's life. All that is true, and honest, and just, and pure, and lovely, and of good report among us has been but a development of the principles which centre in the cross of Calvary; and if the evils that remain are ever to be removed, they can be so only by the conversion of the masses of our fellow-citizens to Jesus; that is, by the building of them into this living temple that has been rising so majestically through all the Christian ages. Nay, wider still, if the world is to be elevated and purified, if the race of men is to be developed to its noblest possibilities of good, whether intellectual, or moral, or social, the Gospel of Christ must still be the instrument which we employ; and that end shall be reached only when the headstone of this holy house shall be brought forth with shoutings, "Grace, grace unto it!"

Having, therefore, all these truths before you, suffer me now to make the appeal of David: "Who then is willing to consecrate his service this day unto the Lord?" Who is *willing*. It is a voluntary thing. The Lord will accept no begrudged laborer. He will have no reluctant toil. Whoso labors for him must labor with a will. "Who is willing to *consecrate* his service?" It is a holy offering—a laying of self, and service, and substance upon the altar of Jehovah; "for the palace is not for man, but for God," of whom riches and honor come. "Who then is willing to consecrate his service *this day* unto the Lord?" This day! this day! "For our days upon the earth are as a shadow, and there is none abiding." Even now it may be almost even-tide with many. The eleventh hour may have struck for some, and the warning of the twelfth may have sounded for others from the clock of destiny; yet as they stand idly in the market-place, there comes even to such the command, "Go, work to-day for me." Make haste that you may do something before the opportunity goes past. And if there should be here some David whom God has intrusted with large possessions or great prosperity, or what is better than either, a great heart, let him, too, hasten to bring forth his gifts for this glorious cause, that so his example may stimulate others, and we may see a revival of life, liberality, and labor in the Church of Christ. As said the great, good Whitefield, in days past, so say I now to you: "I want more tongues, more bodies, more souls for the Lord Jesus. Had I ten thousand, he should have them all. So that had I as many tongues as there are hairs on my head, the ever-loving, ever-lovely Jesus should have them all!" "Who then is willing to consecrate his service this day unto the Lord?"

## XXIII.

### *LAST WORDS.*

1 KINGS ii.; 2 SAMUEL xxiii., 1.

AFTER the solemn assembly of the estates of the realm, at which David publicly inaugurated the reign of Solomon, the strength of the aged monarch seems gradually to have ebbed away until "the days drew near that he must die." During these heart-searching times of silence and retirement, as he lay looking back upon the irrevocable past, and forward into the dread eternity, many thoughts must have filled his mind, and much close communion with God must have been enjoyed by him. He meddled now not much with earthly things, but when he did give any attention to them, the reign of Solomon still came uppermost, and his earnest admonitions to his son concerning the building of the Temple, and the character which he was to choose and cultivate, were renewed. One such occasion appears to have been more important than all the rest; and it is to that the sacred historian refers in the portion of the narrative at which we have now arrived (1 Kings ii., 1-9). Feeling within him the sure premonitions of approaching death, he laid upon Solomon, with all the importance of a last injunction, a most important charge. First he reminded him of the conditional promise which God had given to him through Nathan in these words: "If thy children take heed to their way, to walk before me in truth with all their heart and with all their soul, there shall not fail thee a man on the throne of Israel;" and upon this he founded the following exhortation: "Be thou strong therefore, and show thyself a man; and keep the charge of the Lord thy God, to walk in his ways." We can not read this injunction now without being reminded of Paul's words to Timothy, in somewhat similar circumstances: "Thou, therefore, my son, be strong in the grace that is in Christ Jesus." Nor can we fail to see the appropriateness of the command to ourselves, for God's promises, even in Christ, are conditioned on our acceptance of them, and on our obedience of the precepts in connection with which they are given. It may seem, indeed, strange that we should be commanded to be strong, since, at first sight, strength may not appear to be a thing wholly in our own hands; but we must never forget that God imparts his strength to us only through the strenuous forth-putting of our own. If we would secure his might, we must earnestly employ our own. If we would receive grace from him to resist temptation, we must ourselves show firmness and courage; if we would ultimately, through him, be conquerors in the battle of life, we must zealously carry on the fight ourselves. In the Gospel narrative, the man who had the withered arm received strength to put it forth, by honestly and believingly making the attempt to do what Jesus bade him; and we shall be supported in the discharge of difficult duty only when we endeavor to perform it as heartily as if the whole power required were our own; while at the same time we look up to God for help as sincerely as if all the might were really to come from him, as indeed it always does. When God says "Be strong," we get the strength which we need by acting in such a way as implies that we already possess it. This may seem a paradox, but it is the paradox of faith in every form. Admirably has one said, "The moment religion ceases to command men to attempt the impossible, it ceases to be religion;" and when faith that is really faith attempts the impossible, it changes it forthwith into the possible; for then the strength of God is made perfect in human weakness. For the young especially no axiom is more important than this, contradictory as it may seem, that to gain divine strength we must be strong, and set ourselves defiantly against all evil. Take then, my friends, a decided stand for God, and truth, and duty, and the strength needed to maintain that stand will not be withheld from those who seek it. "Watch ye, stand fast in the faith, quit you like men, be strong."

Appended to this wise paternal counsel, David gave to Solomon sundry injunctions as to the discharge of his governmental duties toward certain individuals. First he spoke of Joab; and, after referring to his murder of Abner and Amasa in circumstances of peculiar atrocity, he said, "Do therefore according to thy wisdom, and let not his hoar head go down to the grave in peace." Next he alluded in kindly terms to the sons of good old Barzillai, and commended them to his tender care thus: "Let them be of those that eat at thy table: for so they came to me when I fled because of Absalom thy brother." Finally he spake of Shimei, who had so shamefully and spitefully cursed him on the same sad occasion; and after acknowledging the oath by which he had bound himself to him, he added, "Now therefore hold him not guiltless: for thou art a wise man, and knowest what thou oughtest to do unto him; but his hoar head bring thou down to the grave with blood." Now, so far as regards his request concerning the sons of Barzillai, we can have no feelings but those of approbation; but it does seem as if his injunctions concerning Joab and Shimei were characterized by a vindictive and revengeful spirit altogether out of harmony with his usual disposition, and utterly inconsistent with the solemn position in which he was placed. A death-bed is a place for forgiveness, and not for implacability; and even those who in their lives have not been conspicuous for their religious principle have, as they lay dying, sent messages of reconciliation to such as have been at variance with them.

At first, therefore, and without going into the consideration of the cases in detail, we are disposed to express our astonishment at the spirit here manifested by David, and to pronounce condemnation on it. In regard to Shimei, indeed, some have supposed that the case is not so bad as our translators have made it appear. Kennicott, the learned Hebraist, has affirmed that it is not uncommon in that language to omit the negative in the second part of a sentence, and consider it as repeated where it has been expressed in the former part of the sentence, if they be connected by the usual conjunctive particle. Therefore he would read David's injunction as to Shimei thus: "Hold him not guiltless, but bring thou not his hoar head to the grave with blood." I am not sufficiently conversant with the niceties of the Hebrew language to be competent to give an opinion on such a point as this; but this proposed rendering has been adopted by such scholars as Dr. Angus, in his "Bible Hand-book," and Dr. Jameson, in his excellent commentary on the historical books of the Old Testament; and it must be confessed that it receives a certain measure of support from Solomon's after-treatment of Shimei, since he did not put him to death at first, but merely confined him within the limits of the city of Jerusalem, and shed his blood only when he had violated the conditions on which his life had been granted to him.

But whatever may be said regarding Shimei, there remains the case of Joab; and when we remember how much David owed him, we are apt to feel that he might now have condoned his faults, and let him go unpunished. All this must be frankly conceded; but when we go below the surface of the narrative and take all the bearings of the subject into our consideration, the case against David is not so bad as it looks. I at least am not disposed to pronounce unqualified censure upon him; nay rather, I am inclined to stand up in his defense, and to maintain that his design in giving these commands was to secure the prosperity of Solomon's reign, and to prevent his son from erring, as he himself had erred, by timidly and weakly passing over the crimes of men simply because they happened to be related to himself, or to be powerful and prominent in the land. Let it be remembered that revenge was not a characteristic feature of David's disposition. He was chivalrous in a high degree. He was a generous enemy. He did not cherish malice, or vindictively plot for a rival's destruction. Once and again, when he might easily have rid himself of Saul, he allowed him to go unharmed; and in his treatment of Joab on the two occasions to which he here makes reference, there was a criminal weakness which was unworthy of a king. We noted the same thing in his dealing with Amnon and Absalom. Hence we can not suppose that when he was on his death-bed, subdued by the feelings which his conscious nearness to the unseen world had produced in him, he would allow himself to be hurried away by a passion which had never moved him at any single period of his history. How, then, shall we account for these injunctions? I answer, by regarding them as deeds of justice, tardily executed, it is true, but yet executed at last on public grounds, for the welfare of the nation and the happiness of his son. He wished Solomon's reign to be undisturbed; and recognizing in Shimei a turbulent and unprincipled man, who might yet give trouble as the leader or abettor of some Benjamite revolt, he put his successor on his guard against him. Then, in regard to Joab, we must remember that all through the old economy the principle is maintained that blood unrighteously shed cries to God for vengeance; and it is everywhere implied that if he who shed it should go unpunished, the slight thus done to justice would certainly bring down calamity on the land. Thus, in the book of the law, in connection with the enactment providing cities of refuge for the accidental man-slayer, we have this injunction: "But if any man hate his neighbor, and lie in wait for him, and rise up against him, and smite him mortally that he die, and fleeth into one of these cities: then the elders of his city shall send and fetch him thence, and deliver him into the hand of the avenger of blood, that he may die. Thine eye shall not pity him, but thou shalt put away the guilt of innocent blood from Israel, that it may go well with thee."*

As an instructive commentary upon this portion of the sacred statute-book, we had before us a few evenings ago the fact that the slaughter of the Gibeonites by Saul, which had continued unatoned for, brought down upon the land, even after the lapse of more than thirty years, a visitation of famine which ceased only when seven of Saul's descendants had been given up to justice. Hence we may suppose that David feared lest some similar judgment should come upon the people in Solomon's time for the unpunished crimes of Joab, and that he sought, by laying these injunctions upon his son, to avert such a calamity from the nation. Besides, though at certain critical times in his history he had been greatly indebted to Joab, yet he had been galled and irritated by his haughty and overbearing character, and may have wished that Solomon should be delivered from a yoke under which he had been fretted and borne down for many years. With our New Testament ideas, indeed, we almost instinctively recoil from these injunctions, given on his deathbed by David to Solomon, but we must place ourselves, like him, under the Mosaic law, with the old ideas of blood-revenge which then prevailed, and which that law sought to regulate rather than to abolish, before we presume to sit in

---

* Deuteronomy xix., 11-13.

judgment upon them. Now, when we thus regard them, we can not condemn David so confidently as many have done. On the contrary, we see, in his anxiety about the disposal of these malefactors, evidence of a quickening of his conscience as a magistrate, which was very natural at the approach of death, while at the same time it indicates the intensity of his desire to relieve Solomon from the evil consequences that would else have resulted from his own failure in the administration of justice. To our thinking, they wrong the dying man most shamefully who would impute to personal malice or cruel revenge recommendations which were given solely on public and judicial grounds by one who felt himself already face to face with his own final account. Nor can I forbear to add, that the disposition which cavils at these injunctions thus understood, is of a piece with the mawkish sentimentalism of these times, which turns every criminal into a simple object of benevolence, when it does not exalt him into a hero, and of which we see the results to-day, when justice is lying torn and bleeding in our streets; when human life, instead of being the most sacred object of protection by society, is almost as little regarded among us as that of the brutes that perish; and when the perpetrators of the most palpable murders contrive, by a thousand plausible pretexts, to elude that penalty which the law has annexed to their crime. Let us not forget that the God of Israel is the God of all nations, and that his providence is still regulated by the principles on which he governed the world in the days of David. Alas! what evils may be even now impending over us, because of the indifference to justice which has characterized so much of our recent so-called judicial procedure! We have had all manner of consideration and pity shown to the criminals; it might be well now if a little of both were manifested to the community at large.

It only now remains, before we come to the last scene of

this eventful history, that we glance a little at the interesting oracle which is introduced by the sacred historian in the twenty-third chapter of 2 Samuel with this phrase: "Now these be the last words of David." It is not necessary to believe that the portion of sacred poetry to which this statement is prefixed was the very latest utterance of the Psalmist before he closed his eyes in death. The meaning of the clause may be that the prediction which it introduces was the last formal communication made by David in the character of an inspired prophet, or it may simply indicate that the oracle belongs to the last illness of the king; and so, over and above its divine inspiration, it may serve to show the current of his thoughts and the support of his heart, as he was passing through the valley of shadow. In any case, it has a character which is quite unique among the productions of David. It is not a Psalm in which we have the element of praise commingled with that of prediction, neither is it a plain declaration of David's spiritual experience in the near prospect of death; but it is a prophecy, or oracle, commencing with a description of the prophet and an assertion of his inspiration, and then proceeding to delineate the nature of Messiah's dominion, with its twofold effect of blessing on the obedient and lowly, and punishment on the rebellious and proud. Then, between the indication of the blessing and the curse, we have a kind of parenthetic reference to David's royal dynasty, the perpetuity of which, as secured in the Messiah, he declares to be all his salvation and all his desire.

Let us attend to each of these portions of this interesting passage. There is, first, the description of the prophet himself. This is usual in the introduction of important predictions. We find it, for example, in the opening verses of the books of Isaiah, Amos, and Jeremiah, and, in particular, we have a strain very similar to that before us in the commencement of Balaam's well-known prophecy. In the passage under consideration, David is called by his simple patronymic, the son of Jesse; and with special allusion to the fact that he was elevated from the lowly life of a shepherd to the lofty glory of a throne, he is styled "the man who was raised up on high." Nor is this all: he is denominated "the anointed of the God of Jacob," in recognition of his having been designated by prophetic anointing for the royal office. Furthermore, he is described as "the sweet Psalmist of Israel." Some have attempted to render the original phrase here by the words, "sweet in the Psalms of Israel;" or, as Bunsen has translated them, "the darling of the songs of Israel;" and they vindicate their view by referring to the victory ode which was sung concerning him after his defeat of the giant, and to other similar songs. But I rather regard the phrase, "the sweet Psalmist of Israel," as a title which, even in his lifetime, David had received, as the author of those sacred hymns which form so large a portion of the book of Psalms; and I am confident that its appropriateness will be thoroughly indorsed by the spiritually-minded even of this latest generation; for the shepherd-king of Israel, when he sang out of his own heart, produced lyrics which have found their way to the heart of humanity itself, and which have been in all ages, as they are in this, the chosen vehicle through which devout spirits have sent alike their joys and their sorrows, their penitence and their praise, their thanksgivings and their petitions up to God. David seems, indeed, to have been led through manifold trials and experiences, and to have been divinely inspired to sing his feelings in them all, just that he might be a leader of psalmody to God's people in every age, and in all circumstances; and so it is that the pious heart even now finds the emotions which are vainly struggling within it for expression already uttered in the book of Psalms, and that, too, to the music of a harp so sweet that as one listens he seems to hear for the time the melody of heaven, and all sorrow and anxiety are charmed away. His joyful odes bear aloft our praises, as on eagles' wings, to heights to which alone and without his assistance we had never soared; his Psalms of penitence and sadness give us minor strains wherewith to humble ourselves before the Lord; while in the sweet simplicity of such pastoral hymns as "The Lord is my shepherd" we have a beauty that never grows dim, a tenderness that never fails to touch the heart, and a music that never palls upon the ear. Truly, therefore, is he styled "the sweet psalmist of Israel."

The next verse sets before us his divine inspiration: "The Spirit of the Lord spake by me, and his word was in my tongue. The God of Israel said, the Rock of Israel spake to me." All his songs, as gathered together in the book with which his name is associated, were divinely inspired; but here, as it seems to me, the reference is specially to the oracle which he is about to utter, and to which he wishes that particular importance should be attached. This was to be his dying prophecy, like that given by Jacob to his sons, or those given by Moses and Joshua to the tribes; and he desired that special attention should be given to it as being not his only, but the utterance of the Divine Spirit through him. How the Spirit spake by him we are not informed; but the assertion of the union of the divine and human in the utterances of the prophet is clearly and emphatically made. David spoke, and the human style had all the characteristics of his usual productions; for the Spirit used not the vocal organs of the prophet alone, but his intellectual and emotional powers as well. But God spoke by David, and that which he uttered was the truth, infallible as he who gave it. The style was natural and human, the thought was supernatural and divine; and no part of it would fall away without fulfillment. Indeed, to make this more striking and impressive, Jehovah is here styled "the Rock of Israel;" for as a rock is immovable in mid-ocean, so God is unchangeable and incorruptible; and the word which he speaks through his servant partakes of his own character, and is a part of that Scripture "which can not be broken."

The oracle thus introduced speaks first of the character of a ruler, whom we easily identify as the Messiah. It is, indeed, the description of an ideal ruler, but the real in whom it is fulfilled is Christ: "He that ruleth over men, just ruling in the fear of God." I have read the clause without the italic supplement in our version, for I take it to be not an affirmation of what a ruler ought to be, but a delineation of the sort of ruler the Messiah should be. It is thus parallel to the prediction in the 72d Psalm. "He shall judge thy people with righteousness, and thy poor with judgment;" and to that of Isaiah: "There shall come forth a rod out of the stem of Jesse, and a Branch shall grow out of his roots. With righteousness shall he judge the poor, and reprove with equity for the meek of the earth: and he shall smite the earth with the rod of his mouth, and with the breath of his lips shall he slay the wicked." Thus the effect of his administration should be different on different individuals. The meek, the righteous, the poor would be blessed; but the unrighteous, the disobedient, the proud would be destroyed. The righteous would be blessed. This is what is affirmed in the fourth verse. The sense of the words, indeed, both in the Hebrew and in the English, is obscure by reason both of the brevity of the expression and the figurative character of the language which is employed; but a slight alteration of the rendering brings out a beautiful and appropriate meaning.

Kennicott found in an old MS. the word Jehovah, and he gives the following version of the passage: "And as the morning light, shall Jehovah the sun arise, even an unclouded morning, and the verdure shall spring out of the earth by the warm, bright splendor, after rain." Now, if this be adopted as the correct rendering, it gives not only an exquisite description of the blessings flowing from the reign of Messiah to his friends—light symbolizing truth and gladness, and the fresh springing of the grass after the shower representing the growth of holiness and peace, which is always consequent upon the reception of the Gospel—but it also furnishes a striking parallel to other prophetic announcements concerning the Son of David. Thus, in Hosea vi., 3, we read, "His going forth is prepared as the morning; and he shall come unto us as the rain, as the latter and former rain unto the earth." And in Malachi iv., 2, it is said, "The Sun of righteousness shall arise with healing in his wings." So again, in the 72d Psalm, the date of which, as we have seen, was near to the time at which the oracle before us was given, we read, "He shall come down like rain upon the mown grass: as showers that water the earth." The full force of such a figure, however, can be realized only when we take into account the physical phenomena of the land of Palestine, in which, as Jameson has said,* "Little patches of grass are seen rapidly springing up after rain; and even where the ground has been long parched and bare, within a few days or hours after the enriching showers begin to fall, the face of the earth is so renewed that it is covered over with a pure fresh mantle of green." Now, could any thing more appropriately illustrate the effects which are everywhere produced when the Gospel has been received and obeyed? Great joy fills the hearts of those who, owning Jesus as their Lord, receive forgiveness at his hands, and forthwith they begin to grow in all that is beautiful, and good, and godlike, so that (to bor-

---

* "Commentary, Critical, Experimental, and Practical, on the Old and New Testaments," by Jameson, Fausset, and Brown, vol. ii., p. 282.

row again from the 72d Psalm) the handful of corn sown even upon the barren mountain top springs up, and its fruit shakes like Lebanon, while "they of the city flourish like grass of the earth." Therefore, they are the greatest benefactors of the race who labor in the missionary enterprise; and the world shall reach its highest excellence when all the nations of men shall own the sceptre of the Prince of Peace.

But while the results of Messiah's administration are thus beneficent to those who willingly submit themselves to him, they are fraught with evil to those who refuse to own his sway; for thus are his enemies spoken of in this prediction (verses 6 and 7), "But the sons of Belial shall be all of them as thorns thrust away, because they can not be taken with hands: but the man that shall touch them must be fenced with iron and the staff of a spear; and they shall be utterly burned with fire in the same place." These words, at first sight, seem obscure; but when you read them properly, they become perfectly clear. Thus, let the last clause of the sixth verse and the first of the seventh be thrown into a parenthesis, and let the first part of the sixth verse be connected with the last of the seventh, and we have this result: "But the sons of Belial, all of them, are as thorns to be thrust out, and to be utterly burned with fire in the place; for they can not be taken by the hand, and the man who shall touch them must be armed with an axe, and with the shaft of a spear." The enemies of Christ are thus compared to the strong, prickly thorns peculiar to Palestine, whose stalks twine together, and whose spines, pointing in every direction, are so troublesome that they can not be touched by the hand without danger, but must be cut down and removed by long-handled instruments of iron. We have here, therefore, a description parallel to that given by the author of the Epistle to the Hebrews (chap. vi., 7, 8): "The earth which drinketh in the rain that cometh oft upon it, and bringeth forth herbs meet for them by whom it is dressed, receiveth blessing from God; but that which beareth thorns and briers is rejected, and is nigh unto cursing; whose end is to be burned;" and both alike bring before us the solemn fact, that while the reception of the Gospel is the means of blessing to those who believe and obey it, its rejection entails the greatest calamities on those who put it from them. Christ has a baptism of the Holy Ghost for his people, but a baptism of fire for his enemies. The wheat he shall gather into his barn, but the chaff he shall burn with fire unquenchable. They who welcome the Messiah with open arms, and receive him into their hearts, have every thing to hope for from his royal administration; but they who defiantly reject him, and refuse to submit themselves to him, are courting their eternal destruction.

Midway between these figurative descriptions of the blessedness of those who receive the Gospel, and the destruction of those who reject it, we have a touching verse, making reference to David's personal feelings in the case: "Although my house be not so with God; yet he hath made with me an everlasting covenant, ordered in all things, and sure: for this is all my salvation, and all my desire, although he make it not to grow." The common interpretation of these words is, that David is alluding to the sad events in his own personal and domestic history, and declaring that, in spite of these, he trusted in God's well-ordered and everlasting covenant. That was all his salvation and desire, though in himself and in his sons it had not been made to grow. Now it is always painful to disturb an old and, it may be, hallowed explanation of such a passage as this; but the objections to this understanding of David's words are so serious, that I fear we must conclusively give it up; for not only does it require us to give to one Hebrew word, which occurs four times in the verse, four different meanings, but it takes the term house in its limited sense of family circle; whereas here, as in all the Messianic prophecies connected with David, it means dynasty or regal lineage. The best expositors, therefore, propose to read it thus, or somehow after this fashion: "For is not my house so with God? for he hath made with me an everlasting covenant, ordered in all things and sure; for this is all my salvation and all my desire; for will he not make it [that is, my house] to grow?" Observe, David has been describing the character of a ruler; and reduplicating on that description, he in effect says, "Is it not to be the distinctive feature of my lineage that it shall rule in justice, and in the fear of the Lord?" a feature which came out not only in Solomon, but also in Asa, Jehoshaphat, Hezekiah, Josiah, and others, and especially and pre-eminently in Jesus Christ, in whom this prophecy culminated, and by whom it was thoroughly fulfilled. Nay, was it not assured to David by God's everlasting covenant that this should be the character of his house, and peculiarly of Him who was its greatest and most illustrious member? In this, therefore, he would rest. This was his salvation, this was his desire; for beyond all doubt God would make it to grow. Thus, as the aged prophet sings his death-song he sees Messiah's glory afar off, and is glad. He rests in the promise of the coming ruler. He looks forward in death to the same Saviour-King to whom now we look backward; and so, stretching through long centuries on either side, our hands meet and touch his, as together we take hold of the same benign Redeemer. Nor is this a mere fanciful interpretation, resting upon no foundation; for what says Peter in reference to the 16th Psalm? "Therefore being a prophet, and knowing that God had sworn with an oath to him, that of the fruit of his loins, according to the flesh, he would raise up Christ to sit on his throne; David, seeing this before, spake of the resurrection of Christ, that his soul was not left in Hades, neither his flesh did see corruption."* David, then, Peter being witness, had a glimpse of Messiah's coming, and on that coming he rested all his hope. It was his salvation and desire. For years he had lived on the prophecy and promise which God gave to him by the mouth of Nathan; and now, as he lay dying, he pillowed his head upon God's covenant that the great righteous Ruler would be sure to come. This was his hope in death; for now we take our leave of him whose checkered history we have followed with such growing interest during these by-gone months. "David slept with his fathers." Slept; for thus early was the good man's death accounted a sleep, not only as bringing rest after "life's fitful fever," but also as predicting an awakening at the resurrection-day. "He was buried in the city of David," and doubtless, as in the case of Samuel, all Israel would mourn beside his grave, which in after-years became the centre of the catacombs wherein were contained the sepulchres of the kings of Judah. Even so late as the Day of Pentecost David's sepulchre was distinguishable, but now it is unknown. Yet it matters not where his tomb is; here is his monument in the history which we have been studying, and in the legacy of sacred song which he has left to the Church of every age, and yonder, on high, is his record. Adieu! thou sweet Psalmist; thou royal prophet; thou tempted, tried, stricken, erring, yet in the main, true-hearted man of God; we shall know thee better when we meet above, now that we have traced thy history so minutely here. Now is thy wish gratified, now is thy prayer answered, for now beholdest thou "the beauty of the Lord," and inquirest "in his Temple." May God make us meet to be there eternally thy fellow-worshipers!

I have time only for two practical reflections, which I

---

*Acts ii., 30, 31.

can do little more than name.  We must have felt, all through our study of this great man's life, how honest the biographies of the Bible are.  Here is no hiding of imperfections, no cloaking of sins, no palliating or excusing of iniquity.  David is spoken of as he was; and we see him to have been a man of like passions with ourselves, very far from being perfect, sorely marked, indeed, by sin, yet in the main a man of God.  Though often falling into errors, he never made his nest in sin; frequently overtaken in a fault, yet not delighting in iniquity, he proved that the polarity of his soul was heavenward.  Who so bitterly bewailed his sins as he did himself?  Who so broken-hearted for his iniquities as he was himself?  If his sins were exceptional, so was his repentance; and He on whom he rested would not cast him out. The voyage of his life had been long and perilous, and at one time such a storm overtook him that he had well-nigh gone down; but after many turnings and tackings, he bore up anew and steered right onward; and now he enters the harbor—not, indeed, with all sails set, and banners flying, and the firing of salutes, and the sound of merry music, but battered and weather-beaten; the canvas torn and the masts broken, and with every evidence of having passed through a fearful gale.  Yet he enters the harbor, and that is a great thing; let the Judge of all determine the measure of his blame.  To be blamed he certainly was; and as we see in all this that he was a man like ourselves, let us remember that there is another life recorded here in which there is no flaw.  Now if we accept the honesty of the sacred biographer in telling us of David's sins, shall we not accept it also when he tells us of the sinlessness of Jesus? and shall we not see in that the evidence that he was more than man? From all our imperfections, let us flee to his perfection; from all our iniquities, let us turn to his spotlessness; and let us be thankful that, amidst our agony in the struggle with self and sin, there is One to whom we can cling who "was in all points tempted like as we are, yet without sin," and who is a human brother indeed, but also and especially a Divine Helper. The more closely we keep to him, the more securely shall we be kept from falling into sin. It is much to get safely to the land at last, even though it should be "on boards, or on broken pieces of the ship." But if we give all diligence to follow him, and determine in all circumstances to adhere to his commands, we shall have "an entrance ministered to us abundantly" into his everlasting kingdom. It is better to be "saved, yet so as by fire," than not to be saved at all. But oh, how much better still it is to be saved in fullness. Be it ours, therefore, to aim after the abundant entrance and the glad "Well done!"

Finally: we may see here the believer's hope in death. David dies not in despair. He has a firm hold of God's covenant. He knows God will bring the Redeemer at the appointed time, and in the administration of the Messiah-King he has his simple trust. Thus his experience in looking forward to Christ's day was singularly parallel to that of Paul looking backward to Christ's work, and upward to Christ's throne, and saying, "I know whom I have believed, and am persuaded that he is able to keep that which I have committed to him against that day." Christ, as the great deliverer of God's covenant and promise, was thus the comforter alike of David and of Paul. Death was easy to both, for they trusted in him, and death will become gain to us also, when we live in him. "It shall come to pass that at evening time it shall be light." Thus it was with Israel's king, and thus it shall be also with us, if all our salvation be in and all our desire be for him who is the righteous ruler and the atoning priest of his believing people. Years ago I used to travel on foot in the winter mornings for five miles, to teach in a country school. I had to set out from home in the dark, and I amused myself with marking the brightest stars, and seeing how one by one they faded into day. There was one that held out always longest—the bright and beautiful planet Venus—and I can remember yet how I used to watch and watch, sure that I would see it in the very act of disappearing. But I was always disappointed. Something would attract my attention elsewhere for a moment, and when I looked again it was gone. So the good man at death goes out of human view.

> "He sets as sets the morning-star,
>   Which goes not down behind the darkened west,
>   Nor hides obscured amid the tempests of the sky,
>   But melts away into the light of heaven."

May God grant to us such a glorious and peaceful exodus! Amen.

# INDEX.

ABIATHAR joins David in the cave of Adullam, 103; is made priest at Jerusalem, 254; joins in the revolt of Adonijah, 400.

Abigail, character of, 157, 159, 160; meets David, 160; marriage of, to David, 161.

Abner makes Ishbosheth king, 191; slays Asahel, 196; quarrels with Ishbosheth, 196; negotiates with David, 197; is slain by Joab, 197.

Absalom, beauty of, 299, 317; causes the death of Amnon, and flees to Geshur, 301; is recalled through Joab's instrumentality, 302; is reconciled to his father, 303, 318; rebels against David, 304; is slain by Joab, 328; lamented by David, 331.

Achish, king of Gath, receives David, 100, 174.

Administration of David: military, 246; civil, 249; ecclesiastical, 253.

Adonijah, revolt against David, 399–403.

Adullam, cave of, described, 102; David's companions in, 103.

Adversity to be expected at an early stage of spiritual life, 72.

Ahimaaz sent by Hushai to David, 325; brings to David the news of Absalom's death, 331.

Ahithophel, adhesion of, to Absalom, accounted for, 308; advice of, to Absalom, 309, 311, 320, 322; commits suicide, 323; lessons from his conduct, 352.

Alexander, Rev. W. L., LL.D., quoted from, 18.

Amasa, appointed to lead David's troops, 348; slain by Joab, 348.

Amnon, sin of, 299; terribly revenged by Absalom, 301.

Anger, evil of, exposed, 165.

Anointing of David, at Bethlehem, 19; at Hebron, 193; influence of, on David, 20.

Apocryphal Psalm on the battle of Elah, 52.

Appropriating faith, 383.

Ark of the covenant at Kirjath-jearim, 215; touched by Uzzah, 216; carried into the house of Obed-edom, 217; taken up to Jerusalem, 218–225.

BARZILLAI the Gileadite joins David at Mahanaim, 327; declines the royal invitation to go to Jerusalem, 343, 354; his sons commended to Solomon by David, 417.

Bath-sheba, her relation to Ahithophel an explanation of his rebellion, 276; appeals to David for Solomon, 401.

# INDEX.

Beauty, personal, right estimation of, 317.
Benevolence, relation of, to personal expenditure, 231.
Bereaved parents admonished and comforted, 289–298.
Bethlehem, situation of, 14; associations with, 14, 15; influence of, upon David, 15; anointing of David at, 16.
Blaikie's "David, King of Israel," quoted from or referred to, 33, 34, 245, 250, 253, 266, 366.
Blood-revenge, right of, 367.
Blunt's "Scriptural Coincidences" referred to, 309, 400.
Book of Jasher, 185.
"Bow," Song of the, 185.
Browning, Robert, lines of, on the power of music, 28.

CARLYLE, Thomas, on David's faults, 274; quotation by, from Richter, 315.
Carmel, village of, 156.
Chandler's "Life of David" referred to, 272, 385.
Character, deterioration of, illustrated from the case of Saul, 188.
Cherubim, symbolic meaning of, 226.
Children, overindulgence of, exposed, 315.
Chimham's place at the royal table, 343.
Christ at the door of the heart, 224.
Commerce stimulated by David, 252.
Communion with God a solace in trial, 357.
Congregational psalmody, importance of, 257.
Consequences of sin can not be arrested, 107.
Convict, letter of a, in illustration of the power of prayer, 127.
Coronation of David at Hebron, 199.
Cush, the slanderer, described, 143.
Cowper, Bishop, on the 119th Psalm, 85.
Cowper, William, on Friendship, 65; hymn of, 131.

DAVID, personal appearance of, 19; anointing of, by Samuel, 19; at Hebron, 191; sent for to the court of Saul, 29; personal courage of, 31; playing before Saul, 33; Psalms of, their peculiar power, 34, 123, 136, 379; return of, to Bethlehem, 41; sent to the camp at Elah, 44; accepts the challenge of Goliath, 47; interviews of, with Jonathan, 58, 94, 96, 124; friendship of, with Jonathan, 58–63; marriage of, to Michal, 69; to Abigail, 161; to Maachah, 195; escape of, from Gibeah, 77; at Ramah, 84; at Nob, 97; at Gath, 99, 174; in the cave of Adullam, 102; provides an asylum for his parents, 105; in the wilderness of Hareth, 116; at Keileh, 119–122; at Ziph, 123; at Engedi, 133; spares Saul magnanimously, 137, 140; contrasted with Rebekah, 146; applies to Nabal for supplies, and is refused, 158; at Ziklag, 174, 177; hears of the deaths of Saul and Jonathan, and sings the "Song of the Bow," 184–188; contrasted with Saul, 188–201; is crowned at Hebron, 199; chooses Jerusalem for his capital, 202-204; builds for himself a cedar palace, 210; defeats the Philistines twice at Rephaim, 212, 213; brings up the ark to Jerusalem, 216; returns to bless his house, 228; desires to build a temple, but is prevented by Nathan, 230; deals kindly with Mephibosheth, 241; administration of, 244-263; victories of, 259; great transgression of, 264; penitence of, 270-275; bereavement of, 284; resignation of, 287; flees from Jerusalem before Absalom, 309; at Mahanaim, 326; laments over the death of Absalom, 331; returns to Jerusalem, 341; is unjust to Mephibosheth, 346; suppresses the revolt of Sheba, 348; gives up seven of Saul's family to the Gibeonites, 368; numbers the people, 371; buys the threshing-floor of Araunah, 373; gives orders for the proclamation of Solomon, 403; gives a last charge to Solomon, 415; last words of, 422-430; death of, 430.

Deception, sin of, exposed, 87-89.

Despair, the forerunner of aggravated sin, 106, 172-174.

Divine holiness, majesty of the, 225.

Divine protection given in many ways to the good man, 86, 382.

Doeg the Edomite a witness of David's deception at Nob, 98; accuses David and Ahimelech to Saul, 104; slays the priests at Nob, 105.

Domestic comfort of the people promoted by David, 252.

Doxology sung by cotton operatives at Staleybridge, 396.

ECCLESIASTICAL arrangements made by David, 256.

Education fostered by David, 250.

Edwards's "Personal Narrative of the Indian Mutiny" referred to, 136.

Elah, valley of, described, 43; battle of, 48; lessons from, 53-57.

Eliab rejected by the Lord as king, 17; rudeness of, to David, 46.

Elisha, effect of music on, 28.

Endor, situation of, 180; witch of, visited by Saul, 180; questions regarding her agency in Samuel's appearance, 181-183.

En-gedi, strongholds of, described, 133.

Esdraelon, vale of, with its branches, described, 178.

Evil spirit from the Lord troubling Saul, 25; soothed by David's music, 33; but only for a time, 39; Christ the true exorciser of, 40.

Ewald's description of the parallelism of Hebrew poetry, 134; his view concerning David's "worthies," 247.

Expiation for sin, necessity of, 376.

Ezel, stone of, 94, 96.

FAIRBAIRN'S "Imperial Bible Dictionary" quoted from, 42.

Faith, lesson of, from David's conflict with Goliath, 55; produces humility, gratitude, and prayer, 239; loss of, is the source of greater sin, 106, 172-174.

Family worship enforced, 228.

Famine, visitation of the land by, 360.

Faraday, Michael, an example of the profitable employment of leisure time, 38.
Farinelli's music, power of, over Philip V., 28.
Free agency of man not interfered with by the purposes of God, 35, 331.
Friends, choice of, 63–65.
Froude's "History of England" referred to, 89, 251.
———— Lectures referred to, 109.

GAD joins David in the cave of Adullam, 103.
Gath, departure of David to, 99.
Gerhardt, Paul, hymns of, 131, 288.
Gibeonites: their history, 364; slain by Saul, 366; Saul's seven descendants given to, 368.
Gilboa, battle of, 184.
"Gloaming of Life," by Wallace, referred to, 335.
God's eternity a source of comfort to the saint, 394.
———— faithfulness tested by David's life, 390; trust in, enforced, 397.
———— gentleness, power of, 391.
———— long-suffering with sinners, 90.
———— moral government, carried on in harmony with natural law, 360; retributive in its character, 386.
———— protection of his people, 86, 382.
———— reception of a sinner contrasted with David's reception of Absalom, 317.
Goliath of Gath, height of, 45; armor of, 45; challenge, the army of Israel, 46; encountered and slain by David, 47; sword of, given to David by Ahimelech, 97.
Guthrie, Rev. John, "Sacred Lyrics," quoted from, 221.
Guthrie, Rev. Dr. Thomas, quoted from, 290.

HACHILAH, David at, 140.
Happiness, how to obtain, 71; compared to sleep, 71, 72.
Hebron, 192.
Holiness of God, majesty of the, 225.
Homer's heroes referred to as illustrating points in the narrative, 48, 59.
Honesty of Scriptural biographies, 277, 341.
Honors in Christ's kingdom, how distributed, 262.
Hume, Sir Patrick, sustained by David's Psalms, 136.
Humility, lesson of, from David's bearing at Elah, 57.
Hushai sent to Jerusalem to defeat Ahithophel, 311.

"I HAVE sinned!" how differently uttered by different men, 150.
Indiscriminate indulgence of children reproved, 399.
Infant salvation, arguments in support of, 292–294; consolation from, 294; appeals from, 297.
———— suffering and death, 284, 285, 289; solace under, 291.

## INDEX.

Imprecatory Psalms, 351.
Ishbosheth made king by Abner, 191; war between David and, 196; quarrels with Abner, 197; is slain by his servants, 199.

JABESH-GILEAD, relieved by Saul, 10; men of, take the bodies of Saul and his sons from the battle-field, 187; David sends a message of thanks to, 194.
Jacox, Francis, "Scripture Texts Illustrated," quotation from, 28.
Jasher, book of, 185.
Jesse, lineage of, 17; children of, 18; character of, 18; sends David to Elah with supplies, 45; sent to Moab by David for safety, 105.
Joab commands David's army against Abner, 195; treacherously slays Abner, 197; contrives to procure Absalom's recall to Jerusalem, 302; slays Absalom, 329; upbraids David for immoderate grief over Absalom, 339; slays Amasa, 348; suppresses the revolt of Sheba, 349; David charges Solomon concerning, 417.
Jonathan, first victory of, 43; interview of, with David after the battle of Elah, 58, 59; friendship with David, 59-63; intercession of, with Saul for David, 75, 76; interview with David at the stone Ezel, 94; in the wood of Ziph, 124; death of, at Gilboa, 184; David's lament over, 185.
Jonathan and Ahimaaz sent by Hushai to David, 325.
Judah, wilderness of, 116.
Judges appointed by David, 249.

"KEIL on 1 Samuel," quoted from or referred to, 45, 51, 204, 233, 234.
Keilah, rescue of, by David, 120; perfidy of the citizens of, 121.
Kingdom of David: its similarity and dissimilarity to that of Christ, 208, 209, 262.
Kingsley, Charles, quotation from, 397.
Kitto's "Cyclopædia," quoted from or referred to, 44, 255.
―――― "Daily Bible Illustrations," quoted from or referred to, 51, 97, 223, 234, 236, 277, 366.
Knighthood, order of, instituted by David, 247.

LEISURE hours, importance of, 36; reasons for the improvement of, 36-38.
Letter of a convict, illustrating the mode in which God answers prayer, 127.
Levites the offerers of the service of song, 218; divided into courses for the musical service, 257.
Liberality of the people for the building of the Temple, 405.
Little things more dangerous to a believer's life than great ones, 165.
Logan's "Words of Comfort for Parents bereaved of Little Children,"[1] referred to, 298.
Long-suffering of God with sinners, 89.
Luther's version of the 46th Psalm, 130.

# 440 INDEX.

MACHIR of Lo-debar joins David, 327.
M'Leod, Dr. Norman, lines from, 74.
Madness feigned by David at Gath, 100.
Mahanaim, arrival of David at, 326; battle of, 328.
Marriage, Christian law of, 166.
Meekness, lesson of, from the bearing of David to Eliab, 55; from the conduct of Mephibosheth, 356.
Mephibosheth, kindly treated by David, 241; grief of, at David's departure from Jerusalem, 343; perfidy of Ziba to, 312, 344; faithfulness of, to David, and its poor requital, 344–346.
Michal, marriage of, to David, 69; device of, to save David's life, 77; images of, 78–80; deceit of, 87–89; punishment of, by David, 224–225.
Miller, Hugh, an instance of the profitable employment of leisure time, 38.
Military organization formed by David, 246.
Milton, "Paradise Lost" of, 130; referred to, 223.
Montgomery, James, lines from, 33.
Music, congregational, how to foster, 257; medicinal effects of, 27–29.
Musical arrangements made by David, 256.

NABAL, character of, 156; rudeness of, to David, 158; death of, 161; contrasted with Samuel, 162.
Nathan, message of, to David in reference to the Temple, 233; visit of, to David after his great transgression, 271; parable of the ewe lamb, 271; agency of, in the defeat of Adonijah, 401.
National prosperity intimately connected with the religious character of the people, 260, 413.
National sins punished by national suffering, 365.
Nee Sima, Rev. Joseph, incidents in his early history, illustrative of the power of prayer, 128.
Newton, Isaac, quoted from, 127.
Nob, David at, 97; massacre of the priests at, 105.

OPPORTUNITY, importance of embracing, 89, 189.

PARAN, wilderness of, 153.
Parents, bereaved, comforted and counseled, 292, 297.
———, care for, enforced on their children, 110.
———, lessons to, from Absalom's rebellion, 316, 333; from Adonijah's revolt, 399.
Pestilence, visitation of, 371.
Philip V. soothed by Farinelli's music, 28.
Philistines, description of, 42; at Elah, 42; complain of Achish for his kindness to David, 100, 176; encamp at the well of Harod, 178; victory of, over Saul, 184; defeated by David at Rephaim, 212.
Plumer's "Studies in the Book of Psalms" quoted from, 85.
Plumtre, Professor, "Biblical Studies of," referred to, 309, 311.

# INDEX.  441

Polygamy, evils of, 167, 195, 266, 315.
Popular favor, fickleness of, 321.
Prayer vindicated from modern objections, 126; illustrations of answers to, 127, 128; answers to, consistent with the uniformity of the laws of nature, 127.
Priests, arrangement of, into courses, 255.
Prophecy of Nathan, interpretation of, 233–237.
Psalm, apocryphal, after the battle of Elah, referred to, 52.
Psalms, passages in, probably referring to Elah, 52.
Psalms, probable origin or occasion of: Psalm iii., 314; iv., 314; v., 350; vii., 142–145; xii., 155; xv., 219; xviii., 379; xxiv., 223; xxx., 210; xxxi., 122; xxxii., 272; xxxiv., 101; xli., 350; xlii., 353; xliii., 353; li., 272, 283; liv., 125; lv., 350; lvi., 101; lvii., 135; lix., 81; lxiii., 117; lxviii., 220; lxix., 307, 350; lxxii., 407; lxxxiv., 353; ci., 193; cx., 253; cxix., 84; cxxxii., 219; cxxxiii., 201; cxlii., 134; cxliii., 350; cxliv., 353.
——, imprecatory, referred to, 351.
Pythagoras, use of music by, 27.

RAHAB compared with Michal, 88.
Ramah, David at, 82.
Rebekah contrasted with David, 146.
Rebellion, Absalom's, accounted for, 304; early success of explained, 305; inauguration of, 308; adhesion of Ahithophel to, 308; suppression of, 329.
Recognition of God's hand in all things by David, 389.
Religion, connection between, and national prosperity, 260, 413.
Repentance, true, distinguished from false, 150–153.
Revolt of Sheba, 348.
—— of Adonijah, 399.
Richter, quotation from, by Carlyle, 315.
Rist, hymns of, 131.
Rizpah's devotion to her son, 369.
Rock of divisions, or escapes, 125.

SACRIFICE, to be sincere, must cost something, 377.
Samuel, character of, 9, 153; commanded to anoint David, 14; visited by David at Ramah, 82–84; death and burial of, 154; contrasted with Nabal, 162–164; appearance of, to Saul at Endor, 180–183.
Saul, chosen king by lot, 9; character of, 10, 12; mistakes of, 10–12; lessons from, 21, 187, 190; troubled by an evil spirit, 24; soothed by David's harp, 28; interview with David after the battle of Elah, 51; jealousy of David, 66; attempts to kill David, 67, 76; "among the prophets," 87, 91; murders the priests at Nob, 105; besieges David, 120, 124; spared by David in the cave, 137, 140; vacillation of feeling in reference to David accounted for, 142; repentance only partial, 150; visit to Endor, 180; appearance of Samuel to, and questions as to that incident, 181–183.

19*

Saunders's "Evenings with the Sacred Poets" referred to, 130.
Schools of the prophets described, 82, 83.
Scott, Sir Walter, reference to, 89 ; quotation from, 99.
Scriptural biographies, honesty of, 277, 431.
Selfism, evil of, illustrated from the case of Saul, 69 ; from that of the men of Keilah, 121.
Sheba, revolt of, 348.
Shew-bread given to David by Ahimelech, 97.
Shimei curses David, 313 ; humbles himself before David, 342 ; is denounced by David to Solomon, 418.
Shobi, of Rabbah, joins David, 327.
Slander, sin of, 147 ; evil of listening to, 149 ; proper demeanor under, 149, 356.
Smith's "Dictionary of the Bible" quoted from or referred to, 42, 133, 218, 345.
Solomon, referred to in Nathan's prophecy, 235 ; wisdom of, an incidental proof of the diffusion of education under David, 251 ; birth of, 299 ; proclaimed king, 401 ; addressed by David, 404 ; receives from him the plans of the Temple, and materials for its construction, 404.
Song born out of trial, 130.
"Song of the Bow," 185.
Song, service of, in the Tabernacle, 218.
Songs in the night, 358.
Staleybridge, incident at, 396.
Stanley, Dean, quoted from or referred to, 13, 52, 134, 136, 193, 245, 247, 373.
Spurgeon's "Treasury of David" quoted from, 387.

TAMAR, beauty of, 299 ; dishonored by Amnon, 300.
Taylor, Isaac, quotation from, 361.
Temple the, David's desire to build, 230 ; Nathan's message regarding, 233 ; a type of the Christian Church, 242 ; lessons from, 408–414.
Tennyson, quotations from, 64, 168.
Teraphim, dissertation on, 78–80.
Thankfulness for God's mercies enforced, 395.
Thirty Years' War in Germany fruitful in noble hymns, 130.
Tholuck, Dr. A., on marriage, 169.
Thomson's "The Land and the Book" quoted from or referred to, 51, 102, 133.
Transgression, the great, of David, 264 ; its precursors, 265 ; its aggravations, 267 ; accounted for, 268 ; David's penitence for, 270 ; the consequences of, 275 ; lessons from, 277.
Trench, Archbishop, quoted from, 26, 130, 183, 187, 188.
Trial, fruitfulness of, 130 ; tendency of David's soul under, 144 ; solace in, 357.
"Trust in God, and do the right !" 73, 74.

# INDEX.

URIM and Thummim, presence of, in the cave of Adullam, 112; place of, in the education of God's people, 114; answers of, contrasted with those of heathen oracles, 214.
Uzzah, death of, 216.

VAINGLORY, national, rebuked, 375.
Voltaire, effect of the 51st Psalm upon, 273.

WHITTIER, J. G., hymn of, 131.
Witch of Endor, Saul's visit to, 180; questions concerning, 181–183.
Wordsworth quoted from, 118.
"Worthies" of David, 247; deeds of, 248.
Wright, Josiah, M.A., quotations from, 191, 375.

YOUNG men exhorted on the improvement of leisure time, 36; on leaving home, 39; on the choice of friends, 63; on making provision for their parents, 110; as to the attainment of success, 146, 206; on marriage, 166; from the history and death of Absalom, 336.
Young's "Night Thoughts" referred to, 223.
Youth not the only dangerous time of life, 278.

ZADOK, priest at Shiloh, 216; assists in suppressing the revolt of Adonijah, 401.
Zibar, perfidy of to Mephibosheth, 312–314; reason for David's treatment of, 347.
Ziklag received by David from Achish, 174; burned by the Amalekites, 177.
Zion, fortress of, taken from the Jebusites, 204.
Ziph, 123; David's interview with Jonathan in the wood of, 124; treachery of the men of, 124.

THE END.

www.ingramcontent.com/pod-product-compliance
Lightning Source LLC
LaVergne TN
LVHW031628070426
835507LV00024B/3387